Young Canada Dictionary

NELSON/CANADA

Contents

What Is a Dictionary?	3
How to Find a Word	3
What the Dictionary Tells You	4
Young Canada Dictionary	6
Appendix:	
Provinces and Capitals	208
Places and People	208
Numbers	210
Metric Symbols	210
Days and Months	211
Holidays and Special Days	211
Pronunciation Key and Abbreviations	212

Editor:	Daniel Liebman
Consultants:	Elizabeth Stenson
	Robert J. Cutting
Designer:	Paul Kaufhold
Illustrator:	Margaret Kaufhold

©Nelson Canada Limited, 1980
All rights reserved

Pupil's edition: ISBN 0-17-600751-2
Teacher's edition: ISBN 0-17-601410-1

Printed and bound in Canada

0 BP 876

What Is a Dictionary?

Sometimes you want to find out how to spell a word. Sometimes you want to know what it means. Your dictionary can help you do these things quickly and easily. It is a book that lists words in alphabetical order, and tells you what each word means.

Alphabetical order helps you find words in the dictionary. All the words beginning with A are at the front of the book. The words beginning with Z are at the back. The words beginning with M are near the middle. In this way, a dictionary is just like a telephone book.

Guide words at the top of each page help you find words even more easily. They guide you to the correct page in the dictionary. An example is **dangerous → dear.** The first guide word tells you the first entry word on that page. The second one tells you the last entry word on that same page.

An *entry* tells you the word and its meaning. It looks like this in your dictionary:

> **pitcher** (pich'ər) *n.* 1. a large jug. 2. the baseball player who tosses or pitches the ball.

The *entry word* is the one in bold type: **pitcher.** If you just want to know how to spell a word, this is sometimes all you need to look at.

The *definition* comes right after the entry word. It tells you the meaning of the word. Sometimes, the same word can have different meanings.

An entry tells you even more about a word — as you will see on the next page.

How to Find a Word

What if you want to look up the word **pitcher**? When you get to know these three steps, you will be able to do it quickly!

1 Think of your dictionary as having two parts — the *front part* (letters **a** to **m**) and the *back part* (letters **n** to **z**).

Front Part **a** to **m**	Back Part **n** to **z**

The word **pitcher** will be under the letter **p**, in the back part of the dictionary. Open your book about halfway.

2 Look at the *guide words* at the top of each page, until you find those beginning with **p**. Guide words look like this in your dictionary:

piece → pitchfork

3 Then look at the *next letter* in the word **pitcher**. It is an **i**.

> **pitcher**

You won't have to look through all the words beginning with **p** to find your word. Just look for the words beginning with **pi**. When you find them, look down the columns of **pi** words until you find **pitcher**.

What the Dictionary Tells You

When you just want to check the spelling of an entry word, the dictionary will help you do it easily. But there is a lot more that an entry will tell you:

Meaning

The definition gives you the meaning of the word. Sometimes, there is more than one meaning. When this happens, the meanings are numbered 1, 2, and so on. Can you think of some words that have two meanings or more?

Often, an example is given to make the meaning clearer. Sometimes, a drawing is given.

> **pitcher** (pich'ər) n. ①a large jug.②the baseball player who tosses or pitches the ball.

> **pollute** v. to make the air, land, or water dirty: *The oil polluted the ocean.* **polluting. polluted.**

Pronunciation

The dictionary helps you to say some difficult words correctly. The word is written again (in brackets) to help you 'sound it out'. Look at the pronunciation guide on page 212, to see how it works. Then look up 'angle' and 'patience' to see how they are pronounced.

> **agency** (ā'jən sē) n. a company that does work for people: *My parents call an agency for a babysitter.* pl. **agencies.**

Different Kinds of Words

After the entry word, there are letters, such as *n., v., adj.* They tell you what kind of word it is.

n. is *noun*, the name of a thing, place, person, or quality, such as 'hat, Canada, Mary, anger'.

pron. is *pronoun*, a word used in place of a noun, such as 'he, she, it, they'.

adj. is *adjective*, a word which describes a noun or pronoun, such as 'red, tall, many'.

v. is *verb*, the active or 'doing' word in a sentence, such as 'go, see, open'.

> **hornet** n. a large wasp that stings.
>
> **horrible** adj. terrible, awful: *When you scrape your nail on the chalkboard, it makes a horrible noise.*

adv. is *adverb*, a word which tells more about a verb, adjective, or another adverb, such as 'badly, slowly, very'.

prep. is *preposition*, a word which begins a group of words that tell about a person, place, or thing, such as, '*with* my friend', '*by* the sea', '*on* the shelf'.

conj. is *conjunction*, a word used for joining words and sentences, such as 'and, but, while, as'.

> **its** *adj.* the one belonging to it: *The cat drank its milk.*
>
> **it's** short for **it is.**
> Note: Do not mix up **its** with **it's**: *It's raining today. The dog lost its collar.*

Special Notes

Sometimes, extra hints are given to help you use the word correctly. What is the difference between 'past' and 'passed', or 'accept' and 'except'? This dictionary tells you.

> **laugh** (laf) *n.* a loud 'ha-ha' sound made when you see or hear something funny. *v.* to make such a sound, to show that you are happy or that something is funny. **laughing. laughed.**

Verbs

Different forms are shown when the entry word is a verb. You will often see the **-ing** ending (*Maria is laughing*) and the **-ed** ending (*Maria laughed* or *Maria has laughed).* Some verbs have special forms, for example 'strike — striking — struck'. Look up the verb 'buy' and see how the verb changes.

> **mouse** *n.* a small, furry animal with a pointed nose and a long tail. *pl.* **mice.**

Plural Forms

Many nouns become plural (more than one) just by adding an 's', for example 'cat — cats'. However, it is not always this simple. What is the plural of 'hero'? Is it 'heros' or 'heroes'? This dictionary tells you.

> Appendix

Appendix

This special section at the back of the book has many words and facts that you may want to find quickly. It begins on page 208.

When you are writing, the dictionary is the most useful book you can have beside you.

a

a *article* one, any, each: *a glass of water, a day of the week, once a month.*

abandon *v.* to leave someone or something, and never return: *The sailors abandoned the sinking ship.* **abandoning. abandoned.**

abbreviation *n.* a shortened form of a word: *P.E.I. is the abbreviation for Prince Edward Island.*

ability *n.* the power or skill to do something: *A fish has the ability to swim.* *pl.* **abilities.**

able *adj.* having the power or skill to do something: *A bird is able to fly.* (*opp.* **unable.**)

aboard *adv.* on or into a ship, plane, bus, or train.

about *prep.* 1. close to: *It was about two o'clock.* 2. to do with: *Ann's book is about games.* *adv.* around: *The boys were running about.*
about to just going to: *Sue was about to go out when Renata came in.*

above *prep.* higher than: *The picture hangs above the table.* *adv.* overhead: *The clouds are above.*

absence *n.* being away: *Jan's absence meant that Pat would have to pitch.*

absent *adj.* not there: *Pat was absent from school.*

absent-minded *adj.* forgetful, not paying attention.

absolute *adj.* complete: *Absolute silence, please!* **absolutely** *adv.*

accent (ak'sent) *n.* a special way of speaking: *Ian speaks with an English accent.* *v.* when speaking, to place more stress on some sounds than on others: *In the word 'accept', we accent the second syllable.* **accenting. accented.**

accept (ak sept') *v.* to take something that is offered: *to accept a gift.* **accepting. accepted.**
Note: Do not mix up **accept** with **except**; **except** means 'other than'.

accident *n.* something that happens suddenly and may be harmful.
by accident not on purpose.

accidental *adj.* not on purpose: *an accidental fall.* **accidentally** *adv.*

accommodate (ə kom'ə dāt) *v.* to have room for: *The hotel can accommodate 50 guests.* **accommodating. accommodated.**

accomplish *v.* to do or to finish: *Lisa can accomplish many jobs in one day.* **accomplishing. accomplished.**

according to from what someone says: *According to Bob it is now one o'clock.*

accordion *n.* a musical instrument, with musical keys, bellows, and buttons.

account *n.* a record of money spent, owed, or saved: *a bank account.*

account for to explain: *Your accident accounts for your not coming.*

accurate (ak'yər it) *adj.* free from mistakes, very exact: *My watch is always accurate.* **accurately** *adv.*

accuse (ə kyüz') *v.* to blame someone: *Maria accused Lee of cheating.* **accusing. accused.**

accustomed to used to: *He can't get accustomed to going to bed so late.*

ace *n.* a playing card with only one spot in the middle.

ache (āk) *n.* a pain, as a *headache, toothache,* or *earache.* *v.* to have a pain. **aching. ached.**

acid *n.* a liquid that can eat away metals.

acorn *n.* the nut-like fruit of the oak tree.

acre (ā'kər) *n.* an area of land, equal to about 4000 m².

acrobat *n.* a person who can do daring leaps and jumps, often on a trapeze.

acrobatic *adj.* as performed by an acrobat: *an acrobatic leap.*

across *prep.* to the other side of: *They swam across the river. adv.* on the other side: *They were safely across.*

act *n.* 1. a deed, a happening: *an act of bravery.* 2. a part in a play: *The school play is in three acts.* 3. a law made by Parliament. *v.* 1. to do something: *That boy needs help. Act now!* 2. to pretend: *Margaret and René acted as if they were ill.* 3. to take part in a play. **acting. acted.**

action *n.* 1. a deed, a happening. 2. movement: *the action of a clock.*

active *adj.* lively: *Andrea is an active girl, always doing things.* **actively** *adv.*

activity *n.* movement, action, or something you do at a certain time: *Baseball is my favourite outdoor activity. pl.* **activities.**

actor (*fem.* **actress**) *n.* a person who performs in the movies, on TV, or on stage.

actual *adj.* real, not imaginary. **actually** *adv.*

ad *n.* short for **advertisement**, an announcement of something to be sold.

Adam's apple *n.* the lump in the front of the neck; it moves up and down when you swallow.

add *v.* 1. to put one thing to another: *to add milk to tea.* 2. to find the total of two or more numbers: *3 added to 4 equals 7.* **adding. added.**

addition *n.* 1. the adding of one thing to another. 2. adding numbers. **in addition** also.

address *n.* 1. the house, street, and town where a person lives. 2. a speech: *The visitor gave the students a short address. v.* 1. to write on a letter or package where it is to go. 2. to give a speech to a group of people. **addressing. addressed.**

adjective *n.* a word that tells you more about somebody or something: *a red rose, an iron gate, a good man.* The adjectives are *red, iron,* and *good.*

adjust *v.* to change something to make it work better or be more comfortable: *Brian adjusts the TV to get a good picture.* **adjusting. adjusted.**

admiral *n.* the highest officer in the navy.

admiration *n.* thinking something or someone is excellent: *I have great admiration for that singer.*

admire *v.* 1. to think highly of something or someone. 2. to look at something with pleasure. **admiring. admired.**

admission *n.* going in: *Admission to the fair is free.*

admit *v.* 1. to let in: *This ticket admits two people.* 2. to confess: *She had to admit that she was wrong.* **admitting. admitted.**

admittance *n.* going in: *The notice on the door read 'No Admittance'.*

adopt *v.* to care for someone else's child or pet, with permission, as your own. **adopting. adopted.**

adorable *adj.* cute and lovable.

adore *v.* to love very much. **adoring. adored.**

adult *n.* a grown-up.

advance *n.* a movement forward: *an advance by soldiers in battle. v.* to move forward. **advancing. advanced.**

advantage *n.* something that puts you ahead of others: *Our football players had the advantage of being bigger than the others.* (*opp.* **disadvantage.**)

adventure *n.* a daring and exciting experience: *I like stories about adventure in the jungle.*

adventurous *adj.* daring, wanting to have an adventure.

adverb *n.* a word that tells you more about a verb, an adjective, or another adverb: *He sneezes loudly on a very cold day.* The adverbs are *loudly* and *very.*

advertise (ad'vər tīz) *v.* to announce something (usually for sale) in the newspaper, on the radio, or on TV. **advertising. advertised.**

advertisement (ad vər'tiz mənt) *n.* an announcement of something to be sold: *We read the newspaper advertisement for the bikes. Then we went to see what they looked like.*

advice (ad vīs') *n.* helpful suggestions: *Father gave Choy advice on choosing new shoes.*

advise (ad vīz') *v.* to offer helpful suggestions. **advising. advised.**

affect *v.* to cause a change: *Louise's illness will affect her holiday plans.* **affecting. affected.**
Note: Do not mix up **affect** with **effect**; **effect** means 'the result of a change'.

affection *n.* a feeling of love: *I have great affection for my grandparents.*

affectionate *adj.* loving.

afford *v.* to spare money or time for something: *I cannot afford to buy a new coat. I cannot afford the time to go to the store.* **affording. afforded.**

afraid *adj.* frightened, full of fear.

African *n.* a person born in or living in Africa. *adj.* having to do with the continent of Africa.

after *prep.* later than, behind: *after dinner; after me.*

afternoon *n.* the time between noon and evening.

afterwards *adv.* later.

again *adv.* once more.

against *prep.* 1. facing: *to walk against the wind.* 2. touching: *Mario leaned against the fence.*

age *n.* 1. how many years a thing has lasted or a person has lived: *Val's age is five years.* 2. a time in history: *the Stone Age.* *v.* to grow old. **aging. aged.**

agency (ā'jən sē) *n.* a company that does work for people: *My parents call an agency for a babysitter. pl.* **agencies.**

agent *n.* a person who works for an agency.

ago *adj.* gone by, in the past: *ten years ago.*
long ago many years past.

agree *v.* to be willing, to say yes: *Ruth agreed to play baseball.* **agreeing. agreed.**

agreement *n.* an understanding between people: *After the argument, they reached an agreement.* (*opp.* **disagreement.**)

agriculture *n.* farming.

ahead *adv.* forward, in front: *The leader went ahead.*

aid *n.* help, assistance. *v.* to help. **aiding. aided.**

ail *v.* to be ill. **ailing. ailed.**

aim *n.* 1. the pointing of a gun or other weapon at a target. 2. a goal: *Joe's aim is to join the team.* *v.* 1. to point a gun or other weapon at something. 2. to try to gain some success: *Jill and Bob aim to be the best dancers.* **aiming. aimed.**

air *n.* the mixture of gases that fills the space around us.

aircraft *n.* any flying machine. *pl.* **aircraft.**

Airedale *n.* a large tan and black dog of the terrier family.

airline *n.* a company that operates aircraft.

airmail *n.* mail carried by aircraft.

airplane *n.* a motor-driven aircraft.

airport *n.* a place where airplanes land and take off.

aisle (īl) *n.* a long, narrow passage, usually between rows of seats.

alarm *n.* 1. a warning of danger: *The alarm was given when the enemy came near.* 2. a bell, as on an alarm clock.

Alberta *n.* province between British Columbia on the west, Saskatchewan on the east; capital is Edmonton. Short form: **Alta.** A person living in or born in Alberta is an **Albertan.**

album *n.* 1. a book to hold a collection: *a stamp album.* 2. a cardboard case for holding a record, or the record itself.

ale *n.* a strong, light-coloured beer.

alert *adj.* ready to act quickly.

alike *adj.* nearly the same: *The sisters are alike in many ways.*

alive *adj.* 1. living, not dead. 2. lively.

all *n.* every one: *All the runners finished the race.*

allergic (ə lər′jik) *adj.* becoming sick when near certain plants, animals, etc., or when you have eaten certain foods: *Ben is allergic to cats. He sneezes when they are around.*

allergy (al′ər jē) *n.* a sickness caused by certain foods, plants, etc.; it happens to some people, but not to others. *pl.* **allergies.**

alley *n.* a narrow lane between buildings. *pl.* **alleys.**

alligator *n.* a large reptile, found in the rivers of some warm places.

allow *v.* to let, to permit: *We must allow him to go.* **allowing. allowed.**

allowance *n.* a regular amount of money: *Carol gets a weekly allowance.*

all right 1. very well, agreed: *All right, I'll go.* 2. in good health: *I'm all right, thanks.* 3. correct: *This is all right. You get 100%.*

ally (al′ī) *n.* a country or person who helps you in a war or struggle. *pl.* **allies.**

almond (a′mənd, ah′mənd) *n.* a nut from a tree that grows in warm places.

almost *adv.* nearly: *We're almost there!*

alone *adv.* with nobody else, with nothing else.

along *prep.* from one end to the other: *We drove along the main street. adv.* 1. on, forward: *Move along!* 2. with yourself: *I took my brother along.*

alongside *prep.* by the side of.

aloud *adv.* loudly, so that all can hear: *John read the story aloud to the class.*

alphabet *n.* the letters of a language; A,B,C, etc.: *There are 26 letters in the English alphabet.*

already *adv.* before this time, by now: *Charles was already there when we arrived.*

also *adv.* too, as well: *Should I also bring my brother?*

altar *n.* a table in a church, used for a religious ceremony.

alter *v.* to change: *Jan has to alter his plans.* **altering. altered.**

alteration *n.* a change.

although (awl тнō′) *conj.* but, even if: *I will go out although I do not like the rain.*

aluminum *n.* a light metal.

always *adv.* for ever, every time: *I shall always try to be early.*

a.m. the time from midnight to noon: *I woke up at 7 a.m.*

am *v.* a form of the verb **be**; used only with 'I': *I am going to sleep.*

amateur (am'ə chər) *n.* a person who does something just for pleasure, not for money: *Amateurs compete in the Olympics.*

amaze *v.* to surprise very much: *The magician amazed us with his tricks.* **amazing. amazed.**

ambassador *n.* someone who represents his or her country in a foreign land.

amber *n.* a deep golden-yellow colour: *Traffic lights are red, green, and amber.* *adj.* having this colour.

ambulance (am'byü ləns) *n.* a van for carrying ill or injured people to hospital.

ambush *n.* a surprise attack on an enemy from a hiding place. *v.* to attack an enemy by surprise after lying in wait. **ambushing. ambushed.**

amen (ah'men', ā'men') *n.* a word at the end of a prayer, meaning 'So be it'.

American *adj.* 1. belonging to or coming from North or South America. 2. belonging to or coming from the United States.

ammunition (am yü nish'ən) *n.* bullets and shells for guns.

among (ə mung') *prep.* 1. surrounded by: *Kim walked among the trees.* 2. to each of: *Share the sandwiches among you.*

amount *n.* 1. quantity: *A large amount of sugar.* 2. total of money: *What is the amount of our bill?* *v.* to add up to: *The bill amounts to $3.50.* **amounting. amounted.**

amphibian (am fib'ē ən) *n.* an animal that is able to live both on land and in the water: *Toads, salamanders, and frogs are amphibians.*

amuse (ə myüz') *v.* to make someone laugh or smile, to entertain. **amusing. amused.**

amusement *n.* 1. entertainment. 2. enjoyment: *We showed our amusement by laughing at the clown's tricks.* 3. a ride at a fair.

amusing *adj.* funny, entertaining.

an *article* one, any, each: *'an' is used in place of 'a' when the next word begins with the letter a, e, i, o, or u (an apple, an egg, an iceberg, an orange, an uncle).*

ancestor (an'ses tər) *n.* a relative who lived a very long time ago.

anchor (ang'kər) *n.* a heavy metal bar with hooks, dropped to the bottom of the water to keep a boat from drifting. *v.* to hold a ship with an anchor. **anchoring. anchored.**

ancient (ān'shənt) *adj.* 1. very old: *an ancient tree.* 2. living or existing long ago: *the ruins of an ancient fort.*

and *conj.* as well as, plus: *Jack and Sue are friends; one and one are two.*

angel (ān'jəl) *n.* a messenger of God.

angle (ang'gəl) *n.* the space between two straight lines or sides that meet.

angrily *adv.* in a bad temper, furiously.

angry *adj.* bad-tempered, in a rage: *an angry witch, an angrier witch, the angriest witch of all.*

animal *n.* any living thing that is not a plant.

ankle *n.* the joint between the foot and leg.

anniversary *n.* a day that is remembered each year, for something important that happened on it: *a wedding anniversary.* *pl.* **anniversaries.**

announce *v.* to let everyone know something: *The principal announced a holiday.* **announcing. announced.**

announcement *n.* a notice given to people about something.

announcer *n.* a person who makes announcements or reads the news, usually on radio or TV.

annoy *v.* to trouble someone; to make someone angry. **annoying. annoyed.**

annual *adj.* happening once each year: *The annual field day takes place each May 15th.* **annually** *adv.*

another *adj.* 1. one more: *Take another piece of cake.* 2. different: *Choose another dress.*

answer (an′sər) *n.* 1. the reply to a question. 2. a reply to a letter. *v.* to reply to a question or a letter. **answering. answered.**

ant *n.* a small insect that lives together with many others in the ground.

antarctic *adj.* at or near the South Pole. **the Antarctic** the south polar region.

anteater *n.* an animal that feeds mostly on ants and has a long nose and a long, sticky tongue.

antelope *n.* a swift, four-legged animal that looks like a deer.

antenna *n.* 1. one of two feelers on the head of a crab, lobster, or insect. *pl.* **antennae** (an ten′ne). 2. a metal wire used for television and radio. *pl.* **antennas.**

anthem *n.* a nation's own song: *The national anthem of our country is 'O Canada'.*

antique (an tēk′) *n.* something made long ago, often a piece of furniture: *This chair is an antique.* *adj.* from times long ago: *This antique chest was carved in Nova Scotia 100 years ago.*

antlers *n. pl.* the horns of a deer, elk, moose, etc.

anxious (ang′shəs) *adj.* 1. worried, fearful. 2. wanting something, but not sure whether you will get it: *Mark was anxious to be on the baseball team.*

any (en′ē) *adj.* 1. one of several: *Come on any day.* 2. some: *Have you any money?*

anybody *n.* any person.

anyone *n.* any person.

anything *n.* 1. any one thing: *Anything will do for the sale.* 2. any thing: *Have you anything to do?*

anyway *adv.* in any case, still: *It was raining, but we held the picnic anyway.*

anywhere *adv.* in any place, or to any place: *I will go anywhere with you.*

apart *adv.* 1. separate, alone: *Leslie stood apart from the others.* 2. in pieces: *Mother took the machine apart.*

apartment *n.* several rooms to live in: *Our apartment is on the third floor.*

ape *n.* a kind of monkey with no tail.

apiece (ə pēs′) *adv.* for each one: *The books cost three dollars apiece.*

apologetic *adj.* full of regret, feeling sorry: *The store sent an apologetic letter because they had made an error.*

apologize *v.* to say you are sorry for something. **apologizing. apologized.**

apology *n.* saying you are sorry. *pl.* **apologies.**

appeal *v.* 1. to interest greatly: *Hockey appeals to Stanley and Rita.* 2. to beg for help: *Tibor appealed for assistance.* **appealing. appealed.**

appear *v.* 1. to come into sight: *Marion appeared from around the corner.* (*opp.* **disappear.**) 2. to seem: *Norman appears to be tired.* **appearing. appeared.**

appearance *n.* 1. coming into sight: *The appearance of the police made the robbers run.* (*opp.* **disappearance.**) 2. how someone or something looks: *The appearance of the building made us feel that it wasn't safe.*

appetite *n.* enjoyment of or desire for food: *Billy has a good appetite, and can eat at any time.*

applaud (ə plawd′) *v.* to cheer, to clap hands. **applauding. applauded.**

applause (ə plawz′) *n.* cheering, clapping hands.

apple *n.* a roundish fruit, red, green, or yellow in colour.

apply *v.* 1. to ask for a job: *When Joe quit, Al applied for the job of coach.* 2. to put on: *Apply the bandage.* **applying. applied.** he **applies.**

approach *v.* to move towards. **approaching. approached.**

approval *n.* agreement, permission: *Don joined the club with his parents' approval.*

approve *v.* to agree to, to give permission: *Mother and Dad approve of Karen's plans.* **approving. approved.** (*opp.* **disapprove.**)

apricot *n.* a soft fruit, pale orange in colour and smaller than a peach.

April *n.* the fourth month of the year.

apron *n.* a piece of clothing worn to keep clothes clean when working.

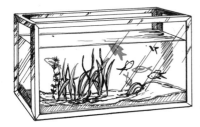

aquarium *n.* a tank holding live fish and water.

Arabian (ə rā′bē ən) *adj.* having to do with Arabs or Arabia.

arch *n.* 1. the curved top of a doorway, tunnel, or bridge. 2. the part of your foot between the heel and toe.

archer *n.* a person who shoots arrows with a bow.

archery *n.* the use of bows and arrows.

arctic *adj.* at or near the North Pole. **the Arctic** the north polar region.

are *v.* a form of the verb **be**; used with 'you' and 'we' and 'they': *You are going to sleep, we are going to sleep, they are going to sleep.*

area *n.* 1. any flat surface. 2. a space, a region: *the area around the city.* 3. an amount of space, measured in squares: *The area of British Columbia is 948 596 km².*

arena (ə rē′nə) *n.* a large space for games or shows, with raised seats all around.

aren't short for **are not.**

argue (ar′gyü) *v.* to disagree with someone, often in a noisy way: *Don't argue with the referee!* **arguing. argued.**

argument (ar′gyü mənt) *n.* 1. a disagreement with someone, in which you tell your opinions strongly. 2. a reason for or against something: *My old bicycle runs well. That is a good argument for not buying a new one.*

arise *v.* to get up. **arising. arose.** I have **arisen.**

arithmetic *n.* working with numbers: *Adding, subtracting, multiplying, and dividing are the main parts of arithmetic.*

ark *n.* in the Bible, the boat in which Noah saved his family and two of every animal from the flood.

arm *n.* 1. the part of your body from the shoulder to the hand. 2. like an arm: *the arms of a chair.* *v.* to supply with weapons. **arming. armed.**

armchair *n.* a chair with an arm on each side of the seat.

armour, armor *n.* iron clothing worn by soldiers in old times.

arms *n. pl.* 1. weapons. 2. a special badge worn by persons of high rank: *a coat of arms.*

army *n.* 1. a great number of soldiers. 2. a very large number: *an army of insects.* *pl.* **armies.**

arose see **arise.**

around *prep., adv.* in a circle, on all sides.

arrange *v.* 1. to set in order: *to arrange books on a shelf.* 2. to make plans: *to arrange to meet a friend.* **arranging. arranged.**

arrangement *n.* 1. a number of things put in order: *an arrangement of flowers.* 2. a plan: *I made an arrangement with Mrs. Smith to walk her dog every day.*

arrest *v.* to take hold of someone and keep him or her as a prisoner: *The police arrested the robber.* **arresting. arrested. under arrest** being kept prisoner.

arrival *n.* coming to a place at the end of a journey: *They waited for the plane's arrival at the airport.*

arrive *v.* to reach a place after a journey. **arriving. arrived.**

arrow *n.* a pointed stick with feathers at one end, shot from a bow.

art *n.* 1. the study of, or the making of, beautiful things. 2. skill, craft: *the art of weaving.* 3. painting or drawing.

article *n.* 1. a single thing, an object. 2. a piece of writing in a newspaper or magazine: *We read an article on fishing.* 3. a part of speech: *The words 'a', 'an', and 'the' are called articles.*

artificial (ar tə fish'əl) *adj.* not real or natural, imitation: *artificial flowers.*

artist *n.* someone who paints pictures or makes or does other beautiful things: *Dancers, painters, singers, and actors are all artists.*

artistic *adj.* 1. fond of art and beautiful things. 2. good at art.

as *adv.* 1. for example: *Some dogs, such as spaniels, have long hair.* 2. the same: *I am as old as Judy.* conj. 1. while: *As they were talking, the snow stopped.* 2. in the way that: *We did just as we were told.*

ash *n.* 1. the black powder left after a fire. 2. a kind of tree.

ashamed *adj.* very sorry for something wrong or silly you have done.

ashore *adv.* on or to the shore: *The ship was driven ashore by the storm.*

Asian (ā'zhən) *n.* a person born in or living in Asia. *adj.* having to do with the continent of Asia.

aside *adv.* on or to one side: *Kay stepped aside to avoid the crowd.*

ask *v.* to question someone: *We were lost and had to ask the way.* **asking. asked.**

asleep *adv.* not awake.

asparagus *n.* a vegetable, green in colour, and sold in bunches.

assemble *v.* to meet, to gather together: *A crowd assembled around the accident.* **assembling. assembled.**

assembly *n.* a meeting: *We saw a movie at this morning's assembly.* *pl.* **assemblies.**

assist *n.* the act of helping another hockey player score a goal. *v.* to help. **assisting. assisted.**

assistance *n.* help: *I fell down and needed assistance.*

assistant *n.* someone who serves and helps: *Sarah is an assistant to the art teacher.*

assortment *n.* a mixture of different kinds: *an assortment of sandwiches.*

astonish *v.* to surprise greatly, to amaze. **astonishing. astonished.**

astronaut *n.* a traveller in a spaceship.

astronomer *n.* someone who studies astronomy.

astronomy *n.* the study of the stars, planets, sun, moon, etc.

at *prep.* 1. in, by, on, or near: *Fran is at her aunt's house.* 2. in the direction of: *Bill pointed his finger at Tim.* 3. for: *I bought two hats at a dollar each.* 4. around the time of: *Wendy wakes up at 9 on Saturdays.*

ate see **eat.**

athlete *n.* a person who is active in sports.

athletic *adj.* good at sports.

Atlantic *n.* the ocean extending from North America and South America to Europe and Africa.
the Atlantic Provinces: New Brunswick, Newfoundland, Nova Scotia, and Prince Edward Island.

atlas *n.* a book of maps. *pl.* **atlases.**

atmosphere (at'məs fēr) *n.* the air around the earth.

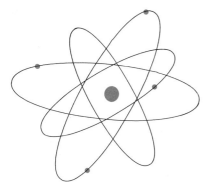

atom (at'əm) *n.* a very small part of anything.

attach *v.* to join together: *The farmer attached the horse to the plough.* **attaching. attached.**

attack *n.* a sudden move forward, a fight. *v.* to move forward and fight. **attacking. attacked.**

attempt *v.* to try to do something: *to attempt to beat a record.* **attempting. attempted.**

attend *v.* to be present at: *to attend school.* **attending. attended.**

attendance *n.* 1. being present. 2. the number of people there: *The attendance at the concert was good.*

attention *n.* care and thought: *Give attention to your work.*

attic *n.* a room just under the roof of a house.

attitude *n.* the way a person thinks, acts, or feels: *a cheerful attitude.*

attract *v.* to pull to itself: *A magnet attracts iron nails.* **attracting. attracted.**

attraction *n.* something that is liked and brings people: *The show was a great attraction.*

attractive *adj.* charming, very pleasant: *Christine's dress is very attractive.* (*opp.* **unattractive**.)

auction *n.* a sale in which each thing is sold to the person who will give the most money for it.

audience *n.* a crowd of people at a performance or meeting.

auditorium *n.* a large room for an audience.

August *n.* the eighth month of the year.

aunt *n.* 1. a sister of your father or mother. 2. the wife of your uncle.

Australian *n.* a person born in or living in Australia. *adj.* having to do with the continent of Australia.

author *n.* a writer of books.

authority *n.* 1. power over other people: *The mayor has the authority to govern the city.* 2. an expert: *Nicholas is an authority on coins and stamps.* *pl.* **authorities.**

autograph (aw'tə graf) *n.* a person's name written by himself or herself.

automatic *adj.* working by itself: *An automatic watch needs no winding.*

automobile *n.* a motor car.

autumn *n.* the season after summer, also called 'fall'.

avalanche *n.* a heavy fall of snow and rocks down a mountain side.

avenue *n.* a road or street, often one lined with trees.

average (av'rij) *adj.* at a halfway point, medium: *George is of average weight for his age.*

aviation *n.* the study of aircraft.

aviator *n.* a pilot of an aircraft.

avoid *v.* to keep clear of, to keep away from. **avoiding. avoided.**

await *v.* to wait for. **awaiting. awaited.**

awake *adj.* not asleep.

award *n.* a prize, honour, or reward. *v.* to give a prize, honour, or reward. **awarding. awarded.**

aware *adj.* knowing, alert to: *Thelma was aware of a smell of burning before she saw the fire.* (opp. **unaware.**)

away *adv.* 1. further off: *The man walked away.* 2. absent: *We have been away on holiday.*

awful *adj.* very bad: *We are having awful weather!*

awfully *adv.* very, terribly: *You are awfully brave!*

awhile *adv.* for a short time: *Could you stay awhile longer and have dinner with us?*

awkward *adj.* clumsy: *He is very awkward, always falling over things.*

axe *n.* a sharp tool for cutting wood.

axis *n.* a line, not always a real one, around which an object turns: *the earth's axis. pl.* **axes** (ak'sēz).

axle *n.* the pole on which a wheel turns.

b

baboon *n.* a kind of large African monkey.

baby *n.* a very young child. *pl.* **babies.**

babysitter *n.* a person who looks after young children.

bachelor (bach'ə lər) *n.* a man who is not married.

back *n.* 1. the part of your body that is opposite to the front part. 2. the part of anything that is opposite to the front part: *the back of the room. adj.* opposite to front: *the back seat. adv.* in return: *Jean gave the ticket back.*

backbone *n.* the spine; a line of little bones down the back of your body.

backpack *n.* a leather or canvas bag that holds clothing and equipment; you carry it on your back.

backwards *adv.* facing the wrong way: *Jeff tried walking backwards.*

backyard *n.* a yard behind a house.

bacon *n.* the meat from the back and sides of a pig.

bad *adj.* 1. not good: *The first song is bad. The second one is worse. The third song is the worst of all.* 2. rotten, decayed: *These plums have gone bad.*

bade see **bid.**

badge *n.* a special sign worn on your clothes, showing that you have a special job or belong to a certain group.

badger *n.* a grey, hairy animal that lives in a hole in the ground.

badly *adv.* wrongly, not well: *It is done badly.*

badminton *n.* a game like tennis, played on a court, with a racket and a 'birdie'.

bag *n.* a sack made of paper, cloth, leather, or soft plastic: *a handbag, a shopping bag.*

bagel (bā'gəl) *n.* a hard bread roll, shaped like a doughnut.

baggage *n.* cases and bags that hold what you need when you take a trip.

baggy *adj.* hanging loose: *baggy pants, baggier pants, the baggiest pants of all.*

bagpipes *n. pl.* a musical instrument with a bag and pipes.

bail *n.* money paid to keep someone out of jail until his or her trial. *v.* to scoop water out of a boat. **bailing. bailed.**

bait *n.* food put on a hook to tempt a fish, or food used to tempt an animal into a trap.

bake *v.* to cook in an oven. **baking. baked.**

baker *n.* someone whose job is to bake bread and cakes.

bakery *n.* a place where bread and cakes are baked or sold. *pl.* **bakeries.**

balance *n.* 1. steadiness: *Keith kept his balance when walking along the painted line.* 2. an instrument for weighing things, used by chemists and others. *v.* to keep steady, as when walking on a tightrope. **balancing. balanced.**

balcony *n.* 1. a platform built outside the upper floor of a building. 2. an upstairs floor of a theatre. *pl.* **balconies.**

bald *adj.* having no hair on the head.

bale *n.* a bundle of hay or straw.

ball *n.* 1. something round, like a sphere: *a ball of wool, a tennis ball.* 2. a big party with dancing.

ballerina (bal ə rē′nə) *n.* a female ballet dancer.

ballet (bal ā′) *n.* a story or play told in the form of graceful dancing.

balloon *n.* an airtight bag filled with hot air or light gas.

bamboo *n.* a tall, woody grass that grows in hot places.

banana *n.* a long, curved fruit with a thick, yellow skin.

band *n.* 1. a narrow strip used for holding things together: *an elastic band.* 2. a group of people working together: *a band of thieves.* 3. a group of musicians playing together: *a dance band.*

bandage *n.* a narrow strip of cloth or other material used to cover wounds. *v.* to cover a wound with strips of cloth or other material. **bandaging. bandaged.**

bandit *n.* a robber.

bang *n.* a loud noise. *v.* to make such a noise. **banging. banged.**

banister *n.* the rail and posts of a staircase.

banjo *n.* a musical instrument with four or five strings. *pl.* **banjos.**

bank *n.* 1. a heap of earth or snow. 2. the side of a river. 3. a place where money is kept safe.

banner *n.* a flag.

banquet *n.* a large feast or dinner party.

bantam *n.* 1. a small barnyard fowl. 2. in sports, a player under 15 years of age.

baptize *v.* to christen, to give a baby a name. **baptizing. baptized.**

bar *n.* a rod, often of metal.

barbecue *n.* 1. an open fireplace for outdoor cooking. 2. an outdoor meal. *v.* to cook over an open fireplace. **barbecuing. barbecued.**

barbed wire wire with sharp spikes, used for fences.

barber *n.* a person who cuts men's and boys' hair.

bare *adj.* 1. plain, without trimmings: *the bare truth.* 2. empty: *a bare room.* 3. naked, without clothes.

barely *adv.* hardly: *He has barely enough time to do all his work.*

bargain (bar′gən) *n.* something that is bought cheaply, and is good value for the money. *v.* to try to get a good buy on something by suggesting the salesperson lower the price. **bargaining. bargained.**

barge *n.* a flat-bottomed boat used on rivers or canals.

bark *n.* 1. the outside skin or cover of a tree trunk or branch. 2. the sharp cry of a dog or wolf. *v.* to make this sound. **barking. barked.**

barley *n.* a grain, grown like wheat, that is used for food.

barn *n.* a farm building used for storing crops or sheltering animals.

barnyard *n.* the yard around a barn.

barometer (bə rom′ə tər) *n.* an instrument that measures air pressure, and shows changes in the weather.

barrel *n.* 1. a wooden tub. 2. the tube of a gun.

barrier *n.* a railing, fence, or other object that stops you from going farther.

base *n.* 1. the part that something rests or stands on; the lowest part. 2. in baseball and other games, a goal or station.

baseball *n.* 1. a game played with bat and ball on a field with four bases. 2. the ball used in this game.

basement *n.* the lowest floor of a building, usually below the ground.

bashful *adj.* shy, timid.

basic (bā′sik) *adj.* simple, but important: *a basic fact.*

basin *n.* a round bowl.

basket *n.* a container usually made of woven straw or twigs.

basketball *n.* 1. a game played with a large ball on a court with two nets. 2. the ball used in this game.

bass (bas) *n.* a fish that can be eaten. *pl.* **bass.**

bass (bās) *n.* 1. in music, the lowest male voice or singing part. 2. a musical instrument with deep tones that looks like a giant violin. *pl.* **basses.**

bat *n.* 1. a wooden club used in baseball and other games. 2. a small winged animal that flies at night. *v.* to use a bat in baseball. **batting. batted.**

batch *n.* a number of things of the same kind: *a batch of cookies.*

bath *n.* the washing of your whole body.

bathe (bāᴛʜ) *v.* to take a bath. **bathing. bathed.**

bathroom *n.* a room with tub, basin, and toilet.

bathtub *n.* a large tub in which you wash your body.

batter *n.* 1. a mixture of eggs, flour, and milk, beaten together and cooked: *pancake batter.* 2. a person who hits a ball with a bat.

battery *n.* a container that keeps or produces electricity: *a car battery.* *pl.* **batteries.**

battle *n.* 1. a fight between two armies in a war. 2. a hard struggle: *a battle against a storm at sea.* *v.* to have such a fight or struggle. **battling. battled.**

bawl *v.* 1. to shout loudly. 2. to weep loudly. **bawling. bawled.**

bay *n.* 1. a big curve of an ocean or a lake into the land. 2. the deep howl of a dog.

be *v.* to stay, to happen, to exist, to belong to a group.
See the following words, all forms of the verb 'to be': **am, is, are, was, were, being, been.**
Note: **be** and its different forms are sometimes used along with other verbs.

beach *n.* the shore of an ocean or lake, either sandy or covered with pebbles.

beacon *n.* a fire or light used as a signal: *A beacon can warn ships of a rocky coast.*

bead *n.* a small piece of glass or metal in a necklace.

beagle *n.* a small hound dog.

beak *n.* the hard, pointed part of a bird's mouth.

beam *n.* 1. a long piece of wood or metal. 2. a ray of light: *a sunbeam.*

bean *n.* 1. a seed from a pod, eaten as a vegetable: *pork and beans.* 2. the pod itself: *green beans.*

beanstalk *n.* the main stem of a bean plant.

bear *n.* a very big, furry animal: *a brown bear, a polar bear.* *v.* 1. to carry: *The mule can bear heavy loads.* 2. to put up with: *I cannot bear the pain.* 3. to produce: *This tree bears many plums.* **bearing. bore.** I have **borne.**

beard *n.* the hair on a man's face.

beast *n.* a four-footed animal.

beat *n.* a stroke made again and again: *the beat of the drums.* *v.* 1. to keep on hitting: *We beat the dirt out of the rug.* 2. to defeat another person or group: *We beat the other team by three goals.* **beating. beat.** I have **beaten.**

beautiful *adj.* lovely, very pretty. **beautifully** *adv.*

beauty (byü ′tē) *n.* 1. loveliness. 2. a lovely thing: *What a beauty! pl.* **beauties.**

beaver *n.* a soft, furry animal that lives in water as well as on land.

because *conj.* for this reason: *Karen came back because it was raining hard.*

become *v.* to come to be: *Barbara wants to become a doctor.* **becoming. became.** I have **become.**

bed *n.* 1. a piece of furniture used to sleep or rest on. 2. a patch of ground in a garden for flowers or vegetables to grow in. 3. the bottom of the sea or a river.

bedroom *n.* a room to sleep in.

bee *n.* an insect that lives with other bees in a beehive, making honey and wax.

beech *n.* a tree with smooth, grey bark.

beef *n.* meat from cattle.

beehive *n.* a hive or house for bees.

been *v.* a form of the verb **be**; always used with 'have', 'had', 'has', or 'having': *I have been.*

beer *n.* a drink made from malt and hops.

beet *n.* a vegetable whose round, dark red root is boiled and eaten.

beetle *n.* an insect with a hard, shiny back to protect its wings.

before *prep.* 1. in front of: *Ted stood before the shop window.* 2. earlier than: *I was here before school started.*

beg *v.* 1. to ask humbly for food or money: *The poor man was begging in the street.* 2. to ask a favour: *I beg you to forgive me.* **begging. begged.**

beggar *n.* a poor person who lives by begging for food or money.

begin *v.* to start to do something. **beginning. began.** I have **begun.**

beginner *n.* someone who is just starting to learn something.

behave *v.* to show good or bad manners in front of others.

behaviour, behavior *n.* the way someone behaves.

behind *prep.* at the back of: *Stand behind me.* *adv.* not on time: *I am behind in my work.*

beige (bāzh) *n.* a light brown colour. *adj.* having this colour.

being *n.* a living creature: *There is not a single being on the moon.* *v.* a form of the verb **be**: *He is being silly.*

belief *n.* something you believe in, an opinion: *It is my belief that tennis is a very good game.*

believe *v.* to think that something is true: *Donald believes that he can win the race.* **believing. believed.**

bell *n.* an object shaped like an upside-down cup, which when struck gives a ringing sound.

bellow *v.* to roar, to shout in an angry way. **bellowing. bellowed.**

belly *n.* the lower part of the front of your body, the stomach. *pl.* **bellies.**

belong *v.* 1. to be owned by: *That book belongs to Billy.* 2. to be a member of: *Marg belongs to the Girl Guides.* **belonging. belonged.**

below *prep., adv.* beneath, under.

belt *n.* a strap worn around your waist, usually made of leather or plastic.

bench *n.* 1. a work table. 2. a long, wooden seat.

bend *n.* a curve: *a bend in the road.* *v.* 1. to curve something: *to bend a wire.* 2. to lean over: *to bend over your desk.* **bending. bent.**

beneath *prep., adv.* lower than, under: *beneath the tree.*

benefit *n.* something good, an advantage: *A warm coat is a great benefit on a cold day.* *v.* to help: *The swimming lessons benefited Ronnie.* **benefiting. benefited.**

berry *n.* a small, juicy fruit: *a raspberry, a blackberry. pl.* **berries.**

beside *prep.* by the side of: *The church is beside the river.*

besides *adv.* also, as well: *Besides our class, several other people were at the dance.*

best *adj.* the very finest: *The blue team is good, the green team is better, and the purple team is the best of all.*

bet *n.* a promise to give something to someone if he or she is right and you are wrong: *We made a bet on who would win the Stanley Cup.* *v.* to gamble that something will happen. **betting. bet.**

better *adj.* finer, worth more: *This ring is good, but that one is better. The gold ring is the best of the three.*

between *prep.* 1. one or the other: *Choose between the two pictures.* 2. with another person: *Share the cake between you.* *adv.* in the middle of two people or things: *There is a distance of two metres between the chairs.*

beware *v.* to be on your guard against, to watch out for: *Beware of the bull!*

beyond *prep.* 1. on the other side of, farther on than: *beyond the village.* 2. too far for: *beyond my reach.*

bib *n.* a little cloth tied around a baby's neck to stop food from falling on his or her clothes.

Bible *n.* the book of the sacred writings of the Christian and Jewish religions.

bicycle *n.* a two-wheeled vehicle.

bid *n.* an offer of money for something, usually at an auction. *v.* 1. to make an offer of money, usually at an auction: *I bid one dollar for that lamp.* 2. to command: *I bid you to stay here.* 3. to say: *I bid you good-bye.* **bidding. bade** (bad or bād). I have **bidden.**

big *adj.* large, tall: *a big cat, a bigger cat, the biggest cat on the street.*

bike *n.* a short name for bicycle.

bill *n.* 1. an account of money that you owe: *Gino paid the gas bill.* 2. a poster: *They pasted bills on the wall.* 3. a bird's beak. *v.* to send a bill. **billing. billed.**

billion *n., adj.* a very large number, a thousand million (1 000 000 000).

bin *n.* a box or barrel for keeping things: *a garbage bin, a bread bin, a grain bin.*

bind *v.* to tie together with thread, string, or rope. **binding. bound.**

binoculars (bə nok'yə lərz) *n. pl.* two very small telescopes fastened side by side: *You look through binoculars with both eyes.*

biography *n.* a written history of a person's life. *pl.* **biographies.**

birch *n.* a tree with smooth bark, often white, which peels off like paper.

bird *n.* a feathered animal that lays eggs and has wings and two legs.

birdie *n.* a light, feather or plastic object, hit in the game of badminton.

birth *n.* being born: *the birth of a baby.*

birthday *n.* the day of the year on which you were born.

biscuit (bis'kit) *n.* a cracker or type of cookie.

bishop *n.* a high-ranking member of the clergy.

bison *n.* a North American wild animal, a buffalo. *pl.* **bison.**

bit *n.* 1. a small piece of something. 2. the metal part of a horse's bridle, held in its mouth. *v.* see **bite.**

bite *v.* to take hold of, or cut off, with your teeth. **biting. bit.** I have **bitten.**

bitter *adj.* 1. having a sharp, sour taste. 2. sharp: *a bitter wind.*

black *n.* the colour of a car tire, opposite to white. *adj.* having this colour.

black-fly *n.* a small, biting insect. *pl.* **black-flies.**

blacksmith *n.* a person who works with iron and makes shoes for horses.

blade *n.* 1. the flat, cutting part of a knife or sword. 2. a long, thin leaf: *a blade of grass.*

blame *n.* responsibility for something bad or wrong: *Fred took the blame for the damage. v.* to find fault with someone: *Doreen blamed Anna for breaking her dish.* **blaming. blamed.**

blank *n.* an empty space. *adj.* empty, not written on: *a blank page in the book.*

blanket *n.* a heavy bed-cover.

blast *n.* 1. a rush of air: *a blast of wind.* 2. an explosion. 3. a loud sound: *a blast of trumpets. v.* to blow up, usually with explosives. **blasting. blasted.**

blast-off *n.* the sending off of rockets and missiles.

blaze *n.* a bright fire throwing out flames.

bleach *n.* something that makes an object white by taking out its colour: *laundry bleach. v.* to make clean or white: *We bleached the dirt out of the clothes.* **bleaching. bleached.**

bleachers *n. pl.* seats at outdoor games such as baseball or tennis, usually with no roof above them.

bleat *v.* to make a noise like a goat or sheep. **bleating. bleated.**

bleed *v.* to lose blood. **bleeding. bled.**

blend *v.* to mix: *Maria blended the paints to make the colour she wanted.* **blending. blended.**

bless *v.* to wish happiness or health: *Bless you all!* **blessing. blessed.**

blessing *n.* 1. a good wish. 2. a good gift: *This rain is a blessing to the farmers.* 3. a prayer: *We say a blessing before the meal.*

blew see **blow.**

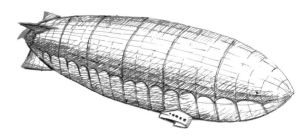

blimp *n.* a small balloon-like airship, filled with gas, that can carry passengers.

blind *adj.* unable to see.

blindfold *n.* a covering put over someone's eyes to keep him or her from seeing. *v.* to wrap a cloth over someone's eyes so that he or she cannot see. **blindfolding. blindfolded.**

blink *v.* to drop and raise your eyelids quickly. **blinking. blinked.**

blister *n.* a watery swelling under your skin.

blizzard *n.* a heavy snowstorm with strong winds.

blob *n.* a lump or drop of something soft or thick: *a blob of chewing gum.*

block *n.* 1. a solid piece: *a block of ice.* 2. a street in a town or city: *Let us walk around the block.* *v.* to get in the way of, to stop: *The car is blocking the way out.* **blocking. blocked.**

blond *adj.* having fair hair and a light skin.

blood (blud) *n.* the red liquid pumped around your body by your heart.

bloodhound *n.* a large dog with a sharp sense of smell.

bloom *n.* a flower, a blossom. *v.* to open up into a flower. **blooming. bloomed.**

blossom *n.* a flower, usually of a fruit tree: *The apple tree is in blossom.* *v.* to open up into a flower. **blossomed. blossoming.**

blot *n.* a stain, especially an ink stain.

blouse (blouz) *n.* a loose outer garment worn above the waist by women and girls.

blow *n.* 1. a hard knock: *a blow with your fist.* 2. sudden bad luck: *Father's accident was a blow to us all.* *v.* 1. to move along: *The wind blows.* 2. to puff at: *to blow a match out.* 3. to play a musical instrument using air from your lungs: *to blow a trumpet.* **blowing. blew.** I have **blown.**

blubber *n.* the fat of whales and some other sea animals: *Blubber is used for making oil.*

blue *n.* the colour of a clear, cloudless sky. *adj.* having this colour.

bluebell *n.* a flower with small blue petals, shaped like a bell.

blueberry *n.* a small, round, blue berry. *pl.* **blueberries.**

bluebird *n.* a small North American bird that has blue feathers on its back.

bluejay *n.* a North American bird with bright blue feathers.

blunder *n.* a silly mistake.

blunt *adj.* 1. not sharp: *a blunt knife.* 2. saying what you think, not being polite: *Mr. Graham was blunt, and told his cousin he was a fool.*

blur *v.* to make something hazy and not easy to see: *Mist blurred the view.* **blurring. blurred.**

blush *v.* to go red in the face because you are shy, excited, or ashamed. **blushing. blushed.**

boar (*fem.* **sow**) *n.* 1. a wild animal like a pig. 2. a male pig.

board *n.* 1. a long, thin piece of wood: *a floor board.* 2. a flat piece of wood used for a certain reason: *a dart board, a diving board.* *v.* 1. to enter a ship, train, or bus. 2. to live somewhere, paying for food and a room: *They boarded at a house near school.* **boarding. boarded.**

boarding school a school where students live during the school year.

boast *v.* to praise yourself or to say how good something is that you own. **boasting. boasted.**

boastful *adj.* always boasting: *a boastful child.*

boat *n.* 1. a small open ship, such as a rowboat. 2. a ship such as a freighter or steamboat.

bob *n.* a float at the end of a fishing line. *v.* to move quickly up or down: *We bob for apples on Halloween.* **bobbing. bobbed.**

bobsled *n.* a long sled with two sets of runners.

body *n.* 1. the whole of any animal or thing. 2. the main part of an animal or thing, the trunk: *Bend your body from the hips.* 3. a group of people: *a body of soldiers.* 4. a mass of something: *a body of water.* *pl.* **bodies.**

bodyguard *n.* someone who protects another person: *the king's bodyguard.*

bog *n.* soft wet ground, a marsh.

boil *n.* a small, painful swelling on the skin. *v.* 1. to heat a liquid until it bubbles and starts to change to a gas. 2. to cook something in boiling water: *to boil potatoes.* **boiling. boiled.**

bold *adj.* brave, confident: *a bold knight.* **boldly** *adv.*

bolt *n.* 1. a sliding bar used to fasten a door or gate. 2. a thick metal pin like a screw without a point. 3. a sudden dash: *The prisoner made a bolt for the woods.* *v.* 1. to fasten with a bolt. 2. to make a sudden dash. **bolting. bolted.**

bomb (bom) *n.* an explosive shell or ball.

bombard *v.* to attack with shells or bombs. **bombarding. bombarded.**

bone *n.* one of the hard white pieces that make up a skeleton.

bonfire *n.* a fire lit outdoors.

bonnet *n.* a head covering, tied under the chin and usually worn by small children.

bony *adj.* made of bone, like a bone: *a bony tail, a bonier tail, the boniest tail of all.*

book *n.* sheets of paper bound together for reading or for writing in: *a library book; a notebook.*

bookcase *n.* a piece of furniture with shelves for books.

booklet *n.* a little book, sometimes having a paper cover.

boom *n.* a deep, rumbling sound. *v.* to make such a sound. **booming. boomed.**

boomerang *n.* a curved stick that can turn in the air and come back to the thrower.

boot *n.* a leather, rubber, or plastic cover for the foot and ankle.

booth *n.* a place at a fair or market where things are shown or sold.

border *n.* 1. an outside edge: *a flower border around a lawn.* 2. the line or frontier where two countries meet.

bore *n.* a person who makes you tired by talking too much about dull things. *v.* 1. to drill a hole. 2. to make someone tired by dull talk. 3. see **bear. boring. bored.**

born *adj.* 1. brought into life. 2. having a special ability: *a born leader.*

borne see **bear.**

borough (bur′ō) *n.* the name given to a large area in some cities.

borrow *v.* to take something for a while, promising to give it back later: *Val borrowed a pen from me.* **borrowing. borrowed.**

boss *n.* someone in charge.

both *adj., pron.* the two: *Both girls went fishing. They both caught trout.*

bother *v.* to cause trouble, to annoy: *Flies bothered the people sitting in the park.* **bothering. bothered.**

bottle *n.* a container for liquids, usually of glass, with a narrow neck: *a medicine bottle.*

bottom *n.* the lowest part: *the bottom of the hill.*

bough (bou) *n.* a main branch of a tree.

bought see **buy.**

boulder (bōl′dər) *n.* a very large, round rock or stone.

boulevard (bůl′ə vard) *n.* a street, often a wide one.

bounce *v.* to throw or toss something so that it will come back. **bouncing. bounced.**

bound *n.* 1. a leap: *The rabbit raced away in great bounds.* 2. a limit, a boundary. *v.* see **bind.**
out of bounds outside the area where you are allowed to walk or play.

boundary *n.* anything marking a limit, a dividing line: *The river was the boundary between the two countries.* *pl.* **boundaries.**

bouquet (bü kā′) *n.* a bunch of flowers.

boutique (bü tēk′) *n.* a small shop, often selling just one kind of item.

bow (bou) *n.* 1. the front part of a ship. (*opp.* **stern.**) 2. a bending forward of the body or head, to show respect: *The knight made a bow to the queen.* *v.* to bend forward to show respect. **bowing. bowed.**

bow (bō) *n.* 1. a weapon for shooting arrows. 2. a stick strung with horsehair, for playing a violin. 3. a ribbon tied in loops.

bowl *n.* a basin, a deep round dish. *v.* to go bowling (5-pin, 10-pin, or lawn-bowling). **bowling. bowled.**

bowling *n.* a game in which a heavy ball is rolled at pins, either along a wooden lane or on a lawn.

box *n.* a container, usually with a cover: *a match box, a box of cookies.* *v.* to fight in a boxing ring with gloves on, for sport. **boxing. boxed.**

boxer *n.* 1. someone who fights for sport using padded gloves. 2. a tall, brown dog.

boy *n.* a male child. *pl.* **boys.**

bracelet *n.* a piece of jewellery worn on the wrist.

brag *v.* to boast, to show off. **bragging. bragged.**

braid *n.* a band formed by weaving together strands of hair, ribbon, rope, etc.

v. to weave together such strands. **braiding. braided.**

brain *n.* the grey mass that is inside the head of people and animals: *The brain lets us think, feel, learn, and remember.*

brake *n.* a piece of machinery, or a system of levers, for stopping a vehicle such as a bicycle, car, or train.

bran *n.* the outer covering of wheat and other grains: *The bran is separated from the flour by sifting.*

branch *n.* 1. an arm of a tree growing out from the trunk, a bough. 2. one of a group of stores or offices, but not the chief one: *a branch of the bank.*

brand *n.* a certain make of a product: *a brand of orange juice.* *v.* to mark by burning the skin with hot metal: *The farmer branded the cattle.* **branding. branded.**

brand new absolutely new.

brass *n.* 1. a yellow metal, made by melting copper and zinc together. 2. certain musical instruments, such as the trumpet or trombone.

brave *adj.* fearless, not afraid of pain or danger. **bravely** *adv.*

bravery *n.* courage, fearlessness.

brawl *n.* a noisy quarrel turning into a fight.

bray *n.* the sound that a donkey makes. *v.* to make such a sound. **braying. brayed.**

bread (bred) *n.* a food made by baking a mixture of flour, yeast, and water.

break *v.* 1. to split, to smash into pieces: *Don't break the cup!* 2. to disobey: *Don't break the rule!* 3. not to carry out: *Don't break a promise!* **breaking. broke.** I have **broken.**
break into to enter by force: *The burglars broke into our house.*
break up to come to an end: *The meeting broke up at ten o'clock.*

breakers *n. pl.* large ocean waves breaking into white foam.

breakfast (brek′fəst) *n.* the first meal of the day.

breast (brest) *n.* the chest.

breath (breth) *n.* air taken into and pushed out of the lungs.
out of breath puffing and panting after running or doing exercises.

breathe (brēTH) *v.* to draw air into or push it out of your lungs. **breathing. breathed.**

breathless *adj.* being short of air after exercising or running.

breed *n.* a particular kind of animal: *Jerseys are a breed of cow, good for milking.* *v.* 1. to raise young animals: *to breed pigs.* 2. to produce young. **breeding. bred.**

breeze *n.* a gentle wind.

breezy *adj.* windy.

brew *v.* to make a drink by soaking and boiling: *To brew tea, add boiling water to the leaves.* **brewing. brewed.**

bribe *v.* to offer money or a gift to a person for doing something dishonest: *The thief bribed the guard to leave the door unlocked.* **bribing. bribed.**

brick *n.* a block of baked clay used for building.

bridal *adj.* belonging to a bride: *the bridal gown.*

bride *n.* a woman on her wedding day.

bridegroom *n.* a man on his wedding day.

bridesmaid *n.* an unmarried woman who helps the bride.

bridge *n.* 1. a road built over a river or valley so that people and vehicles may cross it. 2. a card game.

bridle (brī'dəl) *n.* the part of a harness fitting over a horse's head.

brief (brēf) *adj.* short: *a brief speech.* **briefly** *adv.*

bright *adj.* 1. shining: *a bright light.* 2. intelligent: *Jean is a bright boy.* **brightly** *adv.*

brighten *v.* to make bright or become bright: *Frank's face brightened when he heard the good news.* **brightening. brightened.**

brilliant *adj.* 1. shining brightly: *a brilliant diamond.* 2. very smart: *a brilliant student.*

brim *n.* 1. the edge of a cup or bowl: *The glass was full to the brim.* 2. the edge of a hat.

bring *v.* to fetch. **bringing. brought.**
bring about to cause to happen.
bring up 1. to take care of during childhood: *They brought up a big family.* 2. to vomit.

brink *n.* the edge of the top of a high place: *We stood on the brink of the cliff.*

brisk *adj.* quick, rapid: *We went for a brisk walk.* **briskly** *adv.*

bristle (bris'əl) *n.* a short, stiff hair: *the bristles of a toothbrush.*

British *adj.* having to do with Britain.

British Columbia *n.* province with the Pacific Ocean on the west and Alberta on the east; capital is Victoria. Short form is **B.C.** A person living in or born in British Columbia is a **British Columbian.**

brittle *adj.* easily snapped or broken: *Glass, china, and ice are all brittle.*

broad *adj.* very wide.
broad daylight full daylight.

broadcast *v.* to spread news, especially by radio or television: *The news was broadcast at ten o'clock.* **broadcasting. broadcast.**

broccoli (brok'ə lē) *n.* a large, dark green vegetable.

broke, broken see **break.**

bronco *n.* a western pony. *pl.* **broncos.**

brontosaurus *n.* a huge dinosaur which had a long neck, a small head, and a thick tail.

bronze *n.* a metal made by melting copper and tin together.

brooch (brōch) *n.* a piece of jewellery fastened to clothing by a pin.

brood *n.* 1. a group of birds all hatched together. 2. young animals who have the same parents. *v.* to worry over something in a quiet, moody way: *Lynn was brooding over her lost ring.* **brooding. brooded.**

brook *n.* a small stream.

broom *n.* a long-handled brush used for sweeping.

brother *n.* a man or boy who has the same parents as you do.

brought see **bring.**

brow *n.* the forehead.

brown *n.,* the colour of chocolate or the earth. *adj.* having this colour.

brownie *n.* a small chocolate cake.

Brownie *n.* a junior Girl Guide.

bruise (brüz) *n.* a mark on the skin, caused by a fall or a blow.

brunch *n.* a meal eaten in place of breakfast and lunch, often including foods from both meals.

brush *n.* a cluster of hairs fastened to a handle for cleaning, grooming, or painting: *a clothes brush, a paint brush.* *v.* 1. to clean, groom, or paint with a brush: *Brush your teeth.* 2. to touch lightly: *Lee brushed my shoulder as he walked by.* **brushing. brushed.**

Brussels sprouts very little, green, cabbage-like vegetables.

bubble *n.* a thin balloon of liquid filled with air: *a soap bubble.*

buccaneer *n.* a pirate.

buck *n.* 1. (*fem.* **doe**) a male deer, goat, rabbit, or antelope. 2. (slang) a dollar.

bucket *n.* a large pail.

buckle *n.* a clasp on a belt or shoe. *v.* to fasten with a buckle. **buckling. buckled.** (*opp.* **unbuckle.**)

bud *n.* a young growth on a plant stem that will grow into a leaf, flower, or branch.

Buddhism (büd′iz əm) *n.* the main religion of Japan and other countries in Asia, founded by Buddha (büd′ə).

budge *v.* to move slightly: *He would not budge from·his spot.* **budging. budged.**

budgie *n.* a small bird, usually kept in a cage, with colourful markings.

buffalo *n.* a large, wild, North American animal related to cattle. *pl.* **buffalo.**

bug *n.* an insect: *Bedbugs, flies, and ants are all bugs.*

buggy *n.* a light carriage with one seat. *pl.* **buggies.**

bugle (byü′gəl) *n.* a short trumpet used by soldiers and scouts.

build (bild) *v.* to make something by joining different parts together: *to build a factory.* **building. built.**

building *n.* something built, usually with four walls and a roof, to hold people or things.

bulb *n.* 1. an underground bud that looks like an onion: *Tulips, lilies, daffodils, and onions all grow from bulbs.* 2. a rounded, bulb-shaped object: *a light bulb.*

bulge (bulj) *v.* to swell out or curve outwards. **bulging. bulged.**

bulky *adj.* large and sometimes a little hard to handle: *a bulky sweater, a bulkier one, the bulkiest sweater on the rack.*

bull (*fem.* **cow**) *n.* the male of cattle.

bulldog *n.* a heavy dog with a flattened face.

bulldozer *n.* a powerful tractor that moves soil and rocks.

bullet *n.* a piece of metal fired from a rifle or revolver.

bulletin board a board on which you pin pictures and announcements.

bully *n.* someone who frightens and hurts a smaller or weaker person. *pl.* **bullies.**

bumblebee *n.* a large bee that makes a loud buzz.

bump *n.* 1. a dull thud. 2. a swelling or lump. *v.* to knock into or against. **bumping. bumped.**

bumper *n.* a metal or rubber bar at the front or back of a car.

bun *n.* a sweetened roll.

bunch *n.* a group of things of the same kind, kept together: *a bunch of bananas.*

bundle *n.* a number of things tied or wrapped together: *a bundle of rags. v.* to tie or wrap things together. **bundling. bundled.**

bungalow *n.* a house that has all rooms on the ground floor.

bunk *n.* a narrow bed set against a wall.

bunny *n.* a pet rabbit. *pl.* **bunnies.**

buoy (boi, bü′ē) *n.* a floating object, used to guide swimmers or ships away from danger.

burden *n.* a heavy load.

burglar *n.* someone who breaks into a house to steal.

burglary *n.* breaking in and stealing. *pl.* **burglaries.**

burial (ber′ē əl) *n.* putting a dead body in a grave, tomb, the sea, etc.

buried, buries see **bury.**

burn *n.* a mark on the skin or on cloth, caused by fire or heat. *v.* to be on fire, to set on fire. **burning. burned** or **burnt.**

burr *n.* a prickly part of some plants: *The burrs stuck to Maria's coat as she walked through the woods.*

burrow *n.* a hole in the ground made by an animal and used as its home: *a rabbit-burrow. v.* to make such a hole. **burrowing. burrowed.**

burst *v.* 1. to blow up: *The balloon burst with a loud pop.* 2. to break: *The water pipe burst with the frost.* 3. to enter suddenly: *Paul burst into the room.* **bursting. burst.**

bury (ber′ē) *v.* 1. to cover up and hide: *The squirrel buried the nuts under some leaves.* 2. to place a dead body in the ground or the sea. **burying. buried.** he **buries.**

bus *n.* a large motor vehicle with seats for passengers. *pl.* **buses.**

bush *n.* 1. a shrub, a small tree with many branches. 2. the forest: *The lumberjack went into the bush to cut trees.*

bushy *adj.* looking like a bush: *a bushy tail, a bushier tail, the bushiest tail of all.*

busily (biz′ə lē) *adv.* in a busy way.

business (biz′nis) *n.* 1. a trade, work, shop, factory: *Mr. and Mrs. Shin have a printing business.* 2. something that you look after and attend to: *It is my business to take care of the dog.*

busy (biz′ē) *adj.* hard at work, having plenty to do: *Shirley was busy. Sandy was busier. Sheila was the busiest of all.*

but *conj.* 1. though: *I will go, but I do not want to.* 2. except: *Everyone but Simone saw the movie.*

butcher *n.* 1. a person who kills cattle and other animals for food. 2. a person who cuts up and sells meat.

butler *n.* a male servant, usually the head servant.

butte (byüt) *n.* a flat-topped hill standing by itself.

butter *n.* a yellowish food, separated from milk or cream by churning.

buttercup *n.* a flower with yellow petals.

butterfly *n.* an insect with large, brightly coloured wings. *pl.* **butterflies.**

buttermilk *n.* the liquid left after churning butter from cream or milk.

butterscotch *n.* a candy made from butter and brown sugar.

button *n.* a flat piece of metal, plastic, bone, etc. stitched to your clothes, to hold parts of them together. *v.* to close with buttons. **buttoning. buttoned.** (*opp.* **unbutton**.)

buy (bī) *v.* to get something you want by handing over money for it. **buying. bought.** she **buys.**

buzz *n.* the humming sound made by a fly or bee. *v.* to make such a sound. **buzzing. buzzed.**

buzzer *n.* an electrical button that makes a buzzing noise.

by *prep.* 1. at the side of: *He stood by the door.* 2. because of someone's action or efforts: *It was painted by me.* 3. earlier than: *Finish it by Tuesday.* 4. with the use of: *We travelled by train. adv.* past: *Walk by.*

'bye see **good-bye.**

by-pass *n.* a road going around a busy town to avoid the traffic.

cab *n.* 1. a car that you can hire with a driver: *a taxicab.* 2. the part of a truck or van where the driver sits.

cabbage *n.* a large, round, green vegetable.

cabin *n.* 1. a wooden hut. 2. a small room in a ship.

cabinet *n.* 1. a piece of furniture with drawers. 2. a group of ministers of parliament who help the prime minister to govern.

cable *n.* 1. a strong steel rope: *The ship was tied to the dock with a cable.* 2. a bundle of wires used to carry electric power or telephone messages.

caboose *n.* a railway car at the back of a freight train where the crew works.

cackle *n.* the screeching noise made by a hen, or a noise like it: *the witch's cackle. v.* to make a such a sound. **cackling. cackled.**

cactus *n.* a very prickly plant that grows in the desert. *pl.* **cacti** (kak'tī) or **cactuses.**

cadet *n.* a person in training to be an officer.

cafeteria *n.* a place to eat where people serve themselves.

cage *n.* a box with wires or metal bars, used to hold a bird or animal.

cake *n.* 1. a baked mixture of flour, butter, eggs, sugar, and other things. 2. a flat lump: *a cake of soap, a cake of mud.*

calculate *v.* to figure in numbers: *Gary calculated the number of days to his birthday.* **calculating. calculated.**

calculation *n.* working with numbers (adding, subtracting, multiplying, dividing) to get a result.

calculator *n.* 1. a machine that can add, subtract, multiply, divide, etc. 2. a person who calculates.

calendar *n.* a list of the days, weeks, and months of the year.

calf (kaf) *n.* 1. a young cow, elephant, or whale. 2. the back of your leg, below the knee. *pl.* **calves.**

call *v.* 1. to shout out. 2. to name: *We called our dog 'Tiger'.* 3. to telephone: *The house is on fire. Call the fire department!* **calling. called.**

calm (kahm) *adj.* 1. quiet, still, without wind: *a calm day.* 2. not excited: *A calm police officer directed heavy traffic.*

came see **come.**

camel *n.* a desert animal with one or two humps on its back.

camera *n.* a machine used for taking photographs or making movies.

camouflage (kam'ə flahzh) *n.* something that makes a person, creature, or thing seem to be part of the scenery. *v.* to disguise something so that it blends in with the scenery: *The soldiers camouflaged their camp with netting, branches, and paint.* **camouflaging. camouflaged.**

camp *n.* a number of tents or huts grouped together for soldiers, scouts, and others. *v.* to stay and sleep out of doors. **camping. camped.**

campfire *n.* an outdoor fire.

can *n.* a metal container: *a can of beans.* *v.* 1. a verb placed before another verb to mean 'be able to': *She can skate very well.* **could** (kùd). 2. to store food or drink in cans or jars. **canning. canned.**

Canada goose a large, wild, North American goose.

Canadian *n.* a person born in or living in Canada. *adj.* having to do with Canada.

Canadian Shield an area rich in minerals, surrounding Hudson Bay: *The Canadian Shield covers almost half of Canada's land area.*

canal *n.* a waterway dug across land: *Boats and barges travel through canals.*

canary *n.* a yellow songbird, usually kept in a cage. *pl.* **canaries.**

cancel *v.* 1. to stop something that has been arranged: *They cancelled the concert planned for next month.* 2. to cross out: *to cancel a stamp on an envelope.* **cancelling. cancelled.**

cancer *n.* an illness caused by a harmful growth in the body.

candidate *n.* a person seeking election.

candle *n.* a stick of wax with a wick in it, burned to give light.

candy *n.* something sweet to eat made with sugar and flavouring. *pl.* **candies.**

cane *n.* 1. the hard, springy stem of a bamboo or sugar plant. 2. a walking stick.

cannibal *n.* a person who eats human flesh.

cannon *n.* 1. a large, old-fashioned gun, used to fire iron balls. 2. a large gun that shoots explosive shells.

cannot *v.* to be unable to: *We cannot see through the fog.* **could not.**

canoe *n.* a very light, narrow boat, moved with a paddle.

can't short for **cannot.**

cantaloupe (kant′ə lōp) *n.* a sweet, juicy melon.

canvas *n.* a strong cloth used for shoes, tents, and sails.

canyon *n.* a steep valley.

cap *n.* 1. a soft hat with a peak. 2. a lid for a bottle. 3. a small amount of explosive, used in toy pistols. *v.* to cover with a cap: *to cap a bottle.* **capping. capped.**

capable (kā′pə bəl) *adj.* able to do something well: *Fran is a very capable writer.*

capacity *n.* the amount of space in a room, cup, bowl, etc.: *What is the seating capacity of the auditorium?* *pl.* **capacities.**

cape *n.* 1. a cloak, an overcoat without sleeves. 2. a part of the land sticking out into the water.

capital *n.* 1. a city where the government meets: *Ottawa is Canada's capital. Victoria is British Columbia's capital.* 2. a large letter: *capital B.*

capsize *v.* to overturn: *The canoe capsized in the rough water.* **capsizing. capsized.**

capsule (kap′səl) *n.* 1. a small container: *a medicine capsule.* 2. the front part of a rocket.

captain *n.* 1. a sailor in command of a ship. 2. a soldier in command of a company. 3. someone who leads a sports team.

captive *n.* a prisoner.

captivity *n.* being held in prison.

capture *v.* to seize and hold: *to capture a fort.* **capturing. captured.**

car *n.* a vehicle on wheels, usually an automobile.

card *n.* 1. a piece of stiff paper, often with a printed message: *a birthday card.* 2. a piece of stiff paper used in games.

cardboard *n.* a thick kind of stiff paper, used for making boxes.

cardinal *n.* 1. a high-ranking member of the Roman Catholic clergy, next in line to the Pope. 2. a bright red songbird.

care *n.* worry, trouble: *Steve sang happily, without a care in the world.* *v.* 1. to feel concerned about: *I do not care what he says.* 2. (used with **for**) to look after, to tend: *Mary cares for her cat, feeding him every day.* **caring. cared.**

career *n.* a type of work: *a career in teaching.*

careful *adj.* cautious, taking care: *Always be careful when using matches.* **carefully** *adv.*

careless *adj.* not taking care. **carelessly** *adv.*

caretaker *n.* someone who looks after a building, a janitor.

cargo *n.* goods carried by ship. *pl.* **cargoes.**

Caribbean (ka rib′ē ən, kar ib ē′ən) *adj.* having to do with the Caribbean Sea or the Caribbean islands: *Jamaica and Trinidad are among the Caribbean islands.*

caribou (kar′ ə bü) *n.* a North American reindeer. *pl.* **caribou.**

carnival *n.* an event with amusements, rides, food, etc.

carol *n.* a song of joy: *a Christmas carol.*

carpenter *n.* a person who makes and repairs wooden furniture and the wooden parts of buildings.

carpentry *n.* working with wood: *to study carpentry.*

carpet *n.* a thick, soft covering for floors and stairs.

carriage (kar'ij) *n.* a vehicle, often one pulled by horses.

carrot *n.* a plant with a long, orange root that is eaten as a vegetable.

carry *v.* to take something from one place to another. **carrying. carried.** she **carries.**

cart *n.* a vehicle, usually one pulled by a horse.

cartoon *n.* 1. a funny drawing. 2. a movie made with drawings.

carve *v.* 1. to cut wood or stone into a shape. 2. to cut meat into slices. **carving. carved.**

case *n.* 1. a box in which to keep things: *a pencil case, a jewel case.* 2. a special condition: *Kit has a case of chicken-pox.*
in case if it should happen: *Take your coat in case it rains.*
in any case whatever happens: *Rain or shine, I'll go in any case.*

cash *n.* money in the form of coins or notes: *The teller in the bank handles lots of cash. v.* to get money from a bank or other place: *Marlene cashed her cheque at the bank.* **cashing. cashed.**

cashier (kash ēr') *n.* a person in charge of money, usually in a bank or store.

casserole *n.* 1. a covered dish in which food is baked and served. 2. the food prepared in such a dish.

cast *n.* 1. a plaster support, used to protect broken bones while they are mending.
2. the actors in a play, program, or movie.
v. 1. to throw: *Fred cast his fishing line into the river.* 2. to choose actors for a play, program, or movie. **casting. cast.**

castle *n.* 1. a fort. 2. a palace.

cat *n.* 1. a small, furry animal kept as a pet. 2. a member of the cat family: *Lions, tigers, and leopards are large, wild cats.*

catalogue, catalog *n.* a list of things: *a catalogue of books in a library; a department store catalogue.*

catch *v.* 1. to seize something and hold it: *to catch a ball.* 2. to wait for and enter: *to catch a bus.* 3. to be made ill by: *to catch a cold.* **catching. caught** (cawt).

catcher *n.* in baseball, the player who stands behind home plate.

catching *adj.* able to be passed on from one person to another: *Measles is a catching disease.*

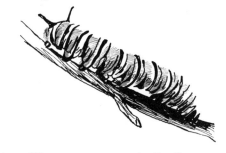

caterpillar *n.* a young butterfly or moth: *The worm-like caterpillar became a bright and beautiful butterfly.*

cathedral (kə thē'drəl) *n.* the main church of a large district.

Catholic *n.* a member of the Roman Catholic church.

cattle *n.* bulls, cows, and steers.

caught see **catch.**

cauliflower *n.* a large white vegetable.

cause *n.* 1. a person or thing that makes something happen: *Careless smoking was the cause of the fire.* 2. a worthy organization to which people give time or money. *v.* to start something happening: *The boys caused a fire by playing with matches.* **causing. caused.**

caution (kaw′shən) *n.* care: *Handle this box of eggs with caution.* *v.* to warn of danger: *The guard cautioned us not to touch the animals in the cage.* **cautioning. cautioned.**

cautious *adj.* careful, watching for danger: *a cautious driver.*

cave, cavern *n.* a large hole in a cliff or hillside.

cavity *n.* a hollow place: *a cavity in a tooth.* *pl.* **cavities.**

C.B. *n.* short for **Citizen's Band** radio.

cease *v.* to stop, to come to an end: *When all the talking ceased, the teacher showed the movie.* **ceasing. ceased.**

cedar *n.* an evergreen tree with spreading branches and fragrant wood.

ceiling (sē′ling) *n.* the inside top surface of a room.

celebrate *v.* to mark or honour an occasion by doing something special: *to celebrate a birthday.* **celebrating. celebrated.**

celebration *n.* a happy event in honour of someone or something.

celery *n.* a vegetable with long, green stems.

cell (sel) *n.* 1. a small room in a prison. 2. a small unit of life: *All animals and plants are made of cells.* 3. an electric battery.

cellar *n.* 1. an underground storeroom. 2. a basement.

cello (chel′ō) *n.* a musical instrument with strings, larger than a violin. *pl.* **cellos.**

Celsius *adj.* the scale on which we measure temperature; °C is the symbol.

cement *n.* a grey powder used for making concrete.

cemetery *n.* a burial ground for the dead. *pl.* **cemeteries.**

cent *n.* a Canadian or American coin, one-hundredth of a dollar.

centimetre *n.* a measure of length; cm is the symbol. 100 cm = 1m

central *adj.* at or near the centre: *Prince George is in central British Columbia.*

centre, center *n.* 1. the middle point. 2. in sports, the position in the middle of the forward line.

century *n.* a hundred years. *pl.* **centuries.**

cereal *n.* 1. corn, rice, wheat, and other grains used for food. 2. a breakfast food made from any of these grains.

ceremony *n.* a formal celebration, sometimes happy, sometimes sad: *a wedding ceremony, a funeral ceremony, a graduation ceremony.* *pl.* **ceremonies.**

certain (sər′tən) *adj.* 1. sure: *Are you certain he will be there?* (*opp.* **uncertain.**) 2. special, particular: *I am looking for a certain flower.*

certainly *adv.* surely, without doubt: *I will certainly be there.*

certificate *n.* a signed statement, written or printed, proving that something is true: *a birth certificate, a doctor's certificate.*

chain *n.* a number of rings or links joined together in length. *v.* to fasten with a chain: *The dog was chained to the tree.* **chaining. chained.**

chair *n.* a seat with a back, for one person.

chalk (chawk) *n.* 1. a white limestone, seen in some cliffs. 2. a marking stick used for writing on chalkboards.

chalkboard *n.* a smooth surface used for drawing or writing on with chalk.

challenge *v.* to dare someone to try to beat you in a contest or game: *Pete challenged Esther to a game of checkers.* **challenging. challenged.**

champion *n.* someone who takes first place in a contest.

championship *n.* first place: *Stella won the school tennis championship.*

chance *n.* 1. luck: *It was only by chance that Sidney found his lost cap.* 2. an opportunity: *He has a good chance of getting that job.*

change *n.* 1. difference: *There is no change in the way the team is playing this year.* 2. money you get back when you pay too much. 3. loose coins: *small change.* *v.* 1. to become different: *You have changed since I saw you last!* 2. to exchange: *Will you change places?* **changing. changed.**

channel *n.* 1. a long, narrow stretch of water: *the English Channel.* 2. a band of frequencies given to a radio or TV station.

chapel *n.* a small church or part of a large church.

chapter *n.* a section of a book or story.

character (kar'ik tər) *n.* 1. the nature of a person or thing: *Tom has a fine character.* 2. a person in a movie or play: *Donald plays the character of Robin Hood in the school play.*

charcoal *n.* a black substance, made of partly burned wood, used in artists' pencils and for barbecues.

charge *n.* 1. an attack. 2. a price: *a charge of one dollar.* 3. an accusation by the police: *a charge of theft.* 4. an explosive put into a gun. *v.* 1. to attack. 2. to put a price on something. 3. to accuse or blame someone: *to charge someone with stealing.* 4. to buy items with a credit card. **charging. charged.**
in charge of taking care of: *Mimi is in charge of the baby while Mother is out.*

charity *n.* help and kindness shown to people. *pl.* **charities.**

Charlottetown *n.* capital city of Prince Edward Island.

charm *n.* 1. a magic spell. 2. an object that is supposed to bring good fortune: *a lucky charm.* 3. a pleasant manner: *a girl of great charm.* *v.* 1. to put under a magic spell. 2. to delight someone. **charming. charmed.**

charred *adj.* scorched, blackened with fire: *charred wood.*

chart *n.* a large piece of paper with information on it.

chase *n.* a running or riding after: *a police chase through the city.* *v.* to run after or ride after: *The dog chased the fire engine.* **chasing. chased.**

chat *n.* a friendly talk between people. *v.* to talk in an easy, friendly way. **chatting. chatted.**

chatter *n.* constant and sometimes silly talk. *v.* to talk in such a way. **chattering. chattered.**

chauffeur (shō fər') *n.* a person paid to drive a car.

cheap *adj.* not costing much. *adv.* **cheaply**

cheat *n.* someone who swindles others or is dishonest. *v.* to swindle someone, to be dishonest. **cheating. cheated.**

check *n.* 1. someone or something that holds back action: *a hockey check.* 2. a mark to show that something is correct (✓). 3. a review to make sure that something is correct. 4. a restaurant bill. *v.* 1. to examine carefully to make sure everything is correct. 2. to stop someone or something, to hold back. 3. to leave for safekeeping: *Check your coat at the door.* **checking. checked.**

checkers *n. pl.* a game played with red and black pieces on a board of 64 squares.

cheek *n.* the side of your face below each eye.

cheer *n.* a chant or shout of joy: *a school cheer.* *v.* 1. to shout applause and encouragement: *They cheered the school team.* 2. to try to make someone feel happier: *We tried to get Harry to cheer up, but he still felt sad.* **cheering. cheered.**

cheerful *adj.* bright and smiling, happy. **cheerfully** *adv.*

cheese *n.* food made from the curds of milk.

chef (shef) *n.* a cook, usually the head cook in a restaurant.

chemical (kem′ə kəl) *n.* a substance used in chemistry.

chemist (kem′ist) *n.* a person who studies chemicals and uses them to make substances, such as dyes and medicines.

chemistry (kem′is trē) *n.* the study of what things are made of: *Chemistry shows us how substances can be mixed to make new substances.*

cheque (chek) *n.* a written order to a bank to pay money to someone.

cherry *n.* a small, round, red fruit with a hard pit inside *pl.* **cherries.**

chess *n.* a game played with black and white pieces on a board of 64 squares.

chest *n.* 1. a large, strong box. 2. the part of your body around your ribs.

chesterfield *n.* a long couch with a back and arms.

chestnut *n.* 1. the brown nut of the chestnut tree. 2. a reddish-brown colour. *adj.* having this colour.

chew *v.* to turn food over in your mouth while digging your teeth into it. **chewing. chewed.**

chick *n.* a very young bird, especially a young chicken.

chicken *n.* a hen or rooster.

chicken-pox *n.* a catching disease: *The chicken-pox patient has a rash and a fever.*

chief *n.* the leader of a group. *adj.* main, most important: *His chief wish is to own a bicycle.*

child *n.* a young boy or girl. *pl.* **children.**

chill *n.* a cold feeling, with shivering.

chilly *adj.* cold: *a chilly day, a chillier day, the chilliest day of the week.*

chime *n.* a kind of bell. *v.* for bells to ring out, or for a clock to strike the hour. **chiming. chimed.**

chimney *n.* a long structure, letting smoke escape from a fireplace or furnace. *pl.* **chimneys.**

chimpanzee *n.* a kind of African ape.

chin *n.* the part of the face below the mouth.

china *n.* fine dishes.

Chinese *n.* the language spoken in China. *adj.* belonging to or coming from China.

chinook (shin ük′) *n.* a warm winter wind that blows across parts of Western Canada.

chip *n.* a piece cut or broken off: *a potato chip.* *v.* to break off a small piece. **chipping. chipped.**

chipmunk *n.* a small, striped squirrel.

chirp *n.* the small squeak of some birds and insects: *the chirp of sparrows.* *v.* to make such a noise. **chirping. chirped.**

chisel *n.* a tool for cutting wood or stone. *v.* to use such a tool. **chiselling. chiselled.**

chocolate *n.* a food made from cacao seeds and used to make candy and cake.

choice *n.* 1. the picking of something: *It is hard to make a choice because I like everything.* 2. the thing chosen: *Vanilla ice cream is my choice.*

choir (kwīr) *n.* a group of trained singers, especially one that sings in a church.

choke *v.* to suffocate, not to be able to breathe properly: *I took too big a bite of the apple, and it nearly choked me.* **choking. choked.**

choose *v.* 1. to pick: *I choose this cake.* 2. to decide: *I chose to go out.* **choosing. chose.** I have **chosen.**

chop *n.* a small piece of meat joined to a bone. *v.* to cut with sharp blows: *to chop down a tree.* **chopping. chopped.**

chore *n.* a task: *Drying the dishes is one of my daily chores.*

chorus (kor'əs) *n.* 1. a group of people singing together: *The chorus on the stage sang popular songs.* 2. the part of a song that is repeated. *pl.* **choruses.**

Christ see **Jesus Christ.**

christen (kris'ən) *v.* to give a baby its Christian name; to baptize a child as a Christian. **christening. christened.**

christening *n.* the ceremony of baptizing a baby.

Christian *n.* a person who believes in Jesus Christ.

Christianity *n.* the religion taught by Jesus Christ and his followers.

Christmas *n.* the yearly festival held on December 25th, to honour the birth of Jesus Christ.

chubby *adj.* plump, a little overweight: *a chubby chimp, a chubbier chimp, the chubbiest chimp of all.*

chuckle *n.* a quiet laugh. *v.* to laugh quietly to yourself. **chuckling. chuckled.**

chum *n.* a close friend, a pal.

chunk *n.* a thick piece: *a chunk of meat for the dog.*

church *n.* a building in which people worship God.

churchyard *n.* the yard around a church.

churn *n.* a container in which cream is shaken or beaten to make butter. *v.* to shake or beat cream into butter. **churning. churned.**

chute (shüt) *n.* a narrow passage through which objects may pass: *a garbage chute.*

cigar *n.* rolled tobacco leaves, for smoking.

cigarette *n.* shredded tobacco rolled in a paper tube, for smoking.

cinders *n. pl.* partly burned pieces of wood or coal left after a fire.

cinnamon *n.* a spice used to flavour cakes and other food.

circle *n.* a perfectly round ring.

circular *n.* a letter, advertisement, or notice sent to a number of people: *Everyone on our street received a circular about the fair.* *adj.* in the shape of a circle.

circus *n.* a travelling show with clowns, acrobats, animals, etc. *pl.* **circuses.**

citizen *n.* a member of a nation, by birth or by choice.

city *n.* a large town. *pl.* **cities.**

claim *n.* 1. a right to something. 2. a prospector's piece of land. *v.* to say that you have a right to something, that it belongs to you: *Bruce claimed the wallet at the lost and found department.* **claiming. claimed.**

clam *n.* a shellfish that lives in sand.

clamp *n.* a piece of metal equipment that holds parts together firmly. *v.* to fasten with this or a similar piece of equipment. **clamping. clamped.**

clang *n.* a deep, ringing sound: *the clang of a bell. v.* to make such a sound. **clanging. clanged.**

clap *n.* a slapping together of the hands. *v.* to slap your hands together, to applaud someone. **clapping. clapped.**

clarinet *n.* a musical wind instrument, shaped like a tube.

clasp *n.* a hook, used to hold something together: *Kate's scarf was fastened by a metal clasp. v.* 1. to fasten something with a clasp. 2. to hug someone, to give a firm handshake. **clasping. clasped.**

class *n.* a group of students who are taught together.

classroom *n.* a room in which school classes are held.

clatter *n.* sharp, rattling sounds: *the clatter of dishes v.* to make such sounds: *The horses' hooves clattered down the road.* **clattering. clattered.**

claw *n.* the hooked nail of a bird and some other animals. *v.* to tear at something with claws: *The tiger clawed at the meat.* **clawing. clawed.**

clay *n.* a smooth, sticky kind of earth, which hardens in a furnace: *Bricks and pottery are made of clay.*

clean *adj.* free from dirt, neat and tidy. *v.* to free from dirt. **cleaning. cleaned.**

clear *adj.* 1. bright, cloudless: *a clear sky.* 2. easily understood: *We heard every word because she had a clear voice.* (*opp.* **unclear.**) **clearly** *adv. v.* to tidy, to clean out: *Al cleared the cupboards.* **clearing. cleared.**

clergy (klər′jē) *n. pl.* persons trained to teach religion and lead services: *Members of the clergy include priests, ministers, pastors, and rabbis.*

clerk *n.* 1. a salesperson in a store. 2. an office worker who looks after files and does other jobs.

clever *adj.* quick at learning, able to do things well.

click *n.* a sharp, little sound: *the click of a camera. v.* to make such a sound. **clicking. clicked.**

cliff *n.* a very steep rock, especially where land meets sea.

climate *n.* the kind of weather that a place usually has.

climb (klīm) *n.* getting up stairs, mountains, etc.: *a mountain climb. v.* 1. to get up stairs or a steep hill, rock, or tree. 2 to rise steeply: *The airplane climbed in the sky.* **climbing. climbed.**

cling *v.* to hold fast to: *The little raccoon clung to its mother.* **clinging. clung.**

clinic *n.* a place where you can see a doctor for treatment and not have to stay overnight.

clip *n.* a fastener: *a hair clip, a paper clip. v.* to trim with scissors or shears: *to clip a hedge.* **clipping. clipped.**

clipper *n.* 1. a large, fast sailing ship, once used for carrying goods across the ocean. 2. a tool used for cutting: *a hair clipper.*

cloak *n.* a cape, a coat without sleeves.

clock *n.* a machine that tells the time.

clog *v.* to choke up: *Grease clogged the pipe, and water would not go down the sink.* **clogging. clogged.**

close (klōz) *v.* 1. to shut: *Close the door, please!* 2. to come to an end: *The meeting closed with a speech.* **closing. closed.**

close (klōs) *adj.* very dear: *Robert and I are close friends. adv.* near: *The bird flew close to them.*

closely *adv.* carefully: *Muriel examined the photograph closely.*

closet *n.* a small room for storing things such as towels, clothes, or sheets.

cloth *n.* woven material of cotton, wool, silk, nylon, or linen threads: *a dish cloth.*

clothe (klōTH) *v.* to dress: *Rena clothed herself in her best summer dress.* **clothing. clothed.**

clothes (klōTHz) *n.* the garments we wear: *Judy always wears nice clothes.*

clothing (klō'THing) *n.* clothes.

cloud *n.* 1. a white or grey mass floating in the sky, made up of tiny water drops. 2. anything like a cloud: *a cloud of smoke. v.* to cover over, to make hazy. **clouding. clouded.**

clover *n.* a meadow plant with leaves in three or sometimes four parts.

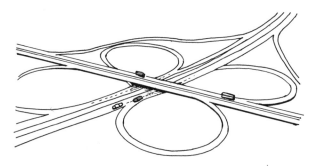

cloverleaf *n.* a road crossing that is in the shape of a four-leaf clover: *A cloverleaf is built so that vehicles may move from one highway to another without having to cross in front of other traffic. pl.* **cloverleaves.**

clown *n.* a circus performer who makes everyone laugh. *v.* to act like a clown. **clowning. clowned.**

club *n.* 1. a short, thick stick used as a weapon. 2. a long stick with a special head for hitting a ball: *a golf club.* 3. a group of people who meet to enjoy some interest together: *a hockey club.* 4. a playing card with one or more (♣) marks on it. *v.* to hit with a club. **clubbing. clubbed.**

cluck *v.* to make a noise like a hen. **clucking. clucked.**

clue *n.* some small thing that helps in solving a mystery or answering a riddle.

clump *n.* a number of flowers or trees growing together.

clumsy (klum'zē) *adj.* awkward in moving about and in doing things: *You are clumsy, but I am clumsier. He is the clumsiest of all.*

clung see **cling.**

cluster *n.* a bunch, a group: *a cluster of grapes.*

clutch *v.* 1. to grab. 2. to hang on to: *The baby clutched his mother's hand.* **clutching. clutched.**

coach *n.* 1. a large, closed, four-wheeled carriage pulled by horses. 2. a railway car. 3. someone who trains a sports team. *v.* to train someone for a sport, or to prepare someone for a test. **coaching. coached.**

coal *n.* a hard, black mineral used as fuel.

coarse *adj.* 1. rough: *coarse sandpaper.* 2. not fine: *coarse sand.*

coast *n.* the seashore. *v.* to travel along in an easy manner: *The boat coasted through the waves.* **coasting. coasted.**

coat *n.* 1. an outer garment with buttons or a zipper down the front. 2. a covering: *a coat of paint.*

coating *n.* a covering: *a coating of paint on wood.*

coax *v.* to persuade gently, using kind words: *We had to coax the puppy to come to us.* **coaxing. coaxed.**

cob *n.* the hard, middle part of an ear of corn.

cobbler *n.* someone who mends boots and shoes.

cobra (kō'brə) *n.* a poisonous snake of Asia and Africa.

cobweb *n.* a spider's net, used for catching flies.

cock (*fem.* **hen**) *n.* a fowl, a rooster.

cocker spaniel a small dog with long hair and drooping ears.

cockpit *n.* the place in an aircraft where the pilot sits.

cockroach *n.* an insect pest, sometimes found near food.

cocoa (kō'kō) *n.* 1. a brown powder made from the seeds of the cacao tree. 2. a hot chocolate drink made from this powder.

coconut *n.* the large nut of the coco palm tree, which grows in hot climates.

cocoon (kə kün') *n.* the silky case spun for protection by some young insects: *The caterpillar spins a cocoon before it changes into a moth.*

cod *n.* a fish that is found in the northern Atlantic Ocean. *pl.* **cod.**

code *n.* 1. signs or secret words used to make a secret message. 2. a set of rules: *the traffic code.*

coffee *n.* a drink made from the roasted seeds of the coffee plant.

coffin *n.* the box in which a dead person is buried.

coil *n.* a wire or rope wound round and round in a spiral. *v.* to wind around in a spiral. **coiling. coiled.**

coin *n.* a piece of metal money.

coincidence (kō in'sə dəns) *n.* two or more things happening by chance at the same time: *By coincidence, my two favourite books were written in the same year.*

cold *n.* an illness causing you to sneeze and cough. *adj.* being without warmth, not hot.

collage (kə lahzh') *n.* a picture made by pasting on different things such as string, newspaper, and glitter.

collapse *v.* to fall down suddenly, to break down: *The old barn collapsed in the storm.* **collapsing. collapsed.**

collar *n.* 1. the part of a garment that fits around the neck. 2. something worn around the neck: *a dog collar.*

collect *v.* 1. to take in: *We collect money for the hospital.* 2. to gather, as a hobby: *John collects stamps.* 3. to meet: *A crowd collected around the accident.* **collecting. collected.**

collection *n.* a number of things collected: *a coin collection.*

collector *n.* a person who collects things for his or her own use or for someone else: *a stamp collector, a tax collector.*

college *n.* 1. a school you can go to after high school: *a community college.* 2. a building that is part of a university.

collide *v.* to bump hard into something. **colliding. collided.**

collie *n.* a large, shaggy dog with a long pointed nose.

collision *n.* a big crash when one thing knocks hard into another.

colon *n.* 1. a punctuation mark (:). 2. the large intestine in your body.

colonel (kər'nəl) *n.* an army officer who commands a regiment.

colony *n.* 1. a group of people settling in a new land. 2. the settlement made by such a group. 3. a group of animals of the same kind, living together: *an ant colony.* *pl.* **colonies.**

colour, color *n.* red, blue, and yellow, or any combination of these. *v.* to give colour to, or change the colour of, something. **colouring. coloured.**

colourful, colorful *adj.* full of colour, bright.

colt (*fem.* **filly**) *n.* a young male horse.

column (kol'əm) *n.* 1. a pillar. 2. a list of numbers, one below the other: *to add up a column of figures.* 3. one of the sections, running from top to bottom, of a newspaper page.

comb (kōm) *n.* 1. a piece of plastic or metal with teeth, used to smooth your hair. 2. the red crest on a cock's head. *v.* to smooth your hair with a comb. **combing. combed.**

combat *n.* a battle, a fight. *v.* to fight. **combatting. combatted.**

combine *v.* to join together: *The two clubs decided to combine to raise money for new equipment.* **combining. combined.**

come *v.* 1. to move near, to approach: *I can hear the train coming.* 2. to arrive: *On which day will they come?* **coming. came.** I have **come.**

comedian *n.* an actor who plays funny parts and tells jokes.

comedy *n.* a funny play, movie, or program. *pl.* **comedies.**

comet *n.* a star-like body in the sky, with a long, glowing tail.

comfort *n.* a relaxed feeling: *Uncle Dennis sat in the armchair in great comfort.* (*opp.* **discomfort.**) *v.* to help someone by kind actions and words: *The nurse tried to comfort the crying child.* **comforting. comforted.**

comfortable *adj.* at ease. (*opp.* **uncomfortable.**)

comic *n.* 1. a comedian. 2. a comic book. *adj.* funny: *a comic actor.*

comical *adj.* funny, amusing.

comma *n.* a punctuation mark (,).

command *n.* 1. an order. 2. charge over: *The captain has command of the ship.* *v.* 1. to order someone to do something. 2. to take charge of: *The captain commands his ship.* **commanding. commanded.**

commander *n.* a leader who takes charge.

commandment *n.* 1. a law. 2. one of the laws called the Ten Commandments, which are found in the Bible.

comment *n.* an opinion or other remark, either spoken or written down. *v.* to make such a remark: *Tim commented that the team could have played a better game.* **commenting. commented.**

commerce *n.* trade, business, buying, and selling.

commercial *n.* an advertisement on radio or television. *adj.* having to do with commerce.

commit *v.* 1. to do something, usually wrong: *to commit a crime.* 2. to promise to do something: *She committed herself to speaking at the meeting.* **committing. committed.**

committee *n.* a small group of people who meet to make rules and plan programs: *The football committee meets on Monday.*

common *adj.* happening or found everywhere, not rare: *Daisies are common flowers.* (*opp.* **uncommon.**)

commotion *n.* a noisy disturbance.

communicate *v.* to tell something to others by talking or writing. **communicating. communicated.**

community *n.* a group of people living in a neighbourhood. *pl.* **communities.**

companion *n.* a friend who goes somewhere or shares time with you.

companionship *n.* friendship.

company *n.* 1. guests: *We had company at our house yesterday.* 2. a business firm: *the firm of Smith and Company.* *pl.* **companies.** 3. companionship: *I like your company when I go shopping.*

compare *v.* to look at things and see the difference: *When you compare these two drawings, you see that Bart's is more colourful than Bill's.* **comparing. compared.**

comparison *n.* the comparing of things.

compartment *n.* a separate section of something: *the compartments in a jewellery box.*

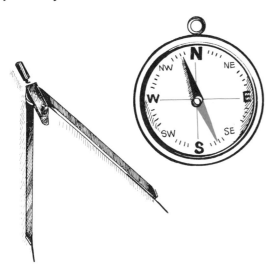

compass *n.* 1. an instrument that shows directions: *The needle of a compass points to the North.* 2. an instrument used for drawing circles or measuring distances on a drawing.

compete *v.* to enter a competition: *Lorna competed in the high jump.* **competing. competed.**

competition *n.* 1. a contest. 2. rivalry: *The players think they did better because the competition was great.*

competitor *n.* someone who takes part in a contest or competition.

complain *v.* to find fault with or object to something: *She complained that the soup was cold.* **complaining. complained.**

complaint *n.* the finding of a fault: *Helen had a complaint about the food at camp.*

complete *adj.* whole, with everything there: *Marc gave Gord his complete train set.* (*opp.* **incomplete.**) *v.* to finish: *Complete your homework before you go out.* **completing. completed. completely** *adv.*

complexion *n.* the appearance of the skin on your face: *Tom has a smooth complexion.*

complicated *adj.* difficult, not simple: *a complicated problem.*

compliment *n.* words of praise, something nice you say to someone: *We paid a compliment to the singer.*

compose *v.* to make up or put together something: *to compose a song, to compose a story or poem.* **composing. composed.**

composer *n.* someone who writes music.

composition *n.* a piece of writing or music.

compute (kəm pyüt′) *v.* to figure out, to calculate: *Please compute this sum.* **computing. computed.**

computer (kəm pyü′tər) *n.* a machine that does calculations quickly and stores information.

conceal *v.* to hide, to keep secret. **concealing. concealed.**

conceited (kən sē′təd) *adj.* having too high an opinion of yourself: *That conceited player thinks he is the best member of the team.*

concentrate *v.* to give careful attention to one thing only: *Concentrate on your work.* **concentrating. concentrated.**

concentration *n.* careful attention to something: *Accidents are often caused by lack of concentration.*

concern *n.* business: *Do not interfere. This is my concern!* *v.* to be important to: *The news today concerns everyone in the club.* **concerning. concerned.**

concert *n.* a performance of music by a number of players.

conclude *v.* to finish, to end. **concluding. concluded.**

conclusion *n.* 1. ending: *the conclusion of a letter.* 2. an opinion: *Mother came to the conclusion that she should send for the doctor.*

concrete *n.* a kind of stone used in building, made from cement, water, and sand or gravel.

condition *n.* 1. the state something is in: *This pony is in poor condition.* 2. part of an agreement: *Father gave Shirley and Gord the puppy on the condition that they look after it.*

conduct (kon'dukt) *n.* behaviour: *Neil's conduct is always excellent.*

conduct (kən dukt') *v.* 1. to lead: *The guide conducted the people through the museum.* 2. to direct a choir or an orchestra. **conducting. conducted.**

conductor *n.* 1. someone who beats time and directs an orchestra or a choir. 2. the person in charge of a train, bus, or streetcar.

cone *n.* 1. anything shaped like a clown's hat, circular at one end and coming to a point at the other: *an ice-cream cone.* 2. the woody fruit of an evergreen tree.

confess *v.* to admit, usually to tell that you have done something wrong: *Pat confessed to eating the last cookie.* **confessing. confessed.**

confession *n.* the admitting of your mistakes.

confetti *n.* tiny bits of coloured paper.

confidence *n.* perfect trust: *I have confidence that they will complete the hike by sunset.*

confident *adj.* bold, sure of yourself: *Denis felt confident that he would pitch a good game.*

confuse (kən fyüz') *v.* 1. to mix up someone: *Edgar confused me with all the things he said.* 2. to mistake one thing for another: *Sue confused the two houses and went to the wrong one.* **confusing. confused.**

confusion *n.* a mix-up: *In the confusion, Tina lost her cap.*

congratulate *v.* to express your happiness to someone over his or her success: *I congratulated Peter when he won the race.* **congratulating. congratulated.**

congratulations *n. pl.* good wishes offered on a person's success.

congregation *n.* a gathering of people.

conjunction *n.* a joining word: *In 'ham and cheese', the word 'and' is the conjunction.*

connect *v.* to join one thing to another. **connecting. connected.** (*opp.* **disconnect.**)

connection *n.* the joining together of two parts.

conquer (kong'kər) *v.* to overcome, to beat in battle. **conquering. conquered.**

conqueror *n.* someone who gains a victory in battle.

conquest *n.* the winning, usually of a battle: *the conquest of the country.*

conscience (kon'shəns) *n.* a feeling that tells you whether something is right or wrong.

conscious (kon'shəs) *adj.* awake and aware of everything around. (*opp.* **unconscious.**)

consent (kən sent') *v.* to agree to something, to give permission. **consenting. consented.**

consequence *n.* a result: *Mike tried to walk on the ledge, and as a consequence he fell.*

consider *v.* to think about, to turn over in your mind: *Consider all the choices before giving your answer.* **considering. considered.**

considerable *adj.* great, important: *A considerable number of people wanted to join the ski club.*

considerate *adj.* kind, thoughtful about others: *Bill is considerate . He's always ready to help others.* (*opp.* **inconsiderate.**)

consist *v.* (used with **of**) to be made up: *The book consists of 120 pages.* **consisting. consisted.**

consonant *n.* any letter of the alphabet that is not one of the five vowels (a, e, i, o, u): *There are 21 consonants in the ' English alphabet.*

constable (kon'stə bəl) *n.* a police officer.

constant *adj.* 1. always happening: *the constant ticking of a clock.* 2. always present: *My dog is my constant companion.* **constantly** *adv.*

construct *v.* to build, to put together: *to construct a model.* **constructing. constructed.**

construction *n.* something built or put together.

consult (kən sult') *v.* 1. to ask the advice of someone: *to consult a doctor about your health.* 2. to seek information from: *to consult a dictionary for the spelling of a word.* **consulting. consulted.**

contact (kon'takt) *v.* to get in touch with: *Contact the newspaper if you want more information.* **contacting. contacted.**

contagious (kən tā'jəs) *adj.* spreading from one person to another: *Measles is a contagious disease.*

contain *v.* to hold: *This box contains nuts and bolts.* **containing. contained.**

container *n.* a box, jar, barrel, etc. used to hold something.

content (kən tent') *adj.* pleased, satisfied: *Kim was content with the prize he won.*

contents (kon'tents) *n. pl.* the things you find in a book or a container: *Towels and sheets were the only contents of the old trunk.*

contest *n.* a game or race that people try to win.

contestant *n.* a person who takes part in a contest: *a contestant on a quiz show.*

continent *n.* a very large mass of land: *Europe, Asia, Africa, North America, South America, Australia, and Antarctica are the seven continents of the world.*

continual *adj.* often happening, frequent: *There were continual breaks in the lesson.*

continue *v.* 1. to keep on doing something: *It continued raining all day.* 2. to start again after stopping: *After a break for lunch, the team continued cycling.* **continuing. continued.**

continuous *adj.* happening without stopping: *the continuous roar of traffic.*

contract (kon'trakt) *n.* an agreement: *The singer signed a contract with the record company.*

contract (kən trakt') *v.* to become smaller, to shrink: *The pupils of your eyes contract in a bright light.* **contracting. contracted.**

contraction *n.* a shortened form of two words: *'Isn't' is the contraction of 'is not'.*

contribute (kən trib'yüt) *v.* to pay or give something: *Eric contributed money to the new hospital.* **contributing. contributed.**

contribution *n.* something paid or put into a fund.

control v. 1. to have power over, to govern: *The ancient Romans controlled a great empire.* 2. to keep in check: *Control your temper!* **controlling. controlled.**

convenience (kən vēn′yəns) n. something that makes things easier: *Buses are a great convenience.*

convenient adj. handy, saving trouble: *This short-cut to school is very convenient.* (opp. **inconvenient.**)

convention n. a large meeting arranged for a certain purpose: *a doctors' convention.*

conversation n. a chat.

convict (kon′vikt) n. someone who has been sent to prison.

convict (kən vikt′) v. to find someone guilty: *He was convicted of the crime.* **convicting. convicted.**

convince v. to persuade someone: *Carol convinced me that she was right.* **convincing. convinced.**

cook n. a person who prepares food. v. to prepare food by heating it. **cooking. cooked.**

cookie n. a small, sweet cake.

cool adj. 1. slightly cold: *The evening air was cool.* 2. calm, not excited: *The lion-tamer entered the lion's cage in a very cool way.*

copper n. a reddish-brown metal.

copy n. 1. anything made to look like something else. 2. one of a number of printed papers or books: *a copy of today's newspaper.* pl. **copies.** v. to make or do a similar thing: *Matthew copies famous pictures.* **copying. copied.** she **copies.**

coral (kor′əl) n. a hard, pink or white substance made up of the skeletons of small ocean creatures.

cord n. a thick string.

corduroy n. a strong, velvety material that has ridges.

corduroys n. pl. trousers made of corduroy cotton, often called 'cords'.

core n. the centre of a thing: *the core of an apple.*

cork n. a stopper for a bottle, made from the bark of a cork tree.

corn n. 1. a grain with yellow kernels: *an ear of corn.* 2. a hard lump on your foot.

corner n. a place where two walls, lines, etc. meet. v. to put into a corner: *The cat tried to corner the mouse.* **cornering. cornered.**

coronation n. the crowning of a king or queen.

corporal n. a soldier higher in rank than a private, lower in rank than a sergeant.

corpse n. a dead body.

corral (kə ral′) n. a closed-in area for horses, cattle, and other farm animals.

correct adj. without an error. (opp. **incorrect.**) v. to put right: *Correct your mistakes.* **correcting. corrected.**

correction n. something that has been made right: *The store made a correction when the manager saw that the price was wrong.*

corridor n. a long hall in a building.

cost n. the price of anything: *What is the cost of this toy train?* v. to sell for: *It costs two dollars.* **costing. cost.**

costly adj. costing a great deal: *a costly hobby, a costlier one, the costliest one of all.*

costume n. 1. clothes worn by an actor in a play. 2. a style of dress: *a display of national costumes.*

cosy, cozy adj. warm and snug, comfortable: *a cosy corner, a cosier one, the cosiest one in the house.*

cot *n.* a small bed, often for a baby.

cottage *n.* a small house, usually in the country.

cotton *n.* 1. the soft, white hairs of the cotton plant. 2. thread or cloth woven from these hairs.

couch *n.* a sofa or long seat for three or four people.

cough (kawf) *n.* the sharp sound made when you clear air from your lungs. *v.* to make such a sound. **coughing. coughed.**

could see **can.**

couldn't short for **could not.**

coulee (kü′lē) *n.* a dry river bed.

council *n.* a group of people called together to discuss something: *the town council.*

count (*fem.* **countess**) *n.* a nobleperson in some countries. *v.* 1. to add numbers. 2. to depend on: *We are counting on Willa to play on the team.* **counting. counted.**

countdown *n.* the time just before the firing of a missile or rocket.

country (kun′trē) *n.* 1. land away from towns: *We had a lovely time at a farm in the country.* 2. a nation: *Canada is my native country. pl.* **countries.**

county *n.* a government district, found in some countries, provinces, and states. *pl.* **counties.**

couple (kup′əl) *n.* two, a pair: *I caught a couple of fish.*

coupon (kü′pon) *n.* a ticket that can be exchanged for goods: *We had a discount coupon for the museum.*

courage (kər′ij) *n.* bravery.

courageous (kə rā′jəs) *adj.* brave, fearless.

course *n.* 1. the direction that something takes when it is moving: *the course of the river.* 2. a series of lessons: *Donald took a course in first aid.* 3. a part of a meal: *The main course was salmon.* 4. an area for a sport or game: *a golf course.*
of course naturally, yes.

court *n.* 1. a place where some game is played: *a tennis court.* 2. a place where justice is given: *a court of law.* 3. a royal palace.

courteous (kər′tē əs) *adj.* polite.

courtesy (kər′tə sē) *n.* politeness, good manners.

cousin (kuz′ən) *n.* the son or daughter of an aunt or uncle.

cove *n.* a small bay.

cover *n.* something put on top of another thing, usually to protect or hide it. *v.* to spread one thing over another: *We covered the firewood with a waterproof sheet.* **covering. covered.**
(*opp.* **uncover.**)

covering *n.* something that covers: *a covering of snow on the ground.*

cow (*masc.* **bull**) *n.* a full-grown female of cattle.

coward *n.* someone who runs away from trouble or danger.

cowboy, cowgirl *n.* a person who looks after cattle or who rides in a rodeo or stampede.

coyote (kī′ōt, kī ō′tē) *n.* a wild prairie animal that looks like a small wolf.

crab *n.* a shellfish with a round body, several legs, and claws. *v.* to complain: *Steve always crabs about supper.* **crabbing. crabbed.**

crack *n.* 1. a split: *a crack in a cup.* 2. a sharp sound: *the crack of a whip.* *v.* 1. to split: *to crack a vase.* 2. to break open: *to crack a nut.* 3. to make a sharp sound: *to crack a whip.* **cracking. cracked.**

cracker *n.* 1. a thin biscuit. 2. a small paper roll used at parties.

crackle *n.* a cracking noise: *the crackle of a fire.* *v.* to make such a sound: *The wood crackled on the fire.* **crackling. crackled.**

cradle *n.* a baby's bed.

craft *n.* the art of making things with your hands: *Macramé, weaving, and pottery are all crafts.*

crafty *adj.* sly, cunning: *a crafty fox, a craftier fox, the craftiest fox of all.*

cram *v.* to stuff: *The monkey crammed the food into its mouth.* **cramming. crammed.**

cramp *n.* a pain from a strained muscle, often in your leg or arm.

cranberry *n.* a sour, dark-red berry that grows in marshes. *pl.* **cranberries.**

crane *n.* 1. a big machine with a long arm for lifting and moving heavy weights. 2. a wading bird with a long beak and long legs.

crash *n.* 1. the noise of something being smashed. 2. falling, breaking, or colliding: *a car crash.* *v.* to fall, break, or collide. **crashing. crashed.**

crate *n.* a large wooden case for holding goods.

crater *n.* the opening of a volcano.

craving *n.* a great longing for something: *He had a craving for chocolate.*

crawl *n.* 1. a very slow pace. 2. an overarm stroke in swimming. *v.* to move on hands and knees, or along the ground. **crawling. crawled.**

crayon *n.* a coloured stick of chalk or wax used for drawing pictures.

crazy *adj.* mad, silly: *a crazy idea, a crazier idea, the craziest idea of all.*

creak *n.* a small, squeaking noise: *the creak of an old door.* *v.* to make such a noise. **creaking. creaked.**

cream *n.* the fatty part of milk, from which butter and other foods are made.

crease *n.* a mark made when cloth or paper is folded and pressed. *v.* to make such a fold. **creasing. creased.**

create (krē āt′) *v.* to make something new: *The inventor created a new kind of engine.* **creating. created.**

creative (krē ā′tiv) *adj.* able to think and make up things: *Creative writing means writing something new.*

creature *n.* a living thing.

credit *n.* 1. honour: *Angela's performance was a credit to her teacher.* 2. time allowed for the payment of goods: *To buy something on credit means to pay for it over a period of time.*

creek *n.* a small stream.

creep *v.* to walk slowly and quietly on your toes: *The cat creeps on its paws.* **creeping. crept.**

crepe paper (krāp pā′pər) thin, crinkled paper used for making decorations.

crest *n.* 1. the highest point: *the crest of a hill.* 2. a bunch of feathers on the head of a bird.

crew *n.* the people who work on a ship, plane, train, etc.

crib *n.* a baby's bed.

cricket *n.* 1. a black or brown insect that looks like a grasshopper. 2. a popular English game played with a ball and bats on a grass field.

cried, cries see **cry.**

crime *n.* breaking of the law in a serious way.

criminal *n.* someone guilty of a crime.

crimson *n.* a deep purplish-red colour. *adj.* having this colour.

crinkle *v.* to make little waves or wrinkles on a surface. **crinkling. crinkled.**

crinkled *adj.* wrinkled or rippled: *an old, crinkled piece of paper.*

crippled *adj.* being unable to move a part of the body in the proper way, because of an injury or disease.

crisp *adj.* fresh, firm, and easily broken: *a slice of crisp toast.*

crisscross *v.* to mark with crossed lines. **crisscrossing. crisscrossed.**

criticize *v.* to examine something and give ideas on what is good and what can be improved. **criticizing. criticized.**

croak *n.* the noise that a frog makes. *v.* to make such a noise. **croaking. croaked.**

crochet (krō shā′) *n.* a form of needlework, in which threads are looped into other loops with a hook. *v.* to do this work. **crocheting. crocheted.**

crocodile *n.* a large reptile with a pointed snout, found in the rivers and lakes of some warm countries.

crocus (krō′kəs) *n.* a small spring flower growing from a bulb. *pl.* **crocuses.**

crook *n.* a swindler, a thief.

crooked (krùk′id) *adj.* twisted, full of bends: *a crooked street.*

crop *n.* plants grown for food: *Wheat is the main crop of the Prairies.*

cross *n.* 1. a mark shaped like + or X. 2. the badge or emblem of Christianity. *adj.* angry, bad-tempered: *My brother was very cross when he burned his fingers.* *v.* to go from one side to another: *to cross the road.* **crossing. crossed.**

crouch *v.* to bend low: *Magda crouched to get under the rail.* **crouching. crouched.**

crow *n.* a big, black bird. *v.* to make a noise like a farmyard cock. **crowing. crowed.**

crowbar *n.* a heavy metal bar with one flattened end.

crowd *n.* a great number of people. *v.* to come together quickly: *The people crowded into the store.* **crowding. crowded.**

crown *n.* the head-dress of gold and jewels worn by a king or queen.

cruel (krü′əl) *adj.* very unkind, causing pain: *a cruel ruler.*

cruelty (krü əl′tē) *n.* the causing of pain or unkindness.

cruise (krüz) *n.* a pleasure trip on a ship.

cruiser *n.* a police car.

crumb (krum) *n.* a tiny bit of bread, cake, cookie, etc.

crumble *v.* to break into small pieces. **crumbling. crumbled.**

crumple *v.* to crush something and make wrinkles in it: *Ruth crumpled the paper bag and threw it away.* **crumpling. crumpled.**

crush *v.* to squeeze hard: *to crush lemons to make lemon juice.* **crushing. crushed.**

crust *n.* a hard outer covering: *a pie-crust, a crust of bread.*

crutch *n.* a thick stick with a padded end to fit under the arm, used by lame people.

cry *n.* a loud call, a loud shout. *pl.* **cries.** *v.* 1. to shout out loudly. 2. to shed tears. **crying. cried.** he **cries.**

crystal (kris′təl) *n.* 1. a hard mineral that looks like ice. 2. a piece of glass cut to look like this mineral.

cub *n.* a young fox, bear, wolf, lion, tiger, etc.

Cub *n.* a junior Boy Scout.

cube (kyüb) *n.* a solid object with six square faces or sides, all alike: *a sugar cube.*

cuckoo *n.* a grey bird that calls, 'cuckoo'.

cucumber (kyü′kum bər) *n.* a long, thin, green vegetable used in salads.

cud *n.* food that comes back into the mouth from the stomach of cows and other animals, to be chewed again.

cuddle *v.* to hug someone. **cuddling. cuddled.**

cuff *n.* 1. the turned-over end of a pant leg. 2. the end of a sleeve near the wrist.

culprit *n.* someone who has done something wrong.

cunning *adj.* sly, clever: *a cunning escape.*

cup *n.* 1. a small container with a handle, used for drinking. 2. anything like a cup: *Our team won the sports cup.*

cupboard (kub′ərd) *n.* a closet with shelves for clothes, books, dishes, or other things.

cupful *n.* as much as a cup will hold. *pl.* **cupfuls.**

curb *n.* the concrete edge of a street. *v.* to hold back, to control: *Curb your appetite.* **curbing. curbed.**

curd *n.* the thickened part of milk: *Cheese is formed from curds.*

curdle *v.* to go sour: *Milk curdles if it is left in a warm place.* **curdling. curdled.**

cure (kyür) *v.* 1. to heal, to make well: *The medicine cured Linda's sore throat.* 2. to preserve meat or skins by drying. **curing. cured.**

curiosity (kyü rē os′i tē) *n.* a desire to learn or know.

curious (kyü′rē əs) *adj.* 1. wanting to know: *Sharon was curious about what I had in my desk.* 2. unusual, interesting: *We found some curious shells on the beach.*

curl *n.* a twisted lock of hair. *v.* 1. to twist something, such as hair. 2. to play the game of curling. **curling. curled.**

curlers *n. pl.* metal or plastic rollers around which hair is wound to make curls.

curling *n.* a game in which heavy stones are slid on ice towards a target.

curly *adj.* in curls, not straight: *Bob's hair is curly. Glen's hair is curlier. Eileen's hair is curliest of all.*

currency *n.* the money of a country: *The 'yen' is the Japanese unit of currency.* *pl.* **currencies.**

current *n.* 1. a stream of air or water flowing quickly: *Wind is a current of air.* 2. a flow of electricity along a wire or cable. *adj.* of the present time: *current events.*

curry *n.* a hot, yellow spice, used in cooking.

curse *n.* an evil wish: *the witch's curse.* *v.* 1. to swear, to use bad language. 2. to wish evil on someone: *The witch cursed the young prince.* **cursing. cursed.**

curtain (kər′tən) *n.* a hanging cloth in front of a window or a theatre stage.

curve *n.* a smooth bend: *a curve in the road.*

cushion *n.* a soft pillow for a chair or chesterfield.

custard *n.* a pudding made of milk, eggs, and sugar.

custom *n.* a habit; a certain way of doing things: *It is John's custom to eat very little at breakfast.*

customer *n.* someone who buys.

customs *n. pl.* 1. taxes on goods brought in from another country. 2. government offices at a border between countries: *When we went to Washington, we had to go through customs.*

cut *n.* an opening made by a sharp object. *v.* to slash or divide with a knife, scissors, or other sharp object. **cutting. cut.**

cute *adj.* clever, lovable, pretty: *The puppy is a cute little thing.*

cycle *n.* beginning and ending in the same place: *the cycle of the seasons. v.* to ride on a bicycle: *We cycled through the park.* **cycling. cycled.**

cyclist *n.* someone riding a bicycle.

cyclone *n.* a heavy storm, with winds moving in a spiral towards the centre.

cylinder (sil'ən dər) *n.* 1. a hollow or solid object that is shaped like a tube. 2. the part of a gasoline engine where the gases are fired.

cymbals (sim'bəlz) *n. pl.* brass plates used by a drummer to make a clashing sound.

d

dab *n.* a small amount of a moist substance: *I put a dab of butter on the peas. v.* to touch lightly: *I dabbed some lotion on the sunburn.* **dabbing. dabbed.**

dachshund (daks'hŭnd) *n.* a small dog with a long body and very short legs.

dad, daddy *n.* father. *pl.* **daddies.**

daddy-longlegs *n.* an insect that looks like a spider: *A daddy-longlegs has six very long legs, and it does not bite.*

daffodil *n.* a tall plant with yellow or white flowers.

dagger *n.* a small knife with a short, pointed blade.

daily *adv.* every day: *The newspaper comes out daily. adj.* coming out or happening every day: *a daily newspaper.*

dainty *adj.* pretty and delicate: *dainty flowers, daintier flowers, the daintiest flowers in the garden.*

dairy *n.* a place where milk and cream are made into cheese and butter. *pl.* **dairies.**

daisy *n.* a small plant with white or pink flowers with a yellow centre. *pl.* **daisies.**

Dalmation *n.* a large dog whose white coat is covered with black or brown spots.

dam *n.* a wall built to hold back the water of a river, stream, creek, etc.

damage (dam'ij) *n.* breaking, injury, harm: *The accident caused great damage to the bike. v.* to break, injure, harm. **damaging. damaged.**

damp *adj.* a little bit wet.

dance *n.* 1. movement in time with music. 2. a party where people dance. *v.* to move feet and body in time to music. **dancing. danced.**

dandelion *n.* a plant with a bright yellow flower.

dandruff *n.* small white pieces of dead skin that fall from the scalp.

danger *n.* risk, something that may cause injury or death: *Fire in a building is a danger to those inside.*

dangerous *adj.* not safe: *Skating on thin ice is dangerous.* **dangerously** *adv.*

dangle *v.* to hang or swing loosely: *The keys dangled from the chain.* **dangling. dangled.**

dare *v.* 1. to risk, to take a chance: *Edward dared to walk up to the bull.* 2. to challenge someone: *I dare you to walk up to the bull.* **daring. dared.**

daredevil *n.* a person who takes risks.

dark *adj.* 1. without light: *a dark room.* 2. deep in colour: *a dark coat.*

darkness *n.* being dark: *My cat is scared of the darkness.*

darling *n.* someone very dear to you.

darn *v.* to fix a hole in cloth: *Please darn my socks.* **darning. darned.**

dart *n.* a small arrow thrown by hand at a board. *v.* to dash forward quickly: *When the rabbit saw me, it darted away.* **darting. darted.**

dash *n.* 1. a rush or quick movement. 2. a small line (–) used in writing. *v.* to move forward quickly: *He dashed by in a rush.* **dashing. dashed.**

dashboard *n.* the part of a car that holds the instruments.

date *n.* 1. the day, month, and year of some event: *What is today's date?* 2. an appointment: *We made a date for next week.* 3. a person with whom you go out. 4. the brown, sticky fruit of a type of palm tree. *v.* to go out with a member of the opposite sex. **dating. dated.**
out-of-date old-fashioned.
up-to-date in fashion, very new.

daughter *n.* a female child: *My grandmother has one daughter. My mother has two daughters.*

dawdle *v.* to waste time, to go slowly. **dawdling. dawdled.**

dawn *n.* sunrise, daybreak.

day *n.* 1. the time between sunrise and sunset. 2. a period of 24 hours, from one midnight to the next.

day-care centre a place where small children are looked after during the day.

daydream *n.* a dream, or imaginary happening, that comes to mind while you are awake.

daylight *n.* sunlight.

daylight-saving time one hour later than standard time: *When we switch to daylight-saving time, in the spring, we have an extra hour of sunlight at the end of the day.*

daytime *n.* the time between sunrise and sunset.

daze *v.* to confuse, to stun: *Jim was so dazed when he fell that he didn't know where he was.* **dazing. dazed.**

dazzle *v.* to blind or confuse someone by shining a bright light in his or her eyes. **dazzling. dazzled.**

dead (ded) *adj.* 1. not alive: *a dead body.* 2. without power: *a dead battery.* 3. complete: *dead silence.*

dead end a street closed at one end.

deadly *adj.* causing death: *a deadly poison, a deadlier one, the deadliest poison of all.*

deaf (def) *adj.* not able to hear.

deal *n.* 1. an amount: *a great deal of cheering.* 2. a sharing out: *a deal of the cards.* 3. a bargain: *We got a real deal on the bike.* 4. an agreement: *I made a deal with my brother.* *v.* 1. to share out playing cards. 2. to carry out business: *This store deals in hardware items.* **dealing. dealt** (delt).

dealer *n.* 1. a trader who buys and sells something. 2. the person who gives out the playing cards to the other players.

dear *n.* a lovable person. *adj.* 1. lovable, kindly. 2. a greeting at the beginning of a

letter: *Dear Grandma and Grandpa.*
3. expensive.

death (deth) *n.* the end of life, being dead.

debate *n.* a discussion between two people or two groups of people who believe different things. *v.* to discuss the reasons for or against something: *The Members of Parliament debated for hours.* **debating. debated.**

debt (det) *n.* something you owe to someone.

decade *n.* ten years: *The time from 1980 to 1990 is one decade.*

decay *n.* rot, or the beginning of a rotting condition: *the decay in the tree.* *v.* to rot and waste away. **decaying. decayed.**

December *n.* the twelfth month of the year.

decent (dē'sənt) *adj.* nice, well-mannered, considerate: *decent behaviour.*

decide *v.* to make up your mind: *It took me a long time to decide what I wanted to do.* **deciding. decided.**

decimal (des'ə məl) *adj.* based on the number 10: *The metric system is a decimal system.*

decision *n.* something that is decided or settled: *The umpire's decision is that Pat hit a foul ball.*

deck *n.* 1. a floor on a ship. 2. a set of playing cards.

declaration *n.* an announcement, a public statement.

declare *v.* to announce, to say something in public: *The official declared our team the winner.* **declaring. declared.**

decorate *v.* 1. to make something look nicer, especially a house or the walls of a room. 2. to pin a medal or ribbon on someone as an honour. **decorating. decorated.**

decoration *n.* 1. something used to decorate: *party decorations.* 2. a badge, medal, or ribbon awarded as an honour.

decrease *v.* to grow smaller, to become less: *In winter, the daylight decreases. In summer, it increases.* **decreasing. decreased.**

deed *n.* an action, the doing of something: *a brave deed.*

deep *adj.* 1. going a long way down from the top: *a deep river.* 2. low: *a deep voice.*

deer *n.* a wild animal that runs very quickly; the male deer has antlers. *pl.* **deer.**

defeat *n.* the loss of a game or battle. *v.* to beat someone in a game or battle. **defeating. defeated.**

defence, defense *n.* 1. a protection against attack: *The wall around the fort was built as a defence.* 2. a team or the players protecting a goal.

defend *v.* to protect, to guard from attack. **defending. defended.**

define *v.* to make clear the meaning of something: *A dictionary defines words.* **defining. defined.**

definite (def'ə nit) *adj.* clear, firm: *Janet made a definite promise to be home early.* **definitely** *adv.*

definition *n.* the meaning of a word: *Some words have more than one definition.*

defy *v.* 1. to refuse to obey: *He defied the orders.* 2. to dare: *I defy you to prove that the job can't be done.* **defying. defied.** she **defies.**

degree *n.* 1. a mark on a thermometer showing how hot or cold it is: *The temperature is 20 degrees Celsius* (20°C). 2. a title given to a university or college student when he or she graduates.

delay *n.* a wait, a putting off: *The coach is late. There will be a delay in the start of the game.* *v.* to put off till a later time: *The test was delayed for a week.* **delaying. delayed.**

deliberate (di lib′ər ət) *adj.* done on purpose: *The teacher made a deliberate mistake on the chalkboard. The class had to find what it was.* **deliberately** *adv.*

delicate (del′i kət) *adj.* weak, tender: *Delicate plants will die in the frost.*

delicatessen *n.* a store that sells prepared foods such as cold meats and salads.

delicious (di lish′əs) *adj.* very enjoyable to eat or smell.

delight (di līt′) *n.* great pleasure: *Charles welcomed his friend with delight. v.* to please a great deal. **delighting. delighted.**

delightful *adj.* very pleasing: *We read a delightful story.* **delightfully** *adv.*

deliver *v.* to hand over something to someone: *to deliver newspapers.* **delivering. delivered.**

delivery *n.* the handing over of something: *The milk delivery is at 7 o'clock.* *pl.* **deliveries.**

delta *n.* a triangle of earth and sand formed at the mouth of some rivers.

demand *n.* a strong request: *Hamburgers are in great demand at our house. v.* to ask firmly for something: *The soldiers demanded to be let in.* **demanding. demanded.**

democracy (də mok′rə sē) *n.* a group that elects its leaders. *pl.* **democracies.**

democratic *adj.* believing in and practising democracy: *We chose our class president the democratic way. We held a vote.*

demon (dē′mən) *n.* an evil spirit.

den *n.* 1. a cave where a wild animal lives. 2. a small room, often used for reading.

denim *n.* a heavy blue cloth.

denims *n. pl.* overalls or jeans made of denim.

denominator *n.* in a fraction, the number below the line.

dense *adj.* 1. tightly packed: *a dense crowd of people.* 2. very thick: *a dense cloud of smoke.*

dent *n.* a small hollow made by pressure: *Don't drop the hammer. You'll make a dent in the wood. v.* to make such a hollow. **denting. dented.**

dental *adj.* having to do with teeth: *Jim went to the dental clinic to have his teeth examined.*

dentist *n.* a doctor who takes care of your teeth.

deny *v.* to say something is not true: *Do you admit saying that? No. I deny it.* **denying. denied.** he **denies.**

deodorant *n.* a preparation that prevents or takes away unpleasant odours.

depart *v.* to go away, to leave: *The train departs from Platform 1.* **departing. departed.**

department *n.* a separate part: *the furniture department of the store; the fire department.*

department store a large store that sells many different types of things.

depend *v.* (used with **on**) 1. to rely on, to trust: *I depend on you to help me.* 2. to have to do with: *It all depends on what you want.* **depending. depended.**

dependable *adj.* reliable, to be trusted: *a dependable person.* (*opp.* **undependable.**)

deposit *n.* 1. something stored in a safe place: *a deposit of money in the bank.* 2. an amount of money you give someone to keep something for you, so that you may buy it later. *v.* 1. to put something down: *Father deposited the luggage on the rack.* 2. to put into a bank: *Cindy deposited some money in her bank account.* **depositing. deposited.**

depot (dē′pō) *n.* a storehouse, a warehouse, or a terminal.

depressed *adj.* very sad: *Charlie was depressed because his dog was ill.*

depth *n.* how deep something is: *The swimming pool has a depth of three metres at the deep end.*

deputy (dep′yə tē) *n.* someone who can take the place of the person he or she works for: *the sheriff's deputy.* *pl.* **deputies.**

descend (di send′) *v.* 1. to go down: *The plane descends onto the runway.* 2. to climb down: *The climbers descended the mountain side.* **descending. descended.**

describe *v.* to tell or write all about something or someone: *We described our summer holidays.* **describing. described.**

description *n.* a picture in words; a statement about some event, place, or person: *They gave the police artist a description of the robber.*

desert (dez′ərt) *n.* dry land on which very few plants grow: *A desert is usually sandy or stony.*

desert (di zərt′) *v.* to leave behind, to run away from: *The cowardly robber deserted his friends when they needed his help.* **deserting. deserted.**

deserve *v.* to have earned a reward or a punishment: *The worker deserves more pay.* **deserving. deserved.**

design (di zīn′) *n.* 1. a drawing or outline that is used as a guide: *The builder showed us the design of the new house.* 2. a pattern: *The wallpaper has a design of flowers. v.* to draw or plan out: *to design a house.* **designing. designed.**

desire *n.* a great wish. *v.* to want very much, to wish for. **desiring. desired.**

desk *n.* a writing table, as used in classrooms.

despair *n.* a feeling of being without hope: *The shipwrecked sailors were in deep despair. v.* to give up hope: *They*

despaired of ever seeing their friends again. **despairing. despaired.**

desperate (des′pər ət) *adj.* made reckless by despair: *The house was on fire, and the desperate man was ready to jump out of the window.*

despise (di spīz′) *v.* to hate very much. **despising. despised.**

dessert (di zert′) *n.* fruit, cake, pudding, etc. served after a meal.

destination *n.* the place you are travelling to: *The train reached its destination ahead of time.*

destroy *v.* to ruin completely: *The fire destroyed the warehouse.* **destroying. destroyed.**

destruction *n.* ruin, the smashing or breaking down of anything.

detail *n.* a tiny part: *Karen told us every detail of her adventure.*

detect *v.* to discover, to notice: *Betty detected water dripping from the pipe.* **detecting. detected.**

detective *n.* someone who tries to solve a crime.

detergent *n.* a liquid or powder used for cleaning dishes or clothes.

determined *adj.* with a sure mind: *Wendy was determined to finish her book before the weekend.*

detest *v.* to hate very much: *Many people detest spiders.* **detesting. detested.**

detour (dē′tür) *n.* a roundabout route, replacing the regular way for a time.

develop *v.* 1. to grow: *Exercise will develop your muscles.* 2. to change from one form to another: *We had the pictures developed.* **developing. developed.**

development *n.* 1. the process of growing into something bigger. 2. a group of buildings put up by the same company: *a housing development.*

device *n.* any tool, instrument, or machine that helps you: *A toaster is a device that toasts bread.*

devil *n.* 1. an evil spirit. 2. a very wicked person.

devote *v.* to give time to a project: *Cheryl devotes a lot of time to her hobby.*

devour *v.* to eat greedily: *The hungry cat devoured its food.* **devouring. devoured.**

dew *n.* drops of water on the ground: *Dew appears at night as the air cools down.*

diagonal *n.* a slanting line, going from one corner of a square or rectangle to the opposite corner.

diagram *n.* a drawing or plan that shows how something works or is made.

dial *n.* the face of a clock, compass, speedometer, phone, or something similar. *v.* to make a phone call by moving the dial or pressing the buttons. **dialling. dialled.**

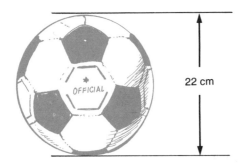
22 cm
OFFICIAL

diameter *n.* a straight line that joins two points of a circle and passes through its centre.

diamond *n.* 1. a precious, clear stone: *Diamond is the hardest substance known.* 2. the shape (♦). 3. a baseball field. 4. a playing card with one or more diamond shapes on it.

diaper (dī′pər) *n.* a piece of cloth or paper, folded and used as underpants for a baby.

diary *n.* a small notebook in which you write down what happens each day. *pl.* **diaries.**

dice *n. pl.* small cubes with a different number of spots marked on each side. *sing.* **die.**

dictate *v.* to say something aloud for other people to write down: *The teacher dictated the spelling words.* **dictating. dictated.**

dictation *n.* the saying or reading of words to another person, who writes them down.

dictionary *n.* a book that lists words in alphabetical order, telling you what each word means. *pl.* **dictionaries.**

did see **do.**

didn't short for **did not.**

die *v.* to stop living, to lose your life. **dying. died.** he **dies.**

diesel engine (dē′zəl en′jən) an engine that burns fuel oil.

diet *n.* 1. the food and drink of a person or animal: *What is the diet of a lion?* 2. special food eaten by a person who is ill, or is trying to lose or gain weight. *v.* to eat only certain foods because you are trying to lose or gain weight. **dieting. dieted.**

difference *n.* 1. the way in which one thing is unlike another: *There is a difference between a pen and a pencil.* 2. the amount left after one number is subtracted from another.

different *adj.* unlike, not the same: *A robin is different from a sparrow.* **differently** *adv.*

difficult *adj.* not easy to do, hard to understand: *The test was difficult.*

difficulty *n.* something hard to do or understand: *The test presented many difficulties.* *pl.* **difficulties.**

dig *v.* to turn over the earth with a shovel. **digging. dug.**

digest (dī jest′) *v.* to change food in the stomach, so that the body can use it. **digesting. digested.**

digestion (dī jes′chən) *n.* the changing of food so that it can pass into the body from the stomach.

dignified *adj.* noble-looking, serious, and proud: *The Queen walked into the palace in a dignified way.*

dike *n.* a ditch or wall, built to protect an area against floods.

dill *n.* a plant whose leaves and seeds are used to flavour pickles and other foods.

dilute (dī lüt′) *v.* to make something

weaker by adding liquid to it: *You dilute orange juice with water. You dilute oil paint with turpentine.* **diluting. diluted.**

dim *adj.* not bright: *a dim light, a dimmer light, the dimmest light in the house.*

dime *n.* a coin of Canada or the United States, worth 10 cents.

dimple *n.* a little hollow in your flesh, usually in your cheek or chin.

dine *v.* to eat dinner. **dining. dined.**

diner *n.* 1. a person who is eating. 2. a small eating place, usually on a main road.

dinghy (ding'ē) *n.* a small boat. *pl.* **dinghies.**

dingy (din'jē) *adj.* dirty-looking, dull and colourless: *a dingy room, a dingier room, the dingiest room in the building.*

dining room a room where meals are eaten.

dinner *n.* the main meal of the day.

dinosaur *n.* a huge reptile that lived millions of years ago.

dip *v.* 1. to put one thing into another for a short time: *to dip your hand into warm water.* 2. to slope down: *The road dipped into the valley.* **dipping. dipped.**

direct *adj.* straight: *What is the most direct way to school? v.* 1. to order, to tell someone what to do: *The police directed the crowds at the game.* 2. to show the

way: *Can you direct me to the station?* **directing. directed.**

direction *n.* the point towards which something faces or moves: *The ship sailed in a westerly direction.*

directions *n. pl.* words that tell you how to do something or how to get to a certain place: *Follow the directions when you build the model.*

directly *adv.* 1. very soon: *I'll be with you directly.* 2. straight, with no stops: *They went directly to the library.*

director *n.* a person who manages something: *the director of a business, an orchestra, a play, a movie, a TV show.*

dirt *n.* filth, mud, dust.

dirty *adj.* covered with dirt: *Muffin's paws are dirty, but Pooch's are dirtier, and Bandit's paws are the dirtiest of all.*

dis- a prefix meaning 'not': **disagree** means not to agree; a **disadvantage** means not an advantage; **dislike** means not to like; **disobey** means not to obey.

disabled *adj.* unable to do certain things because of being injured, crippled, or seriously ill.

disagree *v.* not to agree about something: *We disagreed about which team was the worst one.* **disagreeing. disagreed.**

disappear *v.* to pass out of sight, to go away and vanish. **disappearing. disappeared.**

disappearance *n.* the act of disappearing: *The disappearance of the boat was a great mystery.*

disappointed *adj.* unhappy at not getting what you hoped for: *I was disappointed because the team played badly.*

disappointment *n.* something that is not what you hoped for: *The hockey game was a disappointment. No goals were scored.*

disaster *n.* a great misfortune, accident, or tragedy: *The plane crash was a terrible disaster.*

disastrous *adj.* causing great misfortune and ruin: *a disastrous earthquake.*

disc, disk *n.* a flat, circular plate, or anything like it.

discard *v.* to throw aside: *He discarded the broken record.* **discarding. discarded.**

disciple (di sī'pəl) *n.* a person who follows and learns from a great leader.

discipline (dis'ə plin) *n.* orderly behaviour: *The soldiers showed good discipline during the battle.*

disconnect *v.* to unfasten, to unplug: *Please disconnect the wires.* **disconnecting. disconnected.**

discount *n.* an amount taken off a price: *During the sale there was a discount on the price of cameras.*

discourage (dis kər'ij) *v.* to try to stop someone from doing something: *We discouraged him from driving in the storm.* **discouraging. discouraged.**

discover *v.* to find out, to see for the very first time. **discovering. discovered.**

discovery *n.* the finding of something new: *the discovery of a new star in the sky.* *pl.* **discoveries.**

discuss *v.* to talk about something with other people: *The family discussed plans for the summer holiday.* **discussing. discussed.**

discussion (dis kush'ən) *n.* a talk about something.

disease *n.* illness, sickness.

disgrace *n.* a person or thing that brings shame: *My messy room is a complete disgrace.*

disguise (dis gīz') *n.* a change of clothing and appearance so that people will not recognize you. *v.* to change your appearance so that people will not recognize you. **disguising. disguised.**

disgust *n.* strong dislike: *I look upon cruel people with disgust.*

disgusted *adj.* filled with disgust.

dish *n.* 1. a plate, something to serve food in. 2. a kind of food: *Stew is a meat dish.* *v.* to put into a dish or dishes: *Who will dish out the dessert?* **dishing. dished.**

dishonest (dis on'ist) *adj.* not honest.

disk see **disc.**

dislike *v.* not to like. **disliking. disliked.**

dismiss *v.* to send away: *The teacher dismissed the class earlier than usual.* **dismissing. dismissed.**

disobedient *adj.* not obeying, not doing what you are told.

disobey *v.* not to do what you are told. **disobeying. disobeyed.**

display *n.* a show, an exhibition: *a fireworks display, a Christmas display in the store window.* *v.* to show or exhibit something. **displaying. displayed.**

dispose *v.* to get rid of: *Please dispose of the garbage.* **disposing. disposed.**

disqualify *v.* to make unable to do something: *The team was disqualified from the finals because they had broken an important rule.* **disqualifying. disqualified.** she **disqualifies.**

dissatisfied *adj.* not happy: *The dissatisfied shopper never came back to the store.*

dissolve (di zolv') *v.* to mix something with water or other liquid until it disappears: *to dissolve sugar in a cup of tea.* **dissolving. dissolved.**

distance *n.* 1. the amount of space between two places: *at a distance of ten kilometres from my house.* 2. a place far off: *away in the distance.*

distant *adj.* a long way off: *a distant land.*

distinct *adj.* heard or seen clearly: *The words of the singer are very distinct.*

distinguish (dis ting'gwish) *v.* to see a difference: *to distinguish between one shade of brown and another.* **distinguishing. distinguished.**

distract *v.* to take your mind away from something: *Music distracts me when I'm reading.* **distracting. distracted.**

distribute *v.* to hand out: *The mayor came to school to distribute the prizes.* **distributing. distributed.**

distribution *n.* a sharing out: *The distribution of the prizes took place in the morning.*

district *n.* a part of a town, county, or country.

disturb *v.* to upset, to interfere, to trouble: *Please do not disturb me. I am reading.* **disturbing. disturbed.**

disturbance *n.* an upset, excitement: *The police arrived at the scene of the disturbance.*

ditch *n.* a trench cut in the ground: *A ditch will drain water away.*

dive *n.* a downward plunge, usually into water. *v.* to make such a plunge. **diving. dived** or **dove** (dōv). he has **dived.**

diver *n.* 1. someone who swims under water, usually in a diving suit. 2. someone who dives for sport.

divide *v.* 1. to share out: *Divide the papers among yourselves.* 2. in arithmetic, to separate into equal parts: *8 divided by 2 equals 4.* **dividing. divided.**

division *n.* dividing, seeing how many times one number goes into another.

divorce *n.* the legal ending of a marriage. *v.* to end a marriage legally. **divorcing. divorced.**

dizzy *adj.* confused, not steady: *The ride made me dizzy, but Reen was dizzier, and Sue was the dizziest of all.*

do *v.* to be busy; to make, to work, to start something. **doing. did. done** (dun). he **does** (duz).
Note: **do** is sometimes used with another verb: *I do want to go there.* It is also used to ask a question: *Do you want to go?*

dock *n.* a place by the water where a ship can load, unload, or be repaired. *v.* to bring a boat to such a place. **docking. docked.**

doctor *n.* a person who has a licence to practise medicine.

dodge *v.* to keep away from something by moving to one side quickly. **dodging. dodged.**

doe (*masc.* **buck**) *n.* a female rabbit, deer, or antelope.

does see **do.**

doesn't short for **does not.**

dog *n.* an animal that has four legs and makes a barking noise.

dogcatcher *n.* a person whose job is to pick up stray dogs and take them to the pound or Humane Society.

doghouse *n.* a small, outdoor house for a dog.

dog-sled *n.* a sleigh pulled by dogs.

doll *n.* a toy person.

dollar *n.* the unit of money used in Canada, the United States, and some other countries: *One hundred cents make one dollar ($1.00).*

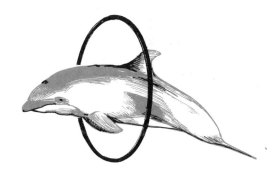

dolphin *n.* a sea mammal that looks like a small whale and has a long snout.

dome *n.* a roof shaped like half a ball.

domestic *adj.* 1. having to do with home: *Domestic duties include cooking and sewing.* 2. tame, not wild: *The cow is a domestic animal.* 3. made in your own country: *I like domestic cheese.*

domino *n.* a flat, black, oblong tile, with dots on one side. *pl.* **dominoes.**

donate *v.* to make a gift: *We donated our time and money to the school fund.* **donating. donated.**

donation *n.* a gift: *The arena was built because of all the donations.*

done see **do.**

donkey *n.* an ass; an animal that has long ears and looks like a small horse. *pl.* **donkeys.**

don't short for **do not.**

donut see **doughnut.**

door *n.* the entrance into a house or room.

doorway *n.* a way into a building or room.

dose (dōs) *n.* the amount of medicine to be taken at one time.

dot *n.* a small spot. *v.* to make such a spot. **dotting. dotted.**

double (dub′əl) *adj.* twice as much: *Frank took a double helping of corn.* *v.* to multiply by two: *What number do you get when you double three?* **doubling. doubled.**

double-cross *v.* to betray someone, to act like a traitor. **double-crossing. double-crossed.**

doubt (dout) *n.* an unsure feeling about something: *I have my doubts about going to the game in this weather.* *v.* to be suspicious of, not to be sure: *I doubt that he is telling the truth.* **doubting. doubted.**

dough (dō) *n.* a stiff mixture of flour, yeast, and water: *Dough is baked to make bread, cake, or cookies.*

doughnut, donut *n.* a small, round piece of fried cake with a hole in the centre.

dove (duv) *n.* a kind of pigeon.

dove (dōv) see **dive.**

down *n.* the very soft feathers of a bird. *prep.* from a higher to a lower place: *They walked down the hill.*

downpour *n.* a heavy rainfall.

downstairs *adv.* down to a lower floor.

downtown *adv.* to the main part of a city: *We go downtown to shop.*

doze *v.* to have a light sleep: *Bobby dozed in the chair.* **dozing. dozed.**

dozen (duz′ən) *adj.* twelve: *a dozen eggs.*

Dr. short for **doctor;** always used with a name: *Dr. Dixon.*

drab *adj.* dull, colourless: *It is a drab day. I wish the sun would come out.*

draft, draught (draft) *n.* a cool breeze blowing from a window, or coming under a door.

drag *v.* 1. to pull something heavy along the ground. 2. to move slowly: *The time seemed to drag.* **dragging. dragged.**

dragon *n.* a made-up monster: *A dragon looks like a lizard with wings. It breathes out fire.*

dragonfly *n.* a large insect that has long legs and two pairs of wings. *pl.* **dragonflies.**

drain *n.* a ditch or large pipe that carries away unwanted water. *v.* to empty unwanted water. **draining. drained.**

drama (dram′ə) *n.* a play that is not a comedy.

dramatic *adj.* 1. having to do with plays: *the dramatic club.* 2. exciting: *a dramatic rescue.*

drank see **drink.**

drapes, draperies *n. pl.* large curtains that hang in folds.

draught see **draft.**

draw *n.* 1. the picking of tickets, for a prize: *a lucky draw.* 2. a tie, the result of a game in which neither side wins. *v.* 1. to pick tickets for prizes. 2. to make a picture on paper with pencil or crayon. 3. to bring to or move in a certain position: *He drew his gun.* **drawing. drew.** I have **drawn.**

drawbridge *n.* a bridge that can be lifted, lowered, or moved.

drawer (dror) *n.* a sliding box in a piece of furniture.

drawing *n.* a picture made with pencil, ink, or crayon.

dread (dred) *v.* to dislike a lot, to be afraid of: *My new puppy dreads the dark.* **dreading. dreaded.**

dream *n.* a picture that comes into your mind while you are asleep. *v.* to imagine things are happening, while you are asleep. **dreaming. dreamed** or **dreamt** (dremt).

dreary *adj.* dull, uninteresting: *a dreary day, a drearier one, the dreariest day of the week.*

drench *v.* to wet completely: *I am drenched!* **drenching. drenched.**

dress *n.* 1. a piece of clothing worn by women and girls. 2. clothes of all kinds: *His dress was always neat and clean.* *v.* to put on your clothes. **dressing. dressed.** (*opp.* **undress.**)

dresser *n.* a piece of bedroom furniture with drawers for clothes.

dressing *n.* 1. a bandage on a cut or wound. 2. a sauce: *salad dressing.* 3. a mixture of bread, vegetables, and herbs, often used to stuff a turkey.

drew see **draw.**

dribble *v.* 1. to drip water. 2. in basketball, to run up the court tapping the ball in front of you. **dribbling. dribbled.**

dried see **dry.**

drier see **dryer** and **dry.**

dries see **dry.**

drift *n.* snow or sand blown into a pile by the wind. *v.* 1. to be heaped into a pile: *The snow is drifting on the road.* 2. to be carried along by the wind: *We drifted along in the boat.* **drifting. drifted.**

driftwood *n.* wood polished by water and washed ashore.

drill *n.* 1. a tool used for making holes. 2. exercises being done over and over again. *v.* 1. to make a hole. 2. to teach by having a student do something over and over again. **drilling. drilled.**

drink *n.* a beverage: *a cold drink.* *v.* to swallow some liquid, such as water. **drinking. drank.** I have **drunk.**

drip *n.* something falling in drops. *v.* to fall in drops: *Water drips from a leaking tap.* **dripping. dripped.**

drive *n.* 1. a wide path leading to a house. 2. a ride in a car. *v.* to steer and control a vehicle: *to drive a train.* **driving. drove.** I have **driven.**

drive-in *n.* a place where you can watch a movie or eat food while sitting in a car.

driveway *n.* a private road that leads from the street to a house or garage.

drizzle *n.* a fall of light rain. *v.* to rain lightly. **drizzling. drizzled.**

droop *v.* to hang down with no strength, to sag. **drooping. drooped.**

drop *n.* 1. a spot of liquid: *drops of water from a spray.* 2. a fall: *a great drop from the top of a tower.* *v.* to fall down from a height. **dropping. dropped.**

drought (drout) *n.* a long period of very dry weather.

drove see **drive.**

drown *v.* to die by being choked by water. **drowning. drowned.**

drug *n.* a medicine.

drugstore *n.* a store where medicines and other things (candy, soap, tissues, etc.) are sold.

drum *n.* 1. a musical instrument that makes a sound when tapped with sticks. 2. a large metal container for liquids: *an oil drum. v.* to beat a drum. **drumming. drummed.**

drumstick *n.* 1. a stick for beating a drum. 2. the lower part of a chicken or turkey leg.

drunk see **drink.**

dry *adj.* not wet or damp: *a dry plant, a drier one, the driest one in the garden. v.* to make dry, to get rid of wetness. **drying. dried.** it **dries.**

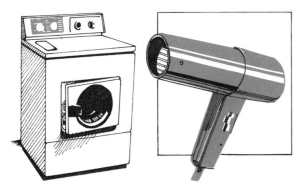

dryer, drier *n.* 1. a machine for drying clothes. 2. a small machine for drying hair.

duchess *n.* 1. the wife of a duke. 2. a woman of very high rank.

duck *n.* 1. a bird with a flat bill and webbed feet that help it to swim. *v.* to dip your head quickly, as a duck does. **ducking. ducked.**

due *adj.* 1. expected: *The train is due now.* 2. owing: *Some money is due to me.*

due to because of: *The train is late due to fog.*

duel (dyü'əl) *n.* a fight between two people with swords or pistols. *v.* to fight a duel. **duelling. duelled.**

dues *n. pl.* a fee paid by members of some groups.

duet (dyü et') *n.* a piece of music for two players or singers.

dug see **dig.**

dug-out *n.* 1. a cave used as a bomb shelter. 2. an area at the side of a baseball field, used by team members waiting to bat. 3. a type of canoe or boat made by hollowing out a log.

duke *n.* a nobleman whose rank is just below that of a prince.

dull *adj.* not bright: *a dull day.* 2. not sharp: *a dull knife.* 3. not interesting: *a dull talk.*

dumb (dum) *adj.* not able to talk.

dummy *n.* a model of a person, seen in a store window. *pl.* **dummies.**

dump *n.* 1. a storage place. 2. a pile of garbage. *v.* to throw into a messy pile. **dumping. dumped.**

dune *n.* a sandhill.

dungeon (dunj'ən) *n.* an underground prison in a castle.

during *prep.* in the time of: *We played football during the morning.*

dusk *n.* the time just before it gets dark in the evening.

dust *n.* fine powdered dirt which floats in the air. *v.* to clean with a cloth or brush: *Wanda and Karl dusted the furniture.* **dusting. dusted.**

dusty *adj.* needing cleaning or dusting: *a dusty table, a dustier one, the dustiest table of all.*

Dutch *n.* the language spoken in the Netherlands. *adj.* belonging to or coming from the Netherlands.

duty *n.* something you have to do: *It is our duty to follow the law. pl.* **duties.**

dwarf *n.* 1. in fairy tales, a bearded little man. 2. any living thing that is much smaller than the usual size. *pl.* **dwarfs.**

dwell *v.* to live in some place: *Fish dwell in the water.* **dwelling. dwelled.** or **dwelt.**

dwelling *n.* a house.

dye *n.* a liquid or powder used to colour materials. *v.* to colour with such a liquid or powder. **dyeing. dyed.**

dying see **die.**

dynamite *n.* a powerful explosive used for breaking up rock. *v.* to use this explosive. **dynamiting. dynamited.**

each *pron., adj.* every single one.

eager *adj.* anxious to have or to do something: *Julius was eager to join in the game of tag.*

eagle *n.* a large and powerful bird that hunts small animals.

ear *n.* 1. the part of the body that allows you to hear. 2. the part of a cornstalk that contains the grain.

early (ər′lē) *adj., adv.* in good time, before the start: *Paul is always early for school. Martin is even earlier. Lillian is the earliest of all.*

earn (ərn) *v.* to get payment for working: *Paul earns money for raking the leaves.* **earning. earned.**

earnings *n. pl.* payment for work.

earring *n.* a small ring or jewel worn on the ear.

earth (ərth) *n.* 1. the world. 2. ground, soil.

earthquake *n.* a shaking of the earth, caused by rocks moving underground.

ease *n.* comfort, rest: *Father sat at ease in his armchair.*

easel *n.* a stand on which to rest a picture.

easily *adv.* without trouble: *I can do the magic trick easily.*

east *n.* the direction of sunrise, opposite to west.

Easter *n.* a Christian festival celebrating the day on which Jesus rose from the grave.

eastern *adj.* in the direction of the east: *Ottawa is in eastern Ontario.*

easy *adj.* not difficult, not hard to do: *an easy puzzle, an easier one, the easiest one of all.*

eat *v.* to take food through the mouth. **eating. ate.** I have **eaten.**

eaves *n. pl.* the lower edge of a roof.

ebony *n.* a black wood, very hard and heavy: *Ebony is used for making the black keys of a piano.*

echo (ek′ō) *n.* a sound that bounces back when you shout at a hill or the wall of a cave. *pl.* **echoes.**

eclipse (ē klips′) *n.* the darkening of the sun or moon: *When the moon comes between the sun and the earth, we have an eclipse of the sun.*

edge *n.* 1. a rim or border: *the edge of the woods.* 2. the sharp side of a blade.

editor *n.* a person in charge of a newspaper, magazine, dictionary, etc.

Edmonton *n.* capital city of Alberta.

educate *v.* to teach or train people. **educating. educated.**

education *n.* schooling, teaching.

eel *n.* a long, thin fish that is shaped like a snake.

effect *n.* the result of a change: *The medicine had a good effect on Arthur.* Note: Do not mix up **effect** with **affect**; **affect** means 'to cause a change'.

effort *n.* using strength or energy to do something, a good try: *The farmer made a great effort to lift the heavy stone.*

egg *n.* a roundish object with a thin shell: *Eggs are laid by birds, fish, and reptiles.*

eggplant *n.* a roundish vegetable that has a shiny, dark purple skin.

eight (āt) *n., adj.* one more than seven (8).

eighteen *n., adj.* ten more than eight (18).

eighth *adj.* following seventh (8th).

eighty *n., adj.* ten times eight (80).

either (ē′THər, ī′THər) *adj.* one or the other of two: *Either Steve or Fred is to be chosen goalie.*

eject *v.* to drive out, force out, turn out: *to eject a missile.* **ejecting. ejected.**

elastic *n.* a rubber band that stretches when pulled. *adj.* stretchy; able to go back to its own shape after being squeezed or pulled.

elbow *n.* the joint between your lower arm and your upper arm.

elderly *adj.* old: *Our group helps elderly people go shopping.*

elect *v.* to choose by voting. **electing. elected.**

election *n.* choosing by vote: *an election for class president.*

electric, electrical *adj.* having to do with electricity: *an electric lamp, an electrical engineer.*

electrician (i lek trish′ən) *n.* a person who builds, puts in, or fixes electrical equipment.

electricity *n.* a powerful form of energy that can produce light and heat.

elementary school a school that begins with kindergarten or grade 1 and goes to grade 6, 7, or 8.

elephant *n.* a huge, grey land animal that lives in Asia and Africa: *An elephant has thick skin, tusks, a trunk, and large ears.*

elevator *n.* 1. a car that carries people or things up and down. 2. a building for storing grain: *a grain elevator.*

eleven *n., adj.* one more than ten (11).

elf *n.* in stories, a small fairy. *pl.* **elves.**

elk *n.* a large deer of North America: *The male elk has broad antlers.*

elm *n.* a tall shade tree.

else *adj.* other: *somebody else.* *adv.* differently: *How else can you do it?*

elsewhere *adv.* in some other place: *It's muddy here. Let's go elsewhere.*

embarrass *v.* to make someone feel shy or ashamed, often because of incorrect or silly behaviour: *Jane was embarrassed because she forgot her mother's birthday.* **embarrassing. embarrassed.**

emblem *n.* a badge or sign: *The maple leaf is an emblem of Canada.*

embroider *v.* to make designs on cloth, using coloured thread. **embroidering. embroidered.**

embroidery *n.* designs sewn on cloth.

emerald *n.* a bright green jewel.

emergency *n.* a sudden happening that must be looked after at once: *A house on fire is an emergency. pl.* **emergencies.**

emperor *n.* a man who is the head of an empire.

empire *n.* a group of countries under one ruler.

employ *v.* to hire someone to work for you: *Stores employ more people before Christmas.* **employing. employed.**

employee *n.* someone who is employed and receives wages.

employer *n.* someone who pays others to work for him or her.

employment *n.* work, a job: *My sister is looking for summer employment.*

empress *n.* 1. a woman who rules over an empire. 2. the wife of an emperor.

empty *adj.* holding nothing: *an empty box.*

enchanted *adj.* charmed, under a magic spell: *an enchanted castle.*

enclose *v.* 1. to shut in on all sides: *The fence encloses the yard.* 2. to put in a wrapping or envelope: *The money is enclosed with my letter.* **enclosing. enclosed.**

encourage (en kər′ij) *v.* to give someone hope and courage to do something: *The coach encouraged Dan to try out for the team.* **encouraging. encouraged.**

encouragement *n.* something given or said to someone to help him or her try harder.

encyclopedia, encyclopaedia *n.* a big book, or set of books, with facts and information on many things.

end *n.* the last part, the finish: *This is the end of the line. v.* to finish: *The story ends on the next page.* **ending. ended.**

enemy *n.* a person or a country that is on the other side in a quarrel or a war. *pl.* **enemies.**

energetic *adj.* full of energy: *After the rest, the swimmers felt energetic again.*

energy *n.* liveliness, force, and power: *The boxer fought with all his energy.*

engage *v.* to promise: *They are engaged to be married in June.* **engaging. engaged.**

engagement *n.* a promise of marriage.

engine (en′jən) *n.* 1. any machine that makes things move. 2. a locomotive: *The engine pulled the train up the hill.*

engineer *n.* 1. a person who works with engines and machinery. 2. the driver of a locomotive.

engineering *n.* the making and using of machines: *My sister is studying engineering at university.*

English *n.* the language spoken in England, Canada, the United States, and other countries. *adj.* belonging to or coming from England.

enjoy *v.* to be pleased by something: *The boys and girls enjoyed the circus.* **enjoying. enjoyed.**

enjoyable *adj.* giving pleasure: *an enjoyable day.*

enjoyment *n.* pleasure, happiness: *Keeping a diary gives Lee a lot of enjoyment.*

enormous *adj.* very big, huge.

enough (ə nuf′) *n., adv.* as much or as many as are needed or wanted: *I have had enough to eat.*

enrol, enroll *v.* to become a member of a group: *Alice enrolled in the tennis club.* **enrolling. enrolled.**

enter *v.* 1. to go in. 2. to join: *Sandy will enter the contest.* **entering. entered.**

entertain *v.* 1. to amuse: *The clowns entertained the children.* 2. to hold a party and have guests: *Rob entertained his class at his birthday party.* **entertaining. entertained.**

entertainment *n.* something that entertains or interests you, such as a movie or play.

entire *adj.* the whole of anything: *The entire crew was saved from the shipwreck.* **entirely** *adv.*

entrance *n.* a way in, a doorway: *the entrance to the theatre.*

entry *n.* 1. a going in, a way in: *Entry to the play is by ticket only.* 2. a person who takes part in a contest: *There are ten entries in the dance contest.* 3. a word that is listed in a dictionary: *The next entry is* **envelope.** *pl.* **entries.**

envelope *n.* a folded and sealed paper cover for a letter.

envious (en′vē əs) *adj.* feeling full of jealousy: *He's so envious! He wants everything I own.*

envy (en′vē) *v.* to feel jealous: *George envies Pete because Pete has a new bike.* **envying. envied.** he **envies.**

epidemic *n.* a disease that spreads from one person to another very quickly: *There is an epidemic of the flu in our school.*

equal *adj.* of the same number or value as something else: *The big cat and the little pup are equal in size.* *v.* in arithmetic, to be the same as; symbol is =. **equalling. equalled.**

equator *n.* an imaginary circle around the middle of the world: *The equator is halfway between the North and South Poles.*

equip *v.* to provide with everything necessary: *to equip a team with uniforms, sticks, and pucks.* **equipping. equipped.**

equipment *n.* items you need in order to do certain jobs or play certain sports: *We used new hockey equipment in our game against the Bisons.*

erase *v.* to rub out: *Please erase the writing on the board.* **erasing. erased.**

eraser *n.* something used for rubbing out writing: *a pencil eraser, a board eraser.*

errand *n.* a small trip made to collect or deliver a message or package.

error *n.* a mistake.

escalator *n.* a moving stairway.

escape *n.* a getting free: *a lucky escape from danger.* *v.* to get away: *to escape from prison.* **escaping. escaped.**

Eskimo *n.* a people living in the Arctic or one of these people. *pl.* **Eskimo** or **Eskimos.**
Note: **Inuit** is the name these people use for themselves.

especially *adv.* most of all: *I like dogs, especially poodles.*

essential *adj.* really necessary: *To play the piano well, it is essential to practise.*

estimate (es′tə mət) *n.* a guess about the size, amount, or value of something: *My estimate is that the tree is five metres tall.*

estimate (es′tə māt) *v.* to guess the size, amount, or value of something: *Donald estimated that there were a hundred people outside.* **estimating. estimated.**

etc. short for **et cetera,** which means 'and other things', 'and so on'.

European (yür ə pē′ən) *n.* a person born in or living in the continent of Europe. *adj.* having to do with the continent of Europe.

evaporate *v.* to change from liquid into vapour or gas when heated. **evaporating. evaporated.**

eve *n.* 1. evening. 2. the day before a special event: *New Year's eve.*

even *adj.* 1. smooth, level: *an even piece of wood*. 2. equal: *At the end of the game, the score was even*. 3. able to be divided by two. *adv.* still, yet: *You play the piano well. If you practise, you'll play even better*.

evening *n.* the time between day and night.

event *n.* 1. some special happening: *current events*. 2. one of the items in a sports program: *The high jump was the third event*.

ever *adv.* at any time: *If you're ever in town, come and see me*.

evergreen *n.* a tree that is always green and does not drop its leaves all at once: *The pine is an evergreen*.

every *adj.* each: *I pass the house every day*.

everybody *pron.* each person, all the people: *Is everybody away?*

everyone *pron.* each person: *Is everyone going to the game?*

everything *pron.* each thing, all the things: *Everything is ready for the party*.

everywhere *adv.* in every place: *We looked everywhere for my lost key*.

evidence *n.* information that proves something: *The lawyer presented her evidence to the judge*.

evil *adj.* harmful, bad: *an evil deed*.

ewe (yü) *n.* a female sheep.

exact (eg zakt′) *adj.* just right, correct: *The exact time is two minutes past one*.

exactly *adv.* without mistake: *The clock is exactly right*.

exaggerate (eg zaj′ər āt) *v.* to say something is bigger, better, or worse than it really is: *The boys exaggerated Al's injury. They said he broke his arm, but he only twisted it*. **exaggerating. exaggerated.**

exam, examination *n.* 1. a careful check: *a physical examination*. 2. a test of what you know: *a history exam*.

examine *v.* 1. to look at closely. 2. to test someone's knowledge of some subject. **examining. examined.**

example *n.* 1. a model to be copied: *to set a good example*. 2. something to use as a sample: *Give me an example of a large city*.

excavate *v.* to dig out from the earth: *Dinosaur bones were excavated from the ground*. **excavating. excavated.**

excellent *adj.* very, very good.

except *prep.* other than; leaving out: *Everyone except Joe went to the fair*. Note: Do not mix up **except** with **accept**; **accept** means 'to take something that is offered'.

exception *n.* something left out or something different: *All the children went to the pool, with the exception of Andy and Randy*.

exchange *v.* to give one thing in return for another: *Alan exchanged an Australian stamp for an old Canadian one*. **exchanging. exchanged.**

excite *v.* to cause activity: *to excite bees by moving their hive*. **exciting. excited.**

excitement *n.* fuss, activity: *There was a lot of excitement when we saw our picture in the newspaper*.

exciting *adj.* thrilling: *The trapeze act was exciting*.

exclaim *v.* to shout out with excitement. **exclaiming. exclaimed.**

exclamation *n.* an excited shout.

exclamation mark a mark (!) put at the end of a sentence to show anger, excitement, or surprise: *Hurray! We have won!*

excuse (eks kyüs′) *n.* a reason you give for something: *an excuse for being late*.

excuse (eks kyüz′) *v.* to forgive: *Please excuse me for leaving early. I'm in a hurry today.* **excusing. excused.**

execute *v.* to put someone to death by law. **executing. executed.**

exercise *n.* 1. something that gives you practice: *a spelling exercise.* 2. an activity for training your body or mind: *Push-ups and sit-ups are good exercises.* *v.* to train the body or mind. **exercising. exercised.**

exhaust *n.* used steam or gas that escapes from an engine. *v.* to tire out: *The long climb exhausted us.* **exhausting. exhausted.**

exhibit *n.* a public display of things such as school projects, paintings, or old cars. *v.* to show or display something. **exhibiting. exhibited.**

exhibition *n.* 1. a show, a display: *an exhibition of pictures in an art gallery.* 2. a large fair: *the Canadian National Exhibition.*

exist *v.* 1. to live: *Rabbits exist on wild plants.* 2. to be real: *Do you believe that Martians exist?* **existing. existed.**

exit *n.* a way out: *The exit from the hall was marked with a sign.*

expand *v.* to grow bigger: *Many objects expand in the heat. They contract in the cold.* **expanding. expanded.**

expect *v.* to think something will happen, to suppose: *I expect to see my brother tomorrow.* **expecting. expected.**

expedition *n.* a journey for some special purpose: *a hiking expedition.*

expel *v.* to send someone away from a school or club for bad conduct. **expelling. expelled.**

expense *n.* a cost: *What were your expenses on the trip?*

expensive *adj.* costing a lot: *an expensive piece of jewellery.* (*opp.* **inexpensive.**)

experience *n.* 1. knowledge gained by having done something for a long time: *Mr. Smith has experience as a builder.* 2. what happens to you: *Doug shared his camp experiences.* *v.* to feel, to have happen to you: *What adventures did you experience at camp?* **experiencing. experienced.**

experienced *adj.* good at something because of practice: *Mrs. Thomas is an experienced carpenter.* (*opp.* **inexperienced.**)

experiment *n.* a test to find what will happen: *a science experiment.* *v.* to test in order to find something: *John experimented by mixing different paints until he got the colour he wanted.* **experimenting. experimented.**

expert *n.* someone who knows a great deal about a subject: *an expert in sewing.*

explain *v.* to describe the meaning of something: *The coach explained the rules carefully.* **explaining. explained.**

explanation *n.* a reason: *I asked why my foot hurt. The doctor gave me a long explanation.*

explode *v.* to burst into pieces, to blow up. **exploding. exploded.**

explore *v.* 1. to look around: *to explore an old castle.* 2. to travel to discover new lands. **exploring. explored.**

explosion (ex plō′zhən) *n.* a bursting into pieces, a blowing up.

explosive *n.* something that can explode: *Gunpowder is an explosive.*

express *n.* a fast bus or train that makes only a few stops. *v.* to tell or show through words, action, or a look on your face: *Jill's frown expressed the way that she felt.* **expressing. expressed.**

expression *n.* a look on your face: *Karen had a worried expression.*

expressway *n.* a divided highway, built for fast travelling.

exterior *n.* the outside of anything: *The exterior of the car was clean and shiny. The interior was filled with junk.*

extinguish *v.* to put out a flame or fire. **extinguishing. extinguished.**

extra *adj.* more than usual: *Mother was given an extra day's holiday.*

extreme *adj.* 1. the greatest: *Take extreme care.* 2. the farthest: *Len stood on the extreme edge of the cliff.*

extremely *adv.* very much so: *Dusty is an extremely playful pup.*

eye (ī) *n.* the part of the body that allows you to see.

eyebrow *n.* the small ridge of hair over each eye.

eyeglasses *n. pl.* a pair of glass or plastic lenses that help you see better.

eyelash *n.* one of the hairs on the edge of your eyelid.

eyelid *n.* the movable cover of skin over each eye.

eyesight *n.* the power to see.

fable (fā′bəl) *n.* a short story that is meant to teach a lesson.

fabric (fab′rik) *n.* cloth.

fabulous (fab′yə ləs) *adj.* amazing, unbelievable.

face *n.* 1. the front of your head. 2. the front of a clock, building, playing card, etc. *v.* to look towards, to have the front towards: *Our house faces a school.* **facing. faced.**

face-off *n.* putting the hockey puck into play.

fact *n.* something that is true or real.

factory *n.* a building in which things are made, most often with the help of machines. *pl.* **factories.**

fade *v.* 1. to lose colour in sunlight or by washing: *The curtains have faded from a dark blue to a pale blue.* 2. to become dim: *The light fades towards evening.* **fading. faded.**

fail *v.* to be unsuccessful, not to do something you try to do: *to fail the test.* **failing. failed.**

failure (fāl′yər) *n.* an unsuccessful try: *I practised hard after my failure to get on the team.*

faint *v.* to feel dizzy and ill, to pass out: *Lee fainted after the accident.* **fainting. fainted.**

fair *n.* a market or a show of farm animals and homemade goods. *adj.* 1. light in colour: *Connie has fair hair.* 2. less than good: *His work is only fair.* 3. honest: *The person was given a fair trial.* 4. not raining: *fair weather.*

fairly *adv.* somewhat, rather: *He's a fairly good ballplayer. He's not the best, but he's not the worst, either.*

fairy *n.* an imaginary little creature with magical powers. *pl.* **fairies.**

fairy tale a story of fairies and other magical creatures.

faith *n.* belief, trust: *I have faith in you.*

faithful *adj.* loyal, to be trusted: *Joanne is a faithful friend. She always keeps her promises.* (*opp.* **unfaithful.**)

fake *adj.* copied, not real, made to look like something better: *fake money, fake jewels.*

falcon *n.* a kind of hawk that is sometimes used for hunting.

fall *n.* 1. the season after summer, also called 'autumn'. 2. coming down from a higher position: *a bad fall.* *v.* 1. to drop from a high place: *Humpty Dumpty fell off the wall.* 2. to happen: *Kristine's birthday falls on Tuesday this year.* **falling. fell.** I have **fallen.**

false *adj.* 1. not true: *a false story.* 2. not real: *false teeth.*

fame *n.* glory, honour, being well-known: *Some people would rather have fame than fortune.*

familiar (fə mil′yər) *adj.* well-known: *Birds are a familiar sight in these woods.* (*opp.* **unfamiliar.**)

family *n.* 1. a parent or parents and their children. 2. close relatives. *pl.* **families.**

famine (fam′in) *n.* a great shortage of food in a district or in a country.

famous (fā′məs) *adj.* very well-known: *a famous actor.*

fan *n.* 1. something to make a cooling breeze: *an electric fan, a paper fan.* 2. someone who very much likes a sports team, a singer, an actor, etc. *v.* to cool with a fan. **fanning. fanned.**

fancy *adj.* special, not plain: *a fancy blouse, a fancier one, the fanciest one in the store.*

fang *n.* 1. a long, sharp tooth of a dog or wolf. 2. a snake's poison-tooth.

fantastic *adj.* amazing, unbelievable.

far *adv.* a long way off: *far away, farther away, the farthest away of all.* *adj.* not near: *the far end of the road.* **so far** until now: *I have not missed any school so far this year.*

fare *n.* the price of a trip on a bus, ship, taxi, train, or plane.

farewell *n.* a good-bye, a parting wish: *We said our farewells, then drove away.*

farm *n.* a piece of land that is used to grow crops and raise animals.

farmer *n.* a person who looks after a farm.

farmyard *n.* a yard enclosed by farm buildings.

farther, farthest see **far.**

fascinate (fas′in āt) *v.* to hold your attention, to be of great interest: *These pictures fascinate me. I can't stop looking at them.* **fascinating. fascinated.**

fashion *n.* an up-to-date style: *Bright colours are now in fashion.*

fast *adj.* quick, speedy: *a fast car.* *adv.* quickly: *Ravi can run fast.* *v.* to go without food. **fasting. fasted.**

fasten (fas′ən) *v.* to tie, join, or close: *Please fasten the string around the box.* **fastening. fastened.** (*opp.* **unfasten.**)

fat *n.* the greasy part of meat. *adj.* plump: *a fat cat, a fatter cat, the fattest cat on the street.*

father *n.* 1. a man who is a parent. 2. a Roman Catholic or Anglican priest.

faucet (faw′sət) *n.* a device used for turning water on or off.

fault *n.* something that is wrong, a mistake: *It is not my fault.*

favour, favor *n.* a kindness: *Will you do me a favour? Please walk my dog.*

favourite, favorite *adj.* most liked: *This is my favourite game.*

fawn *n.* a young deer.

fear *n.* a feeling that something dangerous may happen: *a fear of flying in an airplane.* *v.* to feel afraid of: *The farmer's son fears cows.* **fearing. feared.**

fearful *adj.* full of fear.

fearless *adj.* without fear; sometimes being too brave.

feast *n.* a very large meal, full of good things to eat.

feat *n.* a deed of great courage or strength: *To walk on a tightrope is a great feat.*

feather *n.* one of the many light, fluffy growths that cover a bird's body.

February *n.* the second month of the year.

fed see **feed.**

federal (fed′ər əl) *adj.* having to do with the government of a country, not of a province or city: *Members of Parliament are elected in a federal election.*

fee *n.* a charge: *the doctor's fee.*

feeble *adj.* weak, not strong: *That's a feeble attempt. You could do much better.*

feed *n.* food for animals: *We gave the hens some chicken feed.* *v.* to give food to: *Please feed the baby.* **feeding. fed.**

feel *v.* 1. to touch: *Simon felt the key in his pocket.* 2. to be in a mood: *Ruth feels happy because it's her birthday.* 3. to have an opinion: *I feel this is what we should do.* **feeling. felt.**

feeling *n.* 1. the sense of touch: *By feeling, we can tell what is hard and what is soft.* 2. a mood you are in: *I have a happy feeling.*

feelings *n. pl.* a way you feel about yourself, about someone else, or about something.

feet plural of **foot.**

fell *v.* 1. see **fall.** 2. to cut down: *to fell a tree.* **felling. felled.**

fellow *n.* a friendly name for a man or boy: *He's a good fellow.*

felt *n.* a thick kind of cloth.

felt see **feel.**

female *n.* 1. a girl, a woman. 2. an animal that is, will be, or can be a mother: *A cow is a female. A bull is a male.*

fence *n.* a railing or wall put around a garden or field. *v.* to fight with swords. **fencing. fenced.**

fender *n.* a guard that protects a car or bicycle wheel.

fern *n.* a plant with long, feathery leaves.

ferocious (fə rō′shəs) *adj.* fierce, savage: *a ferocious guard dog.*

Ferris wheel a large wheel, seen at a fair or amusement park, with seats hanging from its rim.

ferry *n.* a boat that carries people and goods across a body of water. *pl.* **ferries.**

fertilizer *n.* a substance added to soil, to make it better for growing crops.

festival *n.* a celebration or time of happiness, often with music, art, or drama.

fever *n.* 1. a body temperature that is higher than usual. 2. the common name for illnesses that make you hot and restless.

few (fyü) *adj.* small in number: *Only a few boys and girls are at the party.*

fibre, fiber *n.* a thread of any kind.

fiction *n.* a made-up story: *I like to read about real people, but my favourite stories are fiction.*

fiddle *n.* a violin. *v.* to play the fiddle. **fiddling. fiddled.**

fiddlehead *n.* the young leaves of certain ferns, used for food.

field (fēld) *n.* 1. a piece of land used for crops or for pasture. 2. a place where sports are played.

fiend (fēnd) *n.* a devil, a monster, or a very cruel person.

fierce (fērs) *adj.* savage, wild.

fifteen *n., adj.* ten more than five (15).

fifth *adj.* following fourth (5th).

fifty *n., adj.* ten times five (50).

fig *n.* a soft, sweet fruit, full of seeds: *Figs grow in warm climates.*

fight (fīt) *n.* a struggle, a quarrel, a battle. *v.* to struggle or battle against someone or something. **fighting. fought** (fawt).

figure (fig'yər) *n.* 1. a number symbol: *2, 9, and 74 are figures.* 2. the shape of someone's body: *Jenny saw the figure of a man in the distance.*

file *n.* 1. a tool with a rough side: *A file is used for smoothing wood or metal.* 2. a box in which you keep important papers. 3. a line of people, one behind another: *single file.*

fill *v.* to put into a container until there is no more room: *to fill a pail with water.* **filling. filled.**

filling *n.* a substance used to fill something.

filly (*masc.* **colt**) *n.* a young female horse. *pl.* **fillies.**

film *n.* 1. a thin layer: *a film of dust on a shelf.* 2. a roll of thin material that you put into a camera.

filmstrip *n.* a roll of film, usually with pictures, to be projected onto a screen.

filthy *adj.* very dirty: *filthy hands, filthier hands, the filthiest hands of all.*

fin *n.* 1. a short wing-like part of a fish: *Fins help fish to keep their balance when swimming.* 2. anything shaped like a fin: *the tail fin of the airplane.*

final *adj.* the last, the end: *the final part of a story.*

finally *adv.* at last: *He finally arrived at the party.*

finch *n.* a small songbird: *The goldfinch, canary, and sparrow are kinds of finches.*

find *v.* to discover, to locate: *Ken found a penny on the street.* **finding. found.**

fine *n.* money paid as a punishment for breaking a rule: *a fine on a library book.* *adj.* 1. sunny, dry: *a fine summer day.* 2. thin, sharp: *Mary made a fine point on her pencil.* 3. very good: *The fisherman had a fine catch.*

finger *n.* one of the five long tips on your hand.

fingernail *n.* the thin, hard layer at the end of each finger.

fingerprint *n.* a mark made by a finger.

finish *n.* the end, the last part: *the finish of a race.* *v.* to complete: *Please finish your breakfast.* **finishing. finished.**

fir *n.* a tall evergreen tree that has needle-like leaves.

fire *n.* the heat and light from something burning. *v.* 1. to shoot with a gun or rifle. 2. to dismiss: *The manager fired the lazy worker.* **firing. fired.**

firecracker *n.* a small cardboard tube filled with gunpowder.

fire engine a truck that has equipment for fighting fires.

fire escape a ladder or stairway used when a building is on fire.

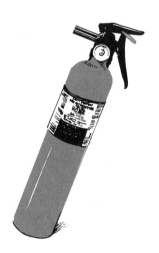

fire extinguisher a container filled with chemicals that will put out a fire.

firefighter, fireman *n.* a person trained to put out fires.

firefly *n.* a small insect that gives off flashes of light. *pl.* **fireflies.**

fire hydrant a wide pipe, sticking out of the ground, that fire hoses can be attached to.

fireplace *n.* a place built to hold a fire: *A fireplace is found under the chimney.*

fireworks *n. pl.* firecrackers, rockets, etc. that make a loud noise or give off a colourful display.

firm *n.* a business: *Mother works for an engineering firm.* *adj.* steady, strong: *The soldier marched with firm steps.*

first *adj.* chief: *first prize.* *adv.* before all others: *Mark came first in the race.*
at first in the beginning: *At first, Kim did not like camp.*

first aid treatment given to a sick or injured person while he or she is waiting for the doctor to arrive.

first-class of the best kind: *Bessie does first-class work.*

fish *n.* an animal that breathes through gills and lives only in water. *pl.* **fish** or **fishes.** *v.* to try to catch fish. **fishing. fished.**

fisherman *n.* a man who catches fish. *pl.* **fishermen.**

fishery *n.* a place for catching fish. *pl.* **fisheries.**

fist *n.* a tightly closed hand.

fit *n.* a sudden attack: *a fit of laughter.* *adj.* in good condition: *Exercising keeps you fit.* *v.* to be of the right size: *The bolt fits into this hole.* **fitting. fit** or **fitted.**

five *n., adj.* one more than four (5).

fix *n.* a difficulty: *I'm in a real fix. I have to go shopping, but I have no money.* *v.* 1. to fasten: *Bill fixed the flag onto the pole.* 2. to repair: *I'll fix the broken bike.* **fixing. fixed.**

fizz *n.* a bubbling sound. *v.* to make such a sound: *The soda is fizzing.* **fizzing. fizzed.**

flabby *adj.* hanging loose, soft: *a flabby cat, a flabbier cat, the flabbiest cat on the street.*

flag *n.* a piece of cloth with an emblem or decoration on it.

flake *n.* a small, thin chip or piece: *a snowflake.*

flame *n.* the glowing, jumping part of a fire. *v.* to burst into a blaze. **flaming. flamed.**

flannel *n.* a soft cloth made of fine wool.

flap *n.* a piece of paper or other material that is attached on one side only: *the flap of the envelope.* *v.* to move up and down, or sideways: *A bird flaps its wings.* **flapping. flapped.**

flare *n.* a very bright blaze of light, which may be used as a signal. *v.* to blaze up suddenly: *The fireworks flared in the darkness.* **flaring. flared.**

flash *n.* a sudden light: *a flash of lightning.* *v.* to shine suddenly: *The car flashed its headlights.* **flashing. flashed.**

flash bulb a bulb that is attached to a camera: *A flash bulb is used for taking pictures indoors or at night.*

flashlight *n.* a small light, powered by batteries, that is used by campers, ushers, doctors, and other people.

flat *adj.* level, even: *flat ground. This field is flat, but that one is flatter. The next field is the flattest of all.*

flatten *v.* to make flat. **flattening. flattened.**

flatter *v.* to say too many nice things to someone: *I don't believe her kind words. She flatters everyone.* **flattering. flattered.**

flavour, flavor *n.* the taste of something: *The drink has an orange flavour.*

flax *n.* 1. a thin plant with small leaves and blue flowers. 2. the fibres from this plant, which are spun into linen thread.

flea *n.* a small, hopping insect without wings.

flee *v.* to go away from trouble or danger: *Catch the thief before he flees!* **fleeing. fled.**

fleet *n.* a number of ships, planes, or cars grouped together.

flesh *n.* the soft part of your body that covers the bones.

flew see **fly.**

flick *v.* to brush lightly with a whip or your finger: *He flicked the dirt off his jacket.* **flicking. flicked.**

flicker *v.* to shine with a blinking light: *The candle's flame flickers just before it goes out.* **flickering. flickered.**

flies see **fly.**

flight *n.* 1. the movement of birds, insects, or airplanes through the air. 2. an airplane trip. 3. a set of stairs.

flinch *v.* to draw back from something threatening: *When Jim raised his hand, I flinched.* **flinching. flinched.**

fling *v.* to throw hard, to hurl: *How far can you fling the stone?* **flinging. flung.**

flint *n.* a very hard kind of stone that makes a spark when rubbed against steel.

flip *v.* to turn over quickly: *Flip a coin.* **flipping. flipped.**

flipper *n.* 1. the flat limb of a seal, walrus, or turtle. 2. a piece of rubber, shaped like a seal's flipper, used by swimmers. 3. a utensil for turning food over while it is cooking.

float *n.* something that stays on top of water. *v.* to rest on water. *Can you float on your back?* **floating. floated.**

flock *n.* a group of animals: *a flock of geese, a flock of sheep.*

flood (flud) *n.* 1. a great overflow of water. 2. anything like this: *a flood of letters came through the mail.* *v.* to become covered or filled with water: *Our house was flooded in March.* **flooding. flooded.**

floor *n.* the bottom of a room, on which we walk.

flop *n.* a failure: *Our play was a flop.* *v.* to drop down heavily: *My mom was so tired, she flopped into an armchair.* **flopping. flopped.**

florist *n.* a person whose job is to sell flowers.

flour *n.* the fine white powder made by grinding grain.

flow (flō) *v.* to move along smoothly: *The river flowed past our home.* **flowing. flowed.**

flower *n.* the blossom of a plant.

flown see **fly.**

flu *n.* short for **influenza**, a sickness that is like a very bad cold.

fluffy *adj.* 1. covered with soft hair or fur. 2. soft and light: *Beat the eggs until they are fluffy.*

fluid (flü'id) *n.* a liquid; a substance that can flow: *Ink, water, and milk are fluids.*

flung see **fling.**

flush *v.* 1. to go red with excitement, to blush. 2. to wash out with water. **flushing. flushed.**

flute *n.* a wind instrument made of wood or metal.

flutter *v.* 1. to wave back and forth in the breeze: *The flags flutter in the wind.* 2. for an insect to flap its wings lightly. **fluttering. fluttered.**

fly *n.* one of several kinds of small insects with two wings: *a black-fly, a housefly.* *pl.* **flies.** *v.* 1. to move through the air on wings. 2. to travel by plane. 3. to make something stay up in the air: *Jo flies a kite.* **flying. flew.** it **flies.** it has **flown** (flōn).

flying *adj.* moving through the air as on wings: *a flying saucer.*

foal *n.* a young horse or donkey.

foam *n.* many small white bubbles: *the foam on a wave.*

foe *n.* an enemy.

fog *n.* a thick cloud of mist.

foggy *adj.* filled with fog: *a foggy day, a foggier day, the foggiest day of the year.*

foil *n.* a thin, silvery sheet of metal: *aluminum foil.*

fold *n.* a crease caused by doubling something over. *v.* to double something over. **folding. folded.** (*opp.* **unfold.**)

folk (fōk) *n. pl.* people: *city folk, country folk.*

folks *n. pl.* relatives: *How are your folks?*

follow *v.* 1. to go after: *to follow a leader.* 2. to understand: *I don't follow what you are saying.* **following. followed.**

fond of liking very much: *Jill is fond of dogs.*

food *n.* what people, animals, and plants eat to keep alive.

fool *n.* a silly person. *v.* to play or joke. **fooling. fooled.**

foolish *adj.* silly, not wise. **foolishly** *adv.*

foot (fŭt) *n.* 1. the part of each leg on which you stand. 2. the bottom part: *the foot of a tower.* 3. a measure of length, equal to about 30 cm. *pl.* **feet.**

football *n.* 1. a large leather ball, used in football and other kicking games. 2. a game in which the football is kicked, passed, or carried to the goal.

foothills *n. pl.* the low hills that are found at the bottom of a mountain.

footprint *n.* the mark of a foot on soft ground or on a clean floor.

footstep *n.* the distance covered or the sound heard when someone takes a step.

for *prep.* 1. in return: *I'll give you a dollar for a hat.* 2. because of: *She was rewarded for her good deed.* 3. as far as, as long as: *We hiked for ten kilometres.* 4. with a purpose: *The tub is for water.*

forbid *v.* to tell someone he or she is not to do something: *I forbid you to go there alone!* **forbidding. forbade** or **forbad.** I have **forbidden.**

force *n.* power, strength. *v.* 1. to make someone do something against his or her wishes: *He tried to force his brother to tell the secret.* 2. to do something using power and energy: *The thief forced open the locked door.* **forcing. forced.**

fore- a prefix meaning 'in front of' or 'before': **forehead** means the front part of your head; to **forecast** the weather means to say in advance what it will be like.

forecast *v.* to say in advance what is likely to happen: *to forecast the result of a ball game.* **forecasting. forecast.**

forefinger *n.* the finger nearest the thumb.

forehead *n.* the part of your face above the eyes.

foreign (for'ən) *adj.* belonging to a country other than your own.

foreman, foreperson *n.* a person in charge of a group of workers.

forest *n.* a large area of country thickly covered with trees.

forest ranger a person whose job is to guard a part of the forest.

forestry *n.* the planting and taking care of trees and forests.

forever *adj.* always: *Bobby is forever laughing.*

forge *n.* a place where metal is made very hot and then hammered into shape: *a blacksmith's forge.* *v.* to copy someone's handwriting. **forging. forged.**

forget *v.* not to remember: *Matthew forgot to take his homework to school.* **forgetting. forgot.** I have **forgotten.**

forgetful *adj.* always or often forgetting something.

forgive *v.* to pardon, to no longer want to punish. **forgiving. forgave.** I have **forgiven.**

fork *n.* 1. a handle with long prongs or points, used to lift food. 2. a big garden tool with prongs, used to lift earth or roots. 3. a place where a road or river divides.

form *n.* 1. a shape: *We piled the sand in the form of a castle.* 2. a sheet of paper with printed questions and spaces for the answers. *v.* to make: *to form a snowman out of snow.* **forming. formed.**

formal *adj.* following certain rules; not familiar or home-like: *It was a formal party. All the guests were wearing their fanciest clothes.* (*opp.* **informal.**)

formula *n.* 1. a mixture used for feeding babies. 2. a recipe used to make some product: *a secret formula.*

fort, fortress *n.* a strong building made for defence.

fortunate (for′chə nət) *adj.* lucky. **fortunately** *adv.*

fortune *n.* 1. wealth, riches: *Jim's father was left a fortune by his uncle.* 2. chance, luck: *Bert won the prize by good fortune.*

forty *n., adj.* ten times four (40).

forward *n.* a player on the front line in some games. *adj.* in front: *the forward position. adv.* ahead: *The soldiers marched forward.*

fossil *n.* the hardened remains of an ancient plant or animal.

foster parents parents who care for a child as their own, even though they are not related to him or her.

fought see **fight.**

foul *adj.* 1. horrible, stormy: *foul weather.* 2. unfair: *foul play.* 3. out of bounds: *a foul ball.*

found see **find.**

fountain *n.* a jet of water shooting upwards and falling back into a pool.

four *n., adj.* one more than three (4).

fourteen *n., adj.* ten more than four (14).

fourth *adj.* following third (4th).

fowl *n.* a bird, especially a chicken.

fox *n.* a wild animal that looks like a dog.

fraction *n.* a part of a whole amount: *One-half (½) and one-quarter (¼) are both fractions.*

fracture *n.* a breaking: *a fracture in a bone. v.* to break, to cause a fracture. **fracturing. fractured.**

fragile (fraj′əl) *adj.* delicate, easily broken: *This glass vase is fragile.*

fragrance (frā′grəns) *n.* a sweet, pleasant smell.

fragrant *adj.* sweet-smelling: *a fragrant rose.*

frail *adj.* weak, delicate in health: *a frail old cat.*

frame *n.* a border of wood or metal around something: *a picture frame, a window frame. v.* to put a border around. **framing. framed.**

frank *adj.* saying what you really think: *She was frank, and told her friend that he had bad manners.*

frankfurter *n.* a hot dog.

frantic *adj.* almost mad with excitement: *The dog gave me a frantic welcome.*

freak *adj.* unnatural, extraordinary: *a freak snowstorm in May.*

freckles *n. pl.* light brown spots on the skin.

Fredericton *n.* capital city of New Brunswick.

free *adj.* 1. loose, not bound: *The dog was free to run.* 2. costing nothing: *a free show.* *v.* to let go: *He freed the trapped animal.* **freeing. freed.**

freedom *n.* being free.

freeze *v.* 1. to become very cold. 2. to turn into ice. **freezing. froze.** it has **frozen.**

freight (frāt) *n.* cargo, the things carried by a truck, train, ship, etc.

freighter *n.* a cargo ship.

French *n.* the language spoken in France, Canada, and other countries.
adj. belonging to or coming from France.

French fries potatoes that have been cut into strips, then fried in deep fat.

French horn a large musical instrument, made of brass.

frequent *adj.* happening or appearing often: *Pat is a frequent visitor. We see him about three times a week.* **frequently** *adv.*

fresh *adj.* 1. new: *fresh news.* 2. not stale: *fresh air.*

Friday *n.* the sixth day of the week.

fried *adj.* cooked in hot fat: *fried eggs.* *v.* see **fry.**

friend (frend) *n.* someone you know well and like.

friendly *adj.* like a friend, nice: *a friendly person, a friendlier one, the friendliest one I have ever met.*

friendship *n.* being and having a friend.

fries see **fry.**

fright *n.* a scare, a fearful shock: *The thunder gave us a fright.*

frighten *v.* to make someone afraid. **frightening. frightened.**

frightening *adj.* scary: *a frightening movie.*

frill *n.* lace or cloth on the edges of material.

fringe *n.* loose threads hanging from the edge of cloth.

frisbee *n.* a piece of plastic, shaped like a saucer and tossed between players.

frog *n.* a small jumping animal that lives in and out of water.

from *prep.* 1. out of: *I took it from the box.* 2. between: *I played from four to five o'clock.* 3. beginning at: *Read from the first line.* 4. because of: *The plant died from the frost.*

front (frunt) *n.* the forward part, not the back: *the front of a train.*

frontier (frun tēr′) *n.* the boundary between two countries. *adj.* the last part of settled land, just before an area is wild: *a frontier town.*

frost *n.* powdered ice you see on the ground on a cold day.

frostbite *n.* the freezing of a part of the body.

frown *n.* a wrinkling together of the eyebrows. *v.* to wrinkle your forehead when you are puzzled or angry. **frowning. frowned.**

froze, frozen see **freeze.**

fruit *n.* 1. a juicy food from a tree, bush, or vine. 2. the part of any plant that contains the seeds.

fry *v.* to cook in oil or fat. **frying. fried.** she **fries.**

frying pan a pan used for frying eggs and other food.

fuel (fyü′əl) *n.* anything that is burned to give heat or energy: *Coal, oil, and wood are fuels.*

full *adj.* filled completely: *The hall is full of people.*

full moon the moon when it appears perfectly round.

fumble *n.* the handling of something in a clumsy way: *We lost the game because of my fumble. v.* 1. to handle something awkwardly: *to fumble the ball.* 2. to feel about: *to fumble for a key in your pocket.* **fumbling. fumbled.**

fumes (fyüms) *n. pl.* unpleasant gases or smoke from something burning.

fun *n.* enjoyment, amusement.

fund *n.* money put away for a special purpose: *a school fund, a holiday fund.*

funeral (fyü′nər əl) *n.* a burial service for a dead person.

fungus *n.* a kind of plant that has no leaves, flowers, or green colour. *pl.* **fungi** (fun′jī) or **funguses.**

funnel *n.* an object that has a thin tube at one end and a wide cone at the other.

funny *adj.* amusing, making you laugh: *My story was funny. Your story is funnier, and his story is the funniest one that I have ever heard.*

fur *n.* the soft, hairy coat of some animals.

furious (fyü′rē əs) *adj.* very, very angry: *My brother spilled paint on my best coat, and I was furious!*

furnace (fur′nəs) *n.* 1. a machine that heats houses and other buildings. 2. a very hot fire, used to heat water for a large boiler, or to melt metals.

furnish *v.* to supply a room with furniture. **furnishing. furnished.**

furniture *n.* the things needed in a room, such as a chair, table, dresser, bed, and lamp.

furry *adj.* made of fur or covered with fur: *a furry bunny, a furrier one, the furriest bunny of all.*

further *adj.* more: *Do you need further help?*

fuss *n.* bother, excitement: *My dog makes a great fuss when I come home from school.*

future (fyü′chər) *n.* what is still to happen, the time that lies ahead: *Val wants to go to England some time in the future.*

g

gag *v.* 1. to put a cloth around someone's mouth so that the person can't call for help: *The burglar gagged the watchman.* 2. to choke on a piece of food. **gagging. gagged.**

gain *v.* to increase: *I gained two kilograms last year.* **gaining. gained.**

galaxy *n.* a large group of stars. *pl.* **galaxies.**

gale *n.* a very strong wind, a storm.

gallery *n.* a building used for showing paintings: *an art gallery. pl.* **galleries.**

gallon *n.* a measure of liquids, equal to about 4.5 L.

gallop *v.* to run at full speed. **galloping. galloped.**

gamble *v.* 1. to play a game for money. 2. to take a risk that is not really necessary: *The sailors gambled their lives. They crossed the ocean in a tiny boat.* **gambling. gambled.**

game *n.* 1. a contest or sport in which the players follow certain rules. 2. wild birds or animals that are hunted.

gander *n.* a male goose.

gang *n.* a group of people going around together, often for a bad purpose: *a gang of robbers.*

gap *n.* an opening or space: *a gap in a wall.*

garage (gə razh′) *n.* a building where cars or buses are kept or repaired.

garbage (gar′bij) *n.* waste, usually from the kitchen.

garden *n.* a piece of ground used for growing flowers, vegetables, or fruit.

gardener *n.* a person paid to look after a garden.

garlic *n.* a strong-smelling plant bulb, used in cooking.

garment *n.* any piece of clothing.

gas *n.* 1. an invisible air-like substance that burns: *Gas is used for heating and cooking.* 2. short for **gasoline.** *pl.* **gases.**

gasp *v.* to open your mouth and breathe in deeply: *The swimmer gasped for air.* **gasping. gasped.**

gate *n.* a hinged door in a fence or wall.

gather (ɢᴀᴛʜ′ər) *v.* 1. to collect: *to gather flowers.* 2. to come together: *A crowd gathered around the movie star.* **gathering. gathered.**

gauze (gawz) *n.* very thin cloth: *Gauze is often used for bandages.*

gave see **give.**

gay *adj.* merry, exciting, full of fun.

gear *n.* a wheel with teeth around the edge; these teeth fit into the teeth of other wheels.

gearshift *n.* the part of a vehicle that connects the motor to the gears.

geese plural of **goose.**

gem (jem) *n.* a jewel or valuable stone: *Rubies, emeralds, and diamonds are gems.*

general *n.* an army commander. *adj.* usual, ordinary: *As a general rule, we begin school at nine o'clock.*

generous *adj.* kind and unselfish in sharing things with others.

genie (jē′nē) *n.* a powerful magician or spirit in fairy tales.

genius (jēn′yəs) *n.* someone who is very smart. *pl.* **geniuses.**

gentle *adj.* 1. quiet: *a gentle voice.* 2. mild, not rough: *a gentle breeze.*

gentleman *n.* a man who is kind, helpful, and polite. *pl.* **gentlemen.**

gently *adv.* mildly, quietly.

genuine (jen′yü ən) *adj.* real, not fake or a copy: *genuine gold.*

geography *n.* the study of the world and the people who live in different places.

gerbil (jər′bəl) *n.* a small pet that looks like a mouse.

germ (jərm) *n.* a tiny living thing that can cause illness and disease.

German *n.* the language spoken in Germany. *adj.* belonging to or coming from Germany.

German shepherd a large dog, brown or grey and black in colour.

get *v.* 1. to receive, to go for: *to get some food to eat.* 2. to become: *to get cold.* **getting. got.** I have **gotten.**
get along with to be friendly with.
get away with to do something wrong without being punished.
get even to pay someone back for a wrong.
get over to recover from a sickness.
get together to have a meeting.
get up 1. to wake up. 2. to stand up.

ghost (gōst) *n.* the spirit of a dead person or animal, which some people think walks about at night.

giant (jī′ənt) *n.* a person of enormous size. *adj.* huge: *a giant apple.*

gift *n.* something given to you, a present.

gigantic (jī gan′tik) *adj.* enormous in size.

giggle (gig′əl) *v.* to laugh in a silly way. **giggling. giggled.**

gills (gilz) *n. pl.* two openings in the head of a fish, used for breathing.

ginger (jin′jər) *n.* the root of a plant that grows in hot places: *Ginger is sometimes ground into a powder and used for cooking.*

gingerbread *n.* a brown cookie or cake flavoured with ginger.

giraffe (jə raf′) *n.* a tall African animal with a very long neck and spotted skin.

girl *n.* a female child.

Girl Guide a member of an organization for girls.

give *v.* 1. to hand over something to someone: *Please give me the book.* 2. to cause: *Don't give them trouble.* 3. to say: *He gave a cry of pain.* **giving. gave.** I have **given.**
to give in, to give up to surrender.

glacier (glā′shər, glā′syər) *n.* a huge river of ice that moves very slowly down a mountain side or along a valley.

glad *adj.* pleased, happy. **gladly** *adv.*

glance *n.* a quick look. *v.* to take a quick look: *I glanced at the library book before I borrowed it.* **glancing. glanced.**

glare *n.* a strong light: *the glare of the sun. v.* to stare at someone in an angry way: *He glared at the man who was talking in the theatre.* **glaring. glared.**

glass *n.* 1. a hard substance you can see through, used in making windows, eyeglasses, etc. 2. a drinking glass.

glasses *n. pl.* short for **eyeglasses.**

gleam *n.* a flash of light: *a gleam of sunshine through the clouds. v.* to shine: *The mirror gleams.* **gleaming. gleamed.**

glee *n.* joy, merriment: *The baby laughed with glee.*

glide *v.* to slide smoothly: *The skaters glided over the ice.* **gliding. glided.**

glider *n.* a light aircraft with no motor.

glisten (glis′ən) *v.* to shine, to sparkle: *Dewdrops glisten in the sun.* **glistening. glistened.**

glitter *v.* to sparkle, to flash: *Diamonds glitter in the light.* **glittering. glittered.**

globe *n.* 1. a ball, or anything in the shape of a ball. 2. the earth, the world.

gloomy *adj.* 1. dark, dim: *a gloomy cave.* 2. miserable, sad: *a gloomy person, a gloomier person, the gloomiest person in the room.*

glorious *adj.* splendid: *a glorious victory; a glorious day.*

glory *n.* beauty, fame, praise: *the glory of victory; the sun in all its glory.*

glove (gluv) *n.* a covering for your hand.

glow (glō) *n.* a shine, often from something hot: *a glow from the campfire. v.* to give out light and warmth, without flames: *The hot coals glowed in the barbecue.* **glowing. glowed.**

glue *n.* a sticky liquid or paste used to hold things together. *v.* to put glue on something. **glueing. glued.**

gnash (nash) *v.* to grind together: *He gnashed his teeth in anger.* **gnashing. gnashed.**

gnat (nat) *n.* a very small fly that can sting.

gnaw (naw) *v.* to chew away at: *The dog loves to gnaw on a bone.* **gnawing. gnawed.**

gnome (nōm) *n.* a little dwarf in fairy tales.

go *v.* 1. to move away: *to go home.* 2. to be moving: *The clock is going.* 3. to last:

Make your money go a long way. 4. to pass: *The time is going very quickly.* 5. to make a sound: *The clock goes 'tick'.* **going. went.** he **goes.** he has **gone** (gon).

goal *n.* 1. a place where players must put the puck or ball in games such as hockey or football. 2. a score in a game of hockey and in some ball games. 3. an aim: *Sandra's goal is to act in a play.*

goalie *n.* the player who defends the goal in hockey, lacrosse, and some other games.

goaltender *n.* the goalie.

goat *n.* a farm animal with horns and long hair.

gobble *v.* to eat something quickly and greedily. **gobbling. gobbled.**

goblin *n.* a mischievous elf in fairy tales.

God *n.* in some religions, the creator of everything.

god (*fem.* **goddess**) *n.* a being thought by some people to have great power over their lives.

godfather (*fem.* **godmother**) *n.* an adult who makes vows for a child when it is baptized.

goes see **go.**

goggles *n. pl.* large glasses worn to protect the eyes.

going see **go.**

gold *n.* 1. a very valuable yellow metal. 2. a yellowish colour. *adj.* having this colour.

golden *adj.* made of gold or looking like gold.

goldfish *n.* a small reddish fish kept as a pet.

golf *n.* a game played on a golf course: *In golf, players use clubs to hit a small white ball.*

gone see **go.**

gong *n.* a large metal plate that gives a booming sound when hit.

good *adj.* kind, excellent, well-behaved, pleasing: *Debbie has done good work. Sara's work is better. Tracy's work is the best of all.*

good-bye, good-by *n.* farewell.

goodness *n.* being good.

goods *n. pl.* property, belongings: *We packed our goods before the move.*

goose (*masc.* **gander**) *n.* a large water bird. *pl.* **geese.**

gorge (gorj) *n.* a narrow valley between high cliffs.

gorgeous (gor'jəs) *adj.* magnificent, beautiful: *a gorgeous sight.*

gorilla *n.* the largest and strongest ape.

gossip *n.* talk about other people that is not always true, and is sometimes unkind. *v.* to talk about others in such a way. **gossiping. gossiped.**

got see **get.**

govern *v.* to rule. **governing. governed.**

government *n.* 1. the act of governing. 2. the people who govern a country: *The government made some new laws.*

governor *n.* someone who rules.

Governor General Canada's representative of the queen (or king).

gown *n.* a long dress.

grab *v.* to snatch: *The thief grabbed the jewels and then fled.* **grabbing. grabbed.**

grace *n.* a short prayer said before a meal.

graceful *adj.* charming, beautiful in movement: *a graceful figure skater.* **gracefully** *adv.*

grade *n.* a level: *He is in Grade 5. This is a better grade of apples than we had before.*

gradual (graj'ü əl) *adj.* gentle, slow: *There has been a gradual improvement in the student's work.* **gradually** *adv.*

graduate (graj'ü ət) *n.* a person who has finished a school or university course.

graduate (graj'ü āt) *v.* to finish a school or university course and receive a diploma: *My brother graduated from university two years ago.* **graduating. graduated.**

graduation *n.* 1. finishing a school or university course. 2. the ceremony that takes place then: *We went to my sister's graduation.*

grain *n.* 1. the seed of corn, wheat, oats, and other cereal plants. 2. a speck: *grains of dust.* 3. the markings on wood.

grain elevator a building in which grain is stored.

gram *n.* a measure of mass; g is the symbol. 1000 g = 1 kg

grammar (gram'ər) *n.* the study of how a language works.

grand *adj.* 1. great in size: *A grand piano is a larger piano than an upright one.* 2. magnificent, splendid: *a grand display of flowers.*

grandchild *n.* a child of a son or daughter; a granddaughter or grandson. *pl.* **grandchildren.**

grandfather, granddad, grandpa *n.* your mother's father or your father's father.

grandmother, grandma *n.* your mother's mother or your father's mother.

grandparent *n.* a grandfather or grandmother.

grandstand *n.* the main seating place on a sports field.

granite (gran'it) *n.* a very hard rock.

grant *v.* to give, to allow: *The wizard granted her three wishes.* **granting. granted.**

grape *n.* a juicy fruit that grows in clusters on a vine; it is red, purple, or green in colour.

grapefruit *n.* a fruit that looks like a large orange and has a yellowish skin.

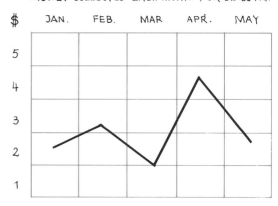

MONEY COLLECTED EACH MONTH FOR CLASS TRIP

graph (graf) *n.* a chart, usually made of lines and dots: *Graphs show changes in weather, mass, height, etc.*

grasp *v.* to seize hold of: *The man grasped the railing to keep from falling down the stairs.* **grasping. grasped.**

grass *n.* the green plant making up a lawn or meadow.

grasshopper *n.* a jumping insect with long back legs.

grate *n.* the part of a fireplace that holds burning coal or wood. *v.* to rub into little pieces: *The cook grated some cheese.* **grating. grated.**

grateful *adj.* thankful: *Shane was grateful to Samantha for helping him finish the puzzle.*

grave *n.* a hole in the earth in which someone is buried. *adj.* serious: *Her grave face showed me that something was wrong.*

gravel (grav'əl) *n.* small pebbles and stones.

graveyard *n.* a place for burying the dead.

gravity (grav'ə tē) *n.* a rule of science that says whatever goes up must come down.

gravy *n.* the juice of cooked meat.

gray see **grey.**

graze *v.* to eat grass: *Cows graze in the fields.* **grazing. grazed.**

grease *n.* soft, oily fat. *v.* to put grease on something: *Steve greased the pan so that the cake wouldn't stick to it.* **greasing. greased.**

greasy *adj.* containing much grease: *a greasy piece of chicken, a greasier one, the greasiest piece of all.*

great (grāt) *adj.* 1. large: *David saw a great big spider.* 2. important: *The automobile is a great invention.* 3. famous, well-known: *a great artist.*

greedy *adj.* wanting more than your share: *a greedy monster, a greedier one, the greediest one of all.*

Greek *n.* the language spoken in Greece. *adj.* belonging to or coming from Greece.

green *n.* the colour of grass. *adj.* having this colour.

greet *v.* to welcome: *The family greeted their friends at the door.* **greeting. greeted.**

greeting *n.* a welcome, a message of welcome or good wishes: *A birthday greeting arrived in the mail.*

grew see **grow.**

grey, gray *n.* a colour made by mixing black and white together: *Grey is the colour of dark clouds.* *adj.* having this colour.

grid *n.* a frame of iron bars; a grating; a grill.

grief (grēf) *n.* sadness, sorrow: *Nina was filled with grief when her canary flew away.*

grim *adj.* stern, hard-faced: *a grim look, a grimmer look, the grimmest look of all.*

grimy (grī'mē) *adj.* dirty, soiled: *grimy hands, grimier hands, the grimiest hands of all.*

grin *n.* a wide smile. *v.* to smile broadly. **grinning. grinned.**

grind *v.* 1. to crush to powder: *The miller ground the wheat into flour.* 2. to rub together: *to grind your teeth.* **grinding. ground.**

grip *v.* to hold tightly. **gripping. gripped.**

grit *n.* a small bit of stone or sand.

grizzly *n.* a large, fierce bear. *pl.* **grizzlies.**

groan *n.* a deep sigh of disappointment or pain. *v.* to make such a sound. **groaning. groaned.**

grocer (grō'sər) *n.* a person who sells food and household goods.

groceries *n. pl.* food and other goods sold at a grocery store.

grocery store a store that sells food and other household goods.

groom *n.* 1. a man on his wedding day. 2. a person who looks after horses. *v.* to make neat and tidy: *to groom a dog.* **grooming. groomed.**

groove *n.* a narrow slot cut into plastic, wood, or metal: *a groove in a record.*

gross *adj.* very bad, very rude: *gross conduct.*

grouch *n.* a miserable, very unhappy person: *You're such a grouch!*

ground *n.* 1. the earth we walk on. 2. a place where some activity happens: *a fairground. v.* see **grind.**

groundhog *n.* a North American animal that digs burrows or holes.

group (grüp) *n.* a number of people doing something together: *a music group.*

grow *v.* 1. to get bigger, to increase: *Acorns grow into oak trees.* 2. to plant: *to grow tomatoes.* **growing. grew.** I have **grown.**

growl *v.* to make a deep, angry noise: *The lion growled in its cage.* **growling. growled.**

grown-up *n.* an adult; a full-grown person.

growth (grōth) *n.* the act of growing: *the growth of a plant.*

grudge *n.* a bad feeling: *That team carries a grudge just because it lost the game.*

grumble *v.* to complain, to find fault: *Vince grumbled because he had to get up early on Saturday.* **grumbling. grumbled.**

grumpy *adj.* miserable, unhappy: *a grumpy person, a grumpier one, the grumpiest person I ever met.*

grunt *n.* the kind of sound that a pig makes. *v.* to make such a sound. **grunting. grunted.**

guarantee (gar ən tē′) *n.* a promise; an agreement that if something goes wrong, it will be fixed: *The store gave me a two-year guarantee on my bike. v.* to make such a promise: *The store guaranteed the stereo for a year.* **guaranteeing. guaranteed.**

guard (gahrd) *n.* someone who keeps watch and protects: *the palace guard. v.* to watch and protect, to defend: *A goalie guards the goal.* **guarding. guarded.**

guess (ges) *n.* a feeling or opinion about something: *My guess is that it will snow tomorrow. v.* to say what you think is true, without knowing for certain: *Jean-Paul guessed my age.* **guessing. guessed.**

guest (gest) *n.* a visitor, someone you invite to your home.

guide (gīd) *n.* a person or thing that shows the way: *When we visit a new city, we pay for a guide to show us around. v.* to lead, to show the way. **guiding. guided.**

Guide see **Girl Guide.**

guilty (gil′tē) *adj.* having done wrong or taken part in a crime: *The prisoner was found guilty of stealing.*

guinea pig (gin′ē) a small animal about the size of a rat: *A guinea pig is kept as a pet and is also used in experiments.*

guitar (gi tar′) *n.* a musical instrument with four, six, or twelve strings.

gulf *n.* a very large bay: *the Gulf of St. Lawrence.*

gull *n.* a grey and white bird, seen near bodies of water.

gulp *v.* to swallow quickly: *Ying gulped down his milk and then went out.* **gulping. gulped.**

gum *n.* 1. a sticky liquid from plants and trees. 2. chewing gum. 3. the red flesh around your teeth.

gun *n.* a cannon, rifle, pistol, or revolver from which shells or bullets are fired.

gunpowder *n.* black explosive powder used in fireworks and guns.

guppy *n.* a very small tropical fish. *pl.* **guppies.**

gush *v.* to burst: *The water gushed out of the tap.* **gushing. gushed.**

gutter *n.* a channel or ditch for carrying off waste water.

guy (gī) *n.* a man, a fellow: *a good guy.*

gym, gymnasium (jim nā'zē əm) *n.* a large room for body exercises and sports.

gymnast *n.* someone who trains to do physical exercises and acrobatics.

gypsy (jip'sē) *n.* a person belonging to a group of wandering people. *pl.* **gypsies.**

habit *n.* something you do the same way all the time: *Denis has the habit of waking up very early.*

had see **have.**

haddock *n.* an ocean fish that can be eaten. *pl.* **haddock.**

hadn't short for **had not.**

hag *n.* an ugly old witch.

hail *n.* frozen rain.

hair *n.* 1. one of the fine threads that grow on the skin. 2. the covering of your head, or of an animal's body.

haircut *n.* the cutting and trimming of your hair.

hairdresser *n.* a person who takes care of or cuts people's hair.

hairy *adj.* covered with hair: *a hairy ape, a hairier ape, the hairiest ape in the cage.*

half (haf) *n.* one of two equal parts that make up a whole. *pl.* **halves** (havz).

halfway *adv.* half the way: *We are halfway home.*

halibut *n.* an ocean fish that can be eaten. *pl.* **halibut.**

Halifax *n.* capital city of Nova Scotia.

hall *n.* 1. the entrance space behind the door of a building. 2. a large room for meetings, concerts, parties, etc. 3. a building for public business: *city hall, town hall.*

Halloween, Hallowe'en *n.* the evening of October 31, when children go trick-or-treating.

hallway *n.* a hall or passage in a building.

halo (hā'lō) *n.* 1. a ring of light around the sun, moon, or a star. 2. a ring of light around the head, shown in some pictures of angels or holy people. *pl.* **halos.**

halt *v.* to stop: *'Halt!' shouted the guard.* **halting. halted.**

ham *n.* 1. cooked meat from a pig's thigh. 2. an amateur radio operator.

hamburger *n.* ground beef, often shaped into a patty and cooked.

hammer *n.* a tool used for driving in nails, shaping metal, or breaking up stone.

hamper *n.* a large container, often a basket with a cover: *a clothes hamper, a picnic hamper.*

hand *n.* 1. the end of your arm. 2. a pointer on a clock. 3. a deal of cards: *I won the card game because I had the best hand.* 4. a member of a ship's crew: *All hands on deck.*
hand in to give to a person in charge: *Hand in your tests.*
hand out to give out: *Hand out the tests to all the pupils.*
hand over to give or return: *Hand over your books to the librarian.*
hands up a call for surrender.
on hand close by, ready: *The tailor has lots of pins on hand.*

handcuffs *n. pl.* steel bracelets used to hold a prisoner's hands together.

handful *n.* as much as your hand will hold. *pl.* **handfuls.**

handicap *n.* something that puts a person at a disadvantage.

handkerchief (hang′ kər chif) *n.* a cloth for wiping your nose. *pl.* **handkerchiefs.**

handle *n.* the part of a cup, pan, or tool by which it is held. *v.* to hold, touch, or move with your hands: *Handle the glasses carefully.* **handling. handled.**

handlebars *n. pl.* the part of a bicycle that the rider holds and uses for steering.

handshake *n.* the clasping of hands between two people as a sign of friendship.

handsome *adj.* good-looking.

handy *adj.* 1. clever with your hands: *Mother is handy at repairs in the house.* 2. useful to have by you: *a handy tool, a handier one, the handiest tool in the workshop.*

hang *v.* 1. to fasten something so that it swings but does not fall: *Please hang your coat on a hook.* **hanging. hung.** 2. to put someone to death with a rope around his or her neck. **hanging. hanged.**

hangar *n.* a shed for aircraft.

hanger *n.* a wooden or wire frame on which to hang clothes.

Hanukkah *n.* an eight-day Jewish holiday in or around December.

happen *v.* to take place, to occur: *The accident happened last night.* **happening. happened.**

happily *adv.* in a happy way: *Kelly went happily to school.*

happiness *n.* being happy.

happy *adj.* pleased, cheerful, glad: *Kim is happy, Sam is happier, and Jamie is the happiest member of the family today.* (*opp.* **unhappy.**)

harbour, harbor *n.* a sheltered place for ships.

hard *adj.* 1. firm, not soft: *hard earth.* 2. difficult: *a hard problem; hard work.*

hardly *adv.* only just: *I can hardly reach it.*

hardware *n.* metal items such as locks, chains, and tools.

hare *n.* an animal with long ears and long back legs: *A hare is very much like a large rabbit.*

harm *v.* to damage, to hurt. **harming. harmed.**

harmful *adj.* causing harm, dangerous: *The berries on that tree are harmful if you eat them.* (*opp.* **harmless.**)

harmonica *n.* a small musical instrument, also called a mouth organ: *The sound of a harmonica is made by blowing into it, and by moving the lips and tongue.*

harmony *n.* 1. a pleasing musical sound. 2. a feeling of friendship, of agreeing on things: *There is perfect harmony between the two cousins.*

harp *n.* a large musical instrument played by plucking its strings.

harpoon *n.* a spear, with a rope fastened to it, fired at whales.

harsh *adj.* rough, unkind: *a harsh winter; harsh punishment.*

harvest *n.* the gathering of grain, fruit, and other crops at the end of the growing season.

has see **have.**

hasn't short for **has not.**

haste (hāst) *n.* a great hurry: *He ran off in haste.*

hat *n.* a covering for the head, usually with a brim.

hatch *v.* to bring baby birds or small fish out of eggs. **hatching. hatched.**

hatchery *n.* a place for hatching eggs. *pl.* **hatcheries.**

hatchet *n.* a small axe.

hate *v.* to dislike very much, to detest. **hating. hated.**

hatred (hā'trəd) *n.* strong dislike.

haul *v.* to drag, to pull: *The horse hauled the logs along the ground.* **hauling. hauled.**

haunted *adj.* believed to be visited by ghosts: *a haunted house.*

have (hav) *v.* 1. to own, to hold: *I have some money.* 2. (used with **to**) must: *I have to go.* 3. used before another verb, to show that something has been finished: *I have eaten. You have slept.* **having. had.** he **has.**

haven't short for **have not.**

hawk *n.* a bird of prey with a strong, hooked beak and long, curved claws.

hay *n.* grass cut and dried as food for animals.

haystack *n.* a large pile of hay.

haze *n.* slight mist or smoke.

hazel (hā'zəl) *n.* 1. a small tree with nuts that can be eaten. 2. a greenish-brown colour. *adj.* having this colour.

hazy (hā'zē) *adj.* misty: *a hazy sky, a hazier sky, the haziest sky I've ever seen.*

he *pron.* a man or boy.

head (hed) *n.* 1. the top part of your body. 2. the top or front of anything: *the head of a parade.* 3. the chief leader: *the head of a country.*

headache (hed'āk) *n.* a pain in the head.

headlights *n. pl.* the main front lights of a car, bus, truck, etc.

headline *n.* the title of an article in a newspaper or magazine.

headquarters *n. pl.* a main office: *police headquarters; army headquarters; the headquarters of a business.*

heal *v.* to make well again: *to heal a cut.* **healing. healed.**

health (helth) *n.* the condition of your mind and body, whether you are well or ill: *If you are well, you enjoy good health.*

healthy (hel'thē) *adj.* in good health: *a healthy pup, a healthier one, the healthiest pup of all.*

heap *n.* a pile: *a heap of papers.*

hear *v.* to receive sounds through the ears. **hearing. heard** (hərd).

hearing *n.* one of the five senses; the ability to hear sounds.

hearse (hərs) *n.* a car used in a funeral, in which the coffin is carried.

heart (hart) *n.* 1. the part of your body that pumps your blood. 2. a playing card with one or more (♥) marks on it. **by heart** from memory; to be able to say the words of a poem, story, or play without looking at a book.

heat *n.* warmth, hotness: *the heat from the sun or from a fire.* *v.* to warm up: *Please heat the potatoes.* **heating. heated.**

heave *v.* to lift up with a great effort: *We heaved the heavy box into the trunk.* **heaving. heaved.**

heaven *n.* 1. according to some religions, the place where good people go after they die. 2. a place of great happiness.

heavy *adj.* 1. more than usual: *heavy rain.* 2. hard to lift: *a heavy box, a heavier one, the heaviest box of all.*

hectare *n.* a unit of measurement for area; ha is the symbol. 1 ha = 10 000 m²

he'd short for **he had** or **he would.**

hedge *n.* bushes that grow close together and form a kind of fence.

heel *n.* 1. the back of your foot, under the ankle. 2. the part of a shoe that is under your heel.

height (hīt) *n.* how high anything is: *Frank's height is 165 centimetres.*

heir (ār) (*fem.* **heiress**) *n.* someone who will become the owner of another person's title, money, or property when that person dies: *The eldest prince is heir to the throne. He will be king when his mother dies.*

held see **hold.**

helicopter *n.* an aircraft without wings: *A helicopter is pulled by large propellers and can rise straight up from the ground.*

hell *n.* 1. according to some religions, the place where wicked people go after they die. 2. a place of misery.

he'll short for **he will.**

hello a greeting.

helmet *n.* a hard hat protecting the head.

help *n. v.* aid: *Can you give me some help?* to share someone's work or troubles by doing something for him or her: *Susan helped her father cut the grass.* **helping. helped.**

helpful *adj.* giving help: *André is very helpful when there is work to be done.*

helping *n.* a share, a portion: *Roger asked for a second helping of ice cream.*

hem *n.* the edge of a piece of cloth, turned over and stitched. *v.* to sew a hem on the edge of cloth. **hemming. hemmed.**

hemlock *n.* an evergreen tree.

hen *n.* 1. a female chicken. 2. the female of other birds.

her *pron., adj.* referring to a girl, woman, or female animal: *Give her the prize. Her coat is wet.*

herb (ərb, hərb) *n.* a plant whose leaves, seeds, or stems are sometimes used in cooking or in making medicine.

herd *n.* a group of cattle or other large animals: *a herd of buffalo.*

here *adv.* 1. in this place: *Here I am.* 2. to this place: *Come here!*

hermit *n.* a person who lives alone and stays away from other people.

hero (hē'rō) *n.* 1. a man or boy who has done something very brave. 2. the chief man or boy in a story. *pl.* **heroes.**

heroic (hi rō'ik) *adj.* brave, as it would be done by a hero or heroine: *a heroic deed.*

heroine (her'ō in) *n.* 1. a girl or woman who has done something very brave. 2. the chief woman or girl in a story.

heroism *n.* (her'ō iz əm) *n.* great bravery.

heron *n.* a large wading bird with a long beak, a long neck, and long legs.

herring *n.* an ocean fish used for food. *pl.* **herring.**

hers *pron.* the one belonging to her: *The prize is hers.*

herself *pron.* she alone: *She built the cabin by herself.*

he's short for **he is.**

hesitate *v.* to pause because you are not sure whether to do or say something: *Erin hesitated about whether to go.* **hesitating. hesitated.**

hesitation *n.* a pause before doing something because you are not sure.

hey a shout made to catch the attention of others.

hi a greeting, hello.

hibernate (hī'bər nāt) *v.* to sleep through the winter as bears and other animals do. **hibernating. hibernated.**

hiccup, hiccough (hik'up) *n.* a short gasp, sometimes made when you eat too much too quickly. *v.* to gasp in such a way. **hiccupping. hiccupped.**

hide *n.* an animal's skin. *v.* 1. to keep out of sight: *Steve is hiding behind a tree.* 2. to put out of sight: *Greg hid the candy under a paper.* **hiding. hid.** I have **hidden.**

hide-and-seek a game in which you hide and someone tries to find you.

high (hī) *adj.* 1. tall, a long way up from the ground: *a high tower.* 2. very great: *a high price.*

high-rise *n.* a tall building with many floors.

high school a secondary school for older boys and girls.

highway *n.* a main road.

hike *n.* a long walk. *v.* to go on such a walk. **hiking. hiked.**

hill *n.* a raised part of the land, lower than a mountain.

him *pron.* the boy, man, or male animal spoken about: *Give him something to eat.*

himself *pron.* he alone: *He built the garage by himself.*

hind *adj.* at the back: *the hind legs of a cow.*

Hindu (hin'dü) *n.* a person who follows Hinduism, a religion of India and other Asian lands.

hinge (hinj) *n.* a joint on which a door or lid can move.

hint *n.* a clue, a helpful piece of advice: *The farmer gave us some hints on how to plant seeds.*

hip *n.* the part that sticks out on each side of your body below the waist.

hippopotamus *n.* a large, thick-skinned animal which lives in and near the waters of Africa. *pl.* **hippopotamuses** or **hippopotami** (hip ə pot'ə mī).

hire *v.* to arrange for someone to do work for pay: *The Smiths hire a babysitter when they go out.* **hiring. hired.**

his *pron., adj.* the one belonging to him: *This coat is his. His hat is here.*

hiss *n.* a sound like an 's'. *v.* to make such a sound: *Geese and snakes hiss when angry.* **hissing. hissed.**

historical *adj.* about history: *a historical story.*

history *n.* the story of what happened in days gone by: *the history of Canada.* *pl.* **histories.**

hit *n.* 1. a blow, a stroke: *a hit on the head.* 2. something popular: *The new song is a hit.* 3. in baseball, a hit by the batter that lets him or her get to at least first base. *v.* to strike, to knock: *Paula hit the ball with the bat.* **hitting. hit.**

hitch *v.* to fasten with a rope: *to hitch a horse to a post.* **hitching. hitched.**

hive (hīv) *n.* 1. the home of bees. 2. a large number of bees living together.

hoard *v.* to store in a secret place: *The squirrels hoard nuts in the ground.* **hoarding. hoarded.**

hoarse *adj.* sounding deep and husky: *a hoarse voice.*

hoax (hōks) *n.* a practical joke, a trick.

hobble *v.* to walk slowly with short steps, to limp. **hobbling. hobbled.**

hobby *n.* a favourite pastime: *My hobby is making model cars.* *pl.* **hobbies.**

hockey *n.* 1. a game played on a skating rink with a goal at each end; the players hit a puck with curved sticks to drive it across the goal. 2. a field game played with curved sticks and a small ball.

hoe *n.* a long-handled tool for loosening the soil.

hog *n.* a full-grown pig.

hoist *v.* to lift up something by ropes: *to hoist a flag.* **hoisting. hoisted.**

hold *v.* 1. to keep something in your hand: *to hold an umbrella.* 2. to contain: *The bag holds flour.* 3. to defend: *They held the castle against enemy attacks.* 4. to have: *to hold a meeting.* **holding. held.**

to hold up 1. to lift. 2. to cause delay: *While riding my bike, I was held up by traffic lights.* 3. to rob: *The bank was held up by robbers.*

hole *n.* 1. an opening: *a hole in the wall.* 2. a pit: *a hole in the ground.*

holiday *n.* a time free from work, a vacation.

hollow *n.* a hole, a pit. *adj.* not solid; empty, having a hole: *a hollow tooth.*

holly *n.* a prickly evergreen shrub with red berries.

holster *n.* a leather case for a pistol, attached to a person's belt.

holy (hō'lē) *adj.* sacred, to do with God.

home *n.* the place where a person lives.

homemaker *n.* a person who looks after a house or apartment and the people who live in it.

home run in baseball, a hit that lets the batter get to home base in one trip.

homesick *adj.* sad because you are away from home.

homework *n.* work done at home, especially schoolwork.

honest (on'ist) *adj.* always truthful and fair, never cheating or stealing. (*opp.* **dishonest.**)

honesty *n.* truthfulness.

honey (hun'ē) *n.* a sweet, thick liquid made by bees.

honeymoon *n.* the holiday taken by a newly married couple.

honk *n.* the cry of a goose, or any sound like this. *v.* to make such a sound: *to honk a horn.* **honking. honked.**

honour, honor (on'ər) *n.* 1. respect, fame: *The soldiers fought for the honour of their land.* 2. honesty: *Mr. Jones is a man of honour. He always keeps his promises.* 3. a title of respect: *Your Honour.* *v.* to praise, to treat with respect. **honouring. honoured.**

honourable, honorable (on'ər ə bəl) *adj.* honest, truthful, fair.

hood *n.* 1. a covering for the head and neck, sometimes fastened to a jacket. 2. a covering over a car engine.

hoof *n.* the horny foot of a horse, cow, sheep, goat, or pig. *pl.* **hoofs** or **hooves.**

hook *n.* a bent and pointed piece of metal made to hold something: *a fish hook.* *v.* to catch or fasten with a hook. **hooking. hooked.**

hoot *n.* the cry of an owl, or a similar sound.

hop *n.* 1. a jump forward on one leg, or with two feet together. 2. a plant whose flowers are used to flavour beer. *v.* to jump on one leg, or with two feet together. **hopping. hopped.**

hope *v.* to wish that something would happen: *Stephanie hoped her cousin would come.* **hoping. hoped.**

hopeful *adj.* full of hope. **hopefully** *adv.*

horizon (hə rī′zən) *n.* the line where sea and sky, or earth and sky, seem to meet.

horizontal (hor ə zon′təl) *adj.* lying flat or level with the ground: *A horizontal line is drawn from left to right. A vertical line is drawn from top to bottom.*

horn *n.* 1. the hard, usually pointed growth on the head of some animals. 2. a musical instrument that you blow. 3. a warning signal: *a car horn.*

hornet *n.* a large wasp that stings.

horrible *adj.* terrible, awful: *When you scrape your nail on the chalkboard, it makes a horrible noise.*

horrify *v.* to upset or shock someone: *We were horrified by the terrible news.* **horrifying. horrified.** it **horrifies.**

horror *n.* great fear, terror, fright.

horse *n.* an animal with hooves that is used for riding and pulling wagons.

horseback *adv.* on the back of a horse: *We will ride horseback to the fair.*

horseshoe *n.* an iron shoe worn by a horse on each hoof.

hose (hōz) *n.* 1. a tube used for carrying water. 2. socks or stockings.

hospital *n.* a building where people who are ill or hurt are cared for by doctors and nurses.

host (*fem.* **hostess**) *n.* a person who entertains visitors.

hot *adj.* full of heat: *a hot day, a hotter one, the hottest day of the summer.*

hot dog a hot wiener in a bun.

hotel (hō tel′) *n.* a large building where travellers stay.

hound *n.* a hunting dog. *v.* to annoy: *Stop hounding me.* **hounding. hounded.**

hour (our) *n.* a length of time equal to 60 minutes; h is the symbol.

house *n.* a building in which people live.

House of Commons the elected government representatives who meet in Ottawa to make laws.

how *adv.* 1. in what way: *How did you do it?* 2. to what amount: *How tall are you?*

however *conj.* and yet: *I fixed the clock; however, it stopped again.*

howl *n.* a long cry: *the howl of a wolf or a dog.* *v.* to make such a cry. **howling. howled.**

huddle *v.* to press close together: *The cows huddled under a tree.* **huddling. huddled.**

hue (hyü) *n.* a shade, a colour: *all the hues of the rainbow.*

huff *n.* a fit of anger: *The angry customer left the store in a huff.*

hug *n.* a close, tight clasp with the arms. *v.* 1. to clasp close in your arms: *Mack hugged his baby sister.* 2. to keep close to: *The boat hugs the shore.* **hugging. hugged.**

huge (hyüj) *adj.* enormous in size: *An elephant is a huge animal.*

hull *n.* the frame or body of a ship.

hum *v.* 1. to make a noise like a bee. 2. to make a singing sound with your lips closed: *Chris hummed a tune as he worked.* **humming. hummed.**

human (hyü′mən) *adj.* having to do with people, not animals: *Men, women, and children are human beings.*

humane (hyü mān′) *adj.* kind, merciful: *Feeding animals is the humane thing to do.*

humble *adj.* feeling not important or less important: *Linda felt humble after the coach had a long talk with her.*

humid (hyü′mid) *adj.* moist, damp: *It was so humid that our clothes took a long time to dry on the line.*

humidity (hyü mid′ə tē) *n.* dampness in the air.

humorous (hyü′mər əs) *adj.* funny, laughable: *Maria told a humorous story and we all laughed for a long time.*

humour, humor (hyü′mər) *n.* 1. fun, joking: *Paul has a good sense of humour.* 2. a mood: *He's in bad humour this morning, so watch what you say.*

hump *n.* a large bulge or bump, usually on the back: *a camel's hump.*

hunch *n.* 1. a hump. 2. a feeling that something will happen: *I just have a hunch that it will snow tomorrow.*

hundred *n., adj.* ten times ten (100).

hundredth *adj.* following ninety-ninth (100th).

hung see **hang.**

hunger *n.* the feeling that you need food.

hungry *adj.* having a wish for food, needing food: *a hungry cat, a hungrier one, the hungriest cat on the street.*

hunt *v.* 1. to chase after something in order to catch or kill it: *to hunt lions.* 2. to search for: *Ryan hunted everywhere for his cap.* **hunting. hunted.**

hunter *n.* someone who hunts.

hurdle *n.* a movable fence for runners or horses to jump over in a race.

hurl *v.* to throw something with all your strength. **hurling. hurled.**

hurrah, hurray a cheer.

hurricane *n.* a storm with a very powerful wind and heavy rain.

hurry *v.* to move fast: *Lee hurried to catch the bus.* **hurrying. hurried.** he **hurries. to hurry up** to move faster.

hurt *n.* a cut, a wound, a pain. *v.* to cause pain or harm to someone. **hurting. hurt.**

husband *n.* a married man.

hush *v.* to keep quiet. **hushing. hushed.**

husky *n.* a strong dog, used in very cold places for pulling sleds. *pl.* **huskies.** *adj.* 1. sounding hoarse: *a husky voice.* 2. big and strong: *a husky lumberjack, a huskier one, the huskiest one in the forest.*

hut *n.* a small shed or cabin.

hyacinth (hī′ə sinth) *n.* a plant that grows from a bulb; it has pink, blue, or white flowers.

hydrant *n.* a wide pipe, sticking out of the ground, that fire hoses can be attached to.

hyena (hī ē′nə) *n.* a wild, wolf-like animal of Africa and Asia.

hymn (him) *n.* a song of praise to God.

hyphen (hī′fən) *n.* a short dash (-) used to separate a word at the end of a line, or to join two words: *Kind-hearted and daddy-longlegs have hyphens.*

hypnotist (hip′nə tist) *n.* a person who can put you into a sleep-like state.

hypnotize (hip′nə tīz) *v.* to put a person into a sleep-like state. **hypnotizing. hypnotized.**

I *pron.* myself, me, the person who is talking or writing.

ice *n.* frozen water. *v.* 1. to cover with ice: *The frost made the pond ice over.* 2. to cover with icing: *to ice a cake.* **icing. iced.**

iceberg *n.* a mountain of ice floating in the sea.

ice cream *n.* a flavoured cream, sweetened and frozen.

ice skate *n.* a skate with a blade that glides on the ice.

ice-skate *v.* to skate on ice. **ice-skating. ice-skated.**

icicle (ī'si kəl) *n.* a pointed stick of hanging ice.

icing (ī'sing) *n.* a mixture of sugar, liquid, and flavours, used to cover cakes.

icy (ī'sē) *adj.* cold as ice : *an icy wind, an icier wind, the iciest wind of the winter.*

I'd short for **I had** or **I would.**

idea (ī dē'ə) *n.* a thought, a plan: *Paul had a good idea for the picnic.*

identical *adj.* exactly the same: *identical twins.*

idiot *n.* a stupid or foolish person.

idle (ī'dəl) *adj.* lazy, not doing anything. *v.* to run slowly without transmitting power: *She left the car idling in the driveway.* **idling. idled.**

idol (ī'dəl) *n.* 1. a statue that is worshipped as a god. 2. a hero or heroine, someone you admire a lot.

if *conj.* 1. on condition that, supposing that: *I will go if you wish.* 2. whether: *Let me know if you are going.*

igloo *n.* an Inuit house or hut: *An igloo is made of blocks of hard snow. pl.* **igloos.**

ignite *v.* to set fire to: *to ignite a match.* **igniting. ignited.**

ignition *n.* 1. the part of the car that starts the engine: *Please turn on the ignition and start the car.* 2. the setting on fire: *Ignition was caused by lightning.*

ignorant *adj.* knowing little or nothing.

ignore *v.* to pretend not to see or hear: *John turned away and ignored me.* **ignoring. ignored.**

iguana (ig waw'nə) *n.* a large, climbing lizard.

ill *adj.* not well, sick: *I felt ill and went to bed.*

I'll short for **I will** or **I shall.**

illegal *adj.* against the law: *It is illegal to drive without a licence.*

illness *n.* sickness, poor health: *a long illness.*

illustrate *v.* to add pictures to: *to illustrate a story in a book.* **illustrating. illustrated.**

illustration *n.* a picture in a book.

illustrator *n.* the person who draws the pictures in a book.

im- a prefix meaning 'not': **impatient** means not patient; **imperfect** means not perfect.

I'm short for **I am.**

imaginary (i maj'in er ē) *adj.* not real, only thought of: *Tina saw an imaginary camel in the clouds.*

imagination (i maj in ā'shən) *n.* being able to picture things in your mind, having ideas: *Louisa has a colourful imagination.*

imagine (i maj' in) *v.* to picture a thing in your mind, to suppose: *Imagine you are a puppet.* **imagining. imagined.**

imitate *v.* to copy: *A parrot can imitate someone's voice.* **imitating. imitated.**

imitation *n.* a copy: *This diamond is not real. It is an imitation.*

immediately *adv.* at once: *Come immediately! The house is on fire!*

immigrant *n.* a person who comes into a new country to live.

impatience (im pā'shəns) *n.* a feeling of restlessness.

impatient *adj.* restless, finding it hard to wait: *Don't be so impatient! We'll be there in half an hour.*

importance *n.* worth, value: *What is the importance of good health?*

important *adj.* meaning a lot; having much value or responsibility: *important news; an important person.* (*opp.* **unimportant.**)

impossible *adj.* not able to be done: *It is impossible to change lead into gold.*

imprison *v.* to put in prison. **imprisoning. imprisoned.**

improve *v.* to make better, or become better: *Joel has improved in spelling.* **improving. improved.**

improvement *n.* a better result: *Deborah shows great improvement in her work.*

in *prep.* 1. inside: *in the cave.* 2. at: *We live in the city.* 3. during, after: *I can do this in a few minutes.* 4. wearing: *dressed in red.*

in- a prefix meaning 'not': **incomplete** means not complete; **inexpensive** means not expensive.

inch *n.* a measure of length, equal to about 2.5 cm.

include *v.* to count in, to put in: *Include the postal code on the envelope.* **including. included.**

increase *v.* to become bigger in size or power: *Increase your speed when you're on the highway. Decrease it when you get back to the city.*

indeed *adv.* certainly: *Yes, indeed, I believe you.*

independent *adj.* not needing or wanting help from anyone else: *That baby won't let anyone help him. He's really independent.*

Index

	Fact and Fancy Books	4
	Fifth Quarter, The	25
	Food For The Eagle	3
	Football Running Backs	30
Acting Rhymes	16	Formidable Enemy, A	26
Against Taffy Sinclair	24	Fourteen Rats and A
All-In-A-Day Books	12	Rat Catcher	19
All The King's Horses	6	Frances and Queen's
Animal Stories From		Golden Angel	17
Africa	15	Freddie's Feet	17
Atush Inlet	3	
Auto Racing Highlights	30	Galapago Islands, The	28
	Gaping Wide-Mouthed
	Frog, A

index *n.* a list in alphabetical order, at the end of a book: *The index tells you the items in the book, and the pages on which you can find them.*

Indian *n.* 1. a member of the race of people that was living in North and South America before the first European explorers came. 2. a person from India. *adj.* 1. having to do with an American Indian. 2. belonging to or coming from India.

indigestion (in'dĭ jes'chən) *n.* a feeling of illness when your body doesn't digest food properly.

individual *n.* a single person or animal: *Every individual must show his or her ticket.*

indoor *adj.* done, played, or used inside: *Basketball is an indoor game.*

indoors *adv.* inside: *Douglas spent the morning indoors.*

industry (in'dəs trē) *n.* all forms of business and manufacturing: *the building industry. pl.* **industries.**

inexpensive *adj.* cheap, not expensive.

infant (in'fənt) *n.* a very young child.

infield *n.* 1. the diamond-shaped part of a baseball field. 2. the players in the field.

inform *v.* to tell, to pass on information: *I will inform the police of what I saw.* **informing. informed.**

information *n.* news, facts, knowledge: *The information about Niagara Falls will help us enjoy our trip there.*

ingredient (in grē'dē ənt) *n.* one of the things you put in a mixture: *How many ingredients do you need for the cake?*

inhabit *v.* to live in a place: *People born in many countries now inhabit Canada.* **inhabiting. inhabited.**

inhabitant *n.* someone who lives in a place: *the inhabitants of a village.*

inherit *v.* to receive money or property from someone who has died: *Uncle Marc inherited some land from his mother.* **inheriting. inherited.**

inheritance *n.* something given to you, often from someone now dead.

initial (i nish′əl) *n.* the first letter of a name: *Eva Helene Smith's initials are E.H.S.* *v.* to put your initials on a piece of paper. **initialling. initialled.**

injection *n.* the forcing of medicine into your body with a needle.

injure (in′jər) *v.* to harm, to damage: *Lisa injured her knee.* **injuring. injured.**

injury (in′jə rē) *n.* harm, damage: *How bad was her injury? pl.* **injuries.**

ink *n.* coloured or black liquid used for writing.

inland *adj.* away from the coast: *an inland town.*

inlet *n.* an arm of the sea; a narrow strip of water running into land or between islands.

inn *n.* a small hotel where travellers can get meals and a room.

inner *adj.* inside: *the inner walls of a house.*

inning *n.* in baseball, the period when each team has a time at bat: *There are nine innings in a baseball game.*

innocent (in′ə sənt) *adj.* not guilty, blameless: *The innocent child was punished by mistake.*

inquire *v.* to ask about something, to try to find something out: *We inquired when the bus would arrive.* **inquiring. inquired.**

insane *adj.* mad, crazy, very foolish.

insect *n.* a small creature such as an ant, bee, or fly: *An insect has six legs and three parts to its body. Many insects have wings.*

inside *n.* the inner side: *the inside of a shed. adv.* within: *Let's go inside before it snows.*

insist *v.* to say firmly and strongly: *Michelle insisted that she was right.* **insisting. insisted.**

inspect *v.* to examine very closely: *The detective inspected the broken lock.* **inspecting. inspected.**

inspector *n.* 1. someone who makes sure that everything is in order: *a licence inspector.* 2. a senior police officer.

install *v.* to put in place: *We installed new wiring when we moved to the old house.* **installing. installed.**

instant *n.* a brief moment of time: *He stopped for an instant, then went on talking. adj.* 1. immediate: *The medicine gave instant relief.* 2. able to be made quickly: *instant coffee.*

instead (in sted′) *adv.* in the place of someone, something, or some time: *I can't go to the gym today. I'll go tomorrow instead.*

instinct *n.* a natural feeling or power that makes living creatures do things without being taught: *Homing pigeons find their way home by instinct.*

instruct *v.* to teach, to show someone how to do something. **instructing. instructed.**

instructions *n. pl.* directions, an explanation of how to do things.

instructor *n.* a teacher.

instrument (in′strə mənt) *n.* 1. a tool: *A thermometer is an instrument that tells how hot or cold it is.* 2. anything that makes music: *Violins and pianos are musical instruments.*

insult (in′sult) *n.* a rude remark.

insult (in sult′) *v.* to be rude to someone. **insulting. insulted.**

intelligence *n.* being able to learn and understand quickly.

intelligent *adj.* quick at learning.

intend *v.* to mean to do something: *Lisa intends to play tennis after school.* **intending. intended.**

intention *n.* what you intend or mean to do: *It is my intention to go to the lake on the weekend.*

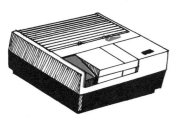

intercom *n.* a system within a building that lets you hear a person's voice in another room.

interest *n.* 1. something you enjoy doing or want to learn more about: *Playing drums is one of my main interests.* 2. money that the bank pays you when you have a savings account; money that you pay the bank if you have a loan. *v.* to attract attention: *This toy interests me.* **interesting. interested.**

interesting *adj.* holding your attention: *I find this book very interesting.*

interfere (in tər fēr′) *v.* to meddle, to get mixed up in: *Do not interfere with my work.* **interfering. interfered.**

interior *n.* the inside: *The interior of the car is kept clean. The exterior could use a wash.*

international *adj.* having to do with all nations: *The Olympic Games are an international sports event.*

interpret *v.* to explain the meaning of something, often another language: *Can you interpret the words of that Spanish song?* **interpreting. interpreted.**

interpreter *n.* a person who can explain the meaning, when someone is speaking or writing in another language.

interrupt *v.* to break into what someone is saying or doing: *Don't interrupt me when I'm talking.* **interrupting. interrupted.**

intersect *v.* to cross each other: *Where do the two streets intersect?* **intersecting. intersected.**

intersection *n.* the place where two or more things cross (such as streets): *Our supermarket is near a busy intersection.*

interview (in′tər vyü) *n.* a meeting arranged among a few people: *My parents arranged to have an interview*

with the teacher. *v.* to meet and talk with someone: *The coach interviewed the player, then gave her the job.* **interviewing. interviewed.**

into *prep.* 1. to the inside of: *The children went into the stadium.* 2. to the form of: *The snow changed into rain.*

introduce *v.* to say the names of people when they meet for the first time: *Please introduce your friend to me.* **introducing. introduced.**

Inuit, Innuit *n.* a member of a people living in northern Canada, Alaska, and other arctic regions: *Inuit means 'people' or 'the people'.*

invade *v.* 1. to enter another country with an army, in order to conquer it. 2. to enter by force: *Ants invaded the garden.* **invading. invaded.**

invalid (in′və lid) *n.* someone who is very ill and cannot get about alone.

invent *v.* to plan or make something for the very first time. **inventing. invented.**

invention *n.* a new thing that has been invented.

inventor *n.* someone who makes something that no one else has ever made.

investigate *v.* to examine carefully: *to investigate a robbery.* **investigating. investigated.**

invisible *adj.* not able to be seen: *The men were invisible in the darkness.*

invitation *n.* a suggestion to come to some place or to do something: *We received a written invitation to Aaron's party.*

invite *v.* to ask someone to join you at home or to do something. **inviting. invited.**

iris (ī′ris) *n.* 1. the coloured part of your eye. 2. a tall garden plant with thin leaves and a purple, white, or yellow flower.

Irish *adj.* belonging to or coming from Ireland.

iron (ī′ərn) *n.* 1. a strong metal from which tools are made. 2. something made of iron or a similar metal: *a steam iron.* *v.* to flatten with a hot piece of smooth iron, usually heated electrically: *to iron clothes.* **ironing. ironed.**

irritate *v.* 1. to annoy, to make angry: *His bad behaviour irritated me.* 2. to make sore: *The rough socks irritated Tim's feet.* **irritating. irritated.**

is *v.* a form of the verb **be**; used with 'he' or 'she' or 'it', or with a person's name: *He is going to sleep. She is going to sleep. Jean is going to sleep. It is a nice day.*

Islam (is lam′) *n.* the religion of the followers of Mohammed. Members of this religion are called **Moslems.**

island (ī′lənd) *n.* a piece of land with water all around it.

isle (īl) *n.* a small island.

isn't short for **is not.**

issue (ish′ü) *n.* 1. something sent out: *a recent issue of the magazine.* 2. a subject or problem to be talked over: *an important issue.* *v.* to deal out, to supply: *The teacher issued pencils to the class.* **issuing. issued.**

it *pron.* a thing or animal.

Italian (i tal′yən) *n.* the language spoken in Italy. *adj.* belonging to or coming from Italy.

itch *v.* for your skin to tickle or feel sore. **itching. itched.** it **itches.**

item (ī′təm) *n.* 1. one thing on a list. 2. an article in a newspaper or magazine: *Did you read the item in the 'Sun'?*

its *adj.* the one belonging to it: *The cat drank its milk.*

it's short for **it is.**
Note: Do not mix up **its** with **it's**: *It's raining today. The dog lost its collar.*

itself *pron.* its own self: *The dog stretched itself out on the rug.*

I've short for **I have.**

ivory (ī′və rē) *n.* 1. a white substance like bone: *Elephants' tusks are made of ivory.* 2. a yellowish white, the colour of a tusk or a piano key. *adj.* having this colour.

ivy (ī′vē) *n.* a climbing plant, often having shiny green leaves.

j

jab *v.* to stab, to poke: *The doctor jabbed the needle into my arm.* **jabbing. jabbed.**

jack *n.* 1. a picture playing card. 2. a tool used for lifting a car or some other heavy load.

jacket *n.* a short coat.

jack-in-the-box *n.* a toy man who jumps from a box when the top is opened.

jack-o'-lantern *n.* a pumpkin hollowed out and carved into a face for Halloween.

jack-rabbit *n.* a large hare with very long ears and long back legs.

jagged (jag′əd) *adj.* with rough, torn edges: *I cut my arm on a jagged piece of wood.*

jaguar (jag′war) *n.* a wild animal like a leopard, but much heavier: *Jaguars live in South America.*

jail *n.* a prison. *v.* to put or keep in prison. **jailing. jailed.**

jam *n.* 1. fruit boiled with sugar until it is thick. 2. a tight crowd of people or traffic: *a traffic jam.* *v.* 1. to press together: *We're jammed in the crowded train.* 2. to stick: *The window is jammed and won't open.* **jamming. jammed.**

jangle *n.* a loud, clashing noise. *v.* to make such a noise. **jangling. jangled.**

janitor *n.* the caretaker of a building.

January *n.* the first month of the year.

Japanese *n.* the language spoken in Japan. *adj.* belonging to or coming from Japan.

jar *n.* a pot or a glass container. *v.* to knock, to clash: *The noise jarred my nerves.* **jarring. jarred.**

javelin (jav′lin, jav′ə lin) *n.* a light spear thrown by hand.

jaw *n.* the upper and lower bones that form the frame of your mouth: *The lower jaw is movable.*

jay *n.* a kind of bird, such as a bluejay or a Canada jay.

jazz *n.* a lively kind of music.

jealous (jel′əs) *adj.* 1. feeling annoyed because someone seems more fortunate than you. 2. afraid that someone you love may love somebody else better.

jealousy (jel′ə sē) *n.* a jealous feeling.

jeans *n. pl.* strong cotton trousers, usually blue.

jeep *n.* a kind of car able to travel over rough country.

jelly *n.* a soft, firm food that is usually made from fruit and sugar. *pl.* **jellies.**

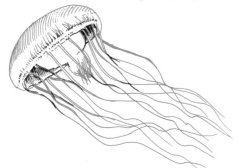

jellyfish *n.* a small sea animal that has a jelly-like appearance. *pl.* **jellyfish.**

jerk *n.* a quick tug.

jester *n.* in old times, a clown who made the king and queen laugh.

Jesus, Jesus Christ *n.* the founder of the Christian religion.

jet *n.* 1. a stream of liquid or gas, sent with force: *A fountain sends up a jet of water.* 2. a type of airplane pushed forward by jets of hot gas.

Jew *n.* a person whose religion is Judaism. **Jewish** *adj.*

jewel *n.* a gem, a valuable stone such as a diamond or ruby.

jeweller, jeweler *n.* a person who sells jewels.

jewellery, jewelry *n.* necklaces, rings, watches, and other ornaments.

jig *n.* a lively dance.

jiggle *v.* to shake slightly. **jiggling. jiggled.**

jigsaw puzzle a picture cut into pieces that have to be put together again.

job *n.* 1. a piece of work: *Inez has the job of sweeping the path.* 2. work done for pay: *My cousin has a job in a factory.*

jockey *n.* a person who rides horses in races. *pl.* **jockeys.**

jog *v.* to run along at a slow pace: *I jogged to the bus stop this morning.* **jogging. jogged.**

join *v.* 1. to fasten, to put together: *to join two ropes.* 2. to become part of a group of people: *to join the Scouts.* **joining. joined.**

joint *n.* a place where two parts meet: *The knuckle is a joint in your finger.*

joke *n.* something said or done to make you laugh. *v.* to say or do something as a joke. **joking. joked.**

jolly *adj.* merry, full of fun: *a jolly clown, a jollier one, the jolliest clown in the circus.*

jolt *v.* to give a sudden jerk: *I jolted the tray and a cup fell off.* **jolting. jolted.**

jot *v.* (used with **down**) to make a quick note in writing: *Jot down the phone number before you forget it.* **jotting. jotted.**

journal (jər′nəl) *n.* 1. a magazine or newspaper. 2. a diary.

journey (jər′ne) *n.* travel from one place to another: *We made a journey across Canada. pl.* **journeys.**

joy *n.* happiness, pleasure.

joyful *adj.* full of joy.

Judaism *n.* the religion of the Jews, based on the belief in one God.

judge *n.* 1. a person in charge of a court of law: *A judge passes a sentence when someone is found guilty.* 2. someone who decides the result of a sports event, such as running or jumping. *v.* to make a judgment. **judging. judged.**

judgment, judgement *n.* an opinion or decision.

judo (jü′do) *n.* a Japanese form of wrestling.

jug *n.* a container for liquids, usually having a handle.

juggle *v.* to toss up several balls or other objects and keep them in the air at the same time. **juggling. juggled.**

juggler *n.* someone skilled at juggling.

juice (jüs) *n.* the liquid in fruits or vegetables, and in meat.

juicy (jü′se) *adj.* full of juice: *a juicy orange, a juicier one, the juiciest one of all.*

July *n.* the seventh month of the year.

jumble *n.* a mixed-up mess: *A jumble of clothing is piled in her room.*

jump *n.* a leap from the ground: *a high jump. v.* to spring up, or over something. **jumping. jumped.**

June *n.* the sixth month of the year.

jungle *n.* land in hot places that is thickly covered with trees and bushes.

junior (jü′nyər) *n.* someone who is younger: *Jason is younger than I am, so he is my junior. adj.* younger or less experienced: *Next year, the junior officer will be a senior officer.*

junk *n.* 1. worthless rubbish. 2. a Chinese sailing ship.

jury (jü′re) *n.* a group of people who sit in a court of law to decide if someone is innocent or guilty. *pl.* **juries.**

just *adj.* fair: *The teacher was very just in deciding who was to blame.*
adv. 1. barely: *The baby was just able to reach the chair.* 2. exactly: *The time is just one o'clock.*

justice (jus′tis) *n.* fair dealing: *The courts give justice in the name of the people.*

juvenile (jü′və nīl) *adj.* having to do with young people: *the juvenile section of the library.*

k

kaleidoscope (kə lī′də scōp) *n.* a tube with small bits of coloured glass and mirrors: *When you turn a kaleidoscope, you see different patterns.*

kangaroo *n.* an Australian animal: *A kangaroo has short front legs and strong back legs which it uses for jumping.* *pl.* **kangaroos.**

kayak (kī′ak) *n.* 1. an Inuit canoe: *A kayak is made of animal skins stretched over a wooden frame.* 2. a light canoe that looks like this.

keen *adj.* 1. eager, enthusiastic: *Mitchell is a keen squash player.* 2. sharp: *a knife with a keen edge.*

keep *v.* 1. to hold: *I will keep the key until it is needed.* 2. not to go bad: *These eggs will keep in the fridge.* **keeping. kept.**

kennel *n.* a shelter for dogs or cats.

kernel *n.* 1. the inside part of a nut, the part you eat. 2. a grain or seed: *a kernel of corn.*

ketchup *n.* a sauce used with meat, French fries, and other food: *Tomato ketchup is made with tomatoes, onions, and other ingredients.*

kettle *n.* a metal container used for boiling liquid.

key *n.* 1. a piece of metal shaped so that it will open a lock. 2. one of the parts pressed down with the fingers on a piano or typewriter. 3. something that explains the symbols in a map, dictionary, etc. *pl.* **keys.**

kick *n.* a hit with the foot: *The player gave the ball a powerful kick.* *v.* to hit with your foot. **kicking. kicked.**

kick-off *n.* the start of a football game.

kid *n.* 1. a young goat. 2. a child. *v.* to pretend, to joke: *Is it true, or are you kidding?* **kidding. kidded.**

kidnap *v.* to carry off a person by force. **kidnapping. kidnapped.**

kidney *n.* one of two small organs in the body: *The kidneys separate waste matter and water from the blood.* *pl.* **kidneys.**

kill *v.* to put to death, to cause someone or something to die. **killing. killed.**

kilogram *n.* a measure of mass; kg is the symbol. 1 kg = 1000 g

kilometre (kil′ō me tər) *n.* a measure of distance; km is the symbol. 1 km = 1000 m

kilt *n.* a pleated skirt, reaching the knees, worn by men in parts of Scotland.

kind *n.* a sort: *A tiger is a kind of wild cat.* *adj.* helpful, friendly, nice. (*opp.* **unkind.**) **kindly** *adj.* or *adv.*

kindergarten *n.* a school or grade for very young children.

kindness *n.* helpfulness: *Helen thanked him for his kindness.*

king *n.* 1. a man who is ruler of a country. 2. a playing card with a picture of a king on it. 3. a piece in the game of chess.

kingdom *n.* a country ruled by a king or queen.

kiss *n.* a touch with the lips. *v.* to touch someone with your lips as a greeting. **kissing. kissed.**

kit *n.* a set of tools or materials needed to do a certain job: *a tool kit, a first-aid kit.*

kitchen *n.* a room where food is prepared.

kite *n.* a light wooden frame with paper, plastic, or cloth over it.

kitten *n.* a young cat.

kitty *n.* a kitten. *pl.* **kitties.**

knapsack (nap′sak) *n.* a bag made of leather or cloth: *A knapsack is worn on the back. It may hold clothes, books, or supplies.*

knead (nēd) *v.* to make a flour mixture into dough by pressing it with your hands. **kneading. kneaded.**

knee (nē) *n.* the joint between the upper and lower part of your leg.

kneecap (nē′kap) *n.* the flat, movable bone over your knee.

kneel (nēl) *v.* to go down on your knees. **kneeling. knelt** or **kneeled.**

knew see **know.**

knife (nīf) *n.* a flat piece of metal, fastened in a handle, that is used for cutting or spreading. *pl.* **knives.**

knight (nīt) *n.* a man with the title 'Sir': *In old times, a knight wore armour and fought for his king or queen.*

knit (nit) *v.* to make wool or other yarn into cloth, using long needles. **knitting. knitted** or **knit.**

knob (nob) *n.* the round handle of a door or drawer.

knock (nok) *v.* to hit with your fist or knuckles: *to knock on a door.* **knocking. knocked.**

knot (not) *n.* 1. a fastening made by tying together pieces of rope, string, cord, etc. 2. the hard section of wood on a tree, where a branch grows out. 3. a measure of the speed of ships.

know (nō) *v.* 1. to understand: *I know how to count to a million.* 2. to have some information: *I know his name.* 3. to tell apart from others: *I know his face, but I can't remember his name.* **knowing. knew. I have known.**

knowledge (nol′ij) *n.* understanding, having information: *He has a great knowledge of history.*

knuckle (nuk′əl) *n.* a joint in a finger.

label *n.* a written or printed ticket: *A label is used to show what something is, who it belongs to, or where it is going.* *v.* to attach a label to something. **labelling. labelled.**

laboratory (lab′rə tor ē, lə bor′ə trē) *n.* a place where scientific work is done. *pl.* **laboratories.**

labour, labor *n.* hard work: *She was paid for her labour.*

Labrador *n.* the mainland area of the Province of Newfoundland.

lace *n.* 1. material made of thin threads that form a pattern. 2. a cord or string: *a shoelace.*

lack *n.* a shortage: *The skinny animals suffered from a lack of food.* *v.* to be without something: *They also lacked water.* **lacking. lacked.**

lacrosse (lə kros′) *n.* a game in which players use netted sticks for passing a rubber ball into the other team's goal.

ladder *n.* a set of steps or rungs fastened between two poles.

ladle (lā′dəl) *n.* a serving spoon with a long handle.

lady *n.* 1. a woman who is kind, helpful, and polite. 2. a noblewoman (*masc.* **lord**). *pl.* **ladies.**

ladybug *n.* a small beetle, red or orange with black spots.

lag *v.* to move slowly behind others: *Dick lagged behind the other hikers.* **lagging. lagged.**

laid see **lay.**

lain see **lie.**

lake *n.* a large body of water with land all around.

lamb (lam) *n.* a young sheep.

lame *adj.* not able to walk correctly.

lamp *n.* a device that provides light.

land *n.* 1. ground, soil: *the farmer's land.* 2. the solid part of the earth's surface: *land and sea.* 3. a country: *Finland is a northern land.* v. 1. to reach earth from the sea or air: *The ship landed at Prince Rupert.* 2. to arrive: *They landed in jail.* **landing. landed.**

landing *n.* 1. a platform at the top of a stairway. 2. an airplane's coming down to earth.

landlady (*masc.* **landlord**) *n.* the owner of a house that is rented to others. *pl.* **landladies.**

landmark *n.* something that stands out from the scenery and can be used as a guide.

lane *n.* a narrow road or pathway.

language (lang'wij) *n.* the speech used by the people of a country: *the English language, the French language.*

lantern *n.* a glass case with a light inside.

lap *n.* 1. the top of your thighs when you are sitting down: *The cat sat on my lap.* 2. once around a track: *The race was four laps around the field.*

lard *n.* pig's fat used in cooking.

large *adj.* big, great in size.

larva *n.* the early form of an insect: *A caterpillar is the larva of a butterfly.* *pl.* **larvae** (lar've).

lash *n.* 1. a stroke from a whip. 2. a hair on an eyelid: *an eyelash.*

lasso (la sü') *n.* a rope with a loop at the end, used for catching cattle. *pl.* **lassos.** v. to catch with a rope. **lassoing. lassoed.**

last *adj.* following all the others, at the end: *the last day of the month.* v. to continue, to serve: *The food must last us several days.* **lasting. lasted.** **at last** finally, after waiting: *The food has arrived at last.*

latch *n.* a fastening for a door or gate.

late *adj.* coming after the usual time: *The bus is late today.* *adv.* after the usual time: *We stayed up late.*

lately *adv.* a little while before: *How have you been feeling lately?*

later *adv.* not now, in the future: *We'll be going to the movies later in the week.*

lather (laтн'ər) *n.* a foam made from soap, shampoo, shaving cream, etc.

laugh (laf) *n.* a loud 'ha-ha' sound made when you see or hear something funny. v. to make such a sound, to show that you are happy or that something is funny. **laughing. laughed.**

laughter (laf'tər) *n.* the sound of laughing.

launch *n.* a small motorboat. v. 1. to send out into the air: *to launch a rocket.* 2. to set afloat: *to launch a boat.* **launching. launched.**

laundromat *n.* a room with coin-operated washing machines and dryers.

laundry (lawn'drē) *n.* 1. clothes to be washed. 2. a room where clothes are washed. *pl.* **laundries.**

lava *n.* hot melted rock flowing from a volcano.

law *n.* 1. a rule made by a government. 2. any rule that is to be obeyed: *the laws of nature.*

lawn *n.* an area of grass by a house, usually well looked after.

lawn mower a machine used for cutting the grass on a lawn.

lawyer (lo'yər) *n.* someone who knows the law and has a licence to give people advice about it.

lay *v.* 1. to place something down. 2. to drop an egg into a nest. 3. past tense of **lie** (definition 2). **laying. laid.**

layer *n.* a thickness, a coating: *a layer of paint on a door.*

lazy (lā'zē) *adj.* unwilling to work or do much: *My dog is lazy, but yours is lazier, and his is the laziest of all.*

lead (led) *n.* a heavy grey metal.

lead (lēd) *n.* a strap with which to hold a dog. *v.* to go in front, to show the way: *The guides lead us through the woods.* **leading. led.**

leader *n.* someone who goes in front and shows the way or takes charge.

leaf *n.* one of the small green, flat parts of a plant or tree. *pl.* **leaves.**

league (lēg) *n.* 1. a group of teams that regularly play one another: *the Canadian Football League.* 2. an old measure of length, equal to about 5 km.

leak *n.* a small hole or crack through which gas or liquid comes in or escapes: *a leak in the boat.* *v.* for gas or liquid to come in or escape through a small hole or crack. **leaking. leaked.**

leaky *adj.* letting something leak out or leak in: *a leaky roof, a leakier one, the leakiest roof on the street.*

lean *adj.* 1. thin: *a tall, lean man.* 2. having little fat: *lean meat.* *v.* 1. to rest: *The ladder leans against a wall.* 2. to slant: *The post leans to one side.* **leaning. leaned.**

leap *n.* a jump over something. *v.* to spring upwards, to jump: *Gregory can leap over the fire hydrant.* **leaping. leaped** or **leapt** (lept).

leap year every fourth year, when February has 29 days instead of 28.

learn *v.* to find out; to get to know new facts by study; to do new things by practice: *Jamie wants to learn how to cook.* **learning. learned** or **learnt.**

least *n.* the littlest amount: *I like football the least of all games. I like hockey the most.*

leather (leтн'ər) *n.* an animal's skin, used to make shoes, gloves, etc.

leave *v.* 1. to go away from: *Please leave the room.* 2. to let something stay where it is: *Don't leave your gloves at school.* **leaving. left.**

leaves see **leaf.**

led see **lead.**

ledge *n.* a narrow shelf: *the window ledge.*

left *adj.* in the direction opposite of right: *When you look at a map of Canada, Alberta is on the left side of Saskatchewan.* *v.* see **leave.**

leg *n.* 1. one of the limbs on which people and animals stand or walk. 2. anything like a leg: *a table leg.*

legal (lē'gəl) *adj.* allowed by the law: *Is it legal to ride your bike on the sidewalk?* (*opp.* **illegal.**)

legend (lej'ənd) *n.* a story from the past that is probably not completely true.

legislature (lej'əs lā chər) *n.* a group of men and women who make laws: *Each province in Canada has a legislature.*

lemon *n.* a yellow fruit with a sour taste.

lemonade *n.* a drink made from lemons, water, and sugar.

lend *v.* to let someone use something of yours for a time. **lending. lent.**

length *n.* how long a thing is.

lengthen *v.* to make longer, to become longer: *Mother lengthened my jeans.* **lengthening. lengthened.**

lens *n.* a curved piece of glass used in eyeglasses, cameras, and telescopes: *A lens may make something appear closer or farther away.* *pl.* **lenses.**

leopard (lep′ərd) *n.* a wild member of the cat family; it lives in Africa and Asia.

leotard (lē′ə tard) *n.* a tight, one-piece garment worn by dancers, gymnasts, and others.

less *adj.* smaller, fewer, not as much.

-less a suffix meaning 'without': **painless** means without pain; **toothless** means without a tooth.

lessen *v.* to make less, to become less: *The thunder lessened as the storm moved away.* **lessening. lessened.**

lesson *n.* something to be learned: *a music lesson.*

let *v.* to permit, to allow: *Let me do it.* **letting. let.**

let's short for **let us.**

letter *n.* 1. one of the symbols of an alphabet: *A, B, C are letters in the English alphabet.* 2. a written message put in an envelope and sent to someone.

letter carrier the person who delivers your mail.

lettuce (let′is) *n.* a green vegetable with large leaves, eaten raw in salads.

level *adj.* smooth and flat, not sloping.

lever (lē′vər, lev′ər) *n.* a bar used for raising or lowering something.

liar (lī′ər) *n.* someone who tells lies.

liberty *n.* freedom, independence: *The prisoners will have their liberty in five years.*

librarian *n.* someone in charge of a library or resource centre.

library *n.* a room or building where books are kept: *Books may be used in the library, or they may be borrowed.* *pl.* **libraries.**

licence, license (lī′səns) *n.* an official paper allowing you to keep, use, or do something: *a dog licence.*

license, licence *v.* to allow by law: *An electrician is licensed to wire a house.* **licensing. licensed.**

lick *v.* to wet with your tongue: *to lick a stamp.* **licking. licked.**

licorice (lik′ə rish, lik′ə ris) *n.* a black candy made from a plant root.

lid *n.* a movable flap: *the lid of a box, an eyelid.*

lie *n.* an untruth. *v.* 1. to tell an untruth: *The thief lied to the police officer.* **lying. lied.** 2. to rest, stretched flat: *Lie down if you are tired.* **lying. lay.** I have **lain.**

lieutenant (lef ten′ənt, lü ten′ənt) *n.* an officer in the armed forces.

Lieutenant-Governor the official head of a province: *The Lieutenant-Governor is appointed by the Governor General.*

life *n.* 1. being alive: *People, animals, and plants have life.* 2. the time you are alive: *Grandma has had a long life.* 3. a human being: *Several lives were lost in the fire.* *pl.* **lives** (līvz).

lifeboat *n.* a boat built for rescuing people in the water.

lifeguard *n.* a trained swimmer who watches to see that swimmers are safe.

lifetime *n.* the time of being alive: *During my lifetime, I hope to see many lands.*

lift *n.* 1. a ride: *May I have a lift to school?* 2. something that takes skiers to the top of a hill. *v.* to raise: *Mother lifted the heavy plank.* **lifting. lifted.**

light *n.* brightness from something burning, such as the sun or a lamp. *adj.* 1. not heavy: *as light as a feather.* 2. not dark: *Mother is wearing a light green scarf.* *v.* 1. to set fire to something. 2. to brighten something. **lighting. lit.**

lighter *n.* something that makes a flame: *a cigarette lighter.*

lighthouse *n.* a tower by a body of water: *A lighthouse has a light that warns ships of dangerous rocks.*

lightning *n.* a flash of electricity in a thunderstorm.

likable *adj.* pleasing, agreeable, popular: *Pat is a likable person. He is always helpful and friendly.*

like *prep.* similar to: *The picture I drew looks just like you.* *v.* to be fond of: *Wendy likes reading.* **liking. liked.**

likely *adj.* probable, to be expected: *It is likely to snow today.*

likeness *n.* a copy: *The photograph is a good likeness of you.*

lilac (lī′lək) *n.* a garden shrub that has white or purple flowers.

lily (lil′ē) *n.* a tall garden flower that grows from a bulb. *pl.* **lilies.**

limb (lim) *n.* 1. an arm or a leg. 2. a tree branch.

lime *n.* 1. a greenish fruit that looks like a small lemon. 2. a white powder made by burning limestone or shells: *Lime is used to improve the soil.*

limit *n.* a point you cannot pass, the edge: *The hills mark the limit of our walk.*

limp *n.* a hobble: *to walk with a limp.* *v.* to walk as if lame, to hobble. **limping. limped.**

line *n.* 1. a long, thin mark: *Connect the dots with a line.* 2. a row: *a line of soldiers.* 3. a cord or rope: *a clothes line.* 4. a track or route: *a railway line.* *v.* 1. to mark with lines. 2. to put a lining in a piece of clothing. **lining. lined.**
line up to stand in line.

linen (lin′ən) *n.* 1. cloth made from fibres of the flax plant. 2. towels and sheets made from this cloth or from a similar material.

line-up *n.* the athletes taking part in a game: *The coach announced the line-up for Saturday's game.*

lining *n.* the thin inside covering in a suit, coat, or dress.

link *n.* one of the rings in a chain.

lion *n.* a wild animal of the cat family; it lives in Africa and southern Asia.

lip *n.* one of the two pink, fleshy edges of your mouth.

lipstick *n.* a stick of make-up, used to colour the lips.

liquid *n.* water, or anything that can be poured like water.

list *n.* a column or columns of names, numbers, words, etc.: *a shopping list.* *v.* to arrange names, numbers, words, etc. in such a column: *How many animals beginning with the letter 'a' can you list?* **listing. listed.**

listen (lis′ən) *v.* to hear, to pay attention to. **listening. listened.**

lit see **light.**

literature (lit′ər ə chər) *n.* stories and poetry: *My brother studies Canadian literature.*

litre (lē′tər) *n.* a liquid measure; L is the symbol. 1 L = 1000 mL

litter *n.* 1. a number of animals all born together: *a litter of pigs.* 2. waste paper and other garbage left lying around. *v.* to leave such garbage around: *Please don't litter.* **littering. littered.**

little *adj.* 1. small: *The white mouse is little, the brown one is littler, and the grey one is the littlest in the cage.* 2. not much: *Sam had little luck in finding someone to help him. Bill had less luck. Tony had the least luck of all.*

live (liv) *v.* 1. to be alive, to have life: *My dog lived to be 15 years old.* 2. to dwell: *Fish live in the sea.* **living. lived.**

live (līv) *adj.* living, not dead: *A zoo keeps live animals. Many museums have stuffed animals.*

lively (līv′lē) *adj.* full of life and pep: *a lively pup, a livelier one, the liveliest pup in the litter.*

liver (liv′ər) *n.* an organ in the body: *The liver helps you to digest food.*

living *n.* regular money earned from a job; it lets people look after themselves and their families: *to make a living.*

living room a family room: *A living room usually has a chesterfield and chairs.*

lizard (liz′ərd) *n.* a small snake-like animal with four short legs.

llama (lah′mə) *n.* a large South American animal with long hair: *A llama looks like a camel, but it has no hump.*

load *n.* a pile of goods to be carried: *a load of hay on a wagon.* *v.* 1. to place goods on a ship, or in a car, truck, train, etc. 2. to put a bullet into a gun. **loading. loaded.**

loaf *n.* a large lump of food baked into a certain shape. *pl.* **loaves.** *v.* to be a little lazy: *I have work to do, but I feel like loafing.* **loafing. loafed.**

loan *n.* a lending: *The loan from the bank helped us pay for the car.*

lobby *n.* a hall or waiting area in an office building or apartment house. *pl.* **lobbies.**

lobe *n.* the fleshy lowest part of your ear.

lobster *n.* a large shellfish with eight legs and two claws.

local *adj.* nearby: *Our local milk store is half a block away.*

locate *v.* 1. to find the exact position of someone or something: *The search party located the lost hikers.* 2. to settle somewhere: *The company located their new factory in Halifax.* **locating. located.**

location (lō kā′shən) *n.* a position or place: *The location of the school is halfway between our houses.*

lock *n.* 1. a fastening for a door or box, often needing a key to open it. 2. a curl of hair. *v.* to fasten a lock in a door or on a lid. **locking. locked.**

locker *n.* a small closet that can be locked.

locomotive *n.* a railway engine.

lodge *n.* a house or an inn, usually in the country.

log *n.* 1. a sawn-off part of a tree trunk or branch. 2. a diary of a voyage: *A ship's captain keeps a daily log.*

log cabin a house made of logs.

logger *n.* someone whose job is to cut down trees and get them to the sawmill.

lollipop *n.* a piece of hard candy at the end of a stick.

lone *adj.* by itself: *We looked at the lone star in the sky.*

lonely *adj.* without companions, feeling sad because you are alone: *a lonely horse, a lonelier one, the loneliest horse on the farm.*

lonesome *adj.* lonely.

long *adj.* 1. a big distance from end to end: *a long road.* 2. taking much time: *a long wait.*

long (used with **for** or **to**) *v.* to want very much, to wish for: *It was very cold and we longed for summer to come.* **longing. longed.**

long ago a long time back.

look *n.* a glance: *He gave me an angry look. v.* 1. to watch, to see. 2. to seem: *He looks tired.* 3. to face: *The house looks east.* **looking. looked.**
look after to take care of.
look forward to to wait for something with pleasure.

loom *n.* a frame on which you weave threads into cloth.

loop *n.* a ring in a string or rope. *v.* to make such a ring. **looping. looped.**

loose (lüs) *adj.* slack, not fastened or tight: *It is easy to untie the loose knot.*

loose-leaf *adj.* having pages with holes that can be put into or taken out of a binder.

loosen *v.* to slacken, to make loose. **loosening. loosened.**

loot *n.* things of value taken by burglars, or by enemy soldiers in war.

lopsided *adj.* uneven, with one side lower than the other.

Lord *n.* 1. God. 2. Jesus Christ.

lord (*fem.* **lady**) *n.* a nobleman.

lose (lüz) *v.* 1. to be without something because you have dropped it or left it somewhere. 2. to be beaten in a game. **losing. lost.**

loss *n.* something lost: *Our team's loss cost us a place in the championships.*

lot *n.* 1. a large number: *a lot of birds.* 2. a piece of ground: *There is an empty lot next to our school.*

lotion (lō'shən) *n.* a cream, put on your skin to heal, clean, or moisten it.

loud *adj.* noisy. **loudly** *adv.*

loudspeaker *n.* the part of a stereo, radio, or TV from which the sound comes.

lounge *n.* a sitting room with easy chairs. *v.* to sit in a comfortable, easy way. **lounging. lounged.**

lovable *adj.* very likable, worth loving.

love *n.* 1. a great liking or affection. 2. in some games such as tennis, a score of nothing. *v.* to like very much, to care a lot about. **loving. loved.**

lovely *adj.* beautiful, fine: *a lovely day, a lovelier one, the loveliest day of the month.*

low *adj.* not high: *a low hill, a low number, a low note in music.*

lower *adj.* more low: *Prices are lower in this store than in that one. v.* to let down: *to lower a flag on a mast.* **lowering. lowered.**

loyal *adj.* faithful and true: *a loyal citizen.*

loyalty *n.* faithfulness: *The dog proved his loyalty when he barked for help.* *pl.* **loyalties.**

luck *n.* chance, fortune: *good luck, bad luck.*

lucky *adj.* having good fortune: *a lucky day, a luckier one, my luckiest day ever.* (*opp.* **unlucky.**)

luggage (lug'ij) *n.* the suitcases and bags that a traveller carries.

lukewarm *adj.* not hot and not cold, slightly warm.

lullaby *n.* a song you sing to make a baby sleep. *pl.* **lullabies.**

lumber *n.* timber, logs, and boards cut and prepared for use.

lumberjack *n.* a man who cuts down trees.

lump *n.* 1. a piece of anything: *a lump of clay.* 2. a swelling or bump on the skin.

lunar (lü'nər) *adj.* having to do with the moon: *a lunar eclipse.*

lunch *n.* the noon meal.

lung *n.* one of the two organs inside the chest that you fill with air when you breathe in.

lure *n.* bait: *a lure for fish.* *v.* to tempt, to attract: *The mouse was lured into the trap by the cheese.* **luring. lured.**

luscious (lush'əs) *adj.* really delicious: *a luscious cherry pie.*

luxury (lug'zhə rē) *n.* something that is enjoyable, but isn't really needed. *pl.* **luxuries.**

lying see **lie.**

lynx (links) *n.* a kind of wild cat; it has pointed ears, a short tail, and large paws.

lyrics (lir'iks) *n. pl.* the words of a song.

ma, mama *n.* mother.

macaroni *n.* a food made of flour paste, often eaten with cheese or a tomato sauce.

machine (mə shēn') *n.* a device that does some particular job: *a sewing machine, a washing machine.*

machinery *n.* 1. engines and machines. 2. the moving parts of a machine.

mackerel *n.* a silvery fish that lives in ocean waters. *pl.* **mackerel.**

mackinaw *n.* a short, heavy, woollen coat, often plaid.

mad *adj.* 1. not in one's right mind, crazy. 2. very angry: *a mad crowd, a madder crowd, the maddest crowd of all.*

made see **make.**

magazine *n.* a thin book with pictures and stories or articles: *A magazine is usually published weekly or monthly.*

magic *n.* the use of clever tricks to make impossible things seem to happen.

magician (mə jish'ən) *n.* a person who can do magic tricks.

magnet *n.* a bar of iron or steel that attracts pieces of iron or other metals towards it.

magnetic *adj.* having the power of a magnet.

magnificent *adj.* wonderful, splendid, grand: *a magnificent palace.*

magnify *v.* to make something look larger: *A microscope is used to magnify objects.* **magnifying. magnified.** it **magnifies.**

magnifying glass a lens that makes things look bigger than they really are.

maid *n.* 1. a young unmarried girl. 2. a woman servant.

mail *n.* letters, cards, packages, and anything else sent by post. *v.* to send letters, etc. by mail. **mailing. mailed.**

mailbox *n.* 1. a box in which to put the mail you are sending. 2. a box in which the mail you receive is placed.

mail carrier, mailman *n.* the person who carries and delivers mail.

main *adj.* chief, most important, greatest in size: *a main road.*

mainland *n.* the major part of a continent or other land area.

maize *n.* a kind of grain that grows on large ears; Indian corn.

Majesty *n.* a title for a king, queen, emperor, or empress: *Your Majesty, His Majesty, Her Majesty. pl.* **Majesties.**

major *n.* an army officer, next in rank above a captain. *adj.* larger, more important: *The ball player moved from the minor league to the major league.*

majority *n.* the greatest number in a group: *The majority of my friends walk to school. pl.* **majorities.**

make *n.* kind, brand: *What make is your family's car? v.* 1. to cause something to be or happen: *I made a model plane. Jokes make me laugh.* 2. to add up to: *One and one make two.* 3. to earn: *How much money do you make?* **making. made.**
to make believe to pretend.
to make sure to be sure.
to make up 1. to invent: *Make up a story.* 2. to become friends again: *Shake hands and make up.*

make-up *n.* powder, rouge, lipstick, etc. put on the face.

male *n.* 1. a boy, a man. 2. an animal that is, will be, or can be a father: *A bull is a male. A cow is a female.*

mallet *n.* a hammer that is made of rubber or wood.

malt *n.* grain, usually barley, that is used to make beverages such as beer.

mammal *n.* a kind of animal that has warm blood and hair or fur: *People, whales, dogs, and other animals are mammals. A female mammal can provide milk to feed her babies.*

man *n.* a grown-up male human being. *pl.* **men.**

manage *v.* 1. to take charge and look after: *to manage a store.* 2. to be able to do something: *Can you manage to carry this package?* **managing. managed.**

manager *n.* a person in charge of something: *The manager of the apartment building is away.*

mane *n.* the long hair on the neck of some animals such as horses and lions.

manhole *n.* a hole through which a worker may enter a sewer or other underground area.

Manitoba *n.* province between Saskatchewan on the west, Ontario on the east; capital is Winnipeg. Short form: **Man.** A person living in or born in Manitoba is a **Manitoban.**

mankind *n.* all people, the human race.

manners *n. pl.* behaviour: *good manners, bad manners.*

mansion *n.* a very large house.

mantelpiece *n.* a shelf above a fireplace.

manual (man′yü əl) *n.* a guide book: *a Scout manual. adj.* done by hand: *Chopping down trees is manual work.*

manufacture (man yə fak′chər) *v.* to make something, usually in a factory. **manufacturing. manufactured.**

manure (mə nyür') *n.* animal droppings and straw put in the ground to make plants grow better.

many *adj.* a great number: *Many Canadians live on farms. More live in towns. Most Canadians live in cities.*

map *n.* 1. a drawing of the earth's surface or of part of it, showing towns, roads, and rivers. 2. any drawing that shows you how to get somewhere.

maple *n.* a tree having broad leaves and wood that is used to make furniture.

maple leaf the leaf of the maple tree, chosen as an emblem of Canada.
pl. **maple leaves.**

maple syrup a sweet, thick liquid made from the sap of a sugar maple tree.

marble *n.* 1. a hard stone used in making statues and buildings. 2. a small glass ball used in the game of **marbles.**

march *n.* 1. the movement of soldiers. 2. a piece of music people can march to. *v.* to walk in step with others as soldiers do. **marching. marched.**

March *n.* the third month of the year.

mare (*masc.* **stallion**) *n.* a female horse.

margarine (mar'jə rin) *n.* a spread made of oils and fats, used instead of butter.

margin (mar'jən) *n.* space left at the top, bottom, and sides of written or printed pages.

marigold *n.* a plant that has orange, red, or yellow flowers.

marina (mə rē'nə) *n.* a place along the waterfront where boats may be docked.

marionette *n.* a doll that can be made to move when strings attached to it are pulled.

maritime *adj.* 1. having to do with the ocean. 2. on or near the ocean: *Halifax and Victoria are maritime cities.*

Maritime Provinces New Brunswick, Nova Scotia, and Prince Edward Island. Also called **the Maritimes.**

mark *n.* 1. a scratch, stain, or cut. 2. a score on a test: *a high mark on a history test. v.* 1. to make a mark on something. 2. to grade a test. **marking. marked.**

market *n.* a place where people meet to buy and sell things.

maroon *n.* a dark red colour. *adj.* having this colour. *v.* to leave someone on a lonely island or coast, usually as a punishment. **marooning. marooned.**

marriage (ma'rij) *n.* 1. a wedding. 2. living together as husband and wife.

marrow *n.* the soft material in the centre of bones.

marry *v.* to become husband and wife. **marrying. married.** she **marries.**

Mars *n.* 1. in ancient times, the Roman god of war. 2. one of the planets.

marsh *n.* wet, swampy ground.

marshmallow *n.* a soft, sticky candy.

marvellous, marvelous *adj.* wonderful: *The circus is a marvellous show.*

mascot *n.* an animal, person, or thing supposed to bring good luck.

mash *v.* to crush and mix to a soft mass: *to mash potatoes.* **mashing. mashed.**

mask *n.* a covering over the face, worn as a disguise or a protection.

mass *n.* a great lump or quantity.

Mass *n.* the main religious ceremony in the Roman Catholic Church, and certain other churches.

massacre (mas'ə kər) *n.* a bloody killing of a large number of people or animals. *v.* to kill in such a way. **massacring. massacred.**

mast *n.* a tall pole, usually one that holds up sails.

master *n.* 1. a great artist or performer. 2. a person who rules people or things.

masterpiece *n.* something that is done with great skill.

mat *n.* 1. a small rug to wipe your feet on. 2. a small cloth used under dishes. 3. a cushion used in gymnastics. 4. a tangled mass. *v.* to become tangled: *The dog's hair is badly matted.* **matting. matted.**

matador *n.* a bullfighter.

match *n.* 1. a small stick of wood or cardboard with a tip that flames up when struck. 2. a game between sides: *a tennis match. v.* to be the same: *Your socks don't match. One is blue and the other is green.* **matching. matched.**

mate *n.* a companion. *v.* to bring together as a pair. **mating. mated.**

material *n.* 1. what something is used for or made of: *Paper is a writing material. My sweater is made of woolly material.* 2. a piece of cloth.

mathematics *n.pl.* the study of numbers and measurement, often called **math** for short.

matinée (mat ən ā′) *n.* an afternoon performance of a play, movie, concert, etc.

matter *n.* 1. something you are concerned about: *This is a serious matter. What's the matter?* 2. what things are made of. *v.* to be of importance, to make a difference: *Does it really matter?* **mattering. mattered.**

mattress *n.* the thick, soft part of a bed.

may *v.* a verb used before another verb to mean 1. 'to be allowed': *She may go if she wants to.* 2. 'to be possible': *She may be able to do it if she tries hard.* **might.**

May *n.* the fifth month of the year.

maybe *adv.* perhaps: *Maybe it will snow this afternoon.*

mayor *n.* the head of a town, village, or city government.

maze *n.* a confusing series of paths or lines in which it is easy to lose your way.

me *pron.* a form of the word I: *Leave me alone.*

meadow (med′ō) *n.* a field of grass or hay in the country.

meal *n.* 1. food eaten each day at a certain time. 2. grain ground into a powder: *oatmeal.*

mean *adj.* unkind: *a mean witch. v.* 1. to have in mind: *I mean to go when I am ready.* 2. to have a certain definition: *To 'touch' means to 'feel'.* **meaning. meant** (ment).

meaning *n.* what someone has in mind when he or she says or writes something.

meantime *n.* the time between two events.

meanwhile *adv.* during the time between two events: *The next game after this one is on Tuesday; meanwhile, we will have to practise very hard.*

measles *n.* a catching disease that causes a rash.

measure (mezh′ər) *n.* the size or amount of something: *a large measure of land; a small measure of sugar. v.* to find the size or amount of something: *to measure someone's height.* **measuring. measured.**

measurement *n.* size or amount: *The measurements of the room are 8 by 5 metres.*

meat *n.* animal flesh used as food.

mechanic (mə kan′ik) *n.* a person who is skilled in repairing and using machinery.

mechanical *adj.* having to do with a machine: *The engineer fixed the mechanical problems.*

medal *n.* a flat piece of metal that is given as a prize or reward.

medical *adj.* having to do with doctors and medicine: *Doctors are trained at medical school.*

medicine (med′ə sin) a liquid, pill, or other substance taken for an illness.

medium *adj.* being in the middle: *Medium height is between the shortest and the tallest.*

meet *n.* a sports competition: *a swimming meet.* *v.* to join, to come together: *We'll meet at my house.* **meeting. met.**

meeting *n.* a coming together of people to talk or listen to someone.

melody *n.* a tune that is easy to hum. *pl.* **melodies.**

melon *n.* a large, sweet, juicy fruit: *A cantaloupe is a melon.*

melt *v.* to change from solid to liquid: *Snow and butter both melt under a hot sun.* **melting. melted.**

member *n.* someone who belongs to a club or group: *Chantal is a member of the Brownies.*

Member of Parliament the title given to each representative elected to the federal parliament; short form is **MP.**

memorize *v.* to learn by heart: *It took me only a day to memorize my part in the play.* **memorizing. memorized.**

memory *n.* 1. the power of remembering things. 2. something you remember: *Stephen had happy memories of his holiday.* *pl.* **memories.**

men plural of **man.**

mend *v.* to fix something that is broken or torn. **mending. mended.**

mental *adj.* having to do with your mind.

mention (men′shən) *v.* to make a remark about: *I mentioned you in my letter.* **mentioning. mentioned.**

menu (men′yü) *n.* a list of the foods that are served in a restaurant. *pl.* **menus.**

meow *n.* the sound that a cat makes. *v.* to make such a sound. **meowing. meowed.**

merchandise *n.* goods that are bought and sold: *Our corner store sells a variety of merchandise.*

merchant *n.* a person who sells things: *a timber merchant.*

mercy *n.* kindness and pity shown to an unfortunate person or creature: *The children showed mercy towards the kitten and took it home.*

merely *adv.* simply, only: *I merely asked a question. Why all the fuss?*

merit *n.* something worth praising: *Tom's idea has great merit.*

mermaid *n.* an imaginary creature who has a fish's tail instead of legs, and a woman's body.

merry *adj.* laughing, happy, full of fun: *Jon was merry, but Nicky was merrier, and Michel was the merriest person at the party.* **merrily** *adv.*

merry-go-round *n.* an amusement that has toy animals on which people ride while the platform turns.

mess *n.* a dirty or untidy group of things. *v.* to make untidy: *to mess up a room.* **messing. messed.**

message (mes′ij) *n.* a notice or some information sent from one person to another.

messenger *n.* someone who takes a message from one person to another.

messy *adj.* sloppy: *a messy room, a messier one, the messiest room of all.*

met see **meet.**

metal *n.* a hard and shiny material such as iron, steel, copper, lead, brass, or gold.

meteor (mē'tē ər) *n.* a large rock that falls from space towards earth: *Shooting stars are meteors.*

meteorology *n.* the science of weather and the atmosphere.

meter *n.* a machine that measures amounts and times: *a parking meter.*

method *n.* a way of doing something: *Watch my method of sewing before you try to make the apron.*

metre *n.* a measure of length; m is the symbol. 1 m = 100 cm

metric system a system of measurements based on the number 10.

Mexican *adj.* belonging to or coming from Mexico.

mice plural of **mouse.**

microphone (mī'krə fōn) *n.* an instrument that carries sounds, sometimes making them much louder.

microscope (mī'krə skōp) *n.* an instrument with a tube holding lenses, which makes tiny things look large.

mid- a prefix meaning 'middle': **midday** means the middle of the day; **midnight** means halfway through the night.

middle *n.* the point that is halfway between two things: *I'll stand in the middle, between Paula and Bob.* *adj.* halfway between: *Sue chose the middle cupcake.*

midget (mij'it) *n.* someone or something that is much smaller than average size.

midnight *n.* 12 o'clock at night.

midway *n.* the place for games and rides at a fair. *adj.* at the middle point, in between.

might (mīt) *n.* power, strength: *Try with all your might! v.* see **may.**

mighty *adj.* powerful, very strong: *a mighty giant, a mightier one, the mightiest of all.*

migrate *v.* to move to another place or country: *Some birds migrate to warmer lands in winter.* **migrating. migrated.**

mild *adj.* 1. gentle: *a mild breeze.* 2. not strong: *Milk has a mild taste.* 3. neither hot nor cold, medium: *a mild day.*

mile *n.* a measure of distance on land equal to about 1610 m.

military *adj.* having to do with an army or war: *a military camp.*

milk *n.* the white liquid that female mammals produce to feed their young: *We use cow's milk for drinking and cooking. v.* to get milk from an animal: *to milk a cow.* **milking. milked.**

milkshake *n.* a drink made of milk, flavoured syrup, and ice cream, shaken or mixed well.

Milky Way a broad band of light that stretches across the sky at night; our galaxy.

mill *n.* 1. a building where there are machines to grind grain into flour. 2. a machine used for grinding or crushing. 3. a factory where cloth or other goods are made. *v.* to grind: *to mill grain into flour.* **milling. milled.**

miller *n.* a person who works in or runs a mill, usually a flour mill.

milligram *n.* a measure of mass; mg is the symbol. 1000 mg = 1 g

millilitre *n.* a liquid measure; mL is the symbol. 1000 mL = 1 L

millimetre *n.* a measure of length; mm is the symbol. 1000 mm = 1 m

million *n., adj.* a thousand thousands (1 000 000).

millionaire *n.* a person who has at least a million dollars.

mime *v.* to act out a story using actions but no words. **miming. mimed.**

mimeograph (mim′ē ə graf) *n.* a machine used for making copies, usually of written material.

mind *n.* the part of a person that feels, thinks, and remembers. *v.* 1. to take care, to look after, to protect: *I will mind the baby for you.* 2. to feel bad about, to dislike: *Do you mind all the snow you get in your city?* **minding. minded.**

mine *pron.* the one belonging to me: *This pen is mine.* *n.* 1. a deep tunnel in the earth from which coal, gold, diamonds, or other minerals are taken. 2. a bomb in the ground or the sea that explodes when something comes near it or touches it.

miner *n.* a person who works in a mine.

mineral *n.* anything dug out from the earth, such as coal, lead, or gold.

mineralogy (min ər ol′ə jē) *n.* the science that has to do with minerals.

miniature (min′ē ə chər) *adj.* very small: *Miniature golf is played on a small course.*

mining *n.* the working of mines: *gold mining, coal mining, nickel mining.*

minister *n.* 1. a member of the clergy. 2. the head of a government department: *the Minister of Finance.*

mink *n.* an animal like a weasel whose valuable fur is used to make coats and other garments.

minnow (min′ō) *n.* a very small freshwater fish.

minor (mī′nər) *n.* a person who, under law, is not considered an adult. *adj.* smaller, less important, not major: *the minor league.*

mint *n.* 1. a plant with a strong scent; its leaves are used as a flavouring. 2. a place where money is made.

minus (mī′nəs) *prep.* less: *20 minus 7 leaves 13;* symbol is – .

minute (min′ət) *n.* 60 seconds of time; min is the symbol: *There are 60 minutes in one hour.*

minute (mī nüt′) *adj.* very tiny: *a minute speck of dust.*

miracle (mir′ə kəl) *n.* a marvellous and unexpected happening: *It is a miracle that no boats were lost in the storm.*

mirage (mə rahzh′) *n.* something you think you see, which is not really there.

mirror *n.* a looking glass that reflects things.

mis- a prefix meaning 'bad', 'badly', or 'wrong': **misbehaving** means behaving badly; to **misspell** a word is to spell it the wrong way.

misbehave *v.* to behave badly. **misbehaving. misbehaved.**

mischief (mis′chif) *n.* bad or silly behaviour that annoys someone.

mischievous (mis′chə vəs) *adj.* full of mischief.

miser (mī′zər) *n.* a greedy person who keeps money and will not spend it.

miserable (miz′ər ə bəl) *adj.* unhappy, sad.

misery (miz′ər ē) *n.* great unhappiness. *pl.* **miseries.**

misfortune *n.* bad luck, a bad accident.

misplace *v.* to put in the wrong place: *I have misplaced my glasses. Will you help me find them?* **misplacing. misplaced.**

Miss a title put in front of the name of an unmarried woman or girl: *Miss Ann Jones.*

miss *v.* 1. to fail to catch, find, reach, hit, or hear something: *to miss the ball.* 2. to be lonely for someone who is away from you: *I miss him.* **missing. missed.**

missile (mis′əl) *n.* 1. something that is fired or thrown, such as a bullet. 2. a self-propelled rocket.

mission (mish′ən) *n.* 1. a special job or task: *a rescue mission.* 2. a group of people sent to do religious work, usually in another country.

missionary *n.* a person who goes to another place to tell about his or her religion. *pl.* **missionaries.**

misspell *v.* to spell a word the wrong way. **misspelling. misspelled.**

mist *n.* a thin fog or haziness in the air.

mistake *n.* something that is wrong, an error: *a spelling mistake.* *v.* to make an error: *It is sometimes easy to mistake plastic for glass.* **mistaking. mistook.** I am **mistaken.**

mistletoe (mis′əl tō) *n.* a climbing plant with white berries, used as a Christmas decoration.

misunderstand *v.* not to understand. **misunderstanding. misunderstood.**

mitt *n.* 1. a baseball glove. 2. a mitten.

mittens *n.pl.* gloves that cover four fingers together and the thumb separately.

mix *v.* to stir together: *to mix paints.* **mixing. mixed.**
mix up 1. to shake up. 2. to mistake one thing for another: *I always mix up the names of the two brothers.*

mixture (mix′chər) *n.* two or more things mixed together: *A mixture of flour and water is used for papier-mâché.*

MLA short for **Member of the Legislative   Assembly**

moan *n.* a low groaning sound, often showing pain. *v.* to make such a sound. **moaning. moaned.**

mob *n.* an uncontrolled crowd of people.

moccasin *n.* a shoe made of soft leather.

mock *v.* to make fun of, to jeer at. **mocking. mocked.**

model *n.* 1. a small copy: *a model plane.* 2. a person who poses for an artist or photographer. 3. a person who sets a good example: *Ben is a model of what a Scout should be.* 4. a style or design: *the latest model of car.* *v.* 1. to make a model. 2. to pose for an artist or photographer. **modelling. modelled.**

modern *adj.* up-to-date, to do with present times: *modern history.*

module *n.* a part of something: *the landing module from the spacecraft.*

moist *adj.* slightly wet, damp.

moisture (mois′chər) *n.* dampness.

mold see **mould.**

mole *n.* 1. a small furry animal that makes tunnels under the ground, leaving molehills on top. 2. a small, dark spot on your skin.

mom, mommy *n.* mother.

moment *n.* an instant of time.

monarch (mon′ərk) *n.* a royal ruler such as a king, queen, or emperor.

Monday *n.* the second day of the week.

money *n.* coins and paper notes used in buying and selling things.

mongrel *n.* a dog of mixed breed: *Our dog is a mongrel. She is half spaniel and half collie.*

monitor *n.* a boy or girl who has special jobs to do for the teacher.

monkey *n.* an animal that lives in the trees in many hot places: *Some monkeys look very much like people.* *pl.* **monkeys.**

monster *n.* a strange and frightening creature.

month *n.* one of the twelve parts of the year.

monthly *adv.* once a month: *The magazine comes out monthly.* *adj.* coming out or happening every month: *a monthly magazine.*

Montréal *n.* largest city in the Province of Québec.

monument *n.* a statue or building put up in memory of someone or some happening.

moo *n.* the long, low sound that a cow makes. *v.* to make such a sound. **mooing. mooed.**

mood *n.* the way that you feel at a certain time: *My brother is in a good mood today. He keeps smiling and laughing.*

moon *n.* the large bright object that shines in the sky at night: *The moon goes around the earth once in about 29½ days.*

moose *n.* a large animal related to the deer; it lives in the forests of Canada and the northern United States. *pl.* **moose.**

mop *n.* a sponge or pieces of cloth joined at the end of a long handle and used for cleaning. *v.* to clean with a mop. **mopping. mopped.**

moral (mor′əl) *n.* a lesson to be learned, often from a story or fable.

more *adj.* extra, a bigger amount of: *Please may I have more cake?* *adv.* again: *Please read that story once more.*

morning *n.* the time between midnight and noon.

morning glory a blue, pink, white, or purple flower that closes up at night. *pl.* **morning glories.**

mosaic (mō zā′ik) *n.* a picture made with bits of coloured glass, stone, or tile.

Moslem see **Islam.**

mosquito (mə skē′tō) *n.* a small, two-winged, stinging insect. *pl.* **mosquitoes.**

moss *n.* a small, smooth, green plant that grows on damp trees and stones.

most *adj.* the greatest number or amount: *Most dogs like bones. adv.* the greatest: *Which sport do you like most?*

motel *n.* a kind of hotel that is built near a main road.

moth *n.* an insect that looks like a butterfly, but flies mostly at night. *pl.* **moths** (moтнz).

mother *n.* a female parent.

motion *n.* movement: *The whistle sounded, and the train went into motion.*

motion picture a series of pictures on a film, projected on a screen; a movie.

motor *n.* a machine that makes other machines work: *an electric motor.*

motorboat *n.* a boat propelled by a motor.

motorcycle *n.* a two-wheeled vehicle powered by a motor.

motorist *n.* a person who drives or rides in an automobile.

motto *n.* a short saying or rule. *pl.* **mottoes.**

mould, mold (mōld) *n.* 1. a hollow form that is made in a special shape: *a plaster mould.* 2. a fuzzy or woolly growth, sometimes seen on old bread or other food. *v.* to make or form into a shape. **moulding. moulded.**

mound *n.* a large heap: *a mound of stones.*

mount *n.* 1. a mountain: *Mount Everest.* 2. a horse for riding. *v.* to climb up: *to mount a horse.* **mounting. mounted.**

mountain *n.* a very high hill.

mountaineer *n.* someone who climbs mountains.

mountainous *adj.* full of mountains: *Switzerland is a mountainous country.*

Mountie *n.* a member of the Royal Canadian Mounted Police.

mourn (morn) *v.* to feel very sorry because someone or something has died or gone far away. **mourning. mourned.**

mouse *n.* a small, furry animal with a pointed nose and a long tail. *pl.* **mice.**

moustache, mustache (məs tash′) *n.* hair that grows above a man's top lip.

mouth *n.* 1. the opening in your face through which you eat. 2. any opening: *the mouth of a cave, the mouth of a bottle.* *pl.* **mouths** (mouᴛʜz).

mouthpiece *n.* 1. the part of a musical instrument that is placed against or in the mouth. 2. the part of a telephone that is held near the mouth.

movable *adj.* able to be moved.

move *n.* 1. in a game, a player's turn: *It's your move.* 2. a movement: *The robber said, 'Don't make a move.'* *v.* to go, or to take something, from one place to another. **moving. moved.**

movement *n.* a change from place to place.

movie *n.* a motion picture.

mow (mō) *v.* to cut grass with a lawn mower or other cutting machine. **mowing. mowed.** he has **mown** or **mowed.**

MP short for **Member of Parliament.**

MPP short for **Member of the Provincial Parliament.**

Mr. short for **Mister**, a title put in front of a man's name.

Mrs. (mis′iz) a title put in front of a married w̄oman's name.

Ms (miz) a title put in front of a woman's name.

much *adj.* great in amount or degree: *much money, more money, the most money of all.*

mud *n.* soft, wet soil or dirt.

muddy *adj.* covered with mud: *muddy paws, muddier paws, the muddiest paws of all.*

muffin *n.* a small round cake, often eaten hot with butter.

muffler *n.* 1. a thick, woollen scarf. 2. something that deadens noises: *a muffler on a car.*

mug *n.* a large drinking cup.

mukluks *n.pl.* high waterproof boots, often made of sealskin, worn by Inuit and others.

mule (myül) *n.* an animal that is half donkey and half horse.

multiplication *n.* multiplying one number by another.

multiply *v.* to make a number several times larger: *When we multiply 6 by 3, we get 18.* **multiplying. multiplied.** he **multiplies.**

mum *n.* mother.

mumble *v.* to speak low and unclearly. **mumbling. mumbled.**

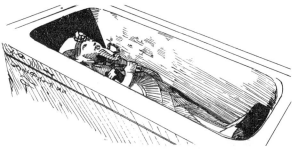

mummy *n.* 1. in ancient times, a dead body treated with chemicals and wrapped in cloths so that it would not decay: *Many mummies have been found in ancient Egyptian tombs.* 2. mother. *pl.* **mummies.**

mumps *n.* a catching illness that makes your face and neck swell up so that it may be hard to swallow.

munch *v.* to chew in a noisy way. **munching. munched.**

mural (myü′rəl) *n.* a large picture painted on a roll of paper or on a wall.

murder *n.* the unlawful killing of a human being. *v.* to kill someone unlawfully. **murdering. murdered.**

murmur *n.* something said softly. *v.* to say something softly. **murmuring. murmured.**

muscle (mus′əl) *n.* one of the parts of your body that can be tightened or loosened, making the body move: *Muscles are made up of strong fibres, and look like cords.*

muscular (mus′kyü lər) *adj.* having strong muscles: *a muscular man.*

museum (myü zē′əm) *n.* a building in which interesting science or art objects are displayed.

mushroom *n.* a plant shaped like a small umbrella: *Some mushrooms may be eaten, but others are poisonous.*

music *n.* a series of pleasant sounds or tones, made by singing or by playing on an instrument.

musical *adj.* having to do with music.

musician (myü zish′ən) *n.* someone who creates or plays music.

muskeg *n.* an area of swamp or marsh.

muskrat *n.* a North American water animal that looks like a large rat.

mussel *n.* a shellfish, something like a clam, with a narrow, black shell.

must *v.* a verb used before another verb to mean 'to have to': *I must go out before the milk store closes.*

mustache see **moustache.**

mustard *n.* a hot-tasting yellow mixture eaten with hot dogs and other foods.

mutiny (myü′tən ē) *n.* the rebelling of soldiers or sailors against their officers. *pl.* **mutinies.**

mutter *v.* to speak or grumble in a low voice. **muttering. muttered.**

muzzle *n.* 1. the jaws and nose of an animal. 2. leather straps put over an animal's mouth to keep it from biting. 3. the open end of a gun barrel. *v.* to put a muzzle on an animal. **muzzling. muzzled.**

my *adj.* belonging to me.

myself *pron.* I alone: *I cut myself.*

mysterious (mis tēr′ē əs) *adj.* very strange, full of mystery.

mystery (mis′tər ē) *n.* 1. something very strange and hard to understand. 2. a story about a crime. *pl.* **mysteries.**

myth (mith) *n.* an old story that deals with strange and magical things.

n

nag *n.* an old and tired horse. *v.* to keep on scolding and finding fault. **nagging. nagged.**

nail *n.* 1. the thin, hard layer at the end of a finger or toe. 2. a small metal spike, pointed at one end and flat at the other. *v.* to hammer a nail into an object. **nailing. nailed.**

naked (nā′kid) *adj.* bare, without clothes.

name *n.* what a person or thing is called. *v.* to give a name to a baby or pet. **naming. named.**

nap *n.* a short sleep. *v.* to take a short sleep. **napping. napped.**

napkin *n.* a piece of cloth or paper used at meals for protecting clothing and for wiping your hands and mouth.

narcissus (nar sis′əs) *n.* a plant that has a white or yellow flower. *pl.* **narcissuses** or **narcissi** (nar sis′ī).

narrate *v.* to tell a story. **narrating. narrated.**

narrator *n.* a person who tells a story.

narrow *adj.* thin, slender; not wide.

nasty *adj.* unpleasant, mean: *a nasty witch, a nastier witch, the nastiest witch in the world.*

nation (nā'shən) *n.* a country, or the people of a country.

national (nash'ən əl) *adj.* belonging to a nation: *A national anthem is the special song of a nation.*

native (nā'tiv) *n.* someone born in a certain place or country: *Tom is a native of Australia.*

natural (nach'ər əl) *adj.* found in nature, not made by people: *Wood is a natural material.*

nature (nā'chər) *n.* 1. the outdoor world of plants and animals: *We go camping because we all enjoy nature.* 2. the character or behaviour of a person or creature: *My puppy has a very gentle nature.*

naughty (naw'tē) *adj.* badly behaved, disobedient: *a naughty child, a naughtier child, the naughtiest child in the room.*

naval (nā'vəl) *adj.* having to do with the navy: *a naval officer.*

navel (nā'vəl) *n.* the little round dent in the centre of the front part of your stomach.

navigate *v.* to guide or plan the route for a ship or an aircraft. **navigating. navigated.**

navigator *n.* someone who guides a ship or aircraft.

navy *n.* a country's warships and their crew. *pl.* **navies.**

near *prep., adv., adj.* not far away from something.

nearby *adv.* very close: *They live nearby.*

nearly *adv.* almost: *It is nearly 12 o'clock.*

neat *adj.* clean and tidy.

necessary (nes'ə ser ē) *adj.* needed, required.

necessity (nə ses'ə tē) *n.* something that we cannot do without: *Food is a necessity.* *pl.* **necessities.**

neck *n.* the part of the body that joins the head to the shoulders.

necklace (nek'ləs) *n.* a string of beads or jewels worn around the neck.

need *v.* to require or want something: *I need a pen to write with.* **needing. needed.**

needle *n.* 1. a thin steel spike, with a hole or 'eye' at one end, used in sewing. 2. an object having this general shape: *a knitting needle.*

negative *n.* a photographic picture on film, in which the light areas and dark areas are switched around: *Photographic prints are made from negatives.* *adj.* meaning 'no' or 'not': *When we asked for a dog, we received a negative answer.*

neglect *v.* to give little attention to someone or something, or to fail to do something: *The plants will die if you neglect them.* **neglecting. neglected.**

neigh (nā) *n.* the noise that a horse makes. *v.* to make such a noise. **neighing. neighed.**

neighbour, neighbor (nā'bər) *n.* someone who lives near you.

neighbourhood, neighborhood *n.* the area or district in which you live.

neither (nē'ᴛʜər, nī'ᴛʜər) *adj.* not one or the other: *Neither Sally nor Connie would go.*
Note: **Neither** is followed by **nor**: *Neither Donald nor Donna is here.* **Either** is followed by **or**: *Either Billy or I will be there.*

nephew (nef'yü) *n.* the son of a brother or sister: *My cousin Alan is my father's nephew.*

nerve *n.* 1. one of the fibres in the body that carries feelings and messages to the brain. 2. courage: *Jamie has plenty of nerve. He will try anything.*

nervous *adj.* tense, easily excited or upset: *My nervous dog hides whenever someone rings the bell.*

nest *n.* a home of twigs, straw, grass, and other materials, made by birds and other creatures.

net *n.* a woven material, usually of string or wire, with large or small spaces between the strings or wires.

neutral (nyü'trəl) *n.* the position of a vehicle that is not in gear. *adj.* not taking sides in a quarrel.

never *adv.* not at any time: *I have never flown in a plane.*
never mind don't worry, it does not matter.

new *adj.* 1. not old. 2. not seen or known before.

New Brunswick province between Québec on the west, Nova Scotia and the Atlantic Ocean on the east; capital is Fredericton. Short form: **N.B.** A person living in or born in New Brunswick is a **New Brunswicker.**

New Canadian 1. a person who has recently come to Canada and plans to live here. 2. a person who has recently become a Canadian citizen.

Newfoundland province on the Atlantic Ocean, with Québec on the west and south; capital is St. John's. Short form: **Nfld.** A person living in or born in Newfoundland is a **Newfoundlander.** The mainland part of Newfoundland is **Labrador.**

news *n.* information about what is going on: *The reporter heard the news of the fire from a friend.*

newspaper *n.* a daily or weekly paper with news, stories, pictures, ads, etc.

next *adj.* 1. the nearest: *the next house.* 2. the one after: *next week. adv.* in the nearest time or place: *Nancy will sing next.*

nibble *n.* a small bite or piece of something. *v.* to eat something in small bites. **nibbling. nibbled.**

nice *adj.* pretty, pleasant, friendly.

nick *n.* a small slit, a scratch.

nickel *n.* 1. a hard, silver-white metal. 2. a five-cent coin in Canada and the United States.

nickname *n.* a name given to someone in fun: *Barry was given the nickname 'Red' by his friends.*

niece *n.* the daughter of a brother or sister: *My cousin Mary is my father's niece.*

night *n.* the time when it is dark, between sunset and sunrise.

nine *n., adj.* one more than eight (9).

nineteen *n., adj.* ten more than nine (19).

ninety *n., adj.* ten times nine (90).

ninth *adj.* following eighth (9th).

nip *v.* 1. to pinch or take a small bite out of something. 2. to snip off. **nipping. nipped.**

no *adv.* the opposite of yes: *Can you swim? No. adj.* not any: *My piggy bank has no money in it.*

noble *n.* someone born into a family of high rank or title. *adj.* 1. splendid, great: *a noble building, a noble deed.* 2. having a rank or title: *a noble family.*

nobody *pron.* no one: *Is nobody here?*

nod *v.* to bend your head forward to say 'yes': *Ted nodded in agreement to my suggestion.* **nodding. nodded.**

noise *n.* a sound, often loud and unpleasant.

noisy *adj.* making a lot of noise: *a noisy truck, a noisier truck, the noisiest truck in town.*

nominate *v.* to choose someone to be a candidate for a position in government, in a club, etc. **nominating. nominated.**

non- a prefix meaning 'no' or 'not': **nonsense** means something that makes no sense; a **non-stop** train does not stop along the way.

none (nun) *pron.* not one, not any.

nonsense *n.* silliness, foolish talk.

noodles *n.pl.* a food made of flour, water, and eggs, shaped in long strips.

nook *n.* a quiet little corner.

noon *n.* twelve o'clock in the daytime, the middle of the day.

no one *pron.* nobody, no person: *No one is home at the Smith house.*

noose *n.* a loop of rope with a slip knot that tightens.

nor *conj.* and not; used after **neither:** *Neither my dog nor my cat can do any tricks.*

normal *adj.* ordinary, usual: *It was a normal day. Nothing special happened.*

north *n.* the direction to your left as you face the sunrise, opposite to south.

North American a person born in or living in Canada, Mexico, or the United States.

northern *adj.* in or towards the north: *Canada is a northern country.*

North Pole the most northern point of the earth.

Northwest Territories territory in northern Canada, east of the Yukon Territory; capital is Yellowknife. Short form: **N.W.T.**

nose *n.* the part of your face that sticks out above your mouth: *The nose has two nostrils or holes through which you smell and breathe.*

nosey, nosy *adj.* curious, always wanting to know what others are doing: *a nosey neighbour, a nosier one, the nosiest one on the street.*

nostril *n.* one of the two openings in your nose.

not *adv.* a word meaning 'no' or 'the opposite'.

notch *n.* a cut, a nick, a little hole: *How many notches are in your belt?*

note *n.* 1. a short message. 2. a musical sound, or a sign that stands for it in music. *v.* to notice closely: *Note all the colours in the picture.* **noting. noted.**

notebook *n.* a book with pages on which to write.

nothing *n.* 1. not anything: *She told me nothing.* 2. in arithmetic, zero (0).

notice *n.* a written or printed announcement or poster: *The notice says, 'Keep off the grass'. v.* to see: *Did you notice that I got my hair cut?* **noticing. noticed.**

notify *v.* to let someone know, to send a note: *The librarian notified Mark that his book was overdue.* **notifying. notified.** he **notifies.**

noun *n.* a word giving the name of a person, place, quality, or thing: *'Alice', 'cat', 'honesty', 'football', and 'Canada' are nouns.*

Nova Scotia province between New Brunswick on the west, the Atlantic Ocean on the east; capital is Halifax. Short form: **N.S.** A person living in or born in Nova Scotia is a **Nova Scotian.**

novel *n.* a long story, in a book form, usually about made-up people and events.

November *n.* the eleventh month of the year.

now *adv.* at present.

nowhere *adv.* in no place, not anywhere.

nudge *v.* to push someone with your elbow to attract his or her attention. **nudging. nudged.**

nugget *n.* a rough lump of metal, usually gold.

nuisance (nyü'səns) *n.* something that is annoying to people, or someone who bothers other people.

numb (num) *adj.* without any feeling: *My feet were numb with cold.*

number *n.* 1. a word or sign saying how many. 2. several: *There are a number of questions on the page.* *v.* to count, to put a number to something: *Number the pages.* **numbering. numbered.**

Numerator → $\dfrac{1}{16}$

numerator *n.* in a fraction, the number above the line.

numerical (nyü mer'i kəl) *adj.* having to do with numbers: *1, 2, 3, 4, 5 are numbers written in numerical order.*

numerous (nyü'mər əs) *adj.* very many: *Do you have time to answer my numerous questions?*

nurse *n.* a person who looks after the sick, the old, and the very young. *v.* to care for these people. **nursing. nursed.**

nursery *n.* 1. a room or building for very young children. 2. a place where young plants are looked after. *pl.* **nurseries.**

nut *n.* 1. a dry fruit or seed with a hard shell: *A chestnut, a walnut, and a peanut are some kinds of nuts.* 2. a small piece of metal with a hole in the centre: *A nut screws onto a bolt.*

nutritious (nyü trish'əs) *adj.* useful as a food: *This cereal is delicious and nutritious.*

nylon *n.* a strong substance made from chemicals, and used to make thread, stockings, and other things.

oak *n.* a tree having nuts called acorns; its hard wood is made into furniture.

oar *n.* a long pole with a flat blade at one end, used for rowing.

oasis (ō ā'sis) *n.* a place in a desert with water and trees. *pl.* **oases** (ō ā'sēz).

oath *n.* a very serious promise to tell the truth or to do something. *pl.* **oaths** (ōTHZ).

oatmeal *n.* a cooked cereal that is made from rolled or ground oats.

oats *n. pl.* a grain, grown like wheat, used for cereal and as feed for animals.

obedience (ō bē'dē əns) *n.* doing as you are told. (*opp.* **disobedience.**)

obedient (ō bē'dē ənt) *adj.* willing to obey. (*opp.* **disobedient.**)

obey (ō bā') *v.* to do what you are told. **obeying. obeyed.** she **obeys.** (*opp.* **disobey.**)

object (ob'jəkt) *n.* 1. a thing you can see and touch. 2. an aim: *David's object in life is to be a sailor like his father.*

object (əb jekt') *v.* to disagree with, to complain against: *Why do you object to taking the boat?* **objecting. objected.**

objection *n.* a disagreement, a complaint: *My objection to going by boat is that I get seasick.*

oblong *adj.* longer than wide: *Do you want a square envelope or an oblong one?*

observant *adj.* quick to notice.

observatory *n.* a building where there are telescopes for studying the stars. *pl.* **observatories.**

observe *v.* 1. to watch carefully: *I observed every move he made.* 2. to celebrate: *We observed Thanksgiving by telling why we were thankful.* 3. to follow, to obey: *Observe the rules of the game.* **observing. observed.**

obstacle *n.* something that is in the way.

obtain *v.* to get something through effort: *Pia obtained the tickets after waiting in line for hours.* **obtaining. obtained.**

obvious (ob'vē əs) *adj.* easy to see or understand: *It is obvious that Riva is taller than David.*

occasion (ə kā'zhən) *n.* a happening, an event: *The fireworks display was a great occasion.*

occasional *adj.* happening now and then: *There were occasional flashes of lightning.* **occasionally** *adv.*

occupation *n.* the work that someone does for a living, a job: *Farming is a farmer's occupation.*

occupy *v.* 1. to fill in space, to live in: *A family of four occupies that apartment.* 2. to fill in time: *Reading occupies most of Sandra's spare time.* **occupying. occupied.** it **occupies.**

occur *v.* 1. to take place, to happen: *New Year's Day occurs on Monday this year.* 2. to come to mind: *It occurs to me that I must visit my friend.* **occurring. occurred.**

ocean (ō'shən) *n.* one of the five large bodies of water: *the Atlantic, Pacific, Indian, Arctic, and Antarctic oceans.*

o'clock short for 'of the clock' (according to the clock).

October *n.* the tenth month of the year.

octopus *n.* an animal that lives in the ocean and has eight arms. *pl.* **octopuses** or **octopi** (ok'tə pī).

odd *adj.* 1. not even in number, not able to be divided exactly by two: *7, 9, and 11 are odd numbers.* 2. not making a perfect pair: *odd socks.* 3. different, strange: *a very odd story.*
odds and ends things left over.

odour, odor (ō'dər) *n.* a smell, usually an unpleasant one.

of (uv) *prep.* 1. made from: *a piece of iron.* 2. belonging to: *a member of the team.* 3. holding: *a shaker of salt.* 4. about: *I heard of it.*

off *prep.* away from: *He pushed the bucket off the roof. adv.* 1. away: *He ran off.* 2. not on: *Please take off your coat.*

offence, offense *n.* 1. a crime, a breaking of the rules: *Is it an offence to ride on the sidewalk?* 2. an attacking team: *Our hockey team has a powerful offence.*

offend *v.* to hurt someone's feelings: *She offended her brother with her unkind remarks.* **offending. offended.**

offensive *n.* an attack, usually in war or sports: *Our team began an offensive. adj.* rude, insulting, unpleasant: *an offensive remark.*

offer *n.* 1. a price suggested by a person who wants to buy something: *What is your offer on this house?* 2. a proposal: *an offer of marriage. v.* to present or hold out for someone to take or refuse: *to offer help.* **offering. offered.**

office *n.* 1. a place where work is done: *a dentist's office.* 2. an important position: *the office of Mayor.*

officer *n.* 1. someone who holds an important position: *a police officer.* 2. someone in command: *an army officer.*

official (ə fish'əl) *n.* an officer: *an official from the hockey league. adj.* having to do with a certain office or important position: *an official uniform.* (*opp.* **unofficial.**)

offshore *adj.* away from the shore.

often (of'ən) *adv.* many times: *We often go swimming in the summer.*

ogre (ō'gər) *n.* in fairy tales, a monster who eats people.

oh 1. used to express feelings such as happiness, surprise, or pain. 2. used when talking to someone before saying his or her name: *Oh, Paul, what are you doing on the weekend?*

oil *n.* a greasy liquid that will not mix with water. *v.* to grease something with oil. **oiling. oiled.**

okay, O.K. *adj., adv.* all right, correct, approved.

old *adj.* 1. having existed or lived for a long time: *an old tree.* 2. having lived for a certain time: *The cat is six years old.*

old-fashioned *adj.* out-of-date, not modern.

olive *n.* a small oily fruit, grown on an evergreen tree in warm places.

Olympic games, Olympics *n. pl.* athletic contests held every four years in a different country: *The 1976 Olympic games were held in Canada.*

omit (ō mit′) *v.* to leave out, to leave undone: *You omitted an important number in your answer.* **omitting. omitted.**

on *prep.* 1. on top of: *The pencil is on the desk.* 2. during: *on Monday.* 3. in the state of: *on fire.* 4. about: *a book on monsters.* *adv.* 1. further: *Let us go on.* 2. not off: *Please turn the light on.*

once (wuns) *adv.* 1. one time: *I have worn these shoes only once before.* 2. in the past: *There was once a castle here.* **at once** now: *Do it at once!*

one *n.* the first whole number after zero (1). *adj.* single: *one thing only.*

one-way street a street with traffic going in one direction only.

onion (un′yən) *n.* a round, strong-smelling bulb that is used as a vegetable.

only *adj.* single: *an only child in a family.* *adv.* simply, merely: *I won only one game of chess.* *conj.* but: *I wanted to go, only I had a cold.*

Ontario *n.* province between Manitoba on the west, Québec on the east; capital is Toronto. Short form: **Ont.** A person living in or born in Ontario is an **Ontarian.**

onto *prep.* to a position on: *He threw the ball onto the roof.*

ooze *v.* to leak, to flow slowly through: *Oil oozed through the crack.* **oozing. oozed.**

open *adj.* 1. not shut: *an open door.* 2. wide and clear: *the open sky.* *v.* 1. to unfasten: *Please open the gate.* 2. to start: *The play opened with a song.* **opening. opened.**

opening *n.* 1. a gap, a space: *an opening in the fence.* 2. a beginning: *The opening of the football season is tomorrow.*

opera (op′ər ə) *n.* a play set to music, with the performers singing their parts.

operate *v.* 1. to work: *to operate a machine.* 2. to perform surgery on a sick or injured person: *The doctor operated on me to remove my tonsils.* **operating. operated.**

operation *n.* 1. the working of a machine. 2. the cutting open of the body in surgery.

operator *n.* a person who looks after a telephone switchboard or other machine.

operetta *n.* a short and funny opera.

opinion *n.* what you think or believe: *It is my opinion that a cat is a better pet than a dog.*

opponent *n.* someone you fight against or play against.

opportunity *n.* a chance: *Tomorrow I will have an opportunity to try out for the team.* *pl.* **opportunities.**

oppose *v.* to fight or argue against: *The people of the town opposed the closing of the swimming pool.* **opposing. opposed.**

opposite *n.* a person or thing that is completely different: *The opposite of 'up' is 'down'.* *prep.* across from: *The house is opposite the church.* *adj.* completely different: *We are going in the opposite direction.*

or *conj.* a word used to show a difference or give a choice: *Is the answer true or false?*

oral *adj.* spoken, not written: *an oral report.*

orange *n.* 1. a reddish-yellow fruit. 2. a reddish-yellow colour. *adj.* 1. having the flavour of the an orange: *orange sherbet.* 2. having a reddish-yellow colour.

orbit *n.* the path that a satellite, planet, or other heavenly body takes around another body in space: *The earth makes an orbit around the sun once a year.* *v.* to move in such a path. **orbiting. orbited.**

orchard *n.* a garden of fruit trees.

orchestra (or′kəs trə) *n.* a group of musicians playing together.

orchid (or′kid) *n.* a plant that has beautiful flowers: *Orchids have three petals and are usually white or purple.*

ordeal *n.* a painful or difficult experience: *It was an ordeal to hike into town after our car broke down.*

order *n.* 1. tidiness, good arrangement: *Laurette always keeps her books in order.* 2. a command: *The general gave the order to move on.* 3. a request: *Please give your order to the waiter.* 4. the way one thing follows another: *The words in a dictionary are arranged in alphabetical order.* *v.* to command or request: *The man ordered the lion to jump through the hoop.* **ordering. ordered.**
in order to for the purpose of: *In order to get on the team, Maryke had to practise daily.*

ordinary *adj.* usual, not special: *Yesterday was an ordinary day. Nothing unusual happened at all.*

ore *n.* rock or earth containing metal.

organ *n.* 1. a musical instrument with pipes and a piano keyboard. 2. a part of an animal or plant that does a certain job: *The ear is the organ of hearing.*

organization *n.* 1. a group of people who work together for a purpose: *Our organization collects newspapers for recycling.* 2. the putting in order of something: *The organization of a Christmas party takes a lot of work.*

organize *v.* to plan and arrange something: *Cheryl organized her record collection.* **organizing. organized.**

original *adj.* brand new, not copied: *This story is original. I made it up myself.*

ornament *n.* a small object that is used for decoration.

orphan (or′fən) *n.* a child whose parents are dead.

ostrich *n.* a bird that has a long neck and long legs: *An ostrich runs fast but it cannot fly.*

other *adj.* 1. different: *I have other things to do.* 2. opposite: *She lives on the other side of town.* 3. left, remaining: *The first story is funny, but the other ones are sad.*

Ottawa *n.* capital city of Canada.

otter *n.* a water animal that has shiny brown fur and eats fish.

ouch a sound that tells of sudden pain.

ought (awt) *v.* a verb used before another verb to mean 'have a duty': *You ought to go.*

ounce *n.* a measure of mass or weight equal to about 28 g.

our *adj.* belonging to us.

ours *pron.* the one belonging to us: *The house is ours.*

ourselves *pron. pl.* we alone: *We shall do it ourselves.*

out *adv.* away, outside, not in: *Father is out. adj.* 1. not burning: *The fire is out.* 2. being seen: *The flowers are out now that spring is here.*
out of bounds in a place that is off limits.
out-of-date old-fashioned, not modern.

out- a prefix meaning 'more than', 'better than', or 'outside of': to **outnumber** means to be greater or more in number; to **outfight** means to fight better than the other person; the **outfield** is outside the playing field.

outboard *n.* a small motor, attached to the outside of the back of a boat.

outdoor *adj.* in the open air: *outdoor games.*

outdoors *adv.* into the open air: *They went outdoors.*

outer *adj.* on the outside: *Open the outer door, but leave the inner door closed.*

outer space space beyond the earth's atmosphere.

outfield *n.* the part of a baseball field beyond the diamond.

outing *n.* a trip out: *The family went on an outing to the park.*

outlaw *n.* a criminal, a lawless person.

outlet *n.* 1. a way out, an opening: *The lake has several outlets.* 2. a place on a wall for putting in an electrical plug.

outline *n.* 1. in drawing, a line showing the shape of an object. 2. a short plan: *an outline of a story.*

outnumber *v.* to be more than: *At the zoo, the tigers outnumber the lions.*
outnumbering. outnumbered.

outport *n.* 1. a small harbour. 2. a small fishing village along the coast of Newfoundland.

outside *n.* the outer part: *the outside of a shed. adv.* outdoors: *Let's go outside.*

outstanding *adj.* 1. very excellent: *I saw an outstanding movie.* 2. not paid: *That bill is outstanding. You owe me a dollar.*

oval *adj.* having the shape of an egg.

oven (uv′ən) *n.* a space in a stove, used for baking.

over- a prefix meaning 'extra' or 'over': **overtime** means extra time; you wear **overshoes** over your regular shoes.

over *prep.* 1. above: *over our heads.* 2. more than: *over a dollar.* 3. above and across: *Jump over the fence. adj.* finished: *The movie is over. adv.* again: *Do the job over.*

overalls *n. pl.* a pair of pants with a bib attached and straps that go over the shoulders.

overboard *adv.* over a ship's side: *The wave swept the crate overboard.*

overdo *v.* to do or try to do too much: *Don't overdo your exercise.*
overdoing. overdid. he **overdoes.** he has **overdone.**

overdue *adj.* behind time, late: *My library book is overdue and must be returned.*

overflow *v.* to spill over, to flood: *Turn off the water! The tub is overflowing.*
overflowing. overflowed.

overhead *adv.* high above, over you: *Birds fly overhead.*

overhear *v.* to hear someone speaking, who does not know you are listening: *I overheard Mary tell William that she felt ill.* **overhearing. overheard.**

overjoyed *adj.* more than happy: *I was overjoyed when I won the contest.*

overlap *v.* to cover part of something. **overlapping. overlapped.**

overseas *adv.* across the sea: *My aunt lives overseas.*

overtime *n.* extra time: *The game was tied, so they played overtime.*

owe (ō) *v.* to be in debt: *I will pay you the money I owe.* **owing. owed.**

owl *n.* a bird with a large head, big eyes, and a hooked beak: *Owls hunt at night.*

own (ōn) *adj.* belonging to: *This is my own watch.* *v.* to have, to possess: *I own five toys.* **owning. owned.**

owner *n.* the one who owns something.

ox *n.* an animal like a cow, kept for its meat or for pulling carts. *pl.* **oxen.**

oxygen *n.* a gas that has no colour or smell: *Oxygen is needed to keep animals and plants alive. It is part of the air we breathe.*

oyster *n.* a round and flat shellfish: *Some kinds of oysters produce pearls, while others are eaten as food.*

p

pa, papa *n.* father.

pace *n.* the speed of moving: *A turtle moves at a slow pace.* *v.* to walk back and forth: *Father paced the room, deep in thought.* **pacing. paced.**

Pacific *n.* the ocean separating North America and South America from Asia and Australia.

pack *n.* 1. a bundle: *a pack on his back.* 2. a group of people or animals: *a pack of thieves; a pack of dogs.* *v.* 1. to put into a bundle, or to put clothes into a case. (*opp.* **unpack.**) 2. to crowd into a room or other area: *There were too many people packed into the elevator.* **packing. packed.**

package *n.* something wrapped in paper which is closed with string or sticky tape.

pad *n.* 1. a number of sheets of paper glued together on one edge. 2. a cushion. 3. the launching area for rocket ships.

paddle *n.* 1. a short oar used to move a canoe. 2. a board used to hit the ball in the game of ping-pong. *v.* to move a canoe with a paddle. **paddling. paddled.**

page *n.* 1. one side of a sheet of paper. 2. a person who does errands at a hotel, or who is a messenger at the House of Commons, the Senate, or the Legislative Assembly.

pageant (paj′ənt) *n.* a parade or play in costume: *a Christmas pageant.*

paid see **pay.**

pail *n.* a bucket with a handle.

pain *n.* an ache, a feeling of being hurt.

painful *adj.* hurting, giving pain: *a painful injury.* (*opp.* **painless.**)

paint *n.* a coloured liquid to be brushed onto a surface. *v.* 1. to cover with paint. 2. to make a picture or a design with paint. **painting. painted.**

painting *n.* a painted picture.

pair *n.* two things of a kind that go together: *a pair of socks; a pair of rabbits.*

pajamas see **pyjamas.**

pal *n.* a close friend.

palace *n.* the home of a king or other ruler, usually very large and beautiful.

pale *adj.* weak in colour: *When I was sick, my face was very pale.*

palm (pahm) *n.* 1. the inside of your hand. 2. a type of tree, found in warm places, with fan-shaped leaves.

palomino *n.* a slim horse, light tan or cream in colour and having a lighter mane and tail. *pl.* **palominos.**

pamper *v.* to give someone whatever he or she wants. **pampering. pampered.**

pamphlet (pamf′lət) *n.* a thin booklet with a paper cover.

pan *n.* a metal dish. *v.* to wash sand in a pan to separate the gold in it. **panning. panned.**

pancake *n.* a thin round cake of eggs, flour, and milk, mixed together and fried.

panda *n.* a large black and white animal, like a bear, that lives in and around China.

pane *n.* a sheet of glass in a window frame.

panel (pan′əl) *n.* 1. a group of people taking part in a discussion or judging a contest. 2. a piece of wood made to cover a wall. *v.* to put such a piece of wood on a wall. **panelling. panelled.**

panic *n.* sudden fear that makes people or animals want to run away. *v.* to have this kind of fear: *The horses panicked when they saw the fire.* **panicking. panicked.**

pansy *n.* a garden flower with flat, round, velvety blossoms. *pl.* **pansies.**

pant *v.* to gasp for breath: *After the race, everyone was panting.* **panting. panted.**

panther *n.* a large wild cat.

pantomime *n.* a play or a game without words in which the players tell the story with movements.

pants *n. pl.* trousers.

paper *n.* a material used for writing, printing, wrapping things, etc.

paperback *n.* a book with a soft cover.

papier-mâché (pā′pər mə shā′) paper strips soaked in a mixture of flour and water and used for modelling: *Papier-mâché becomes very strong and hard when dry.*

papoose *n.* a North American Indian baby.

parachute (par′ə shüt) *n.* a large sheet that is shaped like an umbrella: *A parachute is tied to someone's back so that he or she can jump out of an airplane and float safely to the ground.*

parade *n.* a march or procession in honour of a special occasion.

paradise *n.* heaven.

paragraph (par′ə graf) *n.* a few sentences on a page of writing: *A paragraph begins on a new line. The sentences in a paragraph are usually about the same subject.*

parallel (par′ə lel) *adj.* going in the same direction and never meeting: *Railway lines are parallel.*

paralyse, paralyze *v.* to take away the power to move or feel in part of the body. **paralysing. paralysed.**

parcel *n.* a package.

pardon *n.* forgiveness: *I beg your pardon.* *v.* to forgive, to excuse. **pardoning. pardoned.**

parent *n.* a father or mother.

park *n.* 1. a piece of land with trees, benches, and play areas. 2. a large piece of land protected by the government and used by campers, hikers, and others: *a provincial park, a national park.* *v.* to leave a car somewhere for a time. **parking. parked.**

parka *n.* a warm fur or cloth jacket with a hood.

parking lot a large area near a shopping centre, office building, apartment building, or other busy place where people leave their cars.

parliament *n.* in certain countries, a group of people chosen to make laws: *The House of Commons and the Senate make up the Canadian parliament.*

parrot *n.* a brightly coloured bird that lives in hot places.

parsley *n.* a plant with small leaves that are used to flavour foods.

part *n.* 1. a piece: *Lee and Shirley ate part of the cake.* 2. a person or character in a play: *Jay played the part of a king.* 3. a side: *I took Jim's part in the argument.* 4. a line dividing the hair on your head. *v.* 1. to separate: *to part your hair.* 2. to leave someone: *to part company.* **parting. parted.**

particular *adj.* 1. very careful, very hard to please: *Kay is very particular about her clothes.* 2. very special: *Jan is a particular friend of mine.*

partly *adv.* in part, not completely: *The story is partly true, but I made up the ending.*

partner *n.* 1. someone who shares a business. 2. a husband or wife. 3. someone dancing with another, or playing a game on the same side.

partridge *n.* a wild bird that has grey, white, and brown feathers.

party *n.* a gathering for fun or celebration: *a birthday party. pl.* **parties.**

pass *n.* 1. a way or opening between mountains. 2. a special paper letting you go in or out: *a free pass for the exhibition.* 3. the moving or throwing of a ball or puck between players. *v.* 1. to go past: *We passed the slow car on the highway.* 2. to hand something to someone: *Please pass the salt.* 3. to complete a test successfully: *He passed the driving test.* **passing. passed.**
Note: Do not mix up **passed** with **past**; **passed** is used only as a verb.

passage *n.* 1. a way through, a corridor. 2. a few paragraphs of a book: *Please read the passage at the top of the page.*

passenger *n.* a traveller in a ship, airplane, car, or some other vehicle, who is not the driver or a crew member.

passion (pash′ən) *n.* a strong feeling of love, hate, or excitement.

Passover *n.* a Jewish holiday in March or April, celebrating the Jewish people's freedom from slavery.

passport *n.* special papers that you must have to travel in a foreign country.

past *n.* time gone by: *In the past, people travelled by horse. adj.* gone by, ended: *It has rained a lot during the past month. prep.* beyond, passing by: *past our house.*
Note: Do not mix up **past** with **passed**; **past** is never used as a verb.

paste *n.* a thick mixture, used for sticking things together. *v.* to use this mixture: *We pasted the paper on the wall.* **pasting. pasted.**

pastels *n. pl.* soft, coloured chalks.

pasteurize (pas′chər īz) *v.* to heat milk enough to kill germs. **pasteurizing. pasteurized.**

pastry (pās′trē) *n.* 1. crusts made of dough. 2. sweet baked goods. *pl.* **pastries.**

pasture (pas′chər) *n.* grassland for cattle or other animals to feed on.

pat *n.* a gentle tap: *a pat on the shoulder. v.* to tap gently with your hand: *Sachi patted the friendly dog.* **patting. patted.**

patch *n.* 1. a small piece of cloth that covers a hole: *Mother sewed a patch on my jeans.* 2. a small area: *a vegetable patch. v.* to mend with a patch. **patching. patched.**

path *n.* a narrow lane or track.

patience (pā′shəns) *n.* the ability to wait a long time or work on a hard job without complaining. (*opp.* **impatience.**)

patient (pā′shənt) *n.* a person who is being treated by a doctor or dentist. *adj.* calm; waiting or working steadily without fuss: *Be patient! The guests will be here soon.* (*opp.* **impatient.**)

patio (pat′ē ō) *n.* a paved area attached to a house. *pl.* **patios.**

patriot (pā′trē ət) *n.* a person who loves his or her country and supports it loyally.

patriotic *adj.* loving and serving your country. (*opp.* **unpatriotic.**)

patrol *n.* a small group of soldiers or police officers who are on guard. *v.* to walk about an area, guarding it. **patrolling. patrolled.**

pattern *n.* 1. a model to be copied: *a paper pattern for a dress.* 2. a design: *a pattern of squares on a dress.*

pause (pawz) *n.* a short break: *We took a pause in our hike.* *v.* to stop what you are doing for a short time: *The runner paused for breath.* **pausing. paused.**

pave *v.* to cover a street, driveway, etc. with a flat surface of tar or cement. **paving. paved.**

pavement *n.* a paved area.

paw *n.* the foot of a four-footed animal having nails or claws.

pawn *n.* in chess, one of the 16 pieces of the lowest value.

pay *n.* the money received for work done: *After two weeks, he was given his pay.* *v.* 1. to give money in return for goods, or for work done. 2. to give something other than money: *to pay a compliment.* **paying. paid.** he **pays.**

payment *n.* money that is paid: *The payments on the car are made the first day of each month.*

pea *n.* a round seed that grows in a pod and is used for food.

peace *n.* 1. a time of quiet. 2. a time when there is no war.

peaceful *adj.* quiet and calm. **peacefully** *adv.*

peach *n.* a round, juicy fruit that has a fuzzy skin and a large pit.

peacock *n.* a large male bird with beautiful green, blue, and gold tail feathers.

peahen *n.* the female of the peacock.

peak *n.* 1. a mountain top. 2. the front part of a cap.

peal *n.* a loud sound: *a peal of bells.*

peanut *n.* a nut that grows in a yellowish shell: *One shell usually holds two or three peanuts.*

peanut butter a spread made of ground-up peanuts.

pear *n.* a juicy fruit, round at the bottom and smaller near the stem end.

pearl (pərl) *n.* a precious gem, usually white, found in some oyster shells.

peasant (pez′ənt) *n.* a poor farmer or farm worker.

pebble *n.* a small, round stone.

pecan *n.* a nut that grows in a thin, reddish shell and has a sweet taste.

peck *v.* to jab at food and pick it up with the beak: *a hen pecking at corn.* **pecking. pecked.**

peculiar (pə kyül′yər) *adj.* strange, different: *My cat is peculiar. It's scared of mice!*

pedal *n.* 1. the part on which you place your foot in order to move a vehicle or other machine: *a bicycle pedal.* 2. the part of a piano or organ on which you place your foot. *v.* to make a bicycle move by turning the pedals with your feet. **pedalling. pedalled.**

peddle *v.* to carry from house to house and try to sell: *When my grandfather was a young man, he peddled fruit.* **peddling. peddled.**

peddler, pedlar *n.* a person who peddles.

pedestrian *n.* someone who travels on foot.

peek *n.* a quick and sly look: *Take a peek.* *v.* to take such a look. **peeking. peeked.**

peel *n.* the skin or rind of a fruit or vegetable: *potato peel, orange peel.* *v.* to take off the outer skin of something: *Please peel the orange.* **peeling. peeled.**

peep *n.* 1. a quick, sly look. 2. a short, high sound made by a young bird or chicken. *v.* 1. to take a quick and sly look at something. 2. to make a sound like a peep. **peeping. peeped.**

peewee *n.* 1. a very small person or thing. 2. in sports, a player between the ages of eight and twelve years.

peg *n.* a small metal or wooden pin: *a tent peg.*

pelican *n.* a large bird that has a big pouch under its long beak.

pellet *n.* a tiny ball: *a lead pellet from a shotgun.*

pelt *n.* the skin of an animal, usually with its fur. *v.* to throw or pound: *The rain pelted on the roof.* **pelting. pelted.**

pen *n.* 1. a tool used for writing. 2. an enclosed space in which animals are kept: *a pig pen.*

penalty *n.* a punishment for a crime or for breaking a rule. *pl.* **penalties.**

pencil *n.* a tool used for writing.

penguin *n.* a black and white sea bird that cannot fly, found near the South Pole.

peninsula (pə nin'syə lə) *n.* a piece of land that sticks far out into the water.

pennant *n.* 1. a flag or banner, often long and pointed, used as a signal or a decoration. 2. a flag or trophy that is the emblem of an athletic or other championship: *a baseball pennant.*

penny *n.* a small copper coin worth one cent. *pl.* **pennies.**

people (pē'pəl) *n.* 1. persons; men, women, boys, and girls. 2. a nation: *the Canadian people.*

pepper *n.* 1. a hot-tasting powder that adds flavour to food. 2. a green or red vegetable, to be cooked or used in salads.

peppermint *n.* a plant with a strong scent; its leaves are used to flavour some candies, medicines, and toothpastes.

per cent, percent *n.* parts of a hundred: *Three per cent (3%) means 3 out of every 100.*

perch *n.* 1. a fish that lives in rivers and lakes. *pl.* **perch.** 2. a stick or a twig that a bird can rest on. *v.* to sit on or place on something: *We perched ourselves on the top of the hill.* **perching. perched.**

percussion instrument a musical instrument played by striking it, such as a drum.

perfect (pər'fikt) *adj.* without anything wrong; so good that it cannot be better: *A perfect score is 100%.* **perfectly** *adv.*

perform *v.* 1. to do something in front of an audience: *Jill will perform on the piano.* 2. to carry out or to do: *to perform a chore.* **performing. performed.**

performance *n.* 1. an entertainment: *We saw a performance by dancers.* 2. the carrying out of an action: *The team's performance was excellent.*

performer *n.* an actor or person who entertains by performing.

perfume (pər'fyüm) *n.* a liquid with a nice smell.

perhaps *adv.* it may be, possibly: *Sam isn't at the party; perhaps he's not feeling well.*

period *n.* 1. a length of time: *a period of 30 minutes; a period in a hockey game.* 2. the dot (.) that marks the end of a sentence.

permafrost *n.* ground that is always frozen.

permanent *adj.* always there, long-lasting: *Jane has all her permanent teeth.*

permission (pər mish'ən) *n.* words that allow someone to do something: *We were given permission to go home early.*

permit (pər'mit) *n.* a written form that gives you permission to do something: *a fishing permit.*

permit (pər mit') *v.* to allow, to let: *We are permitted to play here.* **permitting. permitted.**

person *n.* a human being.

personal *adj.* private, your own: *You may not read this letter because it's personal.* **personally** *adv.*

personality *n.* 1. what makes one person act differently from another: *The personalities of the twins are different. He always smiles, but she's very serious.* 2. a well-known person: *a TV personality.* *pl.* **personalities.**

perspiration *n.* wetness that is given off through your skin; sweat.

perspire *v.* to sweat. **perspiring. perspired.**

persuade (pər swād') *v.* to talk to someone and get him or her to agree to something. **persuading. persuaded.**

pest *n.* a person or thing that bothers you or causes trouble.

pester *v.* to annoy or bother: *My brother sometimes pesters me when I'm trying to read.* **pestering. pestered.**

pet *n.* an animal friend that you keep and take care of. *v.* to pat gently: *to pet a dog.* **petting. petted.**

petal *n.* one of the brightly coloured parts of a flower.

pew (pyü) *n.* a long wooden bench in a church.

pharmacy (far'mə sē) *n.* a drug store. *pl.* **pharmacies.**

pheasant (fez'ənt) *n.* a wild bird with long, brightly coloured tail feathers.

phone (fōn) *n., v.* short for **telephone. phoning. phoned.**

phonograph (fō'nə graf) *n.* a record player.

photo, photograph (fō'tō, fō'tə graf) *n.* a picture taken with a camera.

photographer (fə tog'rə fər) 1. any person who takes photographs. 2. a person whose job is to take photographs.

physical (fiz'ə kəl) *n.* a regular visit to your doctor, when he or she checks your health. *adj.* having to do with your body: *Physical exercise is the exercise of your body.*

pianist (pē'ə nist) *n.* a person who plays the piano.

piano *n.* a large musical instrument with black and white keys. *pl.* **pianos.**

pick *n.* a pointed tool used for breaking up hard ground. *v.* 1. to gather, one by one: *to pick berries.* 2. to choose: *Rick picked two library books.* **picking. picked.**

pickerel *n.* a large fish that lives in lakes and rivers. *pl.* **pickerel.**

pickle *n.* 1. the salt water or vinegar in which certain foods are preserved. 2. a cucumber preserved in pickle. *v.* to place vegetables or other foods in pickle to preserve them. **pickling. pickled.**

pickled *adj.* preserved in pickle: *a pickled beet, pickled watermelon rind.*

pickpocket *n.* a thief who steals things from people's pockets.

picnic *n.* an outdoor meal. *v.* to go out and have a meal in the open air. **picnicking. picnicked.**

picture (pik'chər) *n.* a drawing, painting, or photograph. *v.* 1. to draw or paint a picture. 2. to imagine: *Close your eyes and picture yourself in a different land.* **picturing. pictured.**

pie *n.* fruit or meat baked in pastry.

piece (pēs) *n.* 1. a bit or part: *a piece of cake.* 2. one item: *a piece of mail.* 3. one of the movable parts in a board game: *a chess piece.*

pier (pēr) *n.* a road that stretches out into the water.

pierce (pērs) *v.* to stab and make a hole in: *The thorn pierced Indira's skin.* **piercing. pierced.**

pig *n.* a farm animal raised for its meat: *Pork chops, bacon, and ham are from the pig.*

pigeon (pij'ən) *n.* a medium-sized bird, sometimes kept as a pet: *Some pigeons are trained to carry messages.*

pike *n.* 1. a long, thin fish that lives in lakes and rivers. 2. a spear with a heavy steel head.

pile *n.* a number of things, lying one on top of another: *a pile of clothing.* *v.* to heap up: *to pile up papers.* **piling. piled.**

pilgrim *n.* a person who travels, often by walking, to a holy place.

pill *n.* a little tablet or ball of medicine to be swallowed.

pillar *n.* a large post that supports the roof of a building.

pillow *n.* a cushion for resting your head on.

pilot *n.* 1. the person who flies an airplane. 2. the person who steers a ship into port.

pimple *n.* a small bump on the skin.

pin *n.* 1. a small, straight piece of wire with a head at one end and a point at the other. 2. an ornament worn on clothing: *a diamond pin.* 3. one of the pieces to be knocked down in the game of bowling. *v.* to fasten with a pin. **pinning. pinned.** (*opp.* **unpin.**)

pinch *n.* 1. a squeeze with the thumb and a finger. 2. a small amount: *a pinch of salt.* *v.* to squeeze between the thumb and a finger. **pinching. pinched.**

pine *n.* a tall tree with cones, and leaves that look like green needles.

pineapple *n.* a large, sweet fruit that grows in hot places: *The pineapple plant has stiff, prickly leaves.*

ping-pong *n.* table tennis; a game played on a marked table, in which the players use paddles to hit a plastic ball over a net.

pink *n.* a very light red colour. *adj.* having this colour.

pint *n.* a measure of capacity, equal to about 0.5 L.

pinto *n.* a spotted horse or pony. *pl.* **pintos.**

pioneer *n.* 1. one of the first people who go to live in a new place. 2. someone who is the first to do something.

pipe *n.* 1. a long tube that carries gas, water, or other substances. 2. a musical instrument shaped like a tube. 3. a tube with a small bowl at one end in which tobacco is burned: *My uncle smokes a pipe.*

pipeline *n.* a line of pipes, sometimes very long, for carrying gas, oil, and other substances.

piracy (pī'rə sē) *n.* robbery at sea.

pirate *n.* someone who attacks and robs ships while they are on the sea.

pistol *n.* a small gun fired from one hand.

pit *n.* 1. any deep hole in the ground. 2. a hard seed or stone in a fruit: *a peach pit.*

pitch *n.* a throw of the baseball to the batter. *v.* 1. to toss: *to pitch a ball.* 2. to set up: *to pitch a tent.* **pitching. pitched.**

pitcher (pich'ər) *n.* 1. a large jug. 2. the baseball player who tosses or pitches the ball.

pitchfork *n.* a long fork used for tossing hay.

pity *n.* a feeling of sorrow for people in trouble. *v.* to feel sorrow for: *Norman pitied his friend who was in pain.* **pitying. pitied.** he **pities.**

pivot (piv′ət) *n.* a pin or point on which a wheel or other object turns.

pizza (pēt′sə) *n.* a flat dough covered with tomato sauce, cheese, and other foods; it is baked until crusty.

place *n.* a position, spot, or location: *a place at the table; a place of worship.* *v.* to put something in a certain spot: *Ted placed the books on the shelf.* **placing. placed.**
in place of instead of: *I used paints in place of crayons.*
take place to happen: *Describe the events that take place in the story.*

plague (plāg) *n.* a very dangerous disease that spreads quickly.

plaid (plad) *n.* 1. a pattern made of crisscrossed stripes. 2. a cloth woven or printed with such a pattern.

plain *n.* a large area of flat or almost flat, treeless land: *the Saskatchewan plains.* *adj.* 1. clear, easy to see or understand: *It is plain to see that you are not well.* 2. simple, not fancy: *Do you want your cake plain or with ice cream?*

plan *n.* an outline or idea of something to be done: *We made plans for a holiday.* *v.* to think about doing something and to make some arrangements: *to plan a picnic.* **planning. planned.**

plane *n.* 1. a tool used for smoothing wood. 2. short for **airplane.**

planet *n.* one of the heavenly bodies that move around the sun: *The nine planets are Mercury, Venus, Earth, Mars, Jupiter, Saturn, Uranus, Neptune, and Pluto.*

planetarium *n.* a building where there are displays on the stars and planets.

plank *n.* a long, flat piece of wood.

plant *n.* 1. any living thing that is not an animal: *a tomato plant, a house plant.* 2. the buildings and equipment used in manufacturing something: *a steel plant.* *v.* to put in the ground to grow. **planting. planted.**

plaster *n.* a paste of sand, lime, and water, that hardens when dry: *We put plaster in the holes in the wall.* *v.* to use this paste: *to plaster a wall.* **plastering. plastered.**

plastic *n.* a manufactured material that, when heated, can be shaped into different objects. *adj.* made of this material.

plasticine *n.* a soft, clay-like substance used for modelling.

plate *n.* 1. a dish, round and almost flat. 2. in baseball, the home base.

plateau (pla tō′) *n.* a raised area of flat land. *pl.* **plateaus.**

platform *n.* a raised surface: *a railway platform.*

platter *n.* a large plate on which food is often served.

platypus (plat′ə pəs) *n.* an Australian animal that has brown fur, webbed feet, and a wide bill. *pl.* **playtypuses** or **platypi** (plat′ə pī).

play *n.* 1. an action in a game: *Bob made a terrific play and saved the game.* 2. a stage show: *a school play.* *v.* 1. to take part in sports or games: *to play checkers.* 2. to act or pretend: *to play monsters.* 3. to perform on a musical instrument: *to play the drums.* **playing. played.** she **plays.**

player *n.* a person who plays or performs: *a hockey player.*

playful *adj.* full of fun: *a playful kitten.*
playfully *adv.*

playground *n.* a piece of land on which to play.

playoff *n.* 1. an extra game, played to break a tie. 2. a series of games played to decide the championship.

plaza *n.* 1. a shopping centre. 2. a public square in a city or town.

pleasant (plez'ənt) *adj.* nice, friendly, pleasing: *It was a pleasant day. Raju is a pleasant person.* (*opp.* **unpleasant.**)

please *v.* 1. to give someone happiness: *We pleased her with our gift.* 2. to choose, to wish to do: *Do as you please.* 3. a polite word used when you ask for something: *Please may I come in?* **pleasing. pleased.**

pleasure (plezh'ər) *n.* enjoyment, a feeling of being pleased.

pledge *n.* a very serious promise: *a Scout pledge. v.* to make such a promise. **pledging. pledged.**

plenty *n.* a full supply, more than enough.

pliers *n. pl.* a tool used for bending or cutting wire.

plot *n.* 1. a small piece of ground: *a vegetable plot.* 2. the main points of a story: *The plot was about a burglar who was caught by a puppy.* 3. a secret plan: *a plot to rob a bank. v.* to make secret plans. **plotting. plotted.**

plough, plow *n.* 1. a machine used for turning over the soil. 2. a machine used for clearing away substances such as snow. *v.* 1. to turn over the soil. 2. to clear away snow. **ploughing. ploughed.**

pluck *v.* 1. to pull at: *to pluck the guitar strings.* 2. to pull all the feathers off: *to pluck a hen.* **plucking. plucked.**

plug *n.* 1. a piece of solid material that fills a hole. 2. a piece of electrical equipment at the end of a cord: *When a plug is placed into an outlet, it makes an electrical connection. v.* 1. to stop or fill up with a plug. 2. to fit an electrical plug into an outlet. **plugging. plugged.** (*opp.* **unplug.**)

plum *n.* a soft, juicy fruit; it is purple, red, green, or yellow in colour.

plumber (plum'ər) *n.* a person whose job is to work with the pipes and water systems of a building.

plume *n.* a bird's long and colourful feather.

plump *adj.* round and fat: *a plump chicken.*

plunge *v.* to dive, to throw yourself into: *Henry plunged into the water.* **plunging. plunged.**

plural *n.* more than one: *'Boys', 'cherries', 'mice' are the plurals of 'boy', 'cherry', 'mouse'.*

plus *prep.* added to: *3 plus 2 equals 5;* symbol is $+$.

plywood *n.* a strong wood made by gluing together thin layers of wood.

p.m. The time from noon to midnight: *I went to bed at 10 p.m.*

poach (pōch) *v.* 1. to cook an egg, without the shell, in boiling water. 2. to hunt or fish on someone's land without permission. **poaching. poached.**

pocket *n.* a small bag sewn into some clothes, for keeping things in.

pod *n.* a long part of some plants with seeds inside: *a pea pod.*

poem *n.* a piece of writing, usually short; its lines have a rhythm and often a rhyme.

poet *n.* a person who writes poems.

poetry *n.* poems: *a book of poetry.*

point *n.* 1. a small mark or dot. 2. a sharp end: *the point of a blade.* 3. the main idea: *What is the point of the story?* 4. a certain place: *a point of interest.* 5. a score in a game: *We won by a point. v.* 1. to show the direction of a place: *Point the way with your finger.* 2. to aim: *to point a gun.* **pointing. pointed.**

pointed *adj.* sharp, having a point.

pointer *n.* 1. a stick used for pointing at a chalkboard, map, poster, etc. 2. a hunting dog that has long ears and short hair.

poison *n.* a substance that could kill or injure a living creature. *v.* to harm or kill with such a substance. **poisoning. poisoned.**

poison ivy a plant that, when touched, causes people to break out in a rash.

poisonous *adj.* full of poison: *A poisonous snake can pass venom into you with its bite.*

poke *n.* a jab or light punch: *a poke in the ribs. v.* to jab or punch lightly. **poking. poked.**
to poke fun at to tease, to joke about.

poker *n.* 1. a metal rod used for stirring a fire. 2. a card game.

polar *adj.* having to do with the North or South Pole, or both.

polar bear a large white bear of the arctic regions.

pole *n.* 1. a long, thin, rounded piece of wood: *a flagpole.* 2. either of the two ends of a magnet. 3. **Pole** the North or South Pole, the ends of the earth's axis.

police (pə lēs´) *n. pl.* the men and women whose job it is to keep law and order. *v.* to guard or keep order: *to police a territory.* **policing. policed.**

policeman, policewoman, police officer *n.* a member of the police.

polio *n.* a serious illness that can cause the muscles to be paralysed.

polish (pol´ish) *v.* to make something smooth and shiny by rubbing it. **polishing. polished.**

Polish (pō´lish) *n.* the language spoken in Poland. *adj.* belonging to or coming from Poland.

polite *adj.* showing good manners, courteous. (*opp.* **impolite.**) **politely** *adv.*

politician (pol ə tish´ən) *n.* 1. someone busy with politics. 2. an elected government official.

politics *n. pl.* 1. opinions about the government: *My parents often read and talk about politics.* 2. the job of holding public office: *Karen would like to have a career in politics.*

polka *n.* 1. a type of lively dance. 2. the music to which you dance the polka.

polka dot a round dot placed over and over again to make a pattern.

pollen *n.* a yellowish powder in the centre of flowers.

pollute *v.* to make the air, land, or water dirty: *The oil polluted the ocean.* **polluting. polluted.**

pollution *n.* the waste substances in the air, land, or water.

pond *n.* a small lake.

pony *n.* a type of small horse. *pl.* **ponies.**

poodle *n.* a pet dog with very curly hair.

pool *n.* a small pond, sometimes made for swimming in.

poor *adj.* 1. having very little money. 2. not good: *poor work; poor weather.*

poorly *adv.* not well: *The work is poorly done.*

pop *n.* 1. a small bang. 2. a fizzy soft drink. *v.* 1. to make a small, sudden noise. 2. to move about quickly: *to pop out of bed.* **popping. popped.**

popcorn *n.* corn that bursts open and puffs out when heated.

Pope *n.* the leader of the Roman Catholic Church.

poplar *n.* a tree with soft wood, that grows very quickly.

poppy *n.* a wild or garden plant with brightly coloured flowers. *pl.* **poppies.**

popular *adj.* liked by a lot of people: *a popular person; a popular song.* (*opp.* **unpopular.**)

population *n.* the number of people in a place such as a city, province, or country: *The population of my town is about 30 000.*

porch *n.* a covered entrance to a building.

porcupine *n.* a gnawing animal that has sharp quills on its back and tail.

pore *n.* a tiny opening, as in your skin.

pork *n.* meat from a pig.

porpoise (por′pəs) *n.* an intelligent and friendly ocean animal that looks like a small whale.

porridge *n.* a breakfast food made by boiling oatmeal or other cereals in water.

port *n.* 1. a harbour or a town with a harbour. 2. the left side of a ship as you face the front or bow. (*opp.* **starboard.**)

portable (port′ə bəl) *adj.* light enough to be carried easily: *a portable TV.*

portage (por tazh′) *n.* the carrying of canoes, boats, and goods over land between one body of water and another. *v.* to carry such items between bodies of water. **portaging. portaged.**

portion *n.* a part: *Phil ate a small portion of pie.*

portrait (por′trət) *n.* a picture of someone, usually of the face.

pose (pōz) *n.* a position of the body: *Hold that pose until I take your picture!* *v.* to

hold a position for a picture: *Roger posed for the photograph.* **posing. posed.**

position *n.* 1. the place where someone or something is: *the position of the desk; my position on the team.* 2. a job: *My mother has a new position at work.*

positive *adj.* 1. completely sure: *I am positive that my best friend's birthday is in October.* 2. meaning 'yes' or 'all right': *When we asked for a cat, we received a positive answer.*

positively *adv.* for sure: *Positively no bike riding is allowed in this park.*

possess (pə zes′) *v.* to have, to own: *Mrs. Clark possesses two cars.* **possessing. possessed.**

possession *n.* something that you own.

possibility *n.* a chance of happening: *There is a good possibility that it will snow today.* *pl.* **possibilities.**

possible *adj.* able to happen: *It is possible that our team will win the championship.* (*opp.* **impossible.**)

possibly *adv.* perhaps: *Possibly, he has lost the way.*

post *n.* 1. a pole or pillar: *a metal post.* 2. a station or settlement: *a trading post.* 3. the sending or delivery of mail. *v.* 1. to stick on a wall or board: *to post a notice.* 2. to send letters and packages by mail. **posting. posted.**

postage *n.* the charge for sending a letter or package by mail.

postal code numbers and letters of the alphabet that are written on a piece of mail: *The postal code shows a postal delivery area.*

postcard *n.* a card that can be mailed without an envelope: *Some postcards have a picture on one side.*

poster *n.* a large sign or picture put up on a board or wall.

post office a government office where mail is received and sorted, and where you can buy stamps.

postpone *v.* to put off until later: *We postponed our visit until next week.* **postponing. postponed.**

posture (pos'chər) *n.* the way in which you stand: *My friend is trying to improve her posture. She walks with a book on top of her head.*

pot *n.* a deep and often roundish container.

potato (pə tā'tō) *n.* a vegetable that can be baked, boiled, fried, or made into chips: *A potato is a hard underground stem.* *pl.* **potatoes.**

pottery *n.* bowls, cups, flowerpots, and other things made of baked clay.

pouch *n.* a small bag in which to hold things: *A kangaroo carries her young in a pouch.*

poultry (pōl'trē) *n.* chickens, turkeys, geese, and ducks, raised for their meat and often for eggs.

pounce *v.* to swoop down on, to leap on: *The eagle pounced on the rabbit.* **pouncing. pounced.**

pound *n.* 1. a measure of mass or weight, equal to about 0.5 kg. 2. a unit of money used in Britain and some other countries. *v.* 1. to smash or hammer: *He pounded the box until it splintered.* 2. to beat heavily: *Don't pound on the door.* **pounding. pounded.**

pour (por) *v.* 1. to fall or flow: *The milk poured all over the place.* 2. to let liquid flow: *Please pour the milk.* **pouring. poured.**

powder *n.* something made into dust: *milk powder.*

power *n.* strength, force: *electric power.*

powerful *adj.* very strong: *a powerful wind.* **powerfully** *adv.*

practical *adj.* able to be carried out: *a practical plan.*

practical joke a joke in which something is done rather than said.

practically *adv.* almost, nearly: *It is practically time for bed.*

practice *n.* something done many times, so that you improve: *Jean has hockey practice on Tuesdays.*

practise, practice *v.* to do something many times in order to do it better: *Ray practises the piano every day.* **practising. practised.**

prairie *n.* a great stretch of level or rolling land with grass, but few or no trees.

Prairie Provinces Alberta, Saskatchewan, and Manitoba. The treeless area that stretches across these provinces is called **the Prairies.**

praise *n.* words telling that someone or something is very good. *v.* to say such words: *Everyone praised Joanne for rescuing the pup.* **praising. praised.**

prance *v.* to move in a lively way: *Horses prance on their back legs.* **prancing. pranced.**

prank *n.* a trick played on someone.

pray *v.* to speak to God. **praying. prayed.**

prayer (prār) *n.* words used in praying.

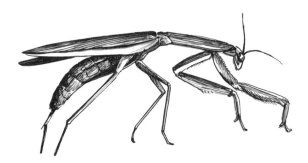

praying mantis an insect that eats grasshoppers and other things: *A praying mantis doubles up its large front legs.* *pl.* **praying mantises.**

preach *v.* 1. to speak on a religious subject. 2. to give advice, but sometimes to give too much. **preaching. preached.**

precious (presh'əs) *adj.* very valuable: *Jewels are precious stones.*

predict *v.* to say in advance that something will happen: *The weather office predicts rain.* **predicting. predicted.**

prediction *n.* an announcement in advance, of something that may happen: *The weather prediction is for heavy rain.*

preface (pref'əs) *n.* a short message found at the beginning of some books.

prefer (pri fər′) *v.* to like one thing more than another: *Joel prefers apples to oranges.* **preferring. preferred.**

prefix *n.* letters put at the beginning of a word to change its meaning: *When you put the prefix 'dis' in front of the word 'appear', you get 'disappear'.*

pregnant *adj.* having a baby developing inside the body.

prehistoric *adj.* living or existing a very long time ago, before history was written down: *a prehistoric animal.*

premier (prēm′yər, prēm′ēr) *n.* the head of a government; in Canada, the head of a provincial government.

preparation *n.* getting ready: *There is a lot of preparation needed for a party.*

prepare *v.* 1. to get ready: *We have to prepare for our visitors.* 2. to make a special food or mixture: *The druggist prepared the medicine.* **preparing. prepared.**

preposition *n.* a word that begins a group of words that tell about a person, place, or thing: *The ball went through the window and landed under the table.* The prepositions are *through* and *under.*

prescribe *v.* to order, usually to order as medicine. **prescribing. prescribed.**

prescription *n.* a doctor's order for medicine.

present (prez′ənt) *n.* 1. a gift to someone. 2. the time now, not the past. *adj.* attending, not absent: *How many people are present at the game?*

present (pri zent′) *v.* to give a prize or gift to someone: *The captain presented her team with T-shirts.* **presenting. presented.**

president *n.* 1. the chief officer of a club, class, company, etc. 2. the title of the head of certain governments: *the President of the United States.*

press *n.* 1. a machine used for printing. 2. a machine used to flatten clothes. *v.* 1. to push or squeeze: *to press a button.* 2. to flatten clothes with an iron. **pressing. pressed.**

pressure (presh′ər) *n.* a force or steady push against something.

pretend *v.* to claim that something is true, when it is not: *Let's pretend we are doctors.* **pretending. pretended.**

pretty *adj.* nice-looking, attractive, charming: *a pretty ring, a prettier one, the prettiest ring in the store.*

pretzel *n.* a hard, salted, and usually twisted cracker.

prevent *v.* to stop something from happening, or to stop someone from doing something: *Penny held on to her little brother to prevent him from falling.* **preventing. prevented.**

previous (prē′vē əs) *adj.* earlier, the one before: *We went by bus on Tuesday, but walked the previous day.*

prey (prā) *n.* an animal or animals hunted by another for food: *Rabbits are the prey of foxes.*

price *n.* the cost of something.

priceless *adj.* beyond any price, so valuable that it cannot be bought: *The paintings in the museum are priceless.*

prick *n.* a small scratch or stab. *v.* to stab with a sharp point: *The thorn pricked me.* **pricking. pricked.**

pride *n.* 1. a feeling of pleasure because you have done well: *She takes pride in her work.* 2. a high opinion of yourself: *His pride keeps him from saying that he is wrong.* *v.* to rate highly: *We pride ourselves on our prize-winning cookies.* **priding. prided.**

pried, pries see **pry.**

priest (prēst) *n.* a minister in certain religions.

primary *adj.* first in time or importance: *The first grades are called the primary grades.*

prime *adj.* first in importance.

Prime Minister the chief officer of some countries, including Canada.

prince *n.* 1. the son of a king or queen. 2. the title given to certain noblemen.

Prince Edward Island province in the Gulf of St. Lawrence, north of New Brunswick and Nova Scotia; capital is Charlottetown. Short form: **P.E.I.** A person living in or born in Prince Edward Island is a **Prince Edward Islander.**

princess *n.* 1. the daughter of a king or queen. 2. the wife of a prince.

principal *n.* the head of a school. *adj.* highest in importance or interest: *The Parliament Buildings are the principal interests of Ottawa.*

principle *n.* 1. an important rule, law, or belief: *a scientific principle.* 2. a rule of conduct: *'Honesty is the best policy' is a famous principle.*

print *n.* 1. printed letters, not script. 2. a mark pressed on the ground by your foot (a footprint), or on paper by an inky finger (a fingerprint). *v.* 1. to make words or pictures, using a printing machine. 2. to write, using separate letters. **printing. printed.**

prison *n.* a jail, a building where criminals are kept.

prisoner *n.* a person kept in prison or captured in war.

private (prī'vət) *n.* a soldier in the army who is not an officer. *adj.* not to be shared with others: *This room is private. Please knock before you come in.*

privilege (priv'ə lij) *n.* a special favour or right.

prize *n.* a reward for doing well or winning a contest.

probable *adj.* likely to happen or to be true: *It is probable that we will win the game, but it is not completely certain.*

probably *adv.* very likely.

problem *n.* a puzzle or question that is not easy to answer.

proceed *v.* to continue, to go on: *Let's proceed with the plan.* **proceeding. proceeded.**

process (pros'es, prō'ses) *n.* 1. a method of manufacture: *a new process for making glass.* 2. the state of being worked on: *The house is in the process of being built.* *v.* to treat in a special way: *We process fruits to make them into jams.* **processing. processed.**

procession (prō sesh'ən) *n.* a large number of people marching or riding on some special occasion.

produce (prə dyüs') *v.* 1. to bring out: *Stefan produced his ticket at the entrance gate.* 2. to make: *The factory produces jam.* **producing. produced.**

produce (prod'yüs) *n.* vegetables and fruit sold in food stores.

product *n.* something that is made: *Milk is a dairy product.*

production *n.* manufacture: *The production of cars is an important industry.*

profession *n.* a job requiring special education, such as that of a doctor, lawyer, accountant, or engineer.

professional *adj.* 1. doing as a job what others do for fun: *a professional musician.* 2. having to do with a job that requires special education: *A doctor is a professional person.*

professor *n.* a teacher having high rank in a university.

profile *n.* a side view, usually of a person's face.

profit *n.* the money you make by selling something for more than you paid.

program, programme *n.* 1. a written outline of the things to be seen or heard at a concert, play, game, etc. 2. a performance: *a TV program.*

progress (prog'res, prō'gres) *n.* a forward movement or improvement: *The students show progress in spelling.*

progress (prə gres') *v.* to move forward, go ahead, or show improvement. **progressing. progressed.**

prohibit *v.* to forbid or prevent: *The notice says, 'Bicycling Prohibited'.* **prohibiting. prohibited.**

project (proj'ekt) *n.* a plan or activity to be done: *Our project is to collect different leaves.*

project (prə jekt') *v.* 1. to throw forward: *Irene projected pictures on a screen. Prem projected his voice from the stage.* 2. to stick out: *The roof projects over the walls of the house.* **projecting. projected.**

projector *n.* a machine used to show a movie or pictures on a screen.

promise *n.* 1. words saying that you are sure to do something: *I made a promise that I would walk the dog.* 2. a reason for hope: *Your story shows promise.* *v.* to say that you will be sure to do something: *Bill promised to return Heidi's book.* **promising. promised.**

promote *v.* 1. to give a higher position to: *The club's vice-president was promoted to president.* 2. to help in the growth or change of something: *Too much sugar promotes tooth decay.* **promoting. promoted.**

promotion *n.* a better job, a higher position: *My dad was given a promotion at work.*

prompt *adj.* quick, done at once: *Ralph received a prompt reply to his letter.* **promptly** *adv.*

prong *n.* one of the pointed ends of a fork.

pronoun *n.* a word used instead of a noun: *Bill said he would ride the bicycle.* The word *he* is a pronoun. Some other pronouns are *I, you, who, what,* and *this.*

pronounce *n.* 1. to say the sound of a word: *The word 'photo' is pronounced 'fō'tō'.* 2. to say that something will be: *The minister said, 'I now pronounce you husband and wife'.* **pronouncing. pronounced.**

pronunciation *n.* the way you say a word: *The pronunciation of 'phone' is 'fōn'.*

proof *n.* something that shows beyond doubt that a thing is true: *The footprints in the mud are proof that someone came here.*

– proof a suffix meaning 'giving protection against': **waterproof** means not letting water pass through; **bullet-proof** means safe from bullets.

prop *n.* 1. a support: *The sagging plant needs a prop.* 2. an object needed for a play: *Niki is in charge of props. She must find a pillow, an old bike, and an armchair.* *v.* to support with a prop: *Prop up the plant with a stick.* **propping. propped.**

propel (prə pel') *v.* to drive forward: *to propel a plane.* **propelling. propelled.**

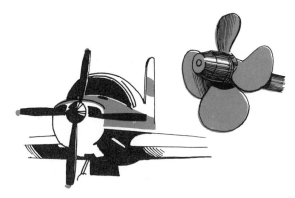

propeller *n.* a device with blades that drives forward a ship or plane.

proper *adj.* right or suitable: *This is the proper way to saw wood.* **properly** *adv.*

property *n.* anything a person owns, especially a building or land: *This property is for sale.* pl. **properties.**

prophet (prof'it) *n.* 1. a person who tells what will happen in the future. 2. a person who believes he or she has received a message from God to be passed on to others.

propose *v.* 1. to suggest something: *Claude proposed that we take a class trip.* 2. to make an offer of marriage. **proposing. proposed.**

prosecute *v.* to bring someone to trial before a court of law. **prosecuting. prosecuted.**

protect *v.* to defend from harm, to guard. **protecting. protected.**

protection *n.* defence, shelter: *An umbrella gives protection from the rain.*

protest *v.* to object, to complain: *The citizens protested against the smoke from the factory.* **protesting. protested.**

Protestant *n.* a member of a Christian but not Roman Catholic or Eastern Orthodox church: *United Church members, Methodists, Presbyterians, Baptists, and many others are Protestants.*

proud *adj.* 1. pleased at having done something well: *Angie was proud of her figure-skating trophy.* 2. conceited, having too high an opinion of yourself: *That proud man thinks he is always right.*

prove (prüv) *v.* 1. to show for certain that something is true. 2. to turn out to be: *Jennifer proved to be a good tennis player.* **proving. proved.**

provide *v.* to supply what is needed: *The teacher provided pencils and paper for the test.* **providing. provided.**

provided *conj.* if, on the condition that: *We'll go to the game, provided it's not raining.*

province *n.* one of the main parts of some countries, such as Canada.

provincial (prə vin'shəl) *adj.* having to do with provinces or a province.

prowl *v.* to move around silently, often looking for something to eat or steal: *The fox prowled around the chicken coop.* **prowling. prowled.**

prowler *n.* a person who prowls around, a thief.

prune *n.* a dried plum. *v.* to cut short the unwanted branches of a tree or bush. **pruning. pruned.**

pry *v.* 1. to look with curiosity: *My cat is always prying in the closet.* 2. to raise or move with force: *Can you pry the lid off the paint can?* **prying. pried.** he **pries.**

P.S. short for **postscript**: *When you want to add a message at the end of a letter, you first write, 'P.S.'*

psalm (sahm) *n.* a religious song or poem.

public *adj.* open to or belonging to everyone: *a public park.*

publish *v.* to prepare a book, newspaper, or magazine for sale. **publishing. published.**

puck *n.* a hard rubber disc used in hockey.

pudding (pǔd'ing) *n.* a soft, sweet dessert: *chocolate pudding.*

puddle *n.* a small pool of water.

puff *n.* a quick blow of breath, smoke, or wind. *v.* 1. to blow out smoke, steam, or air. 2. to swell up. **puffing. puffed.**

pull *v.* 1. to draw towards you: *Pull the door open.* 2. to drag along: *The horse pulled the wagon.* **pulling. pulled.**

pulley *n.* a wheel that has a groove around the outside part: *A pulley is attached to a rope. It is used to pull heavy things.*

pulp *n.* 1. the soft part of fruits. 2. ground-up wood mixed with chemicals, that is used to make paper.

pump *n.* a machine that forces liquid or gases into or out of things: *a bicycle pump.* *v.* to work such a machine. **pumping. pumped.**

pumpkin *n.* a large, roundish, orange fruit, used for pies, for animal feed, and for making jack-o'-lanterns.

punch *n.* 1. a tool used for making holes. 2. a quick hit with the fist. 3. a drink made of a mixture of liquids such as fruit juices. *v.* 1. to stamp a hole in. 2. to hit with the fist. **punching. punched.**

punctuation *n.* the using of periods, commas, and other marks: *Punctuation helps to make the meaning of a sentence clear.*

punctuation marks marks used in writing to help make the meaning clear: *Some punctuation marks are commas, periods, and question marks.*

punish *v.* to make someone suffer for a wrong he or she has done. **punishing. punished.**

punishment *n.* the penalty a person must suffer for doing something wrong.

pup, puppy *n.* a young dog. *pl.* **pups** or **puppies.**

pupa (pyü′pə) *n.* the stage between the larva and the adult in the growth of many insects. *pl.* **pupae** (pyü′pē).

pupil *n.* 1. someone who is being taught at school. 2. the opening in the centre of your eye.

puppet *n.* a doll that can be moved and made to perform, usually on a stage.

puppeteer *n.* a person who makes or works puppets.

purchase (pər′chəs) *v.* to buy something: *I purchased a scarf before the winter.* **purchasing. purchased.**

pure (pyür) *adj.* clean, not mixed with other things: *pure wool.* (*opp.* **impure.**)

purple *n.* a colour made by mixing blue and red. *adj.* having this colour.

purpose (pər′pəs) *n.* the reason for doing something: *The purpose of my visit is to ask for your help.*
on purpose knowing what will happen when you do something: *Did you spill the water on purpose, or was it an accident?*

purr *n.* the sound that a happy cat makes. *v.* to make such a sound. **purring. purred.**

purse *n.* a small bag in which money, keys, and other things are kept.

push *n.* a little shove. *v.* to press against, to try to move something. **pushing. pushed.**

pussycat *n.* a cat.

put *v.* to place something somewhere: *Put the plate on the table.* **putting. put.**
to put off to delay till later: *We put off our visit until our uncle felt better.*
to put up with to make the best of: *At camp we have to put up with hard beds and simple food.*

putty (put′ē) *n.* a soft greyish mixture used for holding glass in a window frame and for filling in cracks.

puzzle *n.* a question that is hard to answer, or a problem that you work out for fun: *a jigsaw puzzle, a crossword puzzle.*

pyjamas, pajamas *n. pl.* a set of clothes to sleep in.

pyramid (pir′ə mid) *n.* a structure that has a square base and four sides shaped like triangles: *The points of the sides of a pyramid meet at the top.*

q

quack *n.* the noise made by a duck. *v.* to make such a noise. **quacking. quacked.**

quaint *adj.* very old-fashioned in a pleasant or interesting way: *My grandparents live in a quaint little cottage.*

quake *v.* to shake, to tremble: *The bridge quaked as the heavy trucks moved along.* **quaking. quaked.**

qualify (kwol′i fī) *v.* to show the ability needed to join certain teams, to get into certain schools, or to join certain professions: *Can you qualify for the team?* **qualifying. qualified.** he **qualifies.**

quality *n.* 1. how good or bad a thing is: *This fruit is of poor quality.* 2. something special that makes a person or animal what it is: *One of the qualities of fur is softness.* pl. **qualities.**

quantity *n.* an amount: *I have a large quantity of records.* pl. **quantities.**

quarrel (kwor′əl) *v.* to disagree and argue, often using angry words. **quarrelling. quarrelled.**

quarry *n.* a place where stone for buildings is dug or cut. pl. **quarries.**

quart *n.* a measure of liquid, equal to about 1 L.

quarter *n.* 1. one of four equal parts: *Divide the paper into quarters.* 2. a 25-cent coin of Canada and the United States.

quarterback *n.* the football player who calls the signals for the team.

quartz *n.* a hard mineral: *Some types of quartz are clear, and other types have brilliant colours.*

quay (kē) *n.* a place where ships load and unload. pl. **quays.**

Québec *n.* province between Ontario on the west, Labrador and New Brunswick on the east; capital is Québec. Short form: **Que.** or **P.Q.** A person born in or living in Québec is a **Quebecker,** or **Québecois** (kā bek wah′).

queen *n.* 1. a woman who is ruler of a country or a king's wife. 2. a playing card with a picture of a queen on it. 3. a piece in the game of chess. 4. a female bee or ant that lays eggs.

queer *adj.* strange, unusual.

quench *v.* to put an end to: *I need another drink to quench my thirst.* **quenching. quenched.**

quest *n.* a search: *The explorers set out on a quest for new lands.*

question *n.* something asked: *Do you have any questions before the test begins?* *v.* to ask in order to get information: *The lawyer questioned the witness.* **questioning. questioned.**

question mark the punctuation mark (?) put at the end of a sentence that asks a question.

quick *adj.* fast, speedy: *a quick train.* **quickly** *adv.*

quicksand *n.* loose, wet sand into which you can sink.

quiet *adj.* noiseless, peaceful, calm. **quietly** *adv.*

quill *n.* 1. a large, stiff feather. 2. one of the stiff, sharp hairs on a porcupine.

quilt *n.* a thick, padded bed covering.

quit *v.* to give up: *My brother quit his job because he had too much homework.* **quitting. quit.**

quite *adv.* 1. completely: *I felt quite alone when my best friend moved away.* 2. very: *It was quite cold.* 3. really: *This is quite a surprise!*

quiver *n.* a case for arrows. *v.* to shake, to tremble: *The dog quivered with fear during the storm.* **quivering. quivered.**

quiz *n.* a short test. pl. **quizzes.** *v.* to give such a test. **quizzing. quizzed.**

quotation *n.* 1. a repeating of someone's

exact words. 2. a short passage from a book: *I write down quotations from my favourite stories.*

quotation marks the punctuation marks ("...") put at the beginning and at the end of a quotation.

quote *n.* a quotation. *v.* to repeat someone's exact words. **quoting. quoted.**

r

rabbi *n.* a Jewish religious leader. *pl.* **rabbis.**

rabbit *n.* a small, furry animal with long ears; it lives in holes which it digs in the ground.

rabies *n.* a very serious disease that some animals get: *People can catch rabies if bitten by an animal that has this disease.*

raccoon *n.* a small greyish-brown animal with dark patches around its eyes; its bushy tail is ringed with bands of dark fur.

race *n.* 1. a contest to see who can go the fastest. 2. a group of living things of the same kind: *the human race. v.* to move or go very fast. **racing. raced.**

rack *n.* a frame on which to hang things: *a towel rack.*

racket *n.* 1. a loud noise: *Don't make such a racket!* 2. a handle and frame with a net of strings, used in tennis and other games.

radiator (rā′dē ā tər) *n.* 1. a heating device used for warming a room. 2. the part of a car that keeps the engine cool.

radio *n.* 1. a way of sending and receiving words and other sounds by electric waves. 2. a machine for sending or receiving such sounds. *pl.* **radios.** *v.* to send a message by radio: *We radioed the ship for help.* **radioing. radioed.** she **radios.**

radish *n.* a small, red-skinned vegetable used in salads.

radius (rā′dē əs) *n.* a straight line going from the centre to the outside of a circle or sphere. *pl.* **radii** (rā′dē ī) or **radiuses.**

raft *n.* logs or planks tied together to make a kind of boat.

rafter *n.* one of the beams that holds up a roof.

rag *n.* a small piece of cloth, usually used for cleaning.

rage *n.* great anger: *He left the room in a rage.*

ragged (rag′əd) *adj.* untidy, having an uneven edge: *Straighten the ragged edge with a pair of scissors.*

raid *n.* a sudden attack: *an enemy raid. v.* to attack suddenly. **raiding. raided.**

rail *n.* 1. a long, narrow bar made of metal or wood: *a fence rail, a rail on a railway track.* 2. railway: *Do you like to travel by rail?*

railing *n.* a fence made of rails.

railway *n.* 1. a track of steel rails on which trains run. 2. tracks, stations, trains, and the people who manage them.

rain *n.* water falling in drops from the clouds. *v.* to fall in drops like rain. **raining. rained.**

rainbow *n.* an arch of colours in the sky: *A rainbow is made by the sun shining through rain or mist.*

raincoat *n.* a waterproof coat.

rainy *adj.* having much rain: *a rainy day, a rainier day, the rainiest day of the year.*

raise *n.* an increase in something, usually money: *Mom got a raise in pay.* *v.* 1. to lift up: *to raise a window.* 2. to grow: *The farmer raises corn.* 3. to bring up: *to raise a family.* 4. to collect: *to raise money.* **raising. raised.**

raisin *n.* a small dried grape, used in cakes, cookies, cereals, etc.

rake *n.* a garden tool that has a row of spikes attached to one end of a long handle. *v.* to move with a rake: *Rosemary raked the leaves off the grass.* **raking. raked.**

rally *n.* a meeting or get-together: *a Cub rally.* *pl.* **rallies.**

ram (*fem.* **ewe**) *n.* a male sheep. *v.* 1. to crash into: *In the chase, one car rammed another.* 2. to force down: *We rammed the post into the ground.* **ramming. rammed.**

ramble *v.* 1. to wander about, to go for a long walk: *We rambled through the forest.* 2. to talk or write in a way that confuses people: *Don't ramble on. Just talk about one thing at a time.* **rambling. rambled.**

ramp *n.* a short, sloping road connecting different levels: *a highway ramp.*

ran see **run.**

ranch *n.* a large farm on which cattle, horses, or sheep are raised.

rang see **ring.**

range *n.* 1. a line, a row: *a range of hills.* 2. land for cattle, sheep, or horses to roam on. 3. a stove for cooking. 4. the distance between certain limits: *a wide range of prices.* *v.* 1. to roam, to wander: *The cattle ranged over the hills.* 2. to vary between certain limits: *The prices range from a quarter to a dollar.* **ranging. ranged.**

ranger *n.* a person whose job is to look after a large area of forest.

Ranger *n.* a senior Girl Guide.

rank *n.* a position, a level: *Jack's father held the rank of captain in the army.*

ransom *n.* money paid for the return of someone who has been taken prisoner or kidnapped.

rap *n.* a quick, sharp tap. *v.* to tap sharply: *to rap at the door.* **rapping. rapped.**

rapid *adj.* very fast. **rapidly** *adv.*

rapids *n. pl.* a part of a river where the water moves very fast, often over rocks.

rare *adj.* 1. not happening often, not often found: *Sally found a rare flower in the woods.* **rarely** *adv.* 2. not cooked very much: *a rare steak.*

rascal *n.* a mischievous or nasty person.

rash *n.* small spots that break out on your skin.

rasp *n.* a harsh, grating sound; the sound of a file moving against wood. *v.* to make such a sound: *He rasped out an order.* **rasping. rasped.**

raspberry *n.* a small, red, juicy fruit that grows on bushes. *pl.* **raspberries.**

rat *n.* a long-tailed, gnawing animal that looks like a large mouse.

rate *n.* 1. speed: *The car went at a fast rate.* 2. a price, an amount: *What is the rate of pay for that job?* *v.* to have a certain rank: *Vicky rates high as a ball player.* **rating. rated.**

rather *adv.* 1. more gladly: *Mark would rather eat meat than fish.* 2. more than a little bit: *I felt rather cold standing outside.*

ration (rash′ən, rā′shən) *n.* a certain amount or share: *All the drivers were given a weekly ration of gas.* *v.* to allow only certain amounts of something: *The government rationed gas.* **rationing. rationed.**

rattle *n.* 1. the sound made by shaking a lot of hard things together. 2. a baby's toy that makes this sound. *v.* to make such a sound. **rattling. rattled.**

rattlesnake *n.* a poisonous snake that makes a rattling sound with its tail.

rave *v.* to talk excitedly, to be very pleased about: *Everyone raved over Bill's excellent performance.* **raving. raved.**

raven *n.* a bird that looks like a crow, but is larger.

ravine (rə vēn′) *n.* a deep, narrow valley.

raw *adj.* 1. not cooked: *raw meat.* 2. very cold: *a raw day.*

ray *n.* a thin beam: *a ray of sunshine through the clouds.*

razor *n.* a sharp cutting instrument used for shaving off hair.

RCMP short for **Royal Canadian Mounted Police.**

re- 1. a prefix meaning 'again': to **reopen** means to open again. 2. a prefix meaning 'back': to **repay** means to pay back.

reach *v.* 1. to stretch out and touch or get: *Can you reach the cereal on the shelf?* 2. to arrive at: *They reached the city in the morning.* **reaching. reached.**

read *v.* to look at words and understand their meaning. **reading. read** (red).

reader *n.* 1. a book that helps to teach reading. 2. a person who reads.

ready (red′ē) *adj.* prepared, willing: *Anna said she was ready to go.*

real *adj.* 1. true, not imaginary: *a real person, not a ghost.* 2. not artificial or made-up: *These are real pearls.*

realize *v.* to understand clearly: *I didn't realize that I was so early.* **realizing. realized.**

really *adv.* truly: *I really mean what I say!*

rear *n.* the back part: *the rear of a train.* *v.* 1. to bring up: *to rear children.* 2. to lift up: *The bull reared its head.* **rearing. reared.**

reason *n.* an explanation: *What is the reason for your absence?*

reasonable (rē′zən ə bəl) *adj.* 1. sensible, not foolish: *a reasonable person.* 2. not expensive: *a reasonable price.* (*opp.* **unreasonable**.)

rebel (reb′əl) *n.* a person who fights against the people in charge and refuses to obey their orders.

rebel (rē bel′) *v.* to refuse to follow orders, to be a rebel. **rebelling. rebelled.**

rebellion *n.* a fight against your own government.

rebound *n.* a bouncing back: *In handball, you hit the ball on the rebound.* *v.* to bounce back: *The ball rebounded from the wall.* **rebounding. rebounded.**

recall *v.* 1. to call someone or something back: *The automobile company recalled a thousand cars.* 2. to remember: *I cannot recall his name.* **recalling. recalled.**

receipt (ri sēt′) *n.* a note saying that you have paid for something.

receive *v.* to take what is given to you: *Dan received many presents.* **receiving. received.**

receiver *n.* 1. the part of a telephone that you put to your ear. 2. a person who receives something.

recent *adj.* made, happened, or done a short while ago: *the recent birth of a baby.* **recently** *adv.*

recess *n.* a short rest period.

recipe (res′ə pē) *n.* directions on how to make something to eat or drink.

recital *n.* a public performance, often by pupils: *a dance recital.*

recite *v.* to tell a story or a poem from memory. **reciting. recited.**

reckless *adj.* being careless and risking danger: *Reckless driving causes many accidents.*

recognize *v.* to know again: *I almost didn't recognize my aunt because she was wearing a wig.* **recognizing. recognized.**

recommend *v.* 1. to speak in favour of someone or something: *I can recommend this cake. It is very good.* 2. to suggest: *I recommend that you try another store.* **recommending. recommended.**

record (rek'ərd) *n.* 1. a written account or diary: *When we have a meeting, we keep a record of everything that is said.* 2. the top performance: *He holds the record for running.* 3. a flat disc, to be played on a record player.

record (ri kord') *v.* 1. to write down events: *He recorded the amount of money he spent.* 2. to put sounds on a tape or record: *Music is recorded in a special room.* **recording. recorded.**

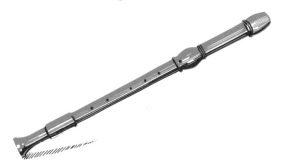

recorder *n.* 1. a wind instrument made of wood. 2. a person whose job is taking notes. 3. a machine that records sounds on a tape.

recover *v.* 1. to get better after an illness. 2. to get something back: *We recovered the stolen car within a week.* **recovering. recovered.**

recovery *n.* 1. getting well after illness: *We wish you a speedy recovery.* 2. getting back something that was lost, stolen, or sent away: *the recovery of a spaceship.* *pl.* **recoveries.**

recreation *n.* games, amusement, something done for enjoyment.

recruit (ri krüt') *n.* a new member of the army, navy, police force, or other group.

rectangle *n.* a figure that has four sides and four square angles: *Oblongs and squares are rectangles.*

rectangular *adj.* having the shape of a rectangle.

recycle *v.* to put into use again: *We recycled the old papers and made bricks.* **recycling. recycled.**

red *n.* the colour of blood. *adj.* having such a colour.

reduce *v.* to make something smaller: *The price of yesterday's bread is reduced today.* **reducing. reduced.**

reduction *n.* a reducing or being reduced: *There was a reduction on the price of that dress.*

reed *n.* a tall grass that grows at the edge of water.

reef *n.* a line of rocks or sand just below the surface of the sea.

reel *n.* 1. a spool-like frame used for winding thread, film, fishing line, etc. 2. a Scottish dance.

re-elect *v.* to elect again. **re-electing. re-elected.**

re-entry *n.* the return of a spacecraft to the earth's atmosphere. *pl.* **re-entries.**

refer (ri fər') *v.* to send or direct for help or information: *I needed to list the oceans. The librarian referred me to an atlas.* **referring. referred.**

referee *n.* someone who takes charge of a game or contest and sees that the rules are obeyed.

reference *n.* 1. something used for information: *A dictionary is a book of reference.* 2. a statement about a person's ability: *My mother has good references from the people she worked for.*

reflect *v.* to give back a picture or light, as water or a mirror does. **reflecting. reflected.**

reflection *n.* a picture or light, reflected from a shiny surface.

refreshments *n.pl.* something to eat or drink.

refrigerate *v.* to keep cool, to put inside a refrigerator: *Please refrigerate the bacon as soon as you get home.* **refrigerating. refrigerated.**

refrigerator *n.* a machine that keeps stored food cold.

refuge (ref'yüj) *n.* shelter: *It was storming, and we took refuge in a shed.*

refugee (ref yü jē') *n.* someone who has fled from one place to another to find safety or protection.

refund (rē'fund) *n.* money paid back: *The pen did not work, so I asked for a refund.*

refund (ri fund') *v.* to pay back money: *The store manager refunded my money because the radio did not work.* **refunding. refunded.**

refuse (ref'yüs) *n.* garbage: *The refuse was thrown into a large green bag.*

refuse (ri fyüz') *v.* to say 'no': *Kim refused to sing, so Rhoda replaced her.* **refusing. refused.**

regain *v.* to win back: *Do you think our team will ever regain the Cup?* **regaining. regained.**

regard *n.* respect, admiration: *I have a great regard for Tom. v.* to think of: *I regard Tom highly.* **regarding. regarded.**

regards *n. pl.* best wishes: *Give my regards to your cousin when you visit her.*

Regina *n.* capital city of Saskatchewan.

region *n.* a large area of land: *The Arctic region is the area around the North Pole.*

register *n.* 1. a machine that keeps a record of certain items: *a cash register.* 2. a written list of names and other information: *The hotel register is located at the main desk. v.* to sign in: *We registered at the hotel desk before going to our room.* **registering. registered.**

regret *v.* to be sorry about something: *I regretted hurting the other player in the game.* **regretting. regretted.**

regular *adj.* 1. even, steady: *the regular ticking of a clock.* 2. usual: *My regular way of getting there is to take a bus.* 3. happening again and again at the same time: *the regular appearance of day and night.* (*opp.* **irregular.**) **regularly** *adv.*

regulation *n.* a rule: *It is against regulations to leave the building.*

rehearsal *n.* a practice to get ready for a performance: *The band had many rehearsals before the parade.*

rehearse (rē hərs') *v.* to practise something, such as a play, in order to prepare for a performance. **rehearsing. rehearsed.**

reign (rān) *n.* the period of time that a king or queen rules: *The reign lasted ten years. v.* to rule, as king or queen: *The queen reigned for many years.* **reigning. reigned.**

reindeer (rān'dēr) *n.* a large deer that has antlers and lives in northern regions. *pl.* **reindeer.**

reins (ranz) *n. pl.* leather straps attached to a horse's bridle: *The rider held the reins to guide her horse.*

rejoice *v.* to show how pleased or happy you are: *We rejoiced when we won the finals.* **rejoicing. rejoiced.**

relate *v.* to tell, to describe: *The sailor related his adventures to the children.* **relating. related.**

related *adj.* 1. connected in some way: *These books are related. They are both about tigers.* 2. belonging to the same family: *Cousins are related to each other.*

relationship *n.* belonging to something, as in a family: *What is your relationship to Sandy? He is my cousin.*

relative *n.* a person who belongs to the same family as someone else: *I have lots of relatives. I have two brothers, two sisters, my parents, four uncles, five aunts, and twelve cousins.*

relax *v.* to take a rest and enjoy yourself: *After work, my mother likes to relax by reading the newspaper.* **relaxing. relaxed.** he **relaxes.**

relaxation *n.* recreation, taking it easy: *Jogging is my favourite form of relaxation.*

relay *v.* to take and pass along: *The messenger relayed the information.* **relaying. relayed.**

relay race a race in which each team member goes only a certain distance, and then another team member takes his or her place.

release *v.* 1. to let go: *Release your hold on the rope.* 2. to set free: *Release the prisoner. She is not guilty.* **releasing. released.**

reliable (ri lī′ə bəl) *adj.* able to be trusted: *Jay is a reliable boy. He will finish his jobs on time.* (*opp.* **unreliable.**)

relief (ri lēf′) *n.* freedom from worry, trouble, or pain: *It was a relief to hear that nobody was hurt in the accident.*

relieve (ri lēv′) *v.* 1. to end worry or pain: *The medicine relieved Barry's headache.* 2. to take over a duty from someone: *The day nurse relieved the night nurse at 7 a.m.* **relieving. relieved.**

religion *n.* the worship of and belief in God, or a god or gods.

religious *adj.* having to do with religion: *a religious service.*

relish *n.* a kind of pickle of chopped vegetables or fruits.

rely (used with **on**) *v.* to depend on, to trust: *We rely on you to show us the way.* **relying. relied.** she **relies.**

remain *v.* 1. to stay behind: *After the party we remained at our friend's house.* 2. to be left over: *All that remains from the party is one piece of cake.* **remaining. remained.**

remainder *n.* 1. what is left over: *We will divide the remainder of the cake.* 2. the number left over when a number cannot be divided evenly.

remark *n.* a short statement: *Marc made a nice remark about my new shirt.* *v.* to say a few words: *Kenneth remarked that he felt tired.* **remarking. remarked.**

remarkable *adj.* surprising, special, worth talking about: *Cathy had a remarkable escape when the ladder fell.* **remarkably** *adv.*

remedy (rem′ə dē) *n.* something that makes you feel better; a cure: *What is a good remedy for a cold?* *pl.* **remedies.**

remember *v.* 1. to bring back to mind: *Do you remember when we went to the zoo?* 2. to keep in mind: *Remember to take a pen to school.* **remembering. remembered.**

Remembrance Day November 11, the day we honour the people who died in the First and Second World Wars.

remind *v.* to help someone remember: *I reminded Tracy about the picnic.* **reminding. reminded.**

reminder *n.* a few words or a note to someone, to help him or her to remember: *Maria sent Rene a reminder about the party.*

remote *adj.* far off: *The North Pole is in a remote part of the world.*

remote control the control of a TV or other machine from a distance, usually by a radio signal.

remove v. to take away: *I removed the library books from the shelf.* **removing. removed.**

renew v. to borrow or get for another period of time: *to renew a book; to renew a driver's licence.* **renewing. renewed.**

rent n. money paid for the use of an apartment, house, or something else you do not own. v. to pay to get the right to use something: *During the summer we rent a cottage.* **renting. rented.**

repair v. to fix something that is broken or torn. **repairing. repaired.**

repeat v. to say or do something again: *I repeated his directions to make sure I understood them.* **repeating. repeated.**

replace v. 1. to take the place of: *When Sue moved away, Jan replaced her on the team.* 2. to put back: *He replaced the book on the shelf.* **replacing. replaced.**

reply n. an answer: *Denis sent a reply to the invitation.* pl. **replies.** v. to answer: *'Did you go to the party?' Lisa asked. 'No, I did not', Sonya replied.* **replying. replied.** she **replies.**

report n. a written or spoken account of something: *a school report.*

reporter n. someone who collects news for a newspaper, magazine, or radio or TV show.

represent v. 1. to stand for, to be a picture of: *This painting represents swans on a pond.* 2. to act for or speak for: *Your Member of Parliament represents your community in Ottawa.* **representing. represented.**

representative n. a person chosen to act or speak for others.

reptile n. a cold-blooded animal that creeps or crawls: *Snakes, turtles, and crocodiles are reptiles.*

republic n. a nation that is headed by a president: *The citizens of a republic elect a president to be the head of their government.*

reputation (rep yü tā′shən) n. what people think and say of you: *Jill has the reputation of being an honest person.*

request v. to ask for something: *Neil requested permission to leave school early.* **requesting. requested.**

require v. to need: *The teacher required more chalk, and sent Kathryn for some.* **requiring. required.**

requirement n. something that is needed: *What are the requirements for joining the club?*

rescue n. the saving from danger or harm: *The cat was in the tree and the firefighters came to the rescue.* v. to save from danger or harm: *The firefighter rescued three people from the burning house.* **rescuing. rescued.**

resemblance n. a similar appearance: *There is a great resemblance between my brother and me.*

resemble (ri zem′bəl) v. to look similar to: *Simone resembles her sister, and sometimes people call her by the wrong name.* **resembling. resembled.**

reservation n. an arrangement made ahead of time: *We made a reservation for dinner at the restaurant.*

reserve (ri zərv′) n. land set aside for a special purpose: *an Indian reserve.* v. to arrange for something to be kept for you: *Before we left, we reserved a room at the motel.* **reserving. reserved.**

reservoir (rez′ər vwar) n. a large tank or pond where water is collected and stored for later use.

residence (rez′i dəns) n. a place where a person lives.

resign (ri zīn′) *v.* to give up a job or position: *My brother resigned from his job because we were moving.* **resigning. resigned.**

resist (ri zist′) *v.* to fight or struggle against: *The robber resisted the police officer.* **resisting. resisted.**

resistance *n.* struggle, opposition: *The burglars showed little resistance when the police caught them.*

resort (ri zort′) *n.* a holiday place.

resource (ri zors′) *n.* 1. a supply of something that will meet a need: *Canada has many natural resources, including minerals, fish, and lumber.* 2. a person or thing that is used for help or information.

respect *n.* a good opinion of someone or something: *My grandmother is a kind person. I have a lot of respect for her.* (*opp.* **disrespect.**) *v.* to admire, to have a good opinion of someone or something: *I respect your ideas.* **respecting. respected.**

respiration *n.* breathing: *Artificial respiration means making a person breathe again by forcing air into and out of the lungs.*

respond *v.* to answer, to reply. **responding. responded.**

responsible *adj.* 1. being in charge: *Ms Woods is responsible for the school play.* 2. being the main cause: *Who was responsible for the fire?* 3. able to be trusted: *Kurt is a responsible boy. He'll water your plants while you're away.* (*opp.* **irresponsible.**)

rest *n.* 1. being still and quiet: *The birds are at rest.* 2. what is left: *You can have the rest of the salad.* 3. in music, a period of silence. *v.* to stop working, to relax or have a nap. **resting. rested.**

restaurant *n.* a place where you buy and eat a meal.

restless *adj.* not able to be still and quiet: *The movie was very long and my little brother became restless.*

restrain *v.* to hold back, to keep in control: *Renata restrained her dog from chasing the cat.* **restraining. restrained.**

result (ri zult′) *n.* 1. the final score or sum: *The result of adding 5 and 4 is 9.* 2. something that happens because of something else: *Her broken arm was the result of a bad fall.*

retire *v.* to give up work, usually because of old age: *My grandfather retired from his job last year.* **retiring. retired.**

retreat *v.* to go back: *The defeated soldiers retreated.* **retreating. retreated.**

retrieve *v.* to get back or to find again: *My brother retrieved my lost watch.* **retrieving. retrieved.**

retriever *n.* a dog that can be trained to retrieve things.

return *v.* 1. to come or go back: *to return home.* 2. to give back: *to return a borrowed book.* **returning. returned.**

reunion (rē yün′yən) *n.* a coming together again of a group of people: *Our family has a reunion each year.*

reveal *v.* to make known: *Don't reveal my secret.* **revealing. revealed.**

revenge *n.* something done to get even with someone who has hurt you: *He swore that he would take revenge.*

reverence *n.* great respect, especially for holy things.

Reverend *n.* a title given to a member of the clergy.

reverse *n.* 1. the opposite: *He did the reverse of what I said. I told him to turn left and he went right.* 2. the position of gears that makes a car move back instead of forward.* *v.* to turn something around. **reversing. reversed.**

review (ri vyü´) *n.* 1. a written or spoken account of a book, play, film, etc. 2. a recall of things learned: *a history review.* *v.* 1. to give a written or spoken account: *Karen reviewed the movie for the class.* 2. to inspect: *The general reviewed the troops.* **reviewing. reviewed.**

revive *v.* to bring someone back to life or to being conscious: *They revived the drowning man by giving him artificial respiration.* **reviving. revived.**

revolt *n.* a refusal to obey orders, a rebellion. *v.* to rebel. **revolting. revolted.**

revolution *n.* 1. a complete changing of government and laws in a country: *There is often much force used when a revolution takes place.* 2. a movement in a circle around a central point: *the revolution of the moon around the earth.*

revolve *v.* to turn around and around: *The earth revolves around the sun.* **revolving. revolved.**

revolver *n.* a pistol that can be fired several times without having to be loaded again.

reward *n.* money or a prize given for something done. *v.* to give a reward: *We rewarded the man who found our dog.* **rewarding. rewarded.**

rhubarb (rü´barb) *n.* a plant with reddish, sour-tasting stalks that can be cooked and eaten.

rhyme (rīm) *n.* a word having the same last sound as another: *'Cat' is a rhyme for 'bat'. 'Able' is a rhyme for 'table'.* *v.* to sound alike in the last part: *'Boy' rhymes with 'toy'.* **rhyming. rhymed.**

rhythm (riTH´əm) *n.* a regular beat or flow of sounds or movements: *the rhythm of a poem, dance, or song.*

rib *n.* one of the bones that curve around your chest, protecting your lungs.

ribbon *n.* a narrow strip of cloth such as silk, velvet, or satin: *a hair ribbon.*

rice *n.* a cereal grass that grows in warm, wet regions.

rich *adj.* 1. having a lot of wealth: *a rich person.* 2. having a lot of sugar, fat, or flavouring: *rich food.*

rid *v.* to get free of something that bothers you: *to rid the garden of weeds.* **ridding. rid** or **ridded.**

riddle *n.* a puzzling question such as: *What goes up when the rain falls down? (An umbrella.)*

ride *n.* a trip in a car or other vehicle, or on a horse. *v.* to travel in a vehicle or on an animal's back. **riding. rode.** I have **ridden.**

ridge *n.* the top of something long and narrow: *the ridges in a field that has been ploughed.*

ridiculous *adj.* very silly or foolish.

riding *n.* an area in Canada represented by a Member of Parliament or a Member of the Legislative Assembly.

rhinoceros (rī nos´ər əs) *n.* a large, thick-skinned African animal, also called a rhino (rī´nō): *A rhinoceros has one or two horns on its snout.* *pl.* **rhinoceroses.**

rifle *n.* a long gun that is fired from the shoulder.

right (rīt) *n.* 1. what is good, the opposite of wrong. 2. a claim: *Everyone has a right to vote in the class election.* *adj.* 1. in the direction opposite of left: *When you look at a map of Canada, Alberta is on the right side of British Columbia.* 2. true, correct: *Your answers are right.*

rim *n.* the outer edge of a cup, bowl, wheel, etc.

rind *n.* a thick peel: *Oranges, watermelons, and lemons have rinds.*

ring *n.* 1. a circle: *The children formed a ring.* 2. a metal band to wear on your finger: *a gold ring.* 3. the sound of a bell: *I hear a ring at the door.* *v.* to sound a bell, or to make a sound like that of a bell. **ringing. rang.** I have **rung.**

rink *n.* 1. a sheet of ice used by hockey players and other skaters. 2. a sheet of ice used in the game of curling. 3. a smooth floor used for roller-skating.

rinse *v.* to use clean water to wash away soap or dirt. **rinsing. rinsed.**

riot *n.* a violent and noisy disturbance caused by a group of people.

rip *n.* a torn place: *a rip in your pants.* *v.* to tear roughly and quickly: *to rip your pants; to rip open an envelope.* **ripping. ripped.**

ripe *adj.* ready to be picked and eaten: *A ripe peach should be a little soft.*

ripple *n.* a tiny wave on smooth water.

rise *v.* 1. to get up: *Ray rises very early each morning.* 2. to move up: *The sun rises in the east.* 3. to slope up: *The road rises from the village.* **rising. rose.** it has **risen.**

risk *n.* a chance of harm or of losing something: *Donald took a risk by petting that unfriendly dog.* *v.* to take such a chance: *Firefighters sometimes risk their lives.* **risking. risked.**

risky *adj.* full of risk: *a risky move, a riskier one, the riskiest move of all.*

rival (rī′vəl) *n.* a person or group that tries to be better than another.

river *n.* a large stream of water that flows into an ocean, bay, or lake, or into another river.

road *n.* a hard path on which vehicles travel.

roam *v.* to wander about: *We roamed through the forest.* **roaming. roamed.**

roar *n.* a deep sound made by a lion, heavy traffic, the waves of the sea, etc. *v.* to make such a sound. **roaring. roared.**

roast *n.* 1. a large piece of meat that has been cooked, or is to be cooked. 2. an outdoor meal where food is cooked over an open fire: *a wiener roast.* *v.* to cook in an oven or over a fire: *to roast meat.* **roasting. roasted.**

rob *v.* to steal by force. **robbing. robbed.**

robber *n.* a thief.

robbery *n.* stealing by force: *a bank robbery.* *pl.* **robberies.**

robe *n.* a long, loose outer garment.

robin *n.* a bird with a reddish breast.

robot (rō′bot) *n.* a machine that sometimes looks like a person and can do some human jobs.

rock *n.* 1. stone. 2. a kind of popular music. *v.* to move gently back and forth: *to rock in a rocking chair.* **rocking. rocked.**

rocket *n.* 1. a firework at the end of a stick, that goes high in the air when lit. 2. a long, tube-shaped machine that is driven into the air or into space by a strong jet of gases.

rocky *adj.* bumpy, or being full of rocks: *a rocky road, a rockier road, the rockiest road in the county.*

Rocky Mountains, the Rockies a mountain range that extends through western Canada and the western United States.

rod *n.* a stick of wood or metal.

rode see **ride.**

rodent *n.* any of a group of animals that have sharp front teeth used in gnawing: *Rats, mice, rabbits, squirrels, and beavers are rodents.*

rodeo (rō'dē ō, rō dā'ō) *n.* a contest of skill in riding horses, roping cattle, etc.: *The Calgary Stampede is the world's biggest rodeo. pl.* **rodeos.**

role *n.* a part played by an actor or actress: *In our school play, Ari has the role of Dr. Pain.*

roll *n.* something in a round shape: *a sausage roll, a bread roll. v.* 1. to turn over and over: *The ball rolled down the stairs.* 2. to wrap around itself: *to roll up a carpet.* 3. to sway from side to side: *The ship rolled in the rough sea.* **rolling. rolled.**

roller *n.* 1. a large, long wave in the ocean. 2. a cylinder that can roll, and may be used to shape something: *hair rollers.*

roller coaster a railway ride at an amusement park or fair.

roller skate a skate that has small wheels on the bottom.

roller-skate *v.* to skate on roller skates. **roller-skating. roller-skated.**

Roman Catholic a person who belongs to the Christian church that has the Pope as its leader.

romance *n.* 1. love. 2. a love story.

romantic *adj.* having to do with romance: *a romantic movie.*

roof *n.* 1. the outside top covering of a building. 2. something like a roof: *the roof of a car. pl.* **roofs** or **rooves.**

rookie *n.* a person who is new to a group and has no experience.

room *n.* 1. one of the inside spaces of a building: *a bathroom, a bedroom.* 2. space: *There is plenty of room on the bus.*

roomy *adj.* full of room or space: *a roomy tent, a roomier tent, the roomiest tent on the grounds.*

rooster (*fem.* **hen**) *n.* a male chicken.

root *n.* 1. the part of a plant which grows in the ground. 2. a word from which other words are made: *'Hair' is the root of 'hairy'.*

rope *n.* a long, thick cord. *v.* 1. to tie with a rope: *We roped the packages together.* 2. to catch with a lasso or rope: *The cowgirl roped the calf.* **roping. roped.**

rose *n.* a sweet-smelling flower that grows on a thorny bush. *v.* see **rise.**

Rosh Hashona the Jewish New Year, celebrated in September or October.

rot *v.* to go bad, to decay. **rotting. rotted.**

rotate *v.* 1. to turn around in circles: *The earth rotates on its axis.* 2. to take turns: *We rotate our crops. This year we planted beets where the beans were last year.* **rotating. rotated.**

rotation *n.* the moving around in a circle: *the rotation of a bicycle wheel.*

rotten *adj.* going bad or gone bad: *rotten eggs, rotten apples.*

rough (ruf) *adj.* 1. not smooth: *rough ground.* 2. stormy: *a rough sea.* **roughly** *adv.*

round *n.* 1. a period of boxing. 2. a short song sung by several people, each singer beginning at a different time. *adj.* 1. in the shape of a circle: *a round ring.* 2. in the shape of a sphere: *a round apple. v.* to make a turn: *I rounded the corner.* **rounding. rounded.**

route (rüt) *n.* 1. a way of getting to a place: *I take a short route to school.* 2. the area that a salesperson has: *a newspaper route.*

routine (rü tēn') *n.* an action done over and over again as a regular thing: *Doing homework is part of my daily routine.* *adj.* regular: *Drying the dishes is one of my routine jobs.*

row (rō) *n.* a line of people or things: *a row of chairs.* *v.* to make a boat move by using oars. **rowing. rowed.**

rowboat *n.* a small boat that is moved with oars.

royal *adj.* having to do with kings or queens or their families: *a royal palace.*

Royal Canadian Mounted Police, RCMP the federal police force of Canada: *In all provinces except Québec and Ontario, the RCMP also act as provincial police.*

royalty *n.* a royal person or royal persons.

R.R. short for **rural route**: *My address is R.R. 3, Peterborough, Ontario.*

rub *v.* to move one thing against another, to wipe: *Marguerite rubbed her shoes on the mat.* **rubbing. rubbed.**

rubber *n.* 1. a springy, elastic material used to make tires, tubing, and other things. 2. a soft piece of this substance used for wiping out pencil marks; an eraser. 3. a low overshoe made of rubber.

rubber band an elastic band, used for holding things together.

rubbish *n.* garbage.

ruby *n.* a clear, red jewel. *pl.* **rubies.**

rucksack *n.* a knapsack.

rudder *n.* a flat, movable piece of wood or metal that is attached to the back of a ship or aircraft: *A rudder is used for steering.*

rude *adj.* bad-mannered, not polite.

ruffle *n.* 1. a wrinkling in a surface. 2. a strip of crinkled cloth or lace attached to a dress or shirt. *v.* to crumple, to wrinkle. **ruffling. ruffled.**

rug *n.* a heavy fabric, used as a floor covering.

rugged (rug'əd) *adj.* rough, strong: *rugged mountains.*

ruin *n.* an old building that has fallen to pieces or is falling down: *Ruins of many ancient buildings are found in Greece and Italy.* *v.* to spoil, to make useless: *The heavy frost ruined the fruit crop.* **ruining. ruined.**

rule *n.* an order: *It is a school rule that you do not ride bicycles in the playground.* *v.* 1. to control or govern: *to rule an empire.* 2. to use a ruler: *Rule a straight line.* **ruling. ruled.**

ruler *n.* 1. a person who controls or governs. 2. a strip of marked wood, plastic, or metal, used for drawing lines or for measuring.

rumble *n.* a deep, rolling sound: *the rumble of thunder.* *v.* to make such a sound: *The train rumbled in the distance.* **rumbling. rumbled.**

rummy *n.* a card game.

rumour, rumor (rü'mər) *n.* a story or information, which may not be true, passed around from one person to another.

run *n.* 1. a quick movement on your feet: *I go for a run every morning.* 2. a tear in a stocking. 3. a caged-in area for a dog. *v.* 1. to move quickly on your feet: *He ran down the street.* 2. to go from place to place: *The road runs from one village to the other.* 3. to travel regularly: *The train runs twice a day.* 4. to be in charge of: *Mrs. Grimaldi runs a gas station.* 5. to compete in a race or in an election: *Mr. Jones is running for mayor.* **running. ran.** I have **run.**
run out of to have none left: *Mother ran out of bread.*

runaway *n.* a person, horse, etc. that runs away.

rung *n.* one of the steps of a ladder. *v.* see **ring.**

runner-up *n.* one who finishes in second or third place in a race or contest. *pl.* **runners-up.**

runway *n.* a wide and long concrete path for airplanes to start from and land on.

rural (rü′rəl) *adj.* having to do with the country, not with the city: *Most of the children in my school come from rural areas.*

rush *v.* to hurry about, to move fast. **rushing. rushed.**

Russian *n.* the language spoken in Russia. *adj.* having to do with Russia.

rust *n.* a reddish-brown coating that forms on metal: *Rust is caused by wetness.*

rustle (rus′əl) *n.* a soft, crackling sound: *the rustle of leaves in the wind.* *v.* to make this sound. **rustling. rustled.**

rustler *n.* someone who steals cattle or horses.

rusty *adj.* covered with rust: *a rusty car, a rustier car, the rustiest car in the garage.*

rut *n.* a deep track made by a wheel.

rye *n.* a grain, grown like wheat, used for making flour and as feed for animals.

S

sabbath *n.* a day of rest and worship: *Sunday is the sabbath for most Christians. Saturday is the sabbath for Jews.*

sabre, saber (sā′bər) *n.* a heavy, curved sword.

sack *n.* a large bag made of strong material.

sacred (sā′krəd) *adj.* holy, having to do with God or a god: *a sacred temple. The church choir sings sacred music.*

sacrifice *n.* 1. a gift to a god. 2. something you value that you give up: *Stephen felt that it was a great sacrifice to give his best stamps to Sharon.*

sad *adj.* not happy: *sad news, sadder news, the saddest news of all.* **sadly** *adv.*

saddle *n.* a seat for the rider of a horse. *v.* to put a saddle on a horse. **saddling. saddled.**

safari (sə far′ē) *n.* an exploring trip, usually in Africa. *pl.* **safaris.**

safe *n.* a strong metal box in which valuable things are locked. *adj.* 1. free from danger or harm: *I feel safe now that I'm off the thin ice.* 2. careful: *My sister is a safe driver.* **safely** *adv.*

safety *n.* freedom from harm, being safe: *The workers wore hard hats for their safety.*

sag *v.* to bend low in the middle: *The old mattress sags in the centre.* **sagging. sagged.**

said see **say.**

sail *n.* a sheet of canvas or cloth that is attached to a ship: *A sail catches the wind and makes the ship move.* *v.* to travel over the water: *We went sailing in Clay's boat.* **sailing. sailed.**

sailboat *n.* a boat that is moved by the wind blowing against its sail or sails.

sailor *n.* a member of a ship's crew.

saint *n.* a man or woman who has lived a very holy life.

Saint John the largest city in New Brunswick.

St. John's capital city of Newfoundland.

sake *n.* a cause, benefit: *I went on the errand for your sake, as you are not well.*

salad *n.* a mixture of raw or cold cooked vegetables, sometimes with cold meat, fish, or eggs: *Salad is often served with a dressing.*

salamander *n.* an animal that looks like a small lizard.

salami *n.* a spicy kind of sausage.

salary *n.* regular payment of money for work done. *pl.* **salaries.**

sale *n.* 1. the selling of something: *the sale of meat by a butcher.* 2. the selling of goods at prices lower than usual: *The store has a sale on books.*

salesperson *n.* a person whose job is selling things.

saliva (sə lī′və) *n.* the liquid in your mouth: *Saliva helps you chew and digest foods.*

salmon (sa′mən) *n.* a large fish with pink flesh, used for food. *pl.* **salmon.**

salt *n.* a white substance used to flavour food: *Salt is found in the earth and in sea water.*

salute *n.* a greeting to someone. *v.* 1. to greet someone. 2. to raise your hand in respect to someone. **saluting. saluted.**

same *adj.* exactly alike, not different: *I have not seen Vicki for two years, but she looks just the same.*

sample *n.* a small piece of something that shows you what the rest is like. *v.* to try: *She sampled the stew.* **sampling. sampled.**

sand *n.* tiny grains of earth or rock.

sandal *n.* a light shoe fastened to your foot by straps.

sand dune a mound of sand on a desert or by the ocean.

sandpaper *n.* a heavy paper that has sand on one side: *Sandpaper is used for smoothing and cleaning wood.*

sandwich *n.* two slices of bread with butter, meat, jam, or some other food in between.

sandy *adj.* 1. having a light brown or beige colour. 2. filled with sand: *a sandy beach, a sandier beach, the sandiest beach in the province.*

sane *adj.* sensible, not mad. (*opp.* **insane.**)

sang see **sing.**

sanitary *adj.* healthy, completely free from dirt: *These clean towels are sanitary.*

sank see **sink.**

Santa Claus the jolly old man said to give out presents on Christmas Eve.

sap *n.* the liquid inside plants and trees: *Sap carries water and food through a tree.*

sardine (sar dēn′) *n.* a small, silvery fish sold for food, usually in cans.

sari (sah′rē) *n.* a piece of clothing worn by women and girls in India and some other countries in Asia. *pl.* **saris.**

sash *n.* 1. a wide ribbon, usually worn around the waist. 2. the frame that holds the glass in a window or door.

Saskatchewan *n.* province between Alberta on the west, Manitoba on the east; capital is Regina. Short form: **Sask.** A person living in or born in Saskatchewan is a **Saskatchewanian**.

Sasquatch *n.* Bigfoot, a heavy, man-like creature said to live in the Rockies.

sat see **sit.**

satellite *n.* 1. a smaller heavenly body moving around a larger one: *The moon is a satellite of the earth.* 2. a spaceship moving regularly around the earth.

satin *n.* a smooth, very shiny cloth.

satisfaction *n.* pleasure, enjoyment: *Reading gives Grandpa a lot of satisfaction.*

satisfactory *adj.* good enough to please: *Your work is satisfactory in every way.* (*opp.* **unsatisfactory.**)

satisfy *v.* to please: *My pitching doesn't satisfy me. I'll have to practise more.* **satisfying. satisfied.** it **satisfies.**

Saturday *n.* the seventh day of the week.

Saturn *n.* the sixth planet of our solar system.

sauce *n.* a liquid or creamy mixture served with food to make it taste better.

saucer *n.* a round dish for a cup to stand on.

sausage *n.* chopped meat that is mixed with spices and stuffed into a thin tube.

savage *adj.* wild and fierce: *The savage bull went after the farmer.*

save *n.* the preventing of a score by a goalie: *He made a great save!* *v.* 1. to free someone from danger: *She saved my life.* 2. to keep something to use it later on: *I'm saving money for Christmas.* 3. to avoid waste: *Let's take a shortcut to save time.* **saving. saved.**

savings *n. pl.* money that has been saved: *My savings are in the bank.*

saw *n.* a tool with sharp metal points along one edge. *v.* 1. see **see**. 2. to cut with a saw. **sawing. sawed.** I have **sawed** or **sawn.**

sawdust *n.* powdered wood from sawing.

sawmill *n.* a place where logs are cut into wooden planks.

saxophone *n.* a musical instrument, played by blowing into a mouthpiece and pushing down the keys.

say *v.* to speak, to tell. **saying. said** (sed). he **says** (sez).

saying *n.* wise words that are often said: *'Haste makes waste' is a wise saying.*

scab *n.* a crust that forms over a wound.

scaffold *n.* a platform that is used to hold window washers and others while they work on a building: *Ropes and pulleys are used to move a scaffold up and down the side of a building.*

scald *n.* a burn from very hot liquid or steam. *v.* to burn with very hot liquid or steam. **scalding. scalded.**

scale *n.* 1. a piece of equipment used to measure the mass of something or someone. 2. one of many thin flakes on the skin of a fish or reptile. 3. a set of musical notes. *v.* to climb: *She scaled the wall quickly.* **scaling. scaled.**

scallop *n.* a shellfish that looks like a clam. *v.* 1. to bake with sauce: *Mother scalloped the potatoes.* 2. to cut with curves. **scalloping. scalloped.**

scalp *n.* the skin and hair on top of your head. *v.* to take a scalp. **scalping. scalped.**

scan *v.* to look at quickly: *June scanned the page for a word.* **scanning. scanned.**

scar *n.* 1. a mark left on your skin after a cut or a burn has healed. 2. any mark like this. *v.* to mark with a scar: *The floor was scarred when Brenda dropped her skates.* **scarring. scarred.**

scarce *adj.* less than is needed: *When there was a shortage of flour, bread became scarce.* **scarcely** *adv.*

scare *n.* a frightening experience: *He had a scare when the window started rattling.* *v.* to frighten: *The noise scared Shane.* **scaring. scared.**

scarecrow *n.* a figure dressed like a person; it is set up in a field to frighten birds from a farmer's crops.

scarf *n.* a piece of cloth worn around the neck or head. *pl.* **scarfs** or **scarves.**

scarlet *n.* a very bright red colour. *adj.* having this colour.

scary *adj.* causing a scare: *a scary story, a scarier one, the scariest one in the book.*

scatter *v.* to throw, fall, or move in all directions: *They scattered seeds on the flower beds.* **scattering. scattered.**

scene (sēn) *n.* 1. a view: *a pretty scene by the river.* 2. a part of a play: *The actors practised the second scene.* 3. a place where something happened: *This is the scene of the fire.*

scenery (sē'nər ē) *n.* 1. what you see outside: *The scenery near my cottage is beautiful.* 2. a painted cloth or board, at the back of a stage; it shows where the play takes place.

scent (sent) *n.* a smell: *The dog followed the fox's scent. I like the scent of roses.*

schedule (shed'yül, sked'yül) *n.* a list of events, usually shown with times: *a TV schedule.* *v.* to make a schedule: *They scheduled the games for the summer holidays.* **scheduling. scheduled.**

scheme (skēm) *n.* a plan: *The thieves had a scheme for robbing the bank.*

scholar (skol'ər) *n.* a person who has a lot of knowledge.

scholarship *n.* money given students to help them continue their studies.

school *n.* 1. a place where people are taught. 2. a large group of fish swimming together.

schooner (skü'nər) *n.* a sailing ship that has two or more masts on it.

science (sī'əns) *n.* knowledge of some part of nature, based on experiments and careful study.

science fiction a story, usually one that takes place in the future: *Many scientific ideas are found in science fiction.*

scientific (sī ən tif'ik) *adj.* having to do with science: *a scientific discovery.*

scientist *n.* someone who studies a science.

scissors (siz'ərz) *n. pl.* a tool used for cutting: *Scissors have two blades joined by a screw in the middle.*

scold *v.* to grumble at someone in an angry way. **scolding. scolded.**

scoop *n.* 1. a little shovel for flour or sugar. 2. a tool shaped like a cup attached to a handle: *I had two scoops of ice cream.* *v.* to take up with a scoop. **scooping. scooped.**

scorch *v.* to burn slightly: *I scorched my shirt with the iron.* **scorching. scorched.**

score *n.* the number of runs, points, or goals made in a game: *The score was two to one.* *v.* 1. to make a goal or a run in games: *Ross scored three goals in the hockey game.* 2. to cut or mark: *Dad scored the steak on the edges before barbecuing it.* **scoring. scored.**

scorn *n.* a feeling that someone or something is worth very little: *The team had nothing but scorn for the cheater.*

scorpion *n.* an animal that looks like a spider with a long tail: *Scorpions can give a poisonous sting.*

Scottish *adj.* belonging to or coming from Scotland.

scour *v.* 1. to scrub, to rub hard: *Father scoured the tub.* 2. to search thoroughly: *They scoured the hills for the missing boy.* **scouring. scoured.**

scout *n.* someone sent ahead to gather information. *v.* to explore an area: *Peg and Jan scouted around for a good campsite.* **scouting. scouted.**

Scout *n.* a person who is a member of the Boy Scouts.

scowl *n.* an angry frown. *v.* to make this kind of frown. **scowling. scowled.**

scramble *v.* 1. to mix together: *We scrambled some eggs for breakfast.* 2. to climb or crawl using hands and feet: *The children scrambled for the ball.* **scrambling. scrambled.**

scrap *n.* a small piece: *a scrap of paper.*

scrape *n.* a scratch or rub: *You have a scrape on your arm from the fall.* *v.* 1. to scratch or rub. 2. to rub smooth with something hard or sharp: *Jennie scraped the mud off her shoes.* **scraping. scraped.**

scratch *n.* a mark left by something sharp: *The cat's claw made a scratch on my arm.* *v.* 1. to make a mark with something sharp: *Barb's cat scratched her.* 2. to rub the part of your skin that itches. **scratching. scratched.**

scrawny *adj.* thin, weak, looking sick: *a scrawny cat, a scrawnier one, the scrawniest cat on the street.*

scream *n.* a high, shrill cry. *v.* 1. to make such a cry. 2. to speak very loudly. **screaming. screamed.**

screech *n.* a high, shrill noise: *the screech of brakes.* *v.* to make such a noise: *He screeched when the bat flew at him.* **screeching. screeched.**

screen *n.* 1. the surface on which television pictures or movies are seen. 2. wire mesh in a frame: *A screen is put on a window to let in air, but to keep out bugs.*

screw *n.* a kind of nail with spiral grooves. *v.* to fix in place by using a twisting movement: *to screw a cap on a bottle of pop.* **screwing. screwed.** (*opp.* **unscrew.**)

screwdriver *n.* a tool used for turning screws.

scribble *v.* to write or draw in a quick and careless way. **scribbling. scribbled.**

script *n.* 1. writing in which the letters are joined together. 2. the written words of a play, movie, or television or radio program: *Everyone received a copy of the script of the play.*

scrub *v.* to clean by rubbing hard: *I scrubbed my hands. I scrubbed the floor.* **scrubbing. scrubbed.**

sculptor *n.* someone who carves statues or shapes.

sculpture *n.* a carving in wood, stone, clay, or some other material: *Vic made a beautiful sculpture of a horse.*

scurry *v.* to run quickly: *The rabbits scurried away when the fox appeared.* **scurrying. scurried.** it **scurries**.

scythe (sīTH) *n.* a long handle with a large curved blade at the end: *A scythe is used for cutting grass and crops.*

sea *n.* 1. the great body of salt water that covers almost three-fourths of the earth's surface. 2. any body of salt water smaller than an ocean: *the Mediterranean Sea.*

sea gull a grey and white bird that lives near a large body of water.

seal *n.* a furry animal that lives in and by the sea: *Seals have flippers instead of feet.* *v.* to join two things tightly together, often by using something sticky: *Wah sealed the envelope.* **sealing. sealed.**

sea lion a large seal that lives in the Pacific Ocean.

seam *n.* a line where two pieces of cloth are sewn together.

search (sərch) *n.* a looking for someone or something: *The search lasted four days.* *v.* to look everywhere for something: *Kelly searched the house for her keys.* **searching. searched.**

searchlight *n.* a special light that gives off a powerful beam: *Lighthouses and airport control towers use searchlights.*

sea shell the shell of a sea animal, such as an oyster or a crab.

seashore *n.* land along the edge of the sea.

season *n.* 1. one of the four parts of the year; spring, summer, autumn, winter. 2. a special time for something: *the football season.* *v.* to add salt, pepper, or other flavours to food. **seasoning. seasoned.**

seat *n.* something to sit on, as a chair or bench. *v.* 1. to give someone a seat: *The smaller children were seated in the front row.* 2. to have seats for: *Our arena seats a thousand people.* **seating. seated.**

seat belt a strong belt that holds a person in the seat of a car or airplane in case of a bump or crash.

seaweed *n.* a green or brown plant that grows in the sea.

second *n.* a very small measure of time; s is the symbol: *There are 60 seconds in a minute.* *adj.* being next after the first: *second place.*

secondary school a school attended after elementary school or junior high school.

second-hand *adj.* used by someone else before you: *My parents bought a second-hand camera.*

secret (sē′krit) *n.* some news that you keep to yourself and one or two friends: *Gene shared the secret with his brother.* *adj.* known to only a few: *a secret cave.*

secretary (sek′rə ter ē) *n.* someone who writes letters and keeps records for another person, a company, or a club. *pl.* **secretaries.**

section *n.* a part: *A section of the roof is leaking.*

secure (sə kyür′) *adj.* 1. safe: *My money is secure in the bank.* 2. firmly fastened: *Tie the box with a secure knot.* **securely** *adv.*

see *v.* 1. to receive a picture of something through your eyes. 2. to understand: *I see what you mean.* **seeing. saw.** I have **seen.**

seed *n.* a small grain or nut from a plant: *New plants grow from seeds.*

seedling *n.* a young plant grown from a seed.

seeing-eye dog a dog trained to guide a blind person.

seek *v.* to look for, to search for: *They sought the plane for a week.* **seeking. sought.**

seem *v.* to look as if something is true: *The baby seems to be asleep.* **seeming. seemed.**

seen see **see.**

seesaw *n.* a long board with a support in the middle, used by children for play.

seize (sēz) *v.* to grasp, to catch hold of: *Lou seized the rope and pulled the boat in.* **seizing. seized.**

seldom *adv.* rarely, not often: *Michael seldom sees his older sister, who lives in another city.*

select *v.* to choose carefully: *Lisa selected two good pears from the box.* **selecting. selected.**

selection *n.* a collection, a choice: *There is a good selection of books in the library.*

selfish *adj.* thinking and caring only about yourself: *He is a very selfish boy, and wants to have everything for himself.* (*opp.* **unselfish.**)

sell *v.* to hand over something in return for money. **selling. sold.**

semi- a prefix meaning 'half': a **semicircle** means half a circle.

Senate *n.* a part of the Canadian government: *Members of the Senate are appointed by the Governor General.*

Senator *n.* a member of the Senate.

send *v.* to make something or someone go somewhere: *to send a letter.* **sending. sent.**

senior (sē′nyər) *n.* someone who is older: *I am older than Jason, so I am his senior.* *adj.* older or more experienced: *The senior train conductor receives more pay than the junior conductor.*

sensation *n.* 1. a feeling: *I had a sensation of cold when I walked into the room.* 2. great excitement: *The school's win in track and field caused a sensation.*

sensational *adj.* exciting: *a sensational story in the newspaper.*

sense *n.* 1. the wisdom to know what is best to say or do: *Susan has a lot of sense.* 2. meaning: *Explain the sense of this paragraph.* 3. one of the five ways we get to know the world: *The five senses are sight, hearing, touch, smell, and taste.* *v.* to feel something, to be aware: *I sense that you are angry.* **sensing. sensed.**

sensible *adj.* full of good sense: *It is sensible to count your change after buying something.* **sensibly** *adv.*

sensitive *adj.* 1. having deep feelings: *Artists are often very sensitive people.* 2. easily upset: *My cousin is a sensitive child. He cries if anyone speaks roughly to him.*

sent see **send.**

sentence *n.* 1. a number of words that make a complete statement or thought. 2. a punishment given in a court of law: *The thief was given a sentence of two years in prison.* *v.* to punish someone with a sentence: *The judge sentenced the criminal to three years in prison.* **sentencing. sentenced.**

separate (sep′ər it) *adj.* not together, different: *A separate pile of books is over there.* **separately** *adv.*

separate (sep′ə rāt) *v.* to divide, to set apart: *We separated the ripe apples from the unripe ones.* **separating. separated.**

September *n.* the ninth month of the year.

sequence *n.* a number of things happening one after the other: *Monday, Tuesday, and Wednesday follow each other in sequence.*

sergeant (sar′jənt) *n.* 1. an officer of the police force. 2. a soldier who is next in rank above a corporal.

series *n.* a number of similar things coming one after the other: *We started the football season with a series of winning games.* *pl.* **series.**

serious *adj.* 1. important and needing attention: *We were given a serious warning about running across busy streets.* 2. very bad: *It was a serious sickness.* **seriously** *adv.*

sermon *n.* a public talk on religion or religious matters.

serpent *n.* a large snake.

servant *n.* someone who is paid to work in someone else's house.

serve *n.* in tennis and other games, the putting into play of the ball: *It's your serve.* *v.* 1. to work for someone or something: *A police officer serves the people.* 2. to give out food to others. 3. to put a ball into play. **serving. served.**

service *n.* 1. a helpful act: *She did us a service by driving the bus.* 2. duty performed in a country's armed forces. 3. a religious meeting or ceremony. *v.* to fix or make ready: *The mechanic serviced our car.* **servicing. serviced.**

serviette *n.* a piece of paper or cloth used to protect clothes and to clean hands and mouth while eating.

serving *n.* a helping of food.

set *n.* 1. a group of things that go together: *a set of golf clubs.* 2. a television or radio receiver. 3. in mathematics, a group of numbers between two brackets: *{1, 2, 3, 4} is a set of numbers. v.* 1. to put things in place: *Please set the table for breakfast.* 2. to go down: *When does the sun set tonight?* 3. to begin: *We set out on our trip in the morning.* **setting. set.**

setter *n.* a long-haired dog that can be trained to remain very still and point with its nose towards something it can smell.

settle *v.* 1. to get comfortable and stay in a place: *Father settled in his chair and went to sleep.* 2. to decide something: *We settled on having a dog.* 3. to make a new home: *People from many countries have settled in Canada.* **settling. settled.**

settler *n.* a person who makes a home in a new area: *The first settlers in Canada experienced many difficulties.*

seven *n., adj.* one more than six (7).

seventeen *n., adj.* ten more than seven (17).

seventh *adj.* following sixth (7th).

seventy *n., adj.* ten times seven (70).

several *adj.* not many, but more than two or three.

severe *adj.* harsh, serious: *It was a severe winter. I have a severe cold.*

sew (sō) *v.* to stitch with a needle and thread. **sewing. sewed.** I have **sewn** or **sewed.**

sewage (sü′ij) *n.* waste material that is carried off by sewers and drains.

sewer (sü′ər) *n.* an underground drain pipe that carries away waste from buildings.

sewer (sō′ər) *n.* a person who sews.

sewing machine a machine for sewing things.

sewn see **sew.**

sex *n.* being male or female: *A bull is of the male sex. A cow is of the female sex.*

shabby *adj.* old and ragged: *shabby clothes, shabbier clothes, the shabbiest clothes in the closet.*

shack *n.* a roughly built wooden hut.

shade *n.* 1. a place hidden from the sun: *We sat in the shade.* 2. something that cuts off strong light: *He pulled down the shade.* 3. the strength of a colour: *a deep shade of blue.*

shadow (shad′ō) *n.* a patch of darkness caused by something standing in the way of a light.

shady (shā′dē) *adj.* full of shadows: *a shady area, a shadier one, the shadiest part of the forest.*

shaft *n.* 1. a long handle, as on a rake or a golf club. 2. a long passage leading down into a mine.

shaggy *adj.* having long, thick, rough hair: *a shaggy dog, a shaggier dog, the shaggiest one in the pet store.*

shake *v.* 1. to move from side to side or up and down: *We shook the tree to make the apples fall.* 2. to tremble: *I am shaking with cold.* **shaking. shook** (shük)**.** I have **shaken.**

shaky *adj.* shaking: *a shaky branch, a shakier one, the shakiest one on the tree.*

shall *v.* a verb placed before another verb, to say what you are going to do: *I shall read. We shall play.*

shallow *adj.* not deep.

shame *n.* a feeling of being unhappy or foolish because you have done wrong: *He felt shame because he had not helped his friend.*

shampoo *n.* a liquid soap for washing hair. *pl.* **shampoos.** *v.* to wash hair, a rug, etc. **shampooing. shampooed.**

shamrock *n.* a plant with bright green leaves that are in three parts.

shape *n.* 1. the outline or form of anything: *The baseball field has a diamond shape.* 2. condition: *The swimmer is in good shape.* *v.* to form or make: *She shaped the clay into a beautiful statue.* **shaping. shaped.**

share *n.* the part of something that is given to one person: *We each had an equal share of the blueberries.* *v.* 1. to divide out: *We shared the cake.* 2. to use together: *The boys shared a bedroom.* **sharing. shared.**

shark *n.* a large, grey ocean fish that has many sharp teeth.

sharp *adj.* 1. with an edge or point that can easily make a cut: *a sharp knife.* 2. sudden: *a sharp bend in the road.* 3. quick to understand or notice something: *sharp eyes.* **sharply** *adv.*

sharpen *v.* to make sharp: *I sharpened my pencil in the morning.* **sharpening. sharpened.**

shatter *v.* to break suddenly into small pieces: *The stone shattered the glass.* **shattering. shattered.**

shave *n.* 1. the cutting off of hair with a razor: *Dad has a shave every morning.* 2. a narrow escape: *We had a close shave when the car started to skid.* *v.* to cut off hair with a razor. **shaving. shaved.**

shawl *n.* a piece of cloth worn around the shoulders or wrapped around a baby.

she *pron.* a woman or girl.

shear *v.* to cut with large scissors. **shearing. sheared.** I have **shorn** or **sheared.**

shears *n. pl.* a cutting tool for trimming hedges or shearing sheep.

shed *n.* a hut for storing tools or materials: *a garden shed.* *v.* to let fall: *Many trees shed their leaves in autumn.* **shedding. shed.**

she'd short for **she had** or **she would.**

sheep *n.* an animal that is raised for its wool and meat. *pl.* **sheep.**

sheer *adj.* 1. very thin, allowing you to see partly through: *sheer curtains.* 2. steep: *There is a sheer drop from the edge of the cliff.*

sheet *n.* 1. a large piece of thin cloth used on a bed. 2. a large, thin piece of something: *a sheet of paper.* 3. a large, flat surface: *a sheet of ice.*

sheik *n.* a leader of a group of Arabs.

shelf *n.* a board on a wall or in a closet for putting things on. *pl.* **shelves.**

shell *n.* 1. a thin, hard covering: *Eggs, nuts, beetles, and many sea animals have shells.* 2. a large bullet that explodes when it hits something. *v.* to take out of a shell: *We shelled all the nuts.* **shelling. shelled.**

she'll short for **she will.**

shellfish *n.* a water animal that has a shell: *Oysters, crabs, and lobsters are shellfish.* *pl.* **shellfish.**

shelter *n.* a place that gives protection or cover: *We need the shed as a shelter from the rain.* *v.* to protect, to cover: *The tent sheltered us from the rain.* **sheltering. sheltered.**

shelves see **shelf.**

shepherd (shep′ərd) *n.* someone who looks after sheep.

sherbet *n.* a frozen dessert made of fruit juice and other ingredients.

sheriff *n.* in Canada, a law officer who carries out certain orders of the court.

she's short for **she is** or **she has.**

shield *n.* 1. a large piece of armour once carried by soldiers. 2. anything that protects you: *An umbrella is a shield against the rain.* *v.* to protect. **shielding. shielded.**

Shield *n.* the **Canadian Shield**; an area rich in minerals, surrounding Hudson Bay.

shift *n.* 1. movement or change: *a shift in the wind.* 2. a group of workers, or the time that they work: *My father is on the night shift at the factory.* *v.* to move something, to change your position. **shifting. shifted.**

shin *n.* the front of your leg between the knee and the ankle.

shine *n.* a brightness: *Wax gave the car a brilliant shine.* *v.* 1. to give out light: *The light shone in my eyes.* **shining. shone** (shon). 2. to polish: *Greg shined his shoes.* **shining. shined.**

shingle *n.* a piece of wood or other material used to cover a roof.

shiny *adj.* bright, glittering: *a shiny floor, a shinier floor, the shiniest floor in the house.*

ship *n.* 1. a large boat. 2. an airplane or spaceship. *v.* to send by ship, bus, train, or plane: *We shipped the presents to my brother in Japan.* **shipping. shipped.**

shipment *n.* goods or materials sent to one place all at once.

shipwreck *n.* a ship that is damaged and sinks at sea.

shirt *n.* a piece of clothing with a collar, sleeves, and buttons down the front.

shiver *v.* to shake with fear or cold: *Rick shivered in the cold house.* **shivering. shivered.**

shock *n.* 1. a sudden fright: *The bang gave me a great shock.* 2. a sharp feeling caused by electricity: *Martin felt a shock when he touched the wire.* *v.* 1. to cause a feeling of surprise or fear. 2. to give an electric shock. **shocking. shocked.**

shoe (shü) *n.* 1. an outer covering for your foot. 2. a bent piece of iron nailed to a horse's hoof to protect it.

shone see **shine.**

shoo *v.* to send away quickly. **shooing. shooed.**

shook see **shake.**

shoot *n.* a new or young plant. *v.* 1. to fire a bullet, shell, or arrow. 2. to move or cause to move fast: *to shoot a puck towards the goal.* 3. to come up from the ground, to grow: *The corn is shooting up all over the field.* **shooting. shot.**

shooting star a meteor.

shop *n.* a building where things are sold or repaired. *v.* to buy from stores. **shopping. shopped.**

shopping centre a place away from the street, where there are many stores together.

shore *n.* land at the edge of an ocean, lake, or large river.

shorn see **shear.**

short *adj.* not measuring a lot from end to end: *a short coat; a short trip.*

shorten *v.* to make shorter: *Mother shortened my dress.* **shortening. shortened.**

shortly *adv.* soon, in a little while: *The game will begin shortly.*

shorts *n. pl.* short pants.

shortstop *n.* the baseball player whose position is between first and second base.

shot *n.* 1. the firing of a gun: *I heard a loud shot.* 2. a person who fires a gun: *Frank is a good shot.* 3. a tiny ball of metal fired from a gun. 4. an injection of medicine: *a measles shot.* 5. the sending off of a spaceship: *a moon shot.* 6. an aimed throw or stroke in some games: *We took some practice shots before the game.* *v.* see **shoot.**

should (shùd) *v.* a verb placed before another verb to mean 'ought to': *I should be doing my work, but I'm not.*

shoulder (shōl'dər) *n.* the part of your body between the neck and the arm.

shouldn't short for **should not.**

shout *n.* a loud call or cry: *a shout of joy.* *v.* to raise your voice and call loudly. **shouting. shouted.**

shove (shuv) *n.* a hard push: *Please give the boat a shove into the lake.* *v.* to push hard: *Ari shoved the boxes away.* **shoving. shoved.**

shovel (shuv'əl) *n.* a tool with a wide scoop. *v.* to use a shovel. **shovelling. shovelled.**

show *n.* an entertainment. *v.* to let someone see something, to point out: *Lena showed the way.* **showing. showed.** I have **shown** (shōn).

shower *n.* 1. a gentle fall of rain. 2. a wash while standing under a spray of water. 3. a party where gifts are brought in honour of someone: *a baby shower.*

shrank see **shrink.**

shred *n.* a tiny strip or scrap of something. *v.* to cut or tear into strips: *Please shred the cabbage for the salad.* **shredding. shredded** or **shred.**

shrew *n.* a small mouse-like animal that feeds on insects.

shriek (shrēk) *n.* a very high scream. *v.* to give a very high scream: *Tim shrieked with pain. John shrieked with laughter.* **shrieking. shrieked.**

shrill *adj.* sounding very high and loud: *We heard a shrill cry for help.*

shrimp *n.* a small, grey shellfish that turns pink when cooked. *pl.* **shrimp.**

shrink *v.* to become smaller: *Some kinds of cloth shrink in the wash.* **shrinking. shrank.** it has **shrunk.**

shrivel *v.* to become very dry and curl up like a dead leaf: *The plants shrivelled in the dry weather.* **shrivelling. shrivelled.**

shrub *n.* a bush with many branches on it, most coming from near the bottom of the plant.

shrug *v.* to move your shoulders in a way that means 'I don't know' or 'I don't care'. **shrugging. shrugged.**

shrunk see **shrink.**

shudder *v.* to shake suddenly with fear or cold. **shuddering. shuddered.**

shuffle *v.* 1. to mix up cards or other things. 2. to walk without lifting your feet. **shuffling. shuffled.**

shut *v.* to move a door or lid to close an opening: *Please shut the door.* **shutting. shut.**

shut-out *n.* a win against a team that scores no points.

shutter *n.* 1. a wooden cover for a window. 2. the part of a camera that opens and closes in front of the lens.

shy *adj.* afraid to speak to or to meet people.

sick *adj.* ill, not well.

sickness *n.* illness, poor health: *There has been a lot of sickness in the class.*

side *n.* 1. a flat surface: *the front side of a house.* 2. a team of players.

sidewalk *n.* a place to walk at the side of a street: *Sidewalks are usually paved.*

sideways *adv.* to one side: *Don't look backwards or forwards. Look sideways.*

siege (sēj) *n.* a time when an enemy surrounds a town or fort and stops help or food from getting in.

sieve (siv) *n.* a fine metal or plastic net that lets only liquids and small pieces pass through: *Shaking flour through a sieve removes the lumps.*

sift *v.* to use a sieve to separate fine powders from lumps or stones. **sifting. sifted.**

sigh (sī) *n.* a heavy breathing out to show that you are tired, bored, or unhappy. *v.* to breathe out in this way. **sighing. sighed.**

sight *n.* (sīt) 1. one of the five senses, the ability to see: *Jonathan has very good sight.* 2. something that is seen: *The sunset was a wonderful sight.*

sign *n.* (sīn) writing, drawing, or movement to show people something: *The sign told us how many kilometres it was to Regina.* *v.* to write your name: *I signed all the papers with a pen.* **signing. signed.**

signal *n.* (sig′nəl) a message sent by movement, sound, or light: *The police officer gave a signal for the traffic to stop.* *v.* to send a signal: *She signalled for the race to begin by blowing a whistle.* **signalling. signalled.**

signature (sig′nə chər) *n.* your name written by yourself in your own way.

silence *n.* the absence of sound.

silent *adj.* not making any sound. **silently** *adv.*

silk *n.* a shiny, smooth cloth made from threads that are spun by silkworms.

sill *n.* a ledge below a window or door.

silly *adj.* foolish: *a silly riddle, a sillier one, the silliest riddle ever.*

silo *n.* a tall, round tower that is used to store farm crops. *pl.* **silos.**

silver *n.* 1. a precious, shiny, white metal. 2. the colour of silver. *adj.* having this colour.

similar *adj.* nearly the same: *My dress is similar to yours.*

similarity *n.* resemblance, looking nearly the same: *There is a similarity between the two hats. pl.* **similarities.**

simmer *v.* to cook at a heat that is just less than boiling. **simmering. simmered.**

simple *adj.* 1. easy: *These problems are very simple.* 2. plain: *This design is very simple.*

simply *adv.* 1. in a simple way: *The teacher spoke simply so that everyone would understand.* 2. really, truly: *I feel simply wonderful today.*

sin *n.* a wrong or bad deed: *It is a sin to steal.* *v.* to do wrong: *He sinned when he stole the coat.* **sinning. sinned.**

since *adv.* from that time until now: *I have been away since Monday. conj.* because: *Since you ask, I will tell you the secret.*

sincere (sin sēr′) *adj.* honest and true: *Neil is a sincere boy. He always means what he says.* (*opp.* **insincere.**)

sincerely *adv.* truly: *Maria ended the letter, 'Sincerely yours'.*

sing *v.* to make a tune with your voice, using sounds or words. **singing. sang.** I have **sung.**

singe (sinj) *n.* a small or slight burn. *v.* to burn slightly: *Lightning singed the branches.* **singeing. singed.**

singer *n.* a person who sings.

single *adj.* 1. one only: *A single apple was left in the bag.* 2. unmarried: *a single man.* 3. for one only: *a single bed.* *v.* (used with **out**) to pick from others: *The coach singled me out as the best catcher.* **singling. singled.**

singular *adj.* referring to one only: *'Dog' is a singular noun; 'dogs' is plural.*

sinister *adj.* evil, or looking evil: *a sinister witch.*

sink *n.* a basin with faucets that is used for washing. *v.* to go under water: *The ship is sinking.* **sinking. sank.** it has **sunk.**

sip *n.* a small drink: *Robin had a sip of water.* *v.* to drink in small amounts: *Grandma sips her tea.* **sipping. sipped.**

Sir *n.* 1. a title given by a king or queen: *Sir John Smith.* 2. a polite name to use when speaking to a man: *Would you like to buy a ticket to the play, sir?*

siren *n.* a machine that makes a loud screaming noise to warn people about something.

sister *n.* a woman or girl who has the same parents as you do.

sit *v.* to rest on your bottom on a chair. **sitting. sat.**

site *n.* the place where something was built or will be built.

sitter *n.* a babysitter.

six *n., adj.* one more than five (6).

sixteen *n., adj.* ten more than six (16).

sixth *adj.* following fifth (6th).

sixty *n., adj.* ten times six (60).

size *n.* how big a thing is.

sizzle *v.* to make a hissing sound because of heat: *The sausages sizzle in the pan.* **sizzling. sizzled.**

skate *n.* a metal blade that can be fastened to a boot or shoe. *v.* to glide or move along on skates. **skating. skated.**

skateboard *n.* a board with wheels on which you balance. *v.* to ride a skateboard. **skateboarding. skateboarded.**

skeleton *n.* the set of bones in a body.

sketch *n.* a quick drawing. *v.* to make a quick drawing. **sketching. sketched.**

ski (skē) *n.* one of two long pieces of wood, metal, or plastic that curve up at the front: *Skis are used for downhill skiing, cross-country skiing, or waterskiing. pl.* **skis.** *v.* to travel on skis: *Jan skied all the way down the hill.* **skiing. skied.** she **skis.**

skid *n.* a sudden slide on something slippery or very smooth. *v.* to slip on a wet or icy surface. **skidding. skidded.**

skier *n.* a person who skis.

skill *n.* the power or ability to do something well: *Martin shows skill at painting pictures of people.*

skim *v.* 1. to remove something from the top of a liquid: *The cook skims the grease from the soup.* 2. to glide: *The boat skimmed over the lake.* 3. to read very quickly: *Al skimmed through the book.* **skimming. skimmed.**

skim milk milk from which the cream has been removed.

skin *n.* the outer covering of people, animals, and of some fruits and vegetables.

skin diver a person who swims under water for long periods of time: *A skin diver wears flippers and a face mask, but not a diving suit.*

skinny *adj.* very thin: *a skinny child, a skinnier child, the skinniest child in my family.*

skip *v.* 1. to jump lightly from one leg to the other, often over a rope. 2. to leave out parts: *I skipped two of the questions on the test.* **skipping. skipped.**

skipper *n.* 1. a captain of a ship. 2. a person who skips.

skirt *n.* a garment hanging down from the waist, worn by women and girls.

skull *n.* the bony part of your head: *The skull protects the brain.*

skunk *n.* a furry, black animal with a white stripe and a bushy tail: *A skunk sprays a bad-smelling liquid when it is frightened or attacked.*

sky *n.* the space above the earth where you can see the sun, moon, stars, and clouds. *pl.* **skies.**

skyline *n.* the outline of buildings against the sky: *As we drove toward Toronto, we saw the city's skyline.*

skyscraper *n.* a building that is very tall.

slab *n.* a flat, thick piece: *a slab of stone; a slab of meat.*

slack *adj.* 1. not tight, loose: *a slack rope.* 2. slow, in an easy way: *We walked at a slack pace.*

slacks *n. pl.* trousers or long pants.

slain see **slay.**

slam *n.* a hard bang. *v.* to bang hard: *The angry man slammed the door when he left.* **slamming. slammed.**

slang *n.* a word or expression that is often used in conversation, but isn't used in proper writing.

slant *n.* a tilt: *The poster is hanging at a slant. v.* to tilt, to lean in a direction that is not straight up and down. **slanting. slanted.**

slap *n.* a hit, usually with an open hand. *v.* to hit with the open hand. **slapping. slapped.**

slash *n.* a long cut made by a sharp object: *a slash in a tire. v.* to make a slash. **slashing. slashed.**

slaughter (slaw'tər) *n.* the killing of animals for food. *v.* to kill animals for food. **slaughtering. slaughtered.**

slave *n.* a person who is owned by another person.

slay *v.* to kill. **slaying. slew.** I have **slain.**

sled *n.* a wooden frame on metal runners; it is used to carry people or things over snow.

sleek *adj.* smooth and shiny: *sleek hair.*

sleep *v.* to rest completely with closed eyes. **sleeping. slept.**

sleepy *adj.* tired, wanting to sleep: *a sleepy baby, a sleepier baby, the sleepiest baby of all.*

sleet *n.* a mixture of rain and fine snow or hail.

sleeve *n.* the part of a garment that covers your arm.

sleigh (slā) *n.* a sled.

slender *adj.* 1. thin, narrow: *a slender branch on a tree.* 2. small in size or number: *a slender chance of winning.*

slept see **sleep.**

slew see **slay.**

slice *n.* a thin, flat piece cut from something: *a slice of bacon. v.* to cut off: *Adam sliced the cheese.* **slicing. sliced.**

slide *n.* 1. a smooth surface for sliding on: *The children had fun going down the slide.* 2. a small photograph or picture to be shown on a screen. 3. a small, thin piece of glass, used with a microscope. *v.* to glide smoothly along: *The boys slid on the ice.* **sliding. slid.**

slight (slīt) *adj.* not big or not important: *Helen has a slight cold.* **slightly** *adv.*

slim *adj.* slender, thin: *a slim dancer, a slimmer dancer, the slimmest dancer on the stage.*

slime *n.* soft, sticky mud or something like it.

slimy *adj.* like mud, covered with mud or slime: *a slimy swamp, a slimier swamp, the slimiest swamp of all.*

sling *n.* 1. a loop of cloth hanging from the neck, which will support an injured arm. 2. a strip of leather used to throw stones.

slip *n.* 1. a loose garment worn under a dress or skirt. 2. a small piece of paper or cloth: *I wrote down Desmond's address on a slip of paper.* 3. a quick fall or slide. *v.* 1. to slide suddenly, losing your balance. 2. to move quietly: *Jo slipped into her seat.* **slipping. slipped.**

slipper *n.* a soft shoe that you wear indoors.

slippery *adj.* having a surface that is hard to hold onto or walk on: *slippery ice.*

slit *n.* a long cut or narrow opening. *v.* to make such a cut: *Hong slit the bag open with a knife.* **slitting. slit.**

slogan *n.* a word or group of words used by a group or business to describe itself.

slope *n.* a line or piece of land that is on a slant: *a ski slope. v.* to tilt, to be higher at one end than at the other. **sloping. sloped.**

sloppy *adj.* 1. wet or slushy. 2. messy or careless: *a sloppy pile of clothes, a sloppier one, the sloppiest pile of all.*

slot *n.* a slit or narrow opening: *Alan put a coin in the slot to get some milk.*

slouch *v.* to walk with your shoulders drooping. **slouching. slouched.**

slough (slü) *n.* a body of fresh water on the Prairies, formed by rain or melting snow.

slow *adj.* taking a long time; moving at less than normal speed: *a slow train.* **slowly.** *adv.* *v.* to move more slowly: *The driver slowed down.* **slowing. slowed.**

slug *n.* 1. a kind of snail with no shell. 2. a piece of lead that is fired from a gun. *v.* to hit hard: *Alicia slugged the ball out of the stadium.* **slugging. slugged.**

sluice (slüs) *n.* a structure with a gate for controlling the flow of water of a river, lake, or canal.

slum *n.* a poor and crowded part of the city.

slump *n.* a heavy or sudden fall or loss: *Our team is having a mid-season slump. v.* to fall or drop heavily: *The dog slumped in the grass after the long run.* **slumping. slumped.**

slush *n.* partly melted snow.

sly *adj.* clever at doing things in a secret way.

smack *n.* 1. a hard hit with the open hand. 2. a sharp, slapping noise. *v.* 1. to hit hard. 2. to make a sharp noise. **smacking. smacked.**

small *adj.* little.

smart *adj.* 1. quick to understand: *He is a smart boy.* 2. neat and well-dressed: *The soldiers looked smart in their new uniforms. v.* to feel a stinging pain: *My eyes smart when I am near smoke.* **smarting. smarted.**

smash *n.* a breaking into pieces: *First I hit the ball, then I heard the smash of glass. v.* to break into pieces: *The ball smashed the glass.* **smashing. smashed.**

smear *n.* a mark left on something: *There is a smear on the table, where I spilled the oil. v.* to rub on, sometimes sloppily: *Be careful that you don't smear the paint.* **smearing. smeared.**

smell *n.* 1. a scent: *the smell of burning wood.* 2. one of the five senses: *Raccoons have a good sense of smell. v.* 1. to give off a smell: *The garbage smells.* 2. to be aware of something by using your nose: *I smell a skunk.* **smelling. smelled** or **smelt.**

smelly *adj.* having a bad smell: *smelly garbage, smellier garbage, the smelliest garbage of all.*

smelt *n.* a small, silvery fish found in lakes and rivers.

smile *n.* a turning up of the corners of your mouth to show you are happy. *v.* to make a smile. **smiling. smiled.**

smock *n.* a loose garment that looks like a long shirt.

smoke *n.* a dark cloud from something burning. *v.* 1. to give off smoke: *The fireplace is smoking.* 2. to draw in and breathe out smoke from tobacco: *Dad smokes a pipe.* **smoking. smoked.**

smooth (smüth) *adj.* even and flat, not rough or bumpy: *a smooth table top. v.* to make even and flat: *Pam smoothed the wooden bowl with sandpaper.* **smoothing. smoothed.**

smother *v.* 1. to stop someone breathing by covering the mouth and nose. 2. to cover all over: *Dave smothered his hamburger with ketchup.* **smothering. smothered.**

smoulder (smōl′dər) *v.* to burn slowly without a flame but with a lot of smoke. **smouldering. smouldered.**

smudge *n.* a dirty mark; a smear: *Daniel has a smudge of ink on his face.*

smuggle *v.* to take goods into or out of a country secretly, against the law. **smuggling. smuggled.**

smuggler *n.* a person who smuggles.

snack *n.* a light meal that is easy to get ready.

snail *n.* a small, slow creature with a shell on its back: *Snails are found on land and in water.*

snake *n.* a long, smooth reptile without legs: *A snake glides over the ground on its body.*

snap *n.* a sudden sharp sound or break: *He gave the twig a snap.* *v.* 1. to make a sudden sound: *He snapped his fingers.* 2. to break suddenly: *The branch snapped.* 3. to speak in a sudden, angry way: *I'm sorry I snapped at you when you lost my book.* 4. to take a photograph. **snapping. snapped.**

snapshot *n.* a photograph.

snare *n.* a trap used to catch animals. *v.* 1. to trap with a snare. 2. to trap: *The police snared the burglar as he was leaving.* **snaring. snared.**

snarl *n.* a low, growling sound. *v.* to make such a sound: *The dog snarled at the stranger.* **snarling. snarled.**

sneak *n.* a sly, dishonest person. *v.* to move, trying not to be seen or heard: *Kristiane was sneaking around the house.* **sneaking. sneaked.**

sneakers *n. pl.* running shoes.

sneer *n.* a look showing hatred or scorn. *v.* to give a sneer: *My brother sneered at my drawings.* **sneering. sneered.**

sneeze *n.* a loud noise made when air rushes out of your nose. *v.* to make a sneeze: *The pepper made Kim sneeze.* **sneezing. sneezed.**

sniff *v.* to breathe air in quickly through your nose: *Mother sniffed the fresh flowers.* **sniffing. sniffed.**

snip *n.* a small piece: *John took a snip off the flower.* *v.* to cut a little bit off: *Pat snipped her nails with the scissors.* **snipping. snipped.**

snore *v.* to breathe noisily while you are asleep. **snoring. snored.**

snorkel *n.* a tube for someone to breathe through while swimming just beneath the surface of the water.

snort *n.* a strong sound, made by forcing the breath through the nose. *v.* to make such a sound: *The pigs snorted at each other.* **snorting. snorted.**

snout *n.* the part of an animal's head that includes the jaws and the nose: *a pig's snout.*

snow *n.* soft, white flakes of ice that fall in cold weather. *v.* to fall as snow: *It snowed on Christmas.* **snowing. snowed.**

snowball *n.* a ball made of tightly packed snow.

snowflake *n.* one piece of snow.

snowmobile *n.* a vehicle with a motor, driven over the snow.

snowplough, snowplow *n.* a machine for clearing snow from roads.

snowshoes *n. pl.* shoes shaped like tennis rackets; they are strapped to the boots and used for walking over deep snow.

snowy *adj.* having to do with or covered with snow: *a snowy day, a snowier day, the snowiest day of the winter.*

so *adv.* 1. in this way: *Hold your pen so.* 2. to such a degree: *Don't cry so much.* 3. very: *I am so glad.* 4. also: *Are you going to the game? So am I.*
conj. therefore, as a result: *We missed the bus, so we had to walk.*

soak *v.* 1. to wet something: *The rain soaked us to the skin.* 2. to stay wet for a long time: *to soak the bread in milk; to soak in the bathtub.* **soaking. soaked.**

soap *n.* a mixture of fat and other things, used with water for washing.

soar *v.* to rise high in the sky: *The jet soared into the sky.* **soaring. soared.**

sob *v.* to cry noisily, with short breaths. **sobbing. sobbed.**

soccer *n.* a game played by two teams of eleven players each: *In soccer, players try to move a round ball into a goal. They can hit the ball with any part of the body except the hands and arms.*

sociable (sō′shə bəl) *adj.* friendly, liking people.

social (sō′shəl) *adj.* having to do with people and how they get along together: *Social studies include history and geography.*

society (sə sī′ə tē) *n.* 1. people who join together because they have the same interest: *Jan's club is called the 'Western Swimming Society'.* 2. human beings living together in a group.

sock *n.* a short stocking. *v.* to hit hard. **socking. socked.**

socket *n.* an opening into which something fits.

sod *n.* a layer of earth with grass growing on it.

soda *n.* a sweet, fizzy drink, sometimes made with ice cream.

sofa *n.* a long, soft seat with arms and a back, for two or more people.

soft *adj.* 1. not hard: *a soft seat.* 2. gentle: *a soft voice.*

softly *adv.* in a soft way: *Walk softly! The baby is sleeping.*

soggy *adj.* wet and messy, soaked: *soggy ground, soggier ground, the soggiest ground in the park.*

soil *n.* ground in which plants grow. *v.* to make or become dirty. **soiling. soiled.**

solar *adj.* having to do with, or coming from, the sun.

solar system the sun and all the planets, satellites, and comets that revolve around it.

sold see **sell.**

soldier (sōl′jər) *n.* someone who belongs to an army.

sole *n.* 1. the part underneath a foot, sock, or shoe. *pl.* **soles.** 2. a kind of flat fish that lives in the ocean. *pl.* **sole.** *adj.* single, only one: *He was the sole witness to the car crash.*

solemn (sol′əm) *adj.* very serious: *They made a solemn promise not to tell the secret.*

solid *adj.* firm right through, not hollow: *a bar of solid iron.*

solo *n.* a piece of music to be played or sung by one person. *pl.* **solos.** *adj.* played or done by one person: *a solo flight.*

solution *n.* 1. the answer to a problem, puzzle, or mystery. 2. a mixture made of a solid dissolved in a liquid.

solve *v.* to find the answer to a puzzle or mystery: *The detective solved the crime.* **solving. solved.**

some (sum) *adj.* 1. a few: *We gathered some berries.* 2. an amount of: *We ate some pie.* 3. one or the other: *We shall find some way out of the forest.*

somebody *pron.* some person: *Will somebody help me?*

somehow *adv.* in a way not known: *We shall finish the job somehow.*

someone *pron.* some person: *Someone opened the letter.*

somersault *n.* a tumble head over heels.

something *pron.* a thing not known: *I have something in my eye.*

sometimes *adv.* once in a while, now and then: *We sometimes visit each other.*

somewhere *adv.* in a place not known: *I left my key somewhere.*

son *n.* a male child: *My grandparents have two sons. My parents have one son.*

song *n.* 1. words that are sung. 2. the musical sounds of a bird.

soon *adv.* in a short time: *Mark ran and was soon at school.*

soot (sút) *n.* black powder that comes from smoke.

soothe (süth) *v.* to comfort, to make someone feel calmer: *Mother soothed Shawn and told him not to worry.* **soothing. soothed.**

sore *n.* a painful place on the body where the skin is hurt. *adj.* painful, tender: *a sore foot.*

sorrow *n.* sadness, unhappiness.

sorry *adj.* feeling unhappy at something that has happened, or something you have done.

sort *n.* a kind: *There are all sorts of flowers in the garden.* *v.* to put things in groups of the same kind: *Jimmy sorted his stamps.* **sorting. sorted.**

sought see **seek.**

soul (sōl) *n.* the part of a person that is thought to be separate from the body: *Many people believe that the soul goes on living after the body dies.*

sound *n.* a noise: *I can hear the sound of drums.* *adj.* deep: *a sound sleep.* *v.* to make sound: *The music sounds lovely.* **sounding. sounded.**

soundproof *adj.* able to keep sound out.

soup (süp) *n.* a liquid food made by boiling meat, fish, or vegetables in water.

sour *adj.* with the kind of taste that lemons and vinegar have: *sour fruit.*

source (sors) *n.* the place where something has come from: *the source of a river.*

south *n.* the direction to your left as you face the setting sun, opposite to north.

South American a person born in or living in South America. *adj.* having to do with the continent of South America.

southern (suth′ərn) *adj.* in the direction of the south: *Niagara Falls is in southern Ontario.*

souvenir (sü və nēr′) *n.* something you keep to remind you of a certain time, place, etc.

sow (sow) (*masc.* **boar**) *n.* a female pig.

sow (sō) *v.* to plant seeds. **sowing. sowed.**

space *n.* 1. the distance between things: *a space of two metres.* 2. a place that is empty: *a space where you can sit.* 3. all the places beyond the earth's atmosphere: *The astronauts shot into space.*

spaceship *n.* a rocket that can carry astronauts through space.

spade *n.* 1. a garden tool used for digging; it has a long handle and a flat blade. 2. a playing card with one or more (♠) marks on it.

spaghetti (spə get′ē) *n.* a white food made with flour and water and often served with a sauce: *In Italian, the word 'spaghetti' means 'little strings'.*

span *n.* the length of something: *the span of the bridge.*

spaniel (span′yəl) *n.* a dog with long hair, drooping ears, and short legs.

spank *v.* to smack with the open hand. **spanking. spanked.**

spanking *n.* a slap, usually on the backside, made with an open hand.

spare *adj.* left over, not being used: *After we painted the fence, we had some spare paint.* *v.* to give or lend something: *Can you spare some matches?* **sparing. spared.**

spark *n.* 1. a speck of something burning: *The burning wood threw up sparks.* 2. a tiny electric flash: *Sparks came from the wire.*

sparkle *n.* a gleam, a glitter: *He had a sparkle in his eyes.* *v.* to glitter: *The diamond ring sparkled in the light.* **sparkling. sparkled.**

sparrow *n.* a small bird with brown, grey, and white feathers.

spat see **spit.**

spatter *v.* to splash with liquid or mud. **spattering. spattered.**

spawn *n.* the eggs of fish, frogs, newts, and other water animals. *v.* to produce these eggs. **spawning. spawned.**

speak *v.* to say something. **speaking. spoke.** I have **spoken.**

speaker *n.* 1. the person who is talking. 2. a device used for making sounds louder.

spear *n.* a weapon with a long handle and a sharp point. *v.* to stab at something with a spear or any other sharp instrument. **spearing. speared.**

special (spesh′əl) *adj.* unusual, different from others in a certain way: *Tricia had some special news for her sister.*

speck *n.* a tiny bit, a small spot: *Sima had a speck of dirt in her eye.*

spectacle *n.* an unusual sight or show: *The parade was a colourful spectacle.*

spectacles *n. pl.* a pair of eyeglasses.

spectacular *adj.* very unusual: *a spectacular display of fireworks.*

spectator *n.* someone who watches a game, sport, or show.

sped see **speed.**

speech *n.* 1. the power of speaking. 2. a talk given to some people: *The famous goalie gave a speech to the team.*

speed *n.* how quickly something moves or happens: *The car went at a slow speed.* *v.* to move quickly: *The car sped down the road.* **speeding. sped.**

speedometer (spē dom′ə tər) *n.* an instrument that shows the speed of a vehicle.

spell *n.* magic words spoken to cause something to happen: *The witch cast a spell on the prince and changed him into a frog.* *v.* to write or say the letters of a word, in the correct order. **spelling. spelled** or **spelt.**

spend *v.* 1. to pay out money: *Kate spent two dollars on a present.* 2. to use time: *Philip spent an hour swimming.* **spending. spent.**

sphere (sfēr) *n.* any object shaped like a ball.

spice *n.* part of a plant used to flavour food: *Ginger, nutmeg, and cinnamon are spices.* *v.* to add spice to food: *Mark spiced the pizza with pepper.* **spicing. spiced.**

spicy *adj.* tasting of spice: *a spicy sauce, a spicier sauce, the spiciest sauce of all.*

spider *n.* a small creature with eight legs and no wings: *Many types of spiders spin webs to catch flying insects.*

spied, spies see **spy.**

spike *n.* a long, sharp nail.

spill *v.* to let a liquid overflow: *Mandy spilled some milk.* **spilling. spilled** or **spilt.**

spin *v.* 1. to turn around quickly: *He spun around on his heels.* 2. to make threads: *to spin thread on a spinning wheel.* **spinning. spun.**

spinach *n.* a dark green, leafy vegetable.

spine *n.* 1. a long set of little bones that fit together down the middle of the back. 2. a spike on a plant or animal.

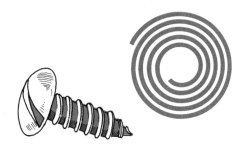

spiral *n.* a curve that keeps winding: *The narrow staircase went around in a spiral.*

spirit *n.* 1. a person's soul. 2. a ghost.

spit *v.* to shoot something out of your mouth: *Bill spat out an orange pit.* **spitting. spat.**

spite *n.* a wish to hurt someone by cruel behaviour: *My cousin broke his brother's toy out of spite.*

splash *n.* the noise made when someone or something heavy falls into water. *v.* to throw liquid about: *The girls splashed about in the pool.* **splashing. splashed.**

splendid *adj.* magnificent, wonderful: *The princess lived in a splendid castle.*

splint *n.* a piece of wood that is used to hold a broken bone in place.

splinter *n.* a thin, sharp piece of wood, metal, or glass: *Toni had a splinter in her thumb.*

split *n.* a crack; a long, thin break: *a split in the board.* *v.* to crack, to break open from end to end. **splitting. split.**

spoil *v.* to make something less good or less useful. **spoiling. spoiled** or **spoilt.**

spoke *n.* one of the rods or bars that connect the rim of a wheel to the centre. *v.* see **speak.**

sponge (spunj) *n.* 1. a soft pad, full of holes, that soaks up liquid. 2. an ocean animal that lives attached to rocks.

spool *n.* a small cylinder on which to wind thread, film, fishing line, etc.

spoon *n.* a small, shallow bowl at the end of a handle.

sport *n.* 1. a game in which a person is active: *Some sports are football, hockey, and bowling.* 2. a person who is cheerful, honest, and brave: *Be a good sport, and come on the roller coaster with us!*

spot *n.* 1. a small mark: *There is a spot on my coat.* 2. a special place: *This is the spot where I fell.* *v.* to see, to notice: *Lorraine spotted an owl in the tree.* **spotting. spotted.**

spotlight *n.* a bright light shining on one spot, as on a stage.

spotted *adj.* covered with spots.

spout *n.* the narrow part of a container through which a liquid flows: *the spout of a kettle.* *v.* to shoot out a liquid through a narrow opening: *The whale spouted water beside the ship.* **spouting. spouted.**

sprain *v.* to twist a part of the body so that it becomes painful: *Deborah sprained her ankle when she fell.* **spraining. sprained.**

sprang see **spring.**

sprawl *v.* to sit or lie with arms and legs spread out carelessly: *Jack sprawled across the couch.* **sprawling. sprawled.**

spray *n.* liquid flying or blowing in tiny drops. *v.* to scatter fine drops of liquid: *Candy sprayed paint on the wall.* **spraying. sprayed.**

spread (spred) *n.* a covering for a surface: *a woollen spread.* *v.* 1. to open out: *The eagle spread its wings.* 2. to cover a surface: *John spread butter on his bread.* **spreading. spread.**

spring *n.* 1. the season after winter. 2. a place where water flows out of the ground. 3. a metal spiral that goes back into shape after it has been pressed or stretched. *v.* to jump up suddenly: *Darren sprang out of bed when the alarm rang.* **springing. sprang.** it has **sprung.**

sprinkle *v.* to scatter powder or drops of liquid: *Chris sprinkled salt on his food.* **sprinkling. sprinkled.**

sprint *v.* to run very quickly for a short distance. **sprinting. sprinted.**

sprout *n.* a new growth on a plant. *v.* to begin to grow: *The beans are sprouting in the water.* **sprouting. sprouted.**

spruce *n.* an evergreen tree with cones, and leaves that look like green needles.

sprung see **spring.**

spun see **spin.**

spur *n.* a spiked wheel on a rider's boot, sometimes used to make the horse go faster.

spurt *v.* to gush out suddenly in a stream: *Water spurted from the hole in the garden hose.* **spurting. spurted.**

spy *n.* someone who tries secretly to find out things about a person or an enemy country. *pl.* **spies.** *v.* 1. to watch secretly. 2. to catch sight of: *Saba spied a rabbit in the field.* **spying. spied.** he **spies.**

squad (skwod) *n.* a small group of people working together: *a police squad.*

squadron *n.* a group of tanks, planes, police cars, etc. and the people who drive them.

square *n.* 1. a flat shape with four equal sides and four equal angles. 2. a four-sided open space in a city or town. *adj.* having the shape of a square.

squash *n.* 1. any of several vegetables that grow on vines along the ground. *pl.* **squash.** 2. a game somewhat like tennis, played with a hollow rubber ball. *v.* to squeeze or crush. **squashing. squashed.**

squat (skwot) *v.* to sit on the floor or the ground with legs bent in front of your body. **squatting. squatted.**

squeak *n.* a short, high sound. *v.* to make this sound: *The mouse squeaked in its cage.* **squeaking. squeaked.**

squeal *n.* a long, high cry. *v.* to make this sound: *The children squealed with joy when they found their dog.* **squealing. squealed.**

squeeze *v.* to press something hard: *Squeeze the tube to make the paint come out.* **squeezing. squeezed.**

squint *v.* to look with partly closed eyes: *The sun shining on the snow made me squint.* **squinting. squinted.**

squirrel *n.* a small animal with a long, fluffy tail: *Squirrels eat nuts and live in trees.*

squirt *v.* to shoot liquid in a fine stream: *Adam squirted water from his water pistol.* **squirting. squirted.**

St. short for **street** or **saint.**

stab *v.* to wound someone with a pointed object. **stabbing. stabbed.**

stable *n.* a building in which horses are kept.

stack *n.* a large pile: *a stack of bricks; a haystack.* *v.* to pile up: *We stacked the boxes in the corner.* **stacking. stacked.**

stadium *n.* a sports ground with rows of seats all around.

staff *n.* 1. a stick or pole: *the staff of a flag.* 2. a group of people who work together: *a hospital staff.*

stage *n.* 1. a raised platform in a theatre. 2. the point someone has reached in doing something: *I am in the last stage of my work.* *v.* to present a play or concert: *Our school staged an Easter concert.* **staging. staged.**

stagecoach *n.* a large, closed coach, pulled by horses: *Stagecoaches were once used for carrying people and mail.*

stagger *v.* to walk in an unsteady way: *The old man felt dizzy and staggered home.* **staggering. staggered.**

stain *n.* a spot that has marked something. *v.* to mark or blot: *I stained my pants with grease.* **staining. stained.**

staircase *n.* a set of steps with a handrail.

stairs *n. pl.* a set of steps leading from one floor of a building to another.

stake *n.* a thick post, pointed at one end and hammered into the ground.

stale *adj.* old, not fresh: *stale bread.*

stalk (stawk) *n.* a stem of a flower or plant. *v.* to hunt quietly, keeping out of sight. **stalking. stalked.**

stall *n.* 1. a place for a cow or horse to stand in a barn or stable. 2. a place for displaying things at a market or fair. *v.* to stop running because there isn't enough power: *The car stalls on very cold mornings.* **stalling. stalled.**

stallion (stal'yən) (*fem.* **mare**) *n.* a male horse.

stamp *n.* a small piece of paper that is sticky on one side: *Stamps are bought at the post office, to be put on letters and packages.* *v.* 1. to stick a stamp on a letter or package. 2. to bang your foot on the ground. **stamping. stamped.**

stampede *n.* 1. a sudden rush of confused people or animals. 2. a rodeo, often with other amusements, at a fair: *the Calgary Stampede.* *v.* to rush madly in confusion: *The buffalo stampeded when they heard the shot.* **stampeding. stampeded.**

stand *v.* 1. to be on your feet or to rise to your feet. 2. to bear, to put up with: *Frances could not stand the pain any longer.* 3. (used with **for**) to mean: *B.C. stands for British Columbia.* **standing. stood.**

star *n.* 1. a heavenly body that looks like a speck of light at night. 2. an outstanding actor, actress, singer, sports player, etc. 3. a performer with a large part in a play, movie, or program. *v.* to have a large part in a play, movie, or program: *My favourite actor is starring in a new movie.* **starring. starred.**

starboard *n.* the right side of a ship looking forward towards the bow. (*opp.* **port.**)

starch *n.* 1. a powder or liquid used to make clothes stiff. 2. a white substance that is found in potatoes and other foods.

stare *v.* to watch someone or something for a long time with a steady look. **staring. stared.**

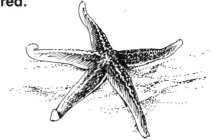

starfish *n.* a small sea creature that has a flat body shaped like a star. *pl.* **starfish.**

starry *adj.* full of stars or shiny like a star: *a starry night, a starrier one, the starriest night this month.*

start *n.* 1. a beginning: *That race had a good start.* 2. a sudden movement of surprise: *Burt gave a start when he saw the bear.* *v.* 1. to begin: *Cathy started to knit.* 2. to move suddenly. **starting. started.**

startle *v.* to make a person or animal feel surprised or frightened. **startling. startled.**

starve *v.* to be very ill or die because there is not enough food to eat. **starving. starved.**

state *n.* 1. how someone or something is: *My old clothes are in a bad state.* 2. one of the parts of certain countries: *There are 50 states in the United States of America.* *v.* to say firmly: *The ranger stated that we could not cycle in the park.* **stating. stated.**

statement *n.* a sentence that tells a fact or an opinion: *My dad made a statement about our vacation. He said, 'This year we'll make a train trip.'*

static *n.* electricity in the air that causes a crackling sound on radios and TV sets.

station (stā'shən) *n.* 1. a stopping place along a route: *a railway station.* 2. a building used for a certain purpose: *a police station.*

stationary *adj.* not moving.

stationery *n.* writing paper and envelopes.

statue (stat′yü) *n.* a figure of a person or animal that is made out of clay, stone, metal, or some other solid material.

stay *v.* 1. to remain behind: *Father stayed at home while we went out.* 2. to live somewhere for a short time: *We stayed at a country cottage for the night.* 3. to keep on being: *We stayed friends after he moved to another province.* **staying. stayed.**

steady (sted′ē) *adj.* 1. firm, not wobbling: *I made sure the ladder was steady.* 2. not changing: *a steady fall of rain.* *(opp.* **unsteady.***)*

steak (stāk) *n.* a slice of meat or fish for cooking.

steal *v.* to take something that is not yours and keep it. **stealing. stole.** I have **stolen.**

steam *n.* water in the form of gas or vapour: *Boiling water gives off steam.* *v.* 1. to give off steam. 2. to loosen or cook with steam. **steaming. steamed.**

steamboat *n.* a boat driven forward by an engine that is powered by steam.

steel *n.* a strong metal, made from iron.

steep *adj.* having a very sharp slope: *a steep hill.*

steeple *n.* the top of a church tower.

steer *n.* a young bull. *v.* to make a ship or vehicle go where you want. **steering. steered.**

stem *n.* the long, thin part of a plant that holds up a leaf, flower, or fruit.

stencil *n.* a thin sheet of material in which letters and patterns are cut.

step *n.* 1. a movement made by putting your foot down in a new place: *She took ten steps forward.* 2. the part of a staircase on which you walk. *v.* to move your feet when walking or dancing: *Ruthie stepped forward and made her speech.* **stepping. stepped.**

stepfather *n.* your new father, if your mother married a second time.

stepmother *n.* your new mother, if your father married a second time.

stereo *n.* a record player that gives different sounds out of two or more speakers. *pl.* **stereos.**

sterile (ster′əl) *adj.* free from germs.

sterilize *v.* to make sterile. **sterilizing. sterilized.**

stern *n.* the back part of a ship. (*opp.* **bow.**) *adj.* strict or harsh: *We were given a stern warning not to lie again.*

stew *n.* meat and vegetables cooked gently together in water.

steward (*fem.* **stewardess**) *n.* a person in charge of food and other services on an airplane, train, or ship.

stick *n.* 1. a thin piece of wood: *a rough stick.* 2. a thin piece of anything: *a stick of chalk.* 3. a shaped piece of wood: *a hockey stick.* *v.* to fasten or be fastened: *The sign was stuck to the board.* **sticking. stuck.**

sticky *adj.* able to stick to something: *sticky glue, stickier glue, the stickiest glue on the shelf.*

stiff *adj.* 1. not easy to move or bend: *The gate was stiff.* 2. strong: *a stiff wind.*

still *adj.* quiet and with no movement: *a still pond.* *adv.* now as before: *He is still in bed.*

stilts *n. pl.* two poles, each with a step part way up, for walking high above the ground.

sting *v.* 1. for an insect or thorn to prick the skin: *Tricia was stung by a wasp.* 2. to hurt like a sting: *The smoke made my eyes sting.* **stinging. stung.**

stingy (stin′jē) *adj.* not willing to spend money or share something: *a stingy person, a stingier one, the stingiest person I ever met.*

stink *n.* a bad smell. *v.* to smell awful: *That old soup really stinks.* **stinking. stank** or **stunk.**

stir *v.* 1. to mix soft or liquid things by moving them around with a spoon: *Dad stirred sugar into his tea.* 2. to start to move: *Do not stir. There is a mouse near you.* **stirring. stirred.**

stirrups *n. pl.* a rider's footrests hanging from each side of a horse's saddle.

stitch *n.* 1. in sewing and knitting, a loop of thread made with a needle. 2. thread used by doctors to hold skin together after an operation or an injury. *v.* to join with stitches. **stitching. stitched.**

stock *n.* 1. a supply of things kept to be used or sold: *The corner store has a large stock of cereals.* 2. broth from cooked meat, fish, or vegetables. *v.* to keep a supply: *We stocked our cottage with firewood.* **stocking. stocked.**

stocking *n.* a long, close-fitting cover for your leg and foot.

stole, stolen see **steal.**

stomach (stum′ək) *n.* a muscular bag in your body where food goes when you have eaten it.

stone *n.* 1. a small piece of rock. 2. a jewel: *a precious stone.* 3. the hard seed of some fruits: *a peach stone, a cherry stone.*

stood see **stand.**

stool *n.* a small seat with no back or arms.

stoop *v.* to bend forward and downward: *Owen stooped to pick up the coin.* **stooping. stooped.**

stop *n.* a place where a bus or train halts for passengers: *a bus stop.* *v.* to end, to bring to an end: *Denise stopped reading. The referee stopped the game.* **stopping. stopped.**

store *n.* a shop: *a grocery store.* *v.* to put away for use in the future: *The squirrels stored nuts for the winter.* **storing. stored.**

storey, story *n.* a floor of a building with all its rooms. *pl.* **storeys** or **stories.**

stork *n.* a bird with a long beak, a long neck, and long legs.

storm *n.* bad weather with heavy rain or snow, strong winds, and sometimes thunder.

stormy *adj.* having to do with a storm: *a stormy day, a stormier day, the stormiest day of the year.*

story *n.* 1. words that tell about something that has really happened: *a newspaper story about the new zoo.* 2. words that tell about something that someone has imagined: *We read a story about ghosts and witches.* *pl.* **stories.**

stout *adj.* big and strong: *a stout cow.*

stove *n.* a large object made of heavy metal, used for cooking or heating.

stowaway *n.* someone who hides in a ship or plane to travel free.

straight (strāt) *adj.* not bent or curved: *Can you walk in a straight line?* *adv.* 1. in a way that is not bent or curved: *Stand up straight!* 2. without delay: *Go straight home after school.*

strain *n.* an injury caused by too much effort. *v.* to stretch, pull, push, or try too much: *The heavy box strained the ropes.* **straining. strained.**

strait (strāt) *n.* a narrow channel between two large bodies of water.

strand *n.* one of many threads or wires twisted together to make a rope or cable.

v. to leave in a helpless way: *The sailors were stranded on a lonely island.* **stranding. stranded.**

strange *adj.* 1. unusual: *a strange feeling.* 2. not known to you: *a strange bird.*

stranger *n.* someone you do not know: *A stranger asked me the way to the church.*

strangle *v.* 1. to kill by squeezing the throat. 2. to choke. **strangling. strangled.**

strap *n.* a strip of leather or cloth. *v.* 1. to hit with a strap. 2. to close with a strap: *Ray strapped his books to his bike.* **strapping. strapped.**

strategy (strat'ə jē) *n.* a plan for getting something you want: *The players' strategy surprised the other team.* *pl.* **strategies.**

straw *n.* 1. the dried stems of corn and other cereals. 2. a thin tube used for sucking up a liquid.

strawberry *n.* the juicy red fruit of a plant that grows close to the ground. *pl.* **strawberries.**

stray *n.* a lost child or animal. *adj.* lost: *We found a stray animal in the park.* *v.* to wander about and get lost: *Tina's dog strayed from home.* **straying. strayed.**

streak (strēk) *n.* a stripe: *a streak of paint.* *v.* 1. to paint stripes. 2. to move quickly: *A jet streaked across the sky.* **streaking. streaked.**

stream *n.* 1. a small river. 2. a movement of things or people: *a steady stream of cars.* *v.* to flow or move steadily: *People streamed out of the stadium.* **streaming. streamed.**

street *n.* a road with buildings on each side.

streetcar *n.* a vehicle that can carry many passengers: *Streetcars are powered by electricity and run on rails.*

strength *n.* the quality of being strong; power.

stress *n.* pressure, strain: *The bridge almost collapsed under the stress of the trucks.* *v.* to give importance to something: *We stress the first syllable when we say the word 'birthday'.* **stressing. stressed.**

stretch *v.* 1. to make something longer by pulling it: *Chan stretched the piece of elastic.* 2. to reach: *Verna stretched out her hand for the book.* **stretching. stretched.**

stretcher *n.* a frame of poles and material for carrying a sick or wounded person.

strict *adj.* following a rule very carefully.

strike *n.* 1. the finding of a large amount of oil or of metal ore. 2. a stopping of work: *The factory workers went on strike for higher pay.* 3. a pitch in baseball that counts against the batter. *v.* 1. to hit with a lot of force: *Don't strike the dog.* 2. to rub: *to strike a match.* 3. to find suddenly: *to strike oil.* 4. to stop work: *The workers are striking for more pay.* 5. to give the time by sounding bells: *The clock struck three.* **striking. struck.**

string *n.* 1. a thin cord for tying things. 2. a long line of things: *a string of lights.* 3. a cord or wire on a musical instrument. *v.* to put on a string: *Marsha strung the beads at summer camp.* **stringing. strung.**

stringed instruments musical instruments that have strings and are played with a bow or with the fingers: *Some stringed instruments are the violin, harp, and cello.*

strip *n.* a long, narrow piece of anything: *a strip of cloth.* *v.* to take off: *to strip wallpaper from a wall.* **stripping. stripped.**

stripe *n.* a long, narrow streak of colour: *stripes of red and white paint.*

stroke *n.* 1. a hard hit: *a stroke of an axe.* 2. a swimming movement: *Patsy swims the breast stroke well.* 3. a mark made by a pen, crayon, or brush. *v.* to rub gently: *Alberto stroked his dog.* **stroking. stroked.**

stroll *n.* a slow, quiet walk. *v.* to walk slowly and easily: *The girls strolled in the park.* **strolling. strolled.**

strong *adj.* powerful, having strength.

struck see **strike.**

structure *n.* anything that is built: *A bridge, school, house, or barn is a structure.*

struggle *n.* 1. a fight. 2. a great effort. *v.* 1. to fight: *The soldiers struggled against the enemy.* 2. to make a great effort: *Pete struggled with the math problem.* **struggling. struggled.**

strung see **string.**

stub *n.* a short piece that is left: *the stub of an old pencil.* *v.* to bang your toe into something. **stubbing. stubbed.**

stubborn *adj.* not easily giving in: *John is a stubborn boy. He never says that he made a mistake.*

stuck see **stick.**

student *n.* someone who is learning things, usually at school.

studio *n.* 1. a place where an artist or photographer works. 2. a place where movies are filmed, or where radio or television programs are made. *pl.* **studios.**

study *v.* 1. to try to learn: *Jennifer is studying for the history test.* 2. to look at carefully: *The scouts studied the map to find their way.* **studying. studied.** she **studies.**

stuff *n.* 1. material that a thing is made of: *This coat is made of good stuff.* 2. a thing or things, often useless: *There is a lot of old stuff in the basement.* *v.* to pack full: *to stuff a drawer with socks.* **stuffing. stuffed.**

stuffing *n.* 1. padding in a pillow or cushion. 2. a filling to be stuffed into a chicken, turkey, or other food before cooking it.

stumble *v.* to trip over something and nearly fall. **stumbling. stumbled.**

stump *n.* the part of a tree left in the ground after the trunk has been cut down. *v.* to puzzle or confuse: *That question stumped our panel.* **stumping. stumped.**

stun *v.* 1. to knock unconscious, or nearly so. 2. to give someone shocking or very surprising news: *Mother was stunned by the bad news.* **stunning. stunned.**

stung see **sting.**

stunk see **stink.**

stunt *n.* an act that shows skill and attracts attention. *v.* to slow down the growth of something: *Lack of water stunted the growth of these plants.* **stunting. stunted.**

stupid *adj.* 1. silly: *a stupid trick.* 2. slow to understand: *a stupid dog.*

sturdy *adj.* strong and healthy: *a sturdy tree, a sturdier one, the sturdiest tree in the yard.*

sty *n.* a place where pigs are kept. *pl.* **sties.**

style *n.* 1. a way of doing something: *I don't like his style of skating. He moves too slowly.* 2. the present way or a fancy way: *Jim always dresses in style.*

sub- a prefix meaning 'under': **sub-zero** means that the temperature is under zero; a **subway** is an underground way.

subject (sub'jəkt) *n.* 1. something thought about, written about, or studied: *The subject of the talk is sport.* 2. a person who is under the control of another: *a subject of the queen.*

submarine *n.* a ship that can travel under water.

submerge *v.* to go beneath the surface of a liquid: *The children submerged their boats in the tub.* **submerging. submerged.**

submit *v.* to give in, to surrender: *Submit your reports after class.* **submitting. submitted.**

subscription *n.* a promise to take and pay for something: *I have a subscription to a nature magazine.*

substance *n.* any material; what a thing is made of: *The can is full of a sticky substance.*

substitute *n.* someone or something used instead of another. *v.* to put someone or something in place of another. **substituting. substituted.**

subtract *v.* to take away: *Subtract 5 from 7, and 2 is left.* **subtracting. subtracted.**

subtraction *n.* the taking of one number from another.

suburb *n.* an area of houses outside or near a city.

subway *n.* 1. an underground passage. 2. an electric railway that travels underground.

succeed (sək sēd′) *v.* 1. to manage to do what you are trying to do: *Jerry succeeded in winning the race.* 2. to follow and take the place of somebody: *George succeeded Ellen as president of the club.* **succeeding. succeeded.**

success *n.* a person or thing that succeeds in what is tried: *The concert was a great success.*

successful *adj.* succeeding, having success. (*opp.* **unsuccessful.**) **successfully** *adv.*

such *adj.* 1. so much: *I have such a lot to do.* 2. of the same kind: *flowers such as these.*

suck *v.* 1. to draw something into your mouth: *to suck lemonade through a straw.* 2. to roll something in your mouth, but not chew it: *to suck a mint.* **sucking. sucked.**

suction *n.* the action of sucking liquid, gas, etc.

sudden *adj.* quick, unexpected: *a sudden fall.* **suddenly** *adv.*

suds *n. pl.* soapy water with bubbles on top.

sue *v.* to use the law when you feel you have been unfairly treated: *The hockey player is suing the team for firing him.* **suing. sued.**

suffer *v.* to feel pain or sorrow: *Tom is suffering from a bad cold.* **suffering. suffered.**

sufficient (sə fish′ənt) *adj.* enough: *I have sufficient money for my trip.* (*opp.* **insufficient.**)

suffix *n.* letters put at the end of a word to change its meaning or form a new word: *When you put the suffix 'proof' at the end of the word 'water', you get 'waterproof'.*

suffocate *v.* to choke, to keep from breathing: *Tim was nearly suffocated by the smoke.* **suffocating. suffocated.**

sugar (shŭg′ər) *n.* a sweet substance used in cooking and put in drinks: *Sugar comes mostly from sugar beets and sugar cane.*

suggest (sə jest′) *v.* to offer an idea to other people: *Terry suggested that we all play ball.* **suggesting. suggested.**

suggestion *n.* an idea or plan.

suit (süt) *n.* 1. a set of clothes to be worn together: *A man's suit has a jacket and trousers.* 2. any of the four types of playing cards: *The four suits are clubs, diamonds, hearts, and spades.* *v.* to be right for: *That dress suits you.* **suiting. suited.**

suitcase *n.* a flat bag for carrying clothes.

sum *n.* 1. a certain amount: *a sum of money.* 2. the total amount when you add things together.

summary *n.* a short description giving the main points. *pl.* **summaries.**

summer *n.* the season after spring.

summit *n.* the top, the highest point: *the summit of a mountain.*

sun *n.* the bright star that we see during the day; it sends us heat and light.

sunbeam *n.* a ray of sunshine.

sunburn *n.* the burning of your skin by the sun.

sundae *n.* ice cream served with a candy sauce, nuts, cherries, and whipped cream.

Sunday *n.* the first day of the week.

sundial *n.* an instrument that shows the time by the position of a shadow on a dial.

sunflower *n.* a large yellow flower that grows on a tall plant.

sung see **sing.**

sunk see **sink.**

sunny *adj.* lit up with sunshine: *a sunny day, a sunnier day, the sunniest day of the summer.*

sunrise *n.* the time when the sun comes up.

sunset *n.* the time when the sun goes down.

sunshine *n.* the light of the sun when it is shining.

super- a prefix meaning 'a lot of'; 'great': a **supermarket** carries a lot of different goods.

superb *adj.* excellent, splendid: *The sunset was a superb sight.*

superintendent *n.* a person who manages or directs something: *an apartment building superintendent.*

superior *adj.* 1. better than: *These apples are superior to those.* 2. higher in rank: *A general is superior to a captain.*

supermarket *n.* a very large store that sells food and household goods: *Shoppers serve themselves in a supermarket.*

supernatural *adj.* not part of the natural world.

supersonic *adj.* travelling faster than sound: *a supersonic jet.*

superstition (sü pər stish'ən) *n.* a belief in magic and spells: *It is a superstition that black cats bring bad luck.*

superstitious (sü pər stish'əs) *adj.* having superstitions.

supper *n.* the last meal of the day.

supply *n.* things kept ready to be used or sold: *The market has a large supply of plums.* pl. **supplies.** *v.* to provide: *The butcher supplies us with good meat.* **supplying. supplied.** he **supplies.**

support *v.* 1. to hold up: *This desk can't support heavy things.* 2. to help, to encourage: *We support the local football team.* **supporting. supported.**

suppose *v.* 1. to imagine, to pretend: *Let us suppose that Janice is queen.* 2. to think something is likely to happen: *I suppose he'll bring it later.* **supposing. supposed.**

sure (shür) *adj.* certain: *John is sure he is right.* **surely** *adv.*

surf *n.* waves breaking on the seashore.

surface *n.* the outside or top part of anything: *The astronauts landed on the surface of the moon.*

surfing *n.* the sport of riding to shore on a wave.

surgeon *n.* a doctor who does operations.

surgery *n.* the treatment of illness and injury by operations on the body.

surprise *n.* something unexpected: *Her uncle's present was a surprise.* *v.* to do something that someone does not expect: *We surprised Maria with our visit.* **surprising. surprised.**

surrender *v.* to give up: *The enemy surrendered when we attacked.* **surrendering. surrendered.**

surround *v.* to be all around: *The house is surrounded by trees.* **surrounding. surrounded.**

survive *v.* to remain alive: *The shrubs survived the cold of last winter.* **surviving. survived.**

survivor *n.* a person who survives something.

suspect (sus'pekt) *n.* someone who is thought to be guilty: *The police arrested a suspect in the robbery.*

suspect (səs pekt') *v.* to be doubtful of, to think there is something wrong: *I suspect Ben is not telling everything.* **suspecting. suspected.**

suspend v. 1. to hang something so that it can swing. 2. to keep out for a time: *to be suspended from school.* **suspending. suspended.**

suspense n. the feeling of being uncertain and worried that something may happen: *I was kept in suspense all through the movie.*

suspicious (səs pish′əs) adj. feeling that something is wrong, not trusting: *My neighbour is suspicious of people she doesn't know well.*

swallow (swol′ō) n. a small bird that can fly very fast: *Swallows are brown or blue.* v. to pass food and drink down your throat. **swallowing. swallowed.**

swam see **swim.**

swamp (swomp) n. an area of soft, very wet ground. v. to flood with water: *Water swamped the boat.* **swamping. swamped.**

swan (swon) n. a very large waterbird, usually white, that has a long neck.

swarm n. 1. a large group of insects: *a swarm of bees.* 2. a large group of people or animals.

sway v. to swing from side to side: *The trees swayed in the wind.* **swaying. swayed.**

swear v. 1. to make a promise or take an oath: *The witness swore on the Bible that she would tell the truth.* 2. to use bad language. **swearing. swore.** I have **sworn.**

sweat (swet) n. the moisture from your skin when you are very hot or ill. v. to give off this moisture. **sweating. sweated.**

sweater (swet′ər) n. a knitted piece of clothing worn on the top part of your body.

sweep v. to clean the floor or ground with a brush or broom: *Lynn swept the floor with a large brush.* **sweeping. swept.**

sweet adj. 1. tasting like sugar. 2. pleasant to smell: *a sweet flower.* 3. pleasant to hear: *a sweet voice.* 4. nice: *a sweet person.*

swell v. to keep growing bigger: *The river swelled during the flood.* **swelling. swelled.** it has **swollen** or **swelled.**

swept see **sweep.**

swerve v. to change direction quickly: *Bob swerved on his bicycle to avoid the little boy.* **swerving. swerved.**

swift adj. fast, speedy, quick: *a swift automobile.* **swiftly** adv.

swim v. to move through water using your arms and legs. **swimming. swam.** I have **swum.**

swimmer n. a person who swims.

swindle v. to cheat, usually over money: *The dishonest banker tried to swindle the old man.* **swindling. swindled.**

swine n. a pig. pl. **swine.**

swing n. a seat hanging on ropes or chains on which you can push yourself. v. 1 to move back and forth: *to swing on a rope.* 2. to turn quickly: *The driver swung around the corner.* **swinging. swung.**

swirl v. to move around and around: *The leaves swirled in the wind.* **swirling. swirled.**

switch n. a little knob or button used to turn something on or off: *a switch for the light.* v. 1. to change from one thing to another: *The robbers switched cars.* 2. to turn on or off with an electrical switch. **switching. switched.**

swollen see **swell.**

swoop v. to move down quickly: *The hawk swooped down on the mouse.* **swooping. swooped.**

sword (sōrd) n. a long steel blade with a handle.

swore, sworn see **swear.**

swum see **swim.**

swung see **swing.**

syllable (sil′ə bəl) *n.* a separate sound in a word: *'Winter' has two syllables. 'Go' has one syllable.*

symbol (sim′bəl) *n.* something that stands for or represents something else: *The lion is a symbol of courage. Red is the symbol for stop or danger.*

sympathy (sim′pə thē) *n.* a feeling of being sorry for someone who is ill, sad, or in trouble. *pl.* **sympathies.**

synagogue (sin′ə gog) *n.* a building for Jewish worship and teaching.

syrup (sēr′əp) *n.* a thick, sweet liquid.

system (sis′təm) *n.* 1. a number of things that form a whole: *a telephone system.* 2. a way of doing things: *My mother has her own system for doing the laundry.*

t

tab *n.* a small flap that is attached to something.

table *n.* 1. a piece of furniture with a flat top and legs. 2. a list of numbers or information: *a multiplication table; a table of contents.*

tablespoon *n.* a large spoon used to measure and serve food.

tablet *n.* 1. a small, flat piece of medicine. 2. a pad of paper.

table tennis a game played on a table with paddles and a plastic ball: *Another name for table tennis is ping-pong.*

tack *n.* a small nail. *v.* to fasten with tacks. **tacking. tacked.**

tackle *n.* the things you need for some kinds of sports or jobs: *fishing tackle.* *v.* 1. to try to do something hard: *The children tackled the job of weeding the garden.* 2. in football, to bring an opponent down. **tackling. tackled.**

tadpole *n.* a very young frog or toad.

taffy, toffee *n.* a kind of candy made with brown sugar and butter.

tag *n.* 1. a label: *a price tag.* 2. a game in which one person has to chase and touch another. *v.* 1. to put a label or ticket on something. 2. to touch someone in the game of tag. **tagging. tagged.**

tail *n.* 1. the movable back end of an animal, fish, or bird. 2. something that has the shape of a tail, such as the back end of an airplane. 3. the side of a coin that does not show the head. *v.* to follow: *The police tailed the car.* **tailing. tailed.**

tailor *n.* a person who makes clothes.

take *v.* 1. to get hold of and carry: *to take an umbrella.* 2. to do something: *to take a photograph.* **taking. took.** I have **taken.**

tale *n.* a story, true or made-up: *a fairy tale.*

talent *n.* a special skill: *Greg has a real talent for acting.*

talk *n.* a speech; something said: *The speaker gave a talk about the planets.* *v.* to speak, to say something. **talking. talked.**

talkative (tawk′ə tiv) *adj.* fond of talking.

tall *adj.* very high: *a tall tower, a taller one, the tallest tower in the world.*

tame *adj.* not wild, living with you as a pet: *a tame rabbit.* *v.* to train a wild animal or bird to be friendly: *Mary tamed a lamb, which followed her everywhere.* **taming. tamed.**

tamper *v.* to meddle, to bother: *Don't tamper with the radio if you don't know what you're doing.* **tampering. tampered.**

tan *n.* a light brown colour. *adj.* having such a colour. *v.* 1. to make animal hides into leather by soaking them in an acid. 2. to become tan from the sun. **tanning. tanned.**

tangerine (tan jə rēn′) *n.* a small, juicy fruit that is like an orange.

tangle *v.* to twist together in a confused way. **tangling. tangled.** (*opp.* **untangle.**)

tank *n.* 1. a large container that holds liquid or gas. 2. a large, powerful vehicle with guns attached to it, used by armies.

tanker *n.* a ship used to carry coal, oil, or other goods.

tantrum *n.* a fit of anger: *a temper tantrum.*

tap *n.* a device for turning gas or water on or off: *the bathtub tap.* *v.* 1. to knock lightly: *She tapped her fingers on the table.* 2. to make a hole in something so that liquid can get out: *They tapped the sugar maple trees for sap.* **tapping. tapped.**

tape *n.* 1. a long, narrow strip of cloth, paper, or plastic. 2. a thin, plastic strip with one sticky side. 3. a thin, narrow strip of plastic film, used for recording sounds. *v.* 1. to close with tape: *Laura taped the pictures into her scrapbook.* 2. to record sounds on a strip of plastic film: *I taped my speech and listened to it several times.* **taping. taped.**

tape measure a long, narrow strip of cloth, plastic, or metal, marked in centimetres or inches: *Tape measures are used to measure length.*

tape recorder a machine that records sounds on a plastic tape, which can be played back later.

tar *n.* a thick, black, sticky substance used in making roads. *v.* to cover with tar. **tarring. tarred.**

tarantula *n.* a large, hairy spider: *A tarantula can give a painful bite, but it is usually not dangerous.*

target *n.* something to aim at: *Kit shot the arrow into the centre of the target.*

tarnish *v.* to lose its shine and become dull, as some metals do: *Silver tarnishes easily.* **tarnishing. tarnished.**

tart *n.* a small pie of fruit, custard, or some other filling. *adj.* sharp in taste: *a tart green apple.*

tartan *n.* woollen cloth with a plaid pattern, sometimes made into kilts.

task *n.* a job to be done: *Andrew has the task of clearing out the shed.*

tassel *n.* a group of threads tied together at one end and left hanging at the other: *a tassel on the end of a scarf.*

taste *n.* the flavour of the food you eat: *a sweet taste.* *v.* 1. to eat or drink a little of something to try its flavour: *Bobbie tasted the soup and liked it.* 2. to have a certain flavour: *This hamburger tastes salty.* **tasting. tasted.**

tasty *adj.* having a good flavour: *a tasty dessert, a tastier one, the tastiest dessert of all.*

tattered *adj.* torn, ragged: *a tattered old coat.*

tattletale *n.* a person who tells secrets.

tattoo *n.* a coloured picture put on the skin. *pl.* **tattoos.** *v.* to put such a picture on the skin. **tattooing. tattooed.**

taught see **teach.**

tax *n.* money that is paid to a government to help pay for roads, education, etc.

taxi *n.* a car that you hire; you pay the driver for the distance he or she takes you. *pl.* **taxis.** *v.* to move slowly over a surface: *The airplane taxied down the runway.* **taxiing. taxied.** it **taxis.**

tea *n.* a drink made by pouring boiling water over dried leaves: *Tea leaves grow in China, India, Sri Lanka, and other countries.*

teach *v.* to show people how to do things, to give lessons. **teaching. taught.**

teacher *n.* someone who teaches, usually in a school.

team *n.* 1. a group of people playing or working together, often in a game: *a football team.* 2. a group of animals working together: *a team of oxen pulling a cart.*

teapot *n.* a container in which tea is made; it has a handle and a spout.

tear (tēr) *n.* a drop of salty water coming from your eye.

tear (tār) *n.* a ripped spot: *Please sew the tear on my jacket.* *v.* 1. to rip: *Jake tore his pants.* 2. to come to pieces when pulled: *That paper tears easily.* **tearing. tore.** I have **torn.**

tease *n.* a person who bothers or makes someone upset: *Don't be such a tease.* *v.* to bother or make fun of in a playful way: *Don't tease the dog. He may bite you.* **teasing. teased.**

teaspoon *n.* a small spoon used for eating, measuring, and stirring.

teenager *n.* a person who is between 13 and 19 years of age.

teepee, tepee *n.* a cone-shaped tent, once used by Indians on the plains.

teeter-totter *n.* a long board with a support in the middle, used by children in play.

teeth plural of **tooth.**

telegram *n.* a message sent by a telegraph.

telegraph *n.* a system used to send messages over a long distance: *A telegraph message is sent by code, over wires.*

telephone *n.* an instrument that lets you speak to anyone else who has a telephone by sending your voice along electric wires. *v.* to call someone by dialling a telephone. **telephoning. telephoned.**

telescope *n.* a tube with glass lenses that make distant things look larger and nearer.

television, TV *n.* an instrument that receives certain kinds of radio signals and turns them into pictures and sound.

tell *v.* to say, to give information by talking. **telling. told.**

temper *n.* the mood someone is in: *a bad temper.*
to lose your temper to be very angry.

temperature *n.* how hot or cold something is.

temple *n.* 1. a building for prayer and worship. 2. one of the two sides of your forehead, just above your cheeks.

tempt *v.* to try to make someone do something, usually something that is foolish or wrong: *I was tempted to spend all my money on candy.* **tempting. tempted.**

ten *n., adj.* one more than nine (10).

tenant *n.* a person who pays money to live in an apartment or building that belongs to someone else.

tender *adj.* 1. soft, not tough: *tender meat.* 2. gentle, loving: *a tender smile.*

tennis *n.* a game in which two or four players hit a ball over a net with a racket.

tent *n.* a canvas or nylon shelter, held up by poles.

tentacle (ten'tə kəl) *n.* a leg or feeler of some animals: *the tentacles of an octopus.*

tenth *adj.* following ninth (10th).

tepee see **teepee.**

term *n.* 1. a certain period of time: *a school term; the mayor's term in office.* 2. part of a contract or agreement: *A term in our lease says we can't have pets.*

terminal *n.* the building in which a railway, bus, or airplane trip starts or ends.

termite *n.* a small, ant-like insect that eats wood.

terrarium *n.* a glass or plastic container, in which to grow plants.

terrible *adj.* awful, causing terror: *a terrible accident.* **terribly** *adv.*

terrier *n.* one of several kinds of small dogs.

terrific *adj.* very great: *a terrific hockey game; a terrific problem.*

terrify *v.* to cause great fear: *Barrie was terrified by the bull.* **terrifying. terrified.** it **terrifies.**

territory *n.* a large area of land: *The pioneers explored new territory.* *pl.* **territories.**

terror *n.* great fear, panic.

test *n.* an examination: *The class had a test in math.* *v.* 1. to find out how much someone knows: *The teacher tested the class in spelling.* 2. to try out: *The driver tested his brakes.* **testing. tested.**

Testament *n.* one of the two main parts of the Bible: *the Old and New Testaments.*

text *n.* 1. the main amount of reading material in a book: *The book has 100 pages of text and 20 pages of pictures.* 2. short for **textbook.**

textbook *n.* a book used for study by pupils.

texture *n.* the feel or look of something: *Sandpaper has a rough texture.*

than *conj.* compared with: *She is older than I am.*
Note: Do not mix up **than** with **then**; **than** is used to compare things.

thank *v.* to say how grateful you are for something: *Debbie thanked her aunt for the present.* **thanking. thanked.**

thankful *adj.* grateful, pleased: *They were thankful to be home again.* (*opp.* **unthankful.**)

thanks *n. pl.* a way of saying thank you.

Thanksgiving Day a holiday on which to give thanks for what we have: *Thanksgiving is celebrated on the second Monday in October.*

that *adj.* being over there: *That tree is beautiful.* *pl.* **those.** *pron.* 1. the one over there: *That is their house.* 2. the one which: *the house that we live in.* *pl.* **those.** *conj.* a word used to connect groups of words: *I know that one and one are two.*

that's short for **that is.**

thaw *n.* the melting of ice and snow in mild weather: *the spring thaw.* *v.* to melt: *The ice thawed in the sun.* **thawing. thawed.**

the *article* 'a certain one' or 'certain ones': *The boys are in the school.*

theatre, theater *n.* a building where plays are acted or movies are shown.

theft *n.* the act of stealing: *They were arrested for the theft of the car.*

their *adj.* belonging to them: *their coats.*

theirs *pron.* the one belonging to them: *The house is theirs.*

them *pron.* those persons, animals, or things: *I like them.*

theme (thēm) *n.* the main topic or subject: *Friendship is the theme of my report.*

themselves *pron.* them alone: *Bob and Ted have only themselves to blame.*

then *adv.* 1. at some time: *We went shopping, and then we came home.* 2. therefore, for that reason: *If you have enough money, then you can go to the movies.*
Note: Do not mix up **then** with **than**; **then** is never used for comparing things.

there *adv.* in that place, to that place: *They went there.*

therefore *adv.* for that reason, because of that: *He felt ill, and therefore, he went to bed.*

there's short for **there is.**

thermometer (thər mom'ə tər) *n.* an instrument that measures temperature in degrees.

these plural of **this.**

they plural of **he**, **she**, or **it**: *They all came to play.*

they're short for **they are.**

thick *adj.* 1. measuring a lot from one side to the other: *a thick slice of bread.* 2. not watery: *thick soup.* 3. hard to see through: *thick fog.*

thicken *v.* to make or become thick: *You can thicken gravy with flour.* **thickening. thickened.**

thickness *n.* being thick: *The thickness of the wall is one metre.*

thief *n.* someone who steals. *pl.* **thieves.**

thigh (thī) *n.* the part of your leg between the knee and hip.

thimble *n.* a metal or plastic cap, worn to protect the end of your finger when sewing.

thin *adj.* 1. slender, slim: *thin wire, thinner wire, the thinnest wire of all.* 2. watery: *thin soup.*

thing *n.* anything that can be seen or touched but is not alive; anything that can be done or thought.

think *v.* 1. to use your mind: *I was thinking about what he said.* 2. to have an opinion: *I think Sam is telling the truth.* **thinking. thought** (thawt).

third *adj.* following second (3rd).

thirst *n.* a feeling that you want to have a drink.

thirsty *adj.* wanting a drink: *a thirsty baby, a thirstier one, the thirstiest baby in the nursery.*

thirteen *n., adj.* ten more than three (13).

thirteenth *adj.* following twelfth (13th).

thirty *n., adj.* ten times three (30).

this *adj.* being here: *This dress is my favourite. pl.* **these.** *pron.* the one here: *This is my camera. pl.* **these.**

thistle (this′əl) *n.* a prickly plant.

thong *n.* a sandal held onto your toes by a narrow piece of leather or plastic.

thorn *n.* a sharp point on a stem or branch.

thorough (thur′ō) *adj.* 1. done properly; careful: *a thorough piece of work.* 2. complete: *You need a thorough rest.* **thoroughly** *adv.*

those plural of **that.**

though (THŌ) *conj.* in spite of the fact that: *We went to the game, even though it was going to rain.*

thought (thawt) *n.* what is in your mind when thinking: *Denise gave a lot of thought to the holiday.* *v.* see **think.**

thoughtful *adj.* 1. thinking deeply: *Tommy was very thoughtful after talking to his father.* 2. thinking of others, kind: *Nicole was very thoughtful of her pets.*

thoughtless *adj.* careless, not thinking about other people or things.

thousand *n., adj.* ten times one hundred (1000).

thread (thred) *n.* a thin string of cotton, silk, or other material used in sewing. *v.* to put thread in a needle: *He threaded the needle.* **threading. threaded.**

threat (thret) *n.* a warning that harm or punishment may be coming.

threaten (thret′ən) *v.* 1. to make threats against. 2. to warn of danger: *The dark clouds threaten a storm.* **threatening. threatened.**

three *n., adj.* one more than two (3).

threw see **throw.**

thrifty *adj.* careful about the way you use money: *thrifty shoppers, thriftier ones, the thriftiest shoppers of all.*

thrill *n.* an excited feeling: *the thrill of riding the roller coaster. v.* to give an excited feeling. **thrilling. thrilled.**

thriller *n.* a scary book, story, play, or movie.

throat *n.* the inside of your neck, used for swallowing food and breathing.

throne *n.* a chair on which a king or queen sits.

through (thrü) *prep.* from the beginning to the end of: *We read through the whole book in one night. adv.* from one side to the other: *She opened the door and we* went through. *adj.* finished: *Are you through with the ink?*

throw *n.* a pitch or toss of something: *That was a good throw!* *v.* to pitch or toss something: *Maria threw the ball very far.* **throwing. threw** (thrü). I have **thrown** (thrōn).

thrust *v.* to push hard and quickly: *The farmer thrust the fork into the hay.* **thrusting. thrust.**

thumb (thum) *n.* the short, thick finger on your hand.

thumbtack *n.* a tack with a large, flat top.

thump *n.* a dull, heavy sound: *He landed with a thump.* *v.* to hit something so that you make a dull, heavy sound: *Tom thumped the table loudly.* **thumping. thumped.**

thunder *n.* the loud noise made by lightning in a storm. *v.* to make a loud, booming sound: *The planes thundered by.* **thundering. thundered.**

Thursday *n.* the fifth day of the week.

tick *n.* 1. the sound that a clock makes. 2. a little mark (√). *v.* 1. to keep on making little sounds: *A clock ticks.* 2. to make a tick: *The teacher ticked the answers that were right.* **ticking. ticked.**

ticket *n.* 1. a small piece of paper or a card that gives the holder certain rights: *José bought two tickets for the movie.* 2. a paper that orders someone to pay a fine: *a traffic ticket.* 3. a label showing the price of something. *v.* to put a ticket on something: *They ticketed all the new boxes.* **ticketing. ticketed.**

tickle *v.* to touch lightly to make someone giggle and laugh. **tickling. tickled.**

ticklish *adj.* quick to laugh when tickled.

tick-tack-toe *n.* a writing game for two players.

tidal wave a powerful ocean wave, caused by an underground earthquake.

tidbit *n.* a small snack or piece of food.

tide *n.* the regular rise and fall of the ocean.

tidy *adj.* neat, with everything in order: *a tidy desk, a tidier one, the tidiest desk in the room.* (*opp.* **untidy.**)

tie *n.* 1. a strip of cloth that is worn around the neck. 2. a draw or even score in a game. 3. a rod that holds together other parts: *a wooden railway tie.* *v.* 1. to join two or more things with a string or rope: *Jackie tied a long string to the kite.* 2. to draw or be even in a game: *The two teams tied, with a score of one goal each.* **tying. tied.** she **ties.**

tiger *n.* a striped wild animal of the cat family, living in India and other parts of Asia.

tight (tīt) *adj.* 1. fitting very closely: *a tight shoe.* 2. firmly joined or stretched: *a tight knot.* **tightly** *adv.*

tighten *v.* to make tight: *Please tighten the string around the box.* **tightening. tightened.**

tightrope *n.* a rope, high above the ground, that acrobats walk on.

tile *n.* a square of plastic, baked clay, or other material, used to cover walls, floors, or ceilings. *v.* to put tiles into place: *My parents tiled the basement floor.* **tiling. tiled.**

till *n.* a drawer where money is kept. *prep.* short for **until**: *Wait here till I come back.* *v.* to plough the land. **tilling. tilled.**

tilt *n.* the leaning of something: *Do you see the tilt in that wall?* *v.* to lean to one side: *The table tilts to one end.* **tilting. tilted.**

timber *n.* large trees in a forest.

timber wolf a large, grey wolf that lives in the northern forests of North America.

time *n.* 1. a moment shown on the clock: *What is the time?* 2. a space in our lives measured in years, months, days, hours, minutes, or seconds: *It is a long time since I saw Joan.*
on time at the correct time: *I arrived on time, but my friend was late.*
time off days or hours missed at work or school.
time out a stopping of play in some games.

timid *adj.* shy, nervous, afraid.

tin *n.* 1. a silvery metal that does not rust easily. 2. a can: *a sardine tin.*

tingle *v.* to have a prickly feeling: *Marie's toes tingled with cold.* **tingling. tingled.**

tinkle *v.* to make a light, ringing sound. **tinkling. tinkled.**

tinsel *n.* small strips of thin metal used for decorating.

tint *n.* a shade of a colour: *Paula's dress had a tint of pale blue.*

tiny *adj.* very small: *a tiny mouse, a tinier mouse, the tiniest mouse in the cage.*

tip *n.* 1. a pointed end: *a finger tip.* 2. extra money given for a service: *Estelle gave the taxi driver a tip.* 3. a piece of helpful information: *Aunt Elsie gave me some useful tips on cooking eggs.* *v.* 1. to tilt or turn: *The baby tipped over the glass of milk.* 2. to give extra money for a service: *She tipped the waitress.* **tipping. tipped.**

tiptoe *v.* to walk quietly on the tip of your toes: *Joel tiptoed past the door.* **tiptoeing. tiptoed. she tiptoes.**

tire *n.* a band of rubber or plastic that fits around the wheel of a car, bicycle, or other vehicle. *v.* to become sleepy or worn-out: *Janet tired of mixing eggs.* **tiring. tired.**

tired *adj.* wanting to rest or sleep.

tissue (tish′ü) *n.* very thin paper or cloth.

title *n.* 1. the name of a book, movie, song, etc. 2. a word before a name to show rank or importance: *The title 'Sir' means that a man has the rank of knight.*

to *prep.* in the direction of, as far as, until.
to and fro backwards and forwards.

toad *n.* an animal that lives on land and in water; it looks like a frog, but has rougher skin.

toadstool *n.* a poisonous mushroom.

toast *n.* bread that is made crisp and brown by heating it. *v.* to make bread crisp and brown with heat: *He toasted the bread in the toaster.* **toasting. toasted.**

toaster *n.* an electrical device that toasts bread.

tobacco *n.* a plant whose leaves are dried and used for smoking in pipes, cigars, or cigarettes.

toboggan *n.* a long, flat sleigh without runners. *v.* to slide down a snowy hill on a toboggan. **tobogganing. tobogganed.**

today *n.* the present day: *Today is my birthday.* *adv.* on this day: *My cousin came today.*

toddler *n.* a small child just learning to walk.

toe *n.* one of the five end parts of your foot.

toffee see **taffy.**

together *adv.* with each other: *They went together for a swim.*

toil *n.* hard work. *v.* to do hard work: *They toiled in the fields all day.* **toiling. toiled.**

toilet *n.* a bowl containing water, used for flushing away body wastes.

told see **tell.**

toll *n.* a tax paid for the right to use something: *We pay a quarter toll when we cross the bridge.* *v.* for bells to sound: *The church bells toll each Sunday morning.* **tolling. tolled.**

tomahawk *n.* a small axe, once used by North American Indians as a tool or weapon.

tomato *n.* a plant with a round, juicy fruit. *pl.* **tomatoes.**

tomb (tüm) *n.* a grave or building in which someone is buried.

tombstone *n.* a stone over a grave.

tomorrow *n.* the day after today: *Tomorrow will be a nice day.* *adv.* on the next day: *My cousin will come tomorrow.*

tone *n.* 1. a musical sound. 2. the sound of someone's voice: *Father spoke in an angry tone.* 3. a shade of colour: *a two-tone car.*

tongue (tung) *n.* the soft, fleshy part of your mouth, used for licking and tasting.

tonight *n.* this night coming: *Tonight is Halloween.* *adv.* on this night: *My favourite program is on tonight.*

tonne *n.* a unit for measuring mass; t is the symbol. 1 t = 1000 kg

tonsil *n.* one of two oval pieces of flesh in the back of a person's throat.

too *adv.* 1. also, as well: *I am going out, and Gary is coming too.* 2. more than enough: *Denis has eaten too much chocolate.*

took see **take.**

tool *n.* something to help you to do work: *Hammers, saws, and axes are tools.*

tooth *n.* one of the bonelike parts in your mouth, used for chewing and biting. *pl.* **teeth.**

toothache *n.* a pain in a tooth.

toothbrush *n.* a small brush on a long handle, used to clean teeth.

toothpaste *n.* a paste for cleaning the teeth.

toothpick *n.* a small, narrow piece of wood, used to clean the teeth.

top *n.* 1. the highest point: *the top of a hill.* 2. the upper side: *the top of a box.* 3. a toy which can be made to spin.

topic *n.* what something is about: *The topic of my speech is, 'My Pet Rabbit'.*

topple *v.* to fall down: *The post toppled over.* **toppling. toppled.**

torch *n.* a stick that burns at one end and can be carried by the other end.

tore, torn see **tear.**

torn *adj.* ripped, having a tear.

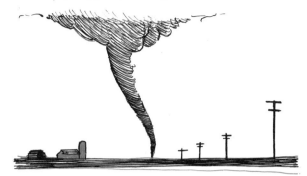

tornado *n.* a violent storm, with dark winds that whirl around at a high speed. *pl.* **tornadoes.**

Toronto *n.* largest city in Canada; capital city of Ontario.

tortoise (tor′təs) *n.* a large turtle that lives on land.

torture *n.* great pain. *v.* to cause horrible pain. **torturing. tortured.**

toss *n.* a throw: *Her toss was quite high.* *v.* 1. to throw up into the air: *Diana tossed the ball as high as she could.* 2. to roll about: *Bruce could not sleep and he tossed in bed.* **tossing. tossed.**

total *n.* the whole amount when two or more numbers are added: *The total of 3 plus 5 plus 2 is 10.*

totem pole a tall pole with many carvings on it, made by the Pacific Coast Indians.

touch (tuch) *n.* one of the five senses; feeling: *We had to describe the touch and taste of different items.* *v.* 1. to feel with your fingers or some other part of your body. 2. to be against: *The back of the chair touches the wall.* **touching. touched.**

touchdown *n.* a score made in football by getting the ball across the other team's goal.

tough (tuf) *adj.* 1. not easily broken or bent: *a tough piece of rubber.* 2. hard to chew: *tough meat.* 3. hard, difficult: *I solved a tough problem in arithmetic.*

tour (tür) *n.* a trip, usually one led by a guide. *v.* to travel about from place to place: *Lee's family will tour France next summer.* **touring. toured.**

tourist (tür′ist) *n.* a person on holiday who travels about to see different places and things.

tournament *n.* a contest among several players or teams: *a tennis tournament.*

tow (tō) *v.* to pull or drag something with a rope: *The car broke down, and a truck towed it away.* **towing. towed.**

towards, toward (tōrds, tōrd) *prep.* in the direction of: *They walked towards the village.*

towel *n.* a cloth or paper that is used for drying or wiping something.

tower *n.* a tall and narrow building or part of a building: *The bells rang from the church tower.* *v.* to stand higher than others: *That building towers over all the others.* **towering. towered.**

town *n.* an area with houses, factories, stores, etc.: *A town is larger than a village and usually smaller than a city.*

township *n.* part of a county: *A township has its own government.*

toy *n.* something to play with. *v.* to play with: *He toyed with his ring.* **toying. toyed.**

trace *n.* a small amount: *There is a trace of grease on the glass.* *v.* 1. to copy a picture by placing transparent paper on top of it and drawing over the lines. 2. to find out about someone or something, using clues: *The police traced the thief to his home.* **tracing. traced.**

track *n.* 1. the set of metal rails a train travels along. 2. marks on the ground left by something moving: *the tracks of a tiger.* 3. the course followed by runners in a race.

tractor *n.* a machine with wheels and a powerful engine that is used on farms for pulling a plough or heavy loads.

trade *n.* 1. the business of buying and selling: *Canada has much trade with foreign countries.* 2. a job needing the use of tools: *the trade of being a carpenter.* *v.* to give one thing in exchange for something else: *Pete traded books with Vera.* **trading. traded.**

tradition *n.* something done over and over, passed on from parents to their children: *Having a Christmas tree is a tradition in our family.*

traffic *n.* the movement of cars, buses, and trucks along the streets.

tragedy (traj′ə dē) *n.* a very sad happening. *pl.* **tragedies.**

tragic (traj′ik) *adj.* very sad, terrible: *The story has a tragic ending.*

trail *n.* 1. marks on the ground showing which way some animal or person has gone. 2. a rough path. *v.* to follow behind: *Our team trailed by one point. The dogs trailed the rabbit.* **trailing. trailed.**

trailer *n.* a vehicle that is pulled by another vehicle: *Some trailers are for people to live in. Others are used to carry goods.*

train *n.* railway cars connected together. *v.* to practise for something: *Lisa is training to be a ballet dancer.* **training. trained.**

trainer *n.* someone who teaches or prepares you for some exercise or sport.

traitor *n.* someone who works against his or her friends or country.

tramp *n.* a poor person who has no home. *v.* 1. to walk heavily. 2. to go for a trip on foot, to hike. **tramping. tramped.**

trample *v.* to walk heavily all over something. **trampling. trampled.**

trampoline *n.* a piece of canvas held to a frame by strong springs.

transfer *n.* a ticket that lets you change from one bus to another without having to pay more money. *v.* to move something or somebody to another place: *My father's company transferred him to another city.* **transferring. transferred.**

transistor (tran zis'tər) *n.* a very small device found in radios, televisions, calculators, and other equipment: *A transistor controls the amount of electric current that is being used.*

translate *v.* to put into another language. **translating. translated.**

translation *n.* a changing of words into another language: *The story is an English translation of a Spanish tale.*

transparent *adj.* clear, able to be seen through: *Glass is transparent.*

transport (trans'port) *n.* a large truck, plane, or ship used for carrying materials.

transport (trans port') *v.* to carry things from one place to another. **transporting. transported.**

transportation *n.* the act of moving someone or something from one place to another.

trap *n.* 1. something made for catching birds or animals: *The mouse escaped from the trap.* 2. a plan for catching someone: *The police officer's question was a trap, and the thief confessed.* *v.* to catch with a trap. **trapping. trapped.**

trapeze *n.* a swinging bar held by two ropes, used by acrobats.

trapper *n.* someone who makes a living by trapping animals.

trash *n.* garbage.

travel *v.* to make a trip. **travelling. travelled.**

traveller, traveler *n.* someone who travels.

trawl *n.* a net dragged along the bottom of the ocean. *v.* to fish with such a net. **trawling. trawled.**

trawler *n.* a ship used for ocean fishing.

tray *n.* a flat piece of wood, plastic, or metal used for carrying things: *a tea tray.*

treason (trē'zən) *n.* helping the enemy: *The spy was guilty of treason.*

treasure (trezh'ər) *n.* something very valuable; great riches: *The pirates hid their treasure on the island.* *v.* to value very highly: *We treasure our friendship.* **treasuring. treasured.**

treasurer *n.* the person in charge of the money of a business or club.

treat *n.* a pleasurable and special thing: *We were taken to the cottage as a treat.* *v.* 1. to give a pleasurable and special thing or time: *Father treated us to lemonade.* 2. to give careful attention to something: *Tina's cut hand was treated at the hospital.* **treating. treated.**

treatment *n.* care given to something: *The doctor gave Raoul treatment for his sore foot.*

treaty *n.* an agreement made between two or more people, cities, countries, etc.: *A peace treaty was signed to end the war.* *pl.* **treaties.**

tree *n.* a large plant with a woody trunk and branches.

trek *n.* a long journey. *v.* to go on a long journey: *We trekked through the Rockies last summer.* **trekking. trekked.**

tremble *v.* to shake or shiver with fear, excitement, or cold. **trembling. trembled.**

tremendous *adj.* huge, enormous: *a tremendous cheer from a crowd; a tremendous elephant.*

trench *n.* a long, narrow ditch.

trespass *v.* to go on someone's property without permission. **trespassing. trespassed.**

trespasser *n.* someone who goes onto private property without permission.

trial *n.* 1. the hearing of a case before a judge in a court of law. 2. a test: *Steve took out his new skateboard for a trial.*

triangle *n.* 1. a space or area enclosed by three straight lines whose ends meet. 2. a musical instrument made from a steel rod bent in this shape.

triangular *adj.* having the shape of a triangle.

tribe *n.* a group of people who have the same customs and leaders: *the Blackfoot tribe.*

trick *n.* 1. a clever act: *The monkey was doing all kinds of tricks.* 2. a quick action that fools people: *a magic trick.* *v.* to fool; to cheat: *He tricked me into paying·too much.* **tricking. tricked.**

trickle *n.* a small flow of something: *Only a trickle of water came out of the tap.* *v.* to flow or fall in drops or a small stream: *The water trickled over my hands.* **trickling. trickled.**

tricycle *n.* a small vehicle with three wheels.

tried, tries see **try.**

trigger *n.* the small lever on a gun or pistol that is pulled to make it fire. *v.* to set off, to begin: *The gun shot triggered the race.* **triggering. triggered.**

trim *adj.* neat and tidy: *a trim lawn, a trimmer one, the trimmest lawn of all.* *v.* to make something neat by clipping it: *to trim a hedge.* **trimming. trimmed.**

trio (trē′ō) *n.* a group of three singers or musicians. *pl.* **trios.**

trip *n.* a short journey: *a trip to the zoo.* *v.* to stumble, to catch your foot on something: *He tripped on the mat.* **tripping. tripped.**

triple *adj.* three times as much: *a triple helping of cake.* *v.* to multiply by three: *When you triple the number two, you get six.* **tripling. tripled.**

triplet *n.* one of three children born at the same time to the same mother.

triumph *n.* a great victory or success: *Our play was a triumph!*

trombone *n.* a brass musical instrument made up of two long tubes.

troop *n.* a group of soldiers or Scouts: *a Scout troop.*

trophy (trō′fē) *n.* a cup, plaque, or other object given to the winner of a contest. *pl.* **trophies.**

tropical *adj.* having to do with the warmest parts of the world.

trot *n.* a light, gentle run. *v.* to run gently: *The horse trotted to the fence.* **trotting. trotted.**

trouble (trub′əl) *n.* anything that bothers or disturbs you: *The trouble with living here is that the bus stop is so far away.* *v.* to bother, to disturb: *Does the noise trouble you?* **troubling. troubled.**

trough (trof) *n.* a long, narrow, open box that holds water or food for animals.

trousers *n. pl.* a pair of long pants.

trout *n.* a fish that lives in fresh water. *pl.* **trout.**

truce *n.* a pause in a battle or disagreement: *During the truce, both sides tried to make peace.*

truck *n.* a large vehicle that carries heavy loads. *v.* to carry heavy loads in a truck: *The cans of vegetables were trucked across the province.* **trucking. trucked.**

trudge *v.* to walk in a tired way: *We trudged slowly along the muddy road.* **trudging. trudged.**

true *adj.* 1. correct, exactly right: *The story I told you is true.* 2. loyal, to be relied on: *Frank is a true friend.* (*opp.* **untrue.**)

truly *adv.* really, honestly: *I am truly sorry I forgot your birthday.*

trumpet *n.* a brass musical instrument; it is made up of a curving tube that widens at one end.

trunk *n.* 1. the main part of a tree. 2. the main part of your body. 3. a big box or chest, used for storing or carrying personal belongings. 4. the nose of an elephant.

trust *n.* a belief in someone or something: *Theo has much trust in this machine.* *v.* to believe that someone is loyal and honest, to have faith: *Tom is an honest boy, and I trust him.* **trusting. trusted.**

truth *n.* what is true, what really happened: *It is the truth that I was sick yesterday.*

truthful *adj.* speaking the truth.

try *n.* an attempt: *You made a good try at jumping over the rope.* *pl.* **tries.** *v.* 1. to aim at doing something, to attempt: *I tried to climb the tree.* 2. to judge someone in a court of law: *The prisoner was tried before a judge and jury.* 3. to test something to see if it works well: *We will try your new idea.* **trying. tried.** he **tries.**

T-shirt *n.* a sports shirt with short sleeves.

tub *n.* a large container for holding water.

tuba *n.* a large, brass musical instrument that produces very low sounds.

tube *n.* 1. a thin pipe. 2. a soft container used for holding toothpaste or other products.

tuck *n.* a fold in cloth. *v.* to fold up, to wrap up: *Father tucked the baby into his bed.* **tucking. tucked.**

Tuesday *n.* the third day of the week.

tug *n.* 1. a sharp pull. 2. short for **tugboat.** *v.* to pull sharply: *Carole tugged at my arm.* **tugging. tugged.**

tugboat *n.* a small, powerful boat used for towing and pushing huge ships in and out of a harbour.

tug of war a contest between two teams pulling a rope.

tulip *n.* a colourful flower that grows from a bulb and is shaped like a cup.

tumble *n.* the act of falling down: *She took a tumble when she tripped on the rope.* *v.* to fall down: *I nearly tumbled downstairs.* **tumbling. tumbled.**

tumbler *n.* 1. a drinking glass. 2. an acrobat.

tuna *n.* a large ocean fish that is caught for food.

tundra *n.* a large area of flat, treeless land in the Arctic: *The ground is always frozen under the tundra.*

tune *n.* a set of notes that make a piece of music.

tunnel *n.* an underground passage: *a railway tunnel.* *v.* to dig a tunnel: *The workers tunnelled through the mountain.* **tunnelling. tunnelled.**

tuque (tük) *n.* a knitted cap, usually made of wool.

turban *n.* a long strip of cloth that is wound around the head: *A turban is worn by men in parts of India and in some other countries.*

turbulence (tər'byü ləns) *n.* moving about with great force: *the turbulence of a hurricane.*

turf *n.* soil with grass growing on it.

turkey *n.* a large bird that is raised for food. *pl.* **turkeys.**

turn *n.* 1. a movement around: *a right turn.* 2. a time for something: *It is my turn.* *v.* 1. to make something go around: *She turned the handle.* 2. to change direction: *Turn right.* 3. to change: *The snow turned to slush.* **turning. turned.**

turnip *n.* a plant with a large, round root that is used as a vegetable.

turnstile *n.* a gate that turns in one direction only.

turpentine *n.* an oil from pine trees, used in paints and varnishes.

turquoise (tər'kwoiz) *n.* 1. a precious stone with a greenish-blue colour. 2. a greenish-blue colour. *adj.* having such a colour.

turtle *n.* an animal that lives on land or in the sea; it has a hard shell, and moves very slowly.

tusk *n.* one of two very long teeth that stick out from the mouth of an elephant, walrus, etc.

tutor *n.* a teacher who gives private lessons to a student.

TV short for **television.**

twelfth *adj.* following eleventh (12th).

twelve *n., adj.* one more than eleven (12).

twenty *n., adj.* ten times two (20).

twice *adv.* two times: *Sydney went to the store twice.*

twig *n.* a small branch on a tree or bush.

twilight *n.* the hazy light just before sunrise or just after sunset.

twin *n.* one of two children born at the same time to the same mother.

twinkle *n.* a sparkle: *We saw the twinkle of the candle. v.* to sparkle: *The stars twinkle in the sky.* **twinkling. twinkled.**

twirl *n.* a twisting or spinning motion. *v.* to spin around quickly. **twirling. twirled.**

twist *n.* a curve or bend. *v.* 1. to wind around, to curve: *The road twisted all the way.* 2. to bend something and change its shape: *Alan twisted the wire into a ring.* **twisting. twisted.**

two *n., adj.* one added to one (2).

tying see **tie.**

type *n.* 1. a kind: *This is a fast type of car.* 2. printed letters. *v.* to write with a typewriter. **typing. typed.**

typewriter *n.* a machine that makes letters in printed type.

typhoon (tī fün′) *n.* a powerful storm, much like a hurricane.

typist *n.* someone who uses a typewriter.

u

udder *n.* the part of the body of a cow where the milk is stored.

UFO short for **unidentified flying object.**

ugly *adj.* not pretty or nice to look at: *an ugly picture, an uglier one, the ugliest picture on the wall.*

Ukrainian *adj.* belonging to or coming from the Ukraine.

ukulele (yü kə lā′lē) *n.* a small guitar that has four strings.

ulcer *n.* an open sore that is not a wound: *Ulcers may occur in or on the body.*

umbrella *n.* a thin steel frame covered with material to give protection from the sun or rain.

umpire *n.* a person who sees that the rules of a game are followed: *a baseball umpire.*

un- a prefix meaning 'not' or 'the opposite of': **unable** means not able; **unfold** means to open out.

unable *adj.* not able: *Alex was unable to go to school because he had the mumps.*

unbelievable *adj.* impossible to believe: *an unbelievable story about dragons.*

uncertain *adj.* not certain: *David was uncertain about which way to go.*

uncle *n.* a brother of your father or mother; the husband of your aunt.

uncomfortable *adj.* not comfortable.

unconscious (un kon′shəs) *adj.* not conscious; stunned and not able to see or feel anything; knocked out.

uncover *v.* 1. to take the cover or wrapping off: *Zandra uncovered the package.* 2. to make known: *to uncover a secret plan.* **uncovering. uncovered.**

under *prep.* below, less than, beneath: *under the sea, under two dollars.*

underground *adj.* under the ground: *an underground tunnel.*

undergrowth *n.* small plants and bushes growing close to the ground.

underhand *adj.* from under instead of above the shoulder: *an underhand pitch of a baseball.*

underline *n.* a line drawn under some writing. *v.* to draw a line under some writing. **underlining. underlined.**

underneath *prep.* directly under: *I found my shoes underneath the table.*

understand *v.* to know the meaning of: *Sally understood the message.* **understanding. understood.**

undertaker *n.* a person whose job is to arrange funerals.

underwater *adj.* growing or used below the surface of the water: *underwater plants. adv.* below the surface of the water: *to swim underwater.*

underwear *n.* clothes you wear under your outer clothes.

undo *v.* to loosen or unfasten something: *Jimmy undid the buttons of his coat.* **undoing. undid.** he has **undone.** he **undoes.**

undress *v.* to take off your clothes. **undressing. undressed.**

unemployed *adj.* out of work.

uneven *adj.* not even or level: *uneven ground.*

unexpected *adj.* not expected, coming as a surprise: *an unexpected present.*

unfair *adj.* not fair.

unfasten *v.* to undo: *to unfasten a seat belt.* **unfastening. unfastened.**

unforgettable *adj.* not to be forgotten: *an unforgettable holiday.*

unfortunate *adj.* not lucky, having bad luck.

unfriendly *adj.* not friendly.

ungrateful *adj.* not grateful or thankful.

unhealthy *adj.* not healthy.

unicorn (yü′ni korn) *n.* an imaginary animal that looks like a horse with a long horn on its forehead.

unidentified *adj.* not recognized, unknown, strange.

uniform (yü′ni form) *n.* special clothes worn to show that people belong to the same group.

unimportant *adj.* not important.

union (yün′yən) *n.* 1. a joining together. 2. a group of workers in the same occupation who have joined together to make sure that they are all treated fairly by the people who employ them.

unit *n.* 1. a single thing, person, or group. 2. an amount used for measuring: *The metre is a unit of length.*

unite *v.* to join together: *The teams united to form a league.* **uniting. united.**

United States a North American country: *There are 50 states in the United States.*

universe *n.* everything that exists, including all the planets and all of space.

university *n.* a school of higher learning. *pl.* **universities.**

unkind *adj.* not kind, cruel.

unknown (un nōn′) *adj.* not known, strange: *The explorers reached an unknown part of the Arctic.*

unless *conj.* except if: *I shall not go unless you come too.*

unlike *prep.* different from: *Unlike most of my family, I like vegetables.*

unlikely *adj.* probably not going to happen: *It is unlikely that he will be there.*

unload *v.* 1. to take off a load: *to unload a truck.* 2. to take the shells from a gun, pistol, etc. **unloading. unloaded.**

unlock *v.* to open a lock by using a key or a combination number. **unlocking. unlocked.**

unlucky *adj.* having bad luck or causing bad luck: *an unlucky man, an unlucky number.*

unnecessary *adj.* not necessary, not needed.

untie *v.* to undo something that has been tied. **untying. untied.**

until *conj.* up to the time when: *Stay here until I come back.*

unusual (un yü′ zhü əl) *adj.* not usual, strange: *It is unusual for Jeannette to be so late.* **unusually** *adv.*

unwrap (un rap′) *v.* to take the wrapping off: *to unwrap a package.* **unwrapping. unwrapped.**

up *prep.* from a lower to a higher place: *We walked up the hill.*

upon *prep.* on or on top of: *Paul stood upon a chair to reach the shelf.*

upper *adj.* higher: *the upper lip of your mouth.*

upset *v.* 1. to knock over: *I upset the jug of milk.* 2. to make very sad: *The bad news upset us.* 3. to make sick: *The second milkshake upset my stomach.* **upsetting. upset.**

upstairs *adv.* up to or on a higher floor.

upstream *adv.* against the current of a river: *The campers swam upstream.*

urban *adj.* having to do with the city, not with the country: *Most of the children in my class come from urban areas.*

urge *n.* a sudden strong wish to do something: *Tai had an urge to go swimming.* *v.* to try to get someone to do something, to persuade. **urging. urged.**

urgent *adj.* needing to be looked after at once: *We received an urgent message for help.*

us *pron.* me and others: *Please help us.*

use (yüs) *n.* 1. the power of using: *When I fractured my arm, I lost the use of it for a month.* 2. value: *This old knife is of no use.*

use (yüz) *v.* to make something help you: *We use knives and forks when eating.* **using. used.**

used *adj.* not new: *a used car.*

useful *adj.* helpful: *a useful idea; a useful tool.*

useless *adj.* not helpful, worth nothing: *You can throw out these useless scissors.*

usher *n.* someone who leads people to their seats in a theatre, stadium, or other place.

usual (yü′zhü əl) *adj.* as generally happens, regular: *Snow is usual for this time of year.* (*opp.* **unusual.**)

usually *adv.* most of the time: *Bret usually has juice, toast, and an egg for breakfast.*

utensil *n.* a piece of equipment, usually one used in the kitchen: *Pots, spoons, and measuring cups are some cooking utensils.*

vacant *adj.* empty, not in use: *The house is vacant.*

vacation *n.* a holiday: *They left for their summer vacation.*

vaccinate (vak′sə nāt) *v.* to inject someone with a vaccine. **vaccinating. vaccinated.**

vaccination *n.* an injection of a vaccine into the body.

vaccine *n.* a preparation that is injected into the body: *Vaccines can protect people against polio, measles, and other diseases.*

vacuum (vak′yüm) *n.* 1. an empty space without even air in it. 2. a vacuum cleaner.

v. to clean with a vacuum cleaner. **vacuuming. vacuumed.**

vacuum cleaner a machine that is used for cleaning carpets, floors, etc. by suction.

vague (vāg) *adj.* uncertain, not clear: *I have only a vague idea of where we are.*

vain *adj.* 1. proud, having too high an opinion of yourself: *My brother is very vain, always admiring himself in the mirror.* 2. useless, not successful: *The runner made a vain attempt to break the record.*
in vain without success: *They tried in vain to win the game.*

valentine *n.* a greeting sent on Valentine's Day, February 14.

valley *n.* an area of low land between hills or mountains. *pl.* **valleys.**

valuable (val'yü bəl) *adj.* having great value; worth much money: *Wendy has a valuable ring.*

value *n.* the amount of money something could be sold for: *What is the value of your ring?*

valve *n.* a part in a pipe that controls the flow of liquid or gas.

vampire *n.* an imaginary creature believed to be a dead body that comes back to life at night.

van *n.* a covered truck.

Vancouver *n.* largest city in the Province of British Columbia.

Vancouver Island a large island just off the west coast of British Columbia.

vandal *n.* someone who destroys property.

vane *n.* a flat or curved metal blade: *The vanes of a windmill are turned by the wind.*

vanilla *n.* a flavouring used in candy, cake, and ice cream: *Vanilla flavouring comes*

from the vanilla bean, which grows in hot places.

vanish *v.* to disappear, to go out of sight: *The magician made the scarf vanish.* **vanishing. vanished.**

vapour, vapor (vā'pər) *n.* steam from boiling water; fog.

variety (və rī'ə tē) *n.* a number of different kinds: *There is a great variety of books in the library. pl.* **varieties.**

various *adj.* different from one another: *Children from various schools watched the events.*

vary *v.* to make different: *Mother varies the meals she cooks each day.* **varying. varied.** she **varies.**

vase (vāz, vahz) *n.* a jar for holding flowers.

vast *adj.* great in size or amount: *A vast number of people watched the soccer game.*

vat *n.* a large container for liquids.

vault *n.* a safe room that is used to store money, jewels, or other things of value. *v.* to leap over using a pole or the hands: *Richard vaulted the low fence.* **vaulting. vaulted.**

veal *n.* the meat of a calf.

vegetable *n.* a plant or part of a plant used for food.

vehicle (vē'ə kəl) *n.* something built to be driven by an engine or pulled by an animal, and to carry people or things over land: *A car is a motor vehicle.*

veil (vāl) *n.* a thin piece of cloth worn to protect or hide the face from the sun, insects, etc.

vein (vān) *n.* one of the thin, long tubes in the body carrying blood to the heart.

velvet *n.* a kind of cloth that is soft and very smooth on one side.

venom *n.* the poison of some snakes and spiders.

vent, ventilator *n.* an opening through which gas or liquid may pass: *We have a vent over the stove.*

ventriloquist *n.* a performer who seems to be able to make a puppet speak.

venture (ven′chər) *v.* to take a risk by doing or saying something, or by going somewhere: *Henry ventured into the long, dark cave.* **venturing. ventured.**

Venus *n.* 1. in ancient times, the Roman goddess of love. 2. one of the planets.

verandah, veranda *n.* an outdoor platform with a roof, joined to a house.

verb *n.* a word in a sentence that says what someone or something is doing: *go, dream, move, fall,* and *open* can all be used as verbs.

verdict *n.* the decision of a jury at the end of a trial: *The jury came to a verdict of guilty.*

verse *n.* 1. poetry: *A poet writes verse.* 2. a group of lines in a poem.

vertical *adj.* straight up and down: *A tower is built in a vertical position. A vertical line is drawn from top to bottom. A horizontal line is drawn from left to right.*

very *adv.* extremely: *Ricardo is a very good singer.*

vessel *n.* 1. a ship or large boat. 2. a container for liquids: *A cup is a drinking vessel.*

vest *n.* a sleeveless piece of clothing worn over a shirt or blouse.

vet *n.* short for **veterinarian**, a doctor who treats animals.

veteran *n.* 1. a person who has served in the armed forces. 2. anyone who has been working at something for a long time.

vibrate *v.* to tremble, to shake: *The bridge vibrated as the train went over.* **vibrating. vibrated.**

vibration *n.* a trembling or shaking feeling.

vicious (vish′əs) *adj.* wicked or evil: *a vicious crime.*

victim *n.* someone who has been killed, hurt, or robbed.

Victoria *n.* capital city of British Columbia.

victory *n.* a win in a battle, game, or contest. *pl.* **victories.**

videotape *n.* a special tape used for television: *Videotape shows pictures and produces sounds when played through a special machine.*

view (vyü) *n.* 1. everything that you can see from one place: *We had a good view of the ocean.* 2. an opinion. *v.* to see or look at: *I viewed some slides of my friend's trip.* **viewing. viewed.**

vigour, vigor *n.* strength, energy: *My old dog is still full of vigour.*

village *n.* a small group of houses and stores: *A village is usually smaller than a town.*

villain (vil′ən) *n.* a wicked person: *The villain in the story scared us.*

vine *n.* a climbing plant: *Grapes and melons grow on vines.*

vinegar (vin′ə gər) *n.* a sour liquid used for giving flavouring and preserving food.

vineyard (vin′yərd) *n.* a large piece of land where grapes are grown.

vinyl *n.* a hard plastic used for making records, floor polishes, and other things.

violence *n.* great force, often causing damage.

violent *adj.* very rough and causing damage: *a violent storm; a violent temper.*

violet *n.* a small plant with blue, purple, or white flowers.

violin *n.* a musical instrument that has four strings and is played with a bow.

violinist *n.* a violin player.

virus *n.* an extremely tiny living thing: *Some viruses can cause disease.* *pl.* **viruses.**

vise (vīs) *n.* a tool that is used to hold an object in place while it is being worked on.

visible (viz′ib əl) *adj.* able to be seen: *The house was hardly visible in the moonlight.* (*opp.* **invisible**.)

vision *n.* being able to see, the sense of sight.

visit *n.* a time spent with someone at his or her home, office, etc.: *Grandpa came on a visit from Scotland last summer.* *v.* to go and see someone or something: *We visited the zoo.* **visiting. visited.**

visitor *n.* someone who visits you, a guest.

vitamin *n.* a substance that is needed for good health, found in sunshine and in many foods.

vocabulary *n.* 1. all the words you know: *Sarah has a large vocabulary.* 2. a list of words and their meanings in the order of the alphabet. *pl.* **vocabularies.**

voice *n.* the sound from your mouth when you are speaking or singing.

volcano (vol kā′nō) *n.* an opening in the surface of the earth through which lava, gases, and flames pour out. *pl.* **volcanoes.**

volleyball *n.* 1. a game in which two teams, standing on either side of a net, hit a large ball back and forth. 2. the ball used in this game.

volume *n.* 1. a book, or one of a set of books or magazines: *The third volume of the encyclopedia is missing.* 2. loudness: *Please turn down the volume of the radio.* 3. the amount of space something fills.

volunteer *n.* someone who offers to do something for no money. *v.* to offer to do something although you do not have to do it: *The Cubs volunteered to carry things to the rummage sale.* **volunteering. volunteered.**

vomit *n.* the substance brought up from the stomach of a person or animal. *v.* to bring up material from the stomach. **vomiting. vomited.**

vote *n.* a choice made in an election: *My vote was for Jerry.* *v.* to say or write your choice in an election: *Penny voted for Angela Brown.* **voting. voted.**

vow *n.* a solemn promise: *Christy made a vow to be early.* *v.* to make a vow: *He vowed not to tell the secret.* **vowing. vowed.**

vowel *n.* any of the five letters a, e, i, o, u.

voyage *n.* a long trip, usually by water or through space.

voyageur (voi ə zhər′) *n.* a boatman, usually a French Canadian, who explored or traded furs long ago.

vulture *n.* a large bird that has dark feathers and a bald head: *Vultures eat dead animals.*

W

waddle (wod′əl) *n.* a swaying kind of walk. *v.* to walk in such a way, as a duck does. **waddling. waddled.**

wade *v.* to walk through shallow water. **wading. waded.**

wafer *n.* a thin, crisp cracker or cookie.

waffle *n.* a light, crisp cake made from a batter.

wag *v.* to move quickly from side to side: *The dog wagged its tail.* **wagging. wagged.**

wage *n.* money people get for doing work, often in weekly payments.

wagon *n.* 1. a vehicle with four wheels, usually one pulled by horses. 2. a little cart for children to pull.

wail *n.* a long, sad cry. *v.* to make such a cry: *The baby wailed after biting her lip.* **wailing. wailed.**

waist *n.* the part of your body between the ribs and hips.

wait *v.* to stay in one place until something happens or someone comes: *We waited a long time for the bus.* **waiting. waited.**

waiter (*fem.* **waitress**) *n.* someone who is paid to serve meals in a restaurant.

wake *v.* 1. to stop someone from sleeping longer: *Father woke John in time for school.* 2. to stop sleeping: *Beth woke up early in the morning.* **waking. woke** or **waked.** I have **woken.**

walk *n.* a trip on foot. *v.* to go on foot: *They walked to the store.* **walking. walked.**

wall *n.* a structure that forms the side of a building or room.

wallet *n.* a flat, folding case for holding money, cards, and pictures.

wallpaper *n.* paper, often with a pattern, that is used to decorate the walls of a room.

walnut *n.* 1. a hard, round nut with a crinkled shell. 2. the tree that produces this nut.

walrus *n.* a large sea animal, something like a seal, that has two long tusks. *pl.* **walruses.**

waltz *n.* a graceful dance with a gliding and whirling motion. *v.* to dance a waltz. **waltzing. waltzed.**

wand *n.* a thin rod: *a magician's magic wand.*

wander *v.* to move from one place to another, not sure of where you want to go. **wandering. wandered.**

want *v.* to wish for: *My brother wants a pair of skis.* **wanting. wanted.**

war *n.* a long fight with weapons and soldiers, usually between countries.

ward *n.* 1. a large bedroom for patients in a hospital. 2. a division or part of a city or town.

warden *n.* 1. a person in charge of a prison. 2. a person who looks after large areas of parkland.

wardrobe *n.* 1. all of a person's clothing: *My sister has a large wardrobe.* 2. a closet for clothes.

warehouse *n.* a large building where goods are stored: *a furniture warehouse.*

warm *adj.* 1. fairly hot, between hot and cold: *a warm climate.* 2. showing happiness: *The winning team received a warm welcome home.*

warmth *n.* the feeling of being warm.

warn *v.* to tell someone about possible danger or trouble: *Tony warned Juan to keep off the ice.* **warning. warned.**

warning *n.* something told or heard, telling of possible danger: *The sailors listened carefully to the storm warning.*

warp *n.* a bend or twist: *a warp in a piece of wood.* *v.* to bend or twist out of shape: *The heat of the radiator warped the wood.* **warping. warped.**

warrant *n.* an official paper that gives an order: *The police had a warrant to search the house.*

warranty *n.* a promise to fix or replace something if anything goes wrong with it before a certain time: *Our new radio has a five-year warranty.* *pl.* **warranties.**

warrior *n.* a person who fights in battles.

wart *n.* a small, hard lump on the skin.

was *v.* a form of the verb **be**; used with 'I', 'he', 'she', or 'it', or with a name or other noun: *I was going to sleep. He was away. She was on holiday. It was raining.*

wash *n.* the act of cleaning: *The car needs a wash.* *v.* to clean with soap and water. **washing. washed.**

washer *n.* 1. a machine for washing. 2. a person who washes. 3. a flat metal or rubber ring placed between a nut and bolt.

washing machine a machine for washing clothes and other things.

wasn't short for **was not.**

wasp *n.* a stinging insect that has a narrow waist and black and yellow stripes.

waste *n.* 1. a poor use of something: *That was a waste of time.* 2. anything that you do not need any more. *v.* to spend more money, or use more time or material, than you should: *Ron wasted a lot of money on candy.* **wasting. wasted.**

watch *n.* a small clock, usually worn on the wrist. *v.* to look at carefully: *I watched a good show last night.* **watching. watched.**

water *n.* the liquid that falls as rain. *v.* to put water on: *Janet forgot to water the plants.* **watering. watered.**

waterfall *n.* a stream of water falling from a high place.

watermelon *n.* a large, juicy fruit that is pink inside and has a thick, green rind.

waterproof *adj.* not letting water through: *a waterproof coat.*

water ski one of a pair of wooden skis used for gliding over water. *pl.* **water skis.**

water-ski *v.* to glide over water on water skis while being pulled by a towing rope attached to a boat. **water-skiing. water-skied.** she **water-skis.**

watery *adj.* having to do with or containing water.

wave *n.* 1. a rippling movement: *an ocean wave.* 2. a movement of the hand and arm meaning hello or good-bye. *v.* to move your hand and arm as a way of saying hello or good-bye. **waving. waved.**

wavy *adj.* looking like waves: *David has wavy hair. Al has wavier hair. Mike has the waviest hair of all.*

wax *n.* 1. a solid substance made by bees. 2. any substance that resembles this: *furniture wax.* *v.* to put wax onto something, to polish: *Jason waxed the furniture on Saturday.* **waxing. waxed.**

way *n.* 1. a road, a direction: *Which way are you going?* 2. how to do something: *This is the way to bake a cake.*

we *pron.* the word used to refer to yourself and one or more other people: *We came to Uncle Jake's house.*

weak *adj.* not strong: *a weak animal; a weak link in a chain.*

wealth (welth) *n.* a lot of money or valuable things.

wealthy *adj.* having much of something, such as money: *a wealthy person, a wealthier one, the wealthiest person in the world.*

weapon (wep′ən) *n.* anything used for fighting or hunting: *Swords, spears, and guns are weapons.*

wear (wār) *v.* 1. to be dressed in something: *Marie wore her new coat.* 2. to become weak or damaged from much use: *The hall rug has worn out.* **wearing. wore.** I have **worn.**

weary (wēr′ē) *adj.* very tired: *a weary horse, a wearier one, the weariest horse on the farm.*

weasel *n.* a small, thin wild animal that lives on smaller animals such as birds and mice.

weather (weᴛʜ′ər) *n.* what it is like outside: *Weather is usually wet or dry, hot or cold, sunny or cloudy.*
Note: Do not mix up **weather** with **whether**; **whether** means 'if'.

weave *v.* to make cloth by putting threads over and under one another. **weaving. wove.** I have **woven.**

weaver *n.* a person who does weaving.

web *n.* 1. a net of sticky threads spun by a spider to catch flying insects. 2. the skin between the toes of some water birds and animals, such as ducks, geese, and otters.

wed *v.* to marry. **wedding. wedded.**

we'd short for **we had** or **we would.**

wedding *n.* the time when a man and woman become husband and wife.

wedge *n.* a piece of wood or metal that is very thin at one end and wider at the other.

Wednesday *n.* the fourth day of the week.

weed *n.* any wild plant that grows in places where it is not wanted. *v.* to take out the weeds from an area: *Betty and Ling weeded the garden.* **weeding. weeded.**

week *n.* a period of seven days.

weekday *n.* any day of the week except Saturday and Sunday.

weekend *n.* Saturday and Sunday.

weekly *adv.* once a week: *The magazine comes out weekly. adj.* coming out or happening every week.

weep *v.* to cry, to sob. **weeping. wept.**

weigh (wā) *v.* to find the mass or heaviness of a person or thing. **weighing. weighed.**

weight (wāt) *n.* 1. the amount of heaviness of a person or thing. 2. something heavy: *The metal weight keeps my papers from blowing off my desk.*

weird (wērd) *adj.* very strange: *Weird noises came from the old house.*

welcome *n.* a friendly greeting: *We gave our visitors a happy welcome. v.* to greet someone in a friendly way: *We welcomed our friends at the bus station.* **welcoming. welcomed.**

welfare *n.* 1. health and happiness: *I am concerned about my grandparents' welfare.* 2. money or other help given by the government to people in need.

well *n.* a deep hole in the ground with water or oil at the bottom: *We pumped water from the well at our cottage. adj.* healthy: *I feel very well. adv.* in a good way: *You did these exercises well.*

we'll short for **we will** or **we shall.**

Welsh *adj.* belonging to or coming from Wales.

went see **go.**

wept see **weep.**

were *v.* a form of the verb **be**; used with 'you', 'they', and 'we', or with names or other nouns: *You were going to sleep. They were skating. We were away.*

we're short for **we are.**

west *n.* the direction of sunset, opposite to east.

western *adj.* in the direction of the west: *Vancouver is in western British Columbia.*

West Indies islands in the Atlantic Ocean between South America and Florida.

wet *adj.* full of a liquid or covered with a liquid: *a wet towel, a wetter one, the wettest towel of all. v.* to make wet: *Wet the cloth and wipe off the car.* **wetting. wetted.**

we've short for **we have.**

whack *n.* a loud smack. *v.* to hit with a loud, smacking sound: *Jeanine whacked the nail into the board.* **whacking. whacked.**

whale *n.* a very large ocean animal that has a body like a fish but is really a mammal.

wharf *n.* a landing place for ships. *pl.* **wharves.**

what *adj.* which: *What time is it? pron.* that which: *He doesn't know what he wants.*

whatever *pron.* anything at all: *I will do whatever I can.*

what's short for **what is** or **what has.**

wheat *n.* a plant that looks like tall grass; its grains are ground to make flour.

wheel *n.* a ring of wood, plastic, or metal that can keep turning around on an axle: *Trains and cars move on wheels. v.* to push on wheels: *Mary wheeled the shopping cart.* **wheeling. wheeled.**

wheelbarrow *n.* a little cart with two handles and one wheel.

wheelchair *n.* a chair on wheels for the use of people who can't walk.

when *adv.* at what time: *When did the game begin? conj.* at the time: *We arrived when everything was over.*

whenever *conj.* at any time: *We will go whenever you are ready.*

where *adv.* 1. at what place: *Where is it?* 2. in the place that: *We will stop where we can rest.*

wherever *adv.* in any place: *I will search for him wherever he is.*

whether *conj.* if: *Carole did not know whether she could go.*

which *adj.* what person or thing: *Which coat is yours? pron.* a word showing the one you are talking about: *His coat, which had a hood, was new.*

while *n.* a space of time: *Mark slept for a short while. conj.* during the time that: *I watched television while dinner was cooking.*

whimper *n.* a soft cry: *The puppy gave a whimper from the corner. v.* to make such a cry. **whimpering. whimpered.**

whine *n.* a long, complaining cry: *The whine from our dog bothered the neighbours. v.* to make such a cry. **whining. whined.**

whip *n.* a long piece of rope or leather joined to a handle and used for hitting things. *v.* 1. to hit with a whip. 2. to stir a liquid so hard that it has a foam. **whipping. whipped.**

whirl *v.* to spin around quickly. **whirling. whirled.**

whirr *n.* a buzzing sound: *the whirr of the birds' wings. v.* to make such a sound: *The flies whirred around us.* **whirring. whirred.**

whiskers *n. pl.* the stiff hair at each side of an animal's mouth.

whisky, whiskey *n.* a strong alcoholic drink made from rye, corn, or other grains.

whisper *n.* a sound made softly. *v.* to speak very softly: *Nadia whispered the secret into my ear.* **whispering. whispered.**

whistle (wis′əl) *n.* 1. a high, sharp sound. 2. a small pipe that makes such a sound. *v.* to make a high, sharp sound by blowing through your lips or using a whistle. **whistling. whistled.**

white *n.* 1. the colour of fresh snow. 2. the part of an egg around the yolk. *adj.* having the colour of fresh snow.

whittle *v.* 1. to cut chips from wood with a knife. 2. to carve wood with a knife. **whittling. whittled.**

who *pron.* 1. which person or persons: *Who left the message?* 2. the person or persons that: *The boy who wrote the story is my cousin.*

whoever *pron.* anyone who: *Whoever believes that story will believe anything.*

whole *adj.* complete, entire: *The whole school had a holiday.*

whom *pron.* which person or persons; used after 'to', 'for', 'from', 'with', or 'by': *To whom did you tell the secret?*

who's short for **who is** or **who has.**

whose *pron.* belonging to what person: *I know whose hat this is.*

why *adv.* for what reason: *Why did you do it?*

wick *n.* a string in a candle or oil lamp.

wicked *adj.* very bad: *The king in that story was a wicked man.*

wide *adj.* measuring a long way from one side to the other: *The St. Lawrence is a wide river. adv.* completely: *The window was wide open.*

widen *v.* to make or become wider: *Workers widened the tunnel. The road widens here.* **widening. widened.**

widow *n.* a woman whose husband is dead.

widower *n.* a man whose wife is dead.

width *n.* how wide something is.

wiener *n.* a reddish sausage, usually made of beef and pork.

wife *n.* a married woman. *pl.* **wives.**

wig *n.* false hair worn on the head, often over someone's own hair.

wiggle *v.* to move with short, quick movements from side to side. **wiggling. wiggled.**

wigwam *n.* a hut that some North American Indians used to live in.

wild *adj.* not controlled by people, not tame.

wildcat *n.* a cougar, lynx, or other wild animal related to the common cat: *A wildcat is smaller than a lion, but bigger than a pet cat.*

wilderness (wil′dər nis) *n.* an open place where no people live.

wildlife *n.* a group of wild animals and birds that live in an area.

will *n.* 1. the power of your mind to choose what to do. 2. a written paper saying who is to have someone's money and things when he or she is dead. *v.* a verb used with another verb to say what is going to happen in the future: *I will go. She will play. They will work.* **would** (wûd).

willing *adj.* glad and ready to do what is wanted: *I am willing to come with you.* (*opp.* **unwilling.**)

willow *n.* a tree that has long, narrow leaves and thin branches that bend easily.

wilt *v.* to droop, to wither: *The plant is wilting because nobody watered it.* **wilting. wilted.**

win *n.* a success, a victory. *v.* to beat someone else in a game or fight: *Our team won two games and lost three.* **winning. won.**

wind (wind) *n.* air moving past quickly.

wind (wīnd) *v.* 1. to twist around or wrap around: *Rick wound the string into a ball.* 2. to tighten the spring of a watch. **winding. wound.** (*opp.* **unwind.**)

windbreaker *n.* a short sports jacket worn outdoors.

windmill *n.* a mill with sails turned by the wind: *Windmills are used to pump water and to grind grain into flour.*

window *n.* an opening in the wall of a building, filled with glass, to let in light and air.

windshield *n.* a glass or plastic screen that protects a driver from wind and rain.

wine *n.* an alcoholic drink made from the juice of grapes or other fruit.

wing *n.* 1. one of the parts of a bird, bat, or insect used for flying. 2. a flat stretch of metal on either side of an airplane that helps to keep it in the air.

wink *n.* a quick opening and closing of an eyelid. *v.* to close and open an eyelid quickly: *Terry winked at me to show that he did not believe the man's story.* **winking. winked.**

winner *n.* a team or person who wins something.

Winnipeg *n.* capital city of Manitoba.

winter *n.* the season after autumn.

wipe *v.* to rub something with a cloth to make it clean or dry. **wiping. wiped.**

wire *n.* a metal thread. *v.* to put in wires for electricity: *The electrician wired the new house.* **wiring. wired.**

wisdom (wiz′dəm) *n.* knowledge of what is right, true, and good: *My grandmother is a person of great wisdom.*

wise (wīz) *adj.* knowing many things, having plenty of sense: *My grandfather is a wise person.*

wish *n.* a want or desire: *My wish came true.* *v.* to want; to say or think what you would like to happen. **wishing. wished.**

witch *n.* a bad woman in fairy tales who is thought to have magic powers.

with *prep.* 1. in the company of: *Joyce walked with Karen.* 2. having: *My cousin is the girl with dark hair.* 3. because of: *Neil shouted with joy.* 4. using: *Richard hit the ball with the bat.*

withdraw *v.* to take back, to remove: *Frieda is withdrawing her offer to coach the team. I withdrew money from the bank.* **withdrawing. withdrew.** I have **withdrawn.**

wither *v.* to become dry and smaller: *The plant withered in the hot sun.* **withering. withered.**

within *prep.* inside: *The tin on the shelf was within Jim's reach.*

without *prep.* not having: *Sheena went to school without her lunch.*

witness *n.* someone who saw something happen: *a witness to an accident.* *v.* to see something happen: *Sheila witnessed the accident.* **witnessing. witnessed.**

wives plural of **wife.**

wizard *n.* a man in fairy tales who is thought to have magic powers.

woke, woken see **wake.**

wolf *n.* a wild animal, usually grey, that looks like a dog. *pl.* **wolves.**

wolverine *n.* a dark brown animal that looks like a large weasel.

woman (wŭm′ən) *n.* a grown-up female human being. *pl.* **women** (wim′in).

won see **win.**

wonder *n.* 1. a surprising or unusual thing: *Niagara Falls is one of the world's great wonders.* 2. a feeling of amazement: *We watched in wonder as the magician did his tricks.* *v.* to want to know: *I wonder where Michel is.* **wondering. wondered.**

wonderful *adj.* amazing, giving a lot of pleasure: *The waterfall is a wonderful sight.*

won't short for **will not.**

wood *n.* the hard part of a tree, under the bark: *The table is made of wood.*

wooden *adj.* made of wood.

woodpecker *n.* a bird that has a strong, pointed bill: *A woodpecker taps on trees to get at the insects under the bark.*

woods *n. pl.* a forest; a large number of trees growing together.

wool *n.* 1. the thick hair of sheep and some other animals. 2. the thread made from this hair.

woollen, woolen *adj.* made of wool.

word *n.* a sound or group of sounds that mean something when spoken, written, or read.

wore see **wear.**

work *n.* 1. something that you have to do: *There is a lot of work to be done for the school play.* 2. something that people do to earn money: *What kind of work does your grandfather do?* 3. something done or made: *a work of art.* *v.* 1. to do or make something through effort: *Billy worked in the yard after school.* 2. to do work for pay: *My father works at a cheese factory.* 3. to run or operate: *I wonder why the radio will not work.* **working. worked.**

worker *n.* someone who works.

workshop *n.* a place in which work is done by hand or by machine.

world *n.* 1. the earth and all the people, animals, and plants that live on it. 2. another planet in space: *Spaceships can travel to other worlds.*

worm *n.* a small, thin animal with a soft body and no legs.

worn see **wear.**

worry (wər′ē) *n.* a troubled feeling. *pl.* **worries.** *v.* to feel upset about something bad that may happen or may have happened: *I was worried because I didn't study long enough for the test.* **worrying. worried.** he **worries.**

worse (wərs) *adj.* more than bad: *Tom's cold is bad. Rob's is even worse.*

worship (wər′ship) *n.* prayers and praise given to God or a god. *v.* to show love for God or a god. **worshipping. worshipped.**

worst (wərst) *adj.* the most bad: *The orange team is bad. The pink team is worse. The grey team is the worst of all.*

worth (wərth) *adj.* 1. equal in value to: *The ring is worth five dollars.* 2. good enough for: *That book is worth reading.*

worthwhile *adj.* good enough to spend time or money on: *Swimming is a worthwhile exercise.*

would see **will.**

wouldn't short for **would not.**

wound (wünd) *n.* an injury such as a cut. *v.* to hurt or injure: *Tom wounded himself when the knife slipped.* **wounding. wounded.**

wound (wownd) see **wind.**

wove, woven see **weave.**

wrap (rap) *v.* to put paper or cloth around something. **wrapping. wrapped.**

wrapping (rap′ping) *n.* a piece of paper or some other material, placed around something.

wreath (rēth) *n.* a large ring of flowers, branches, etc., twisted together.

wreck (rek) *n.* anything destroyed, such as a ship on rocks or a crashed airplane. *v.* to destroy. **wrecking. wrecked.**

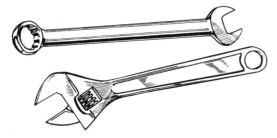

wrench (rench) *n.* a tool that is used to twist nuts on and off bolts. *v.* to twist or pull: *I wrenched a muscle in my arm.* **wrenching. wrenched.**

wrestle (res′əl) *v.* to struggle with someone and try to force him or her to the ground. **wrestling. wrestled.**

wrestling *n.* a sport in which two people struggle hand to hand.

wriggle (rig′əl) *v.* to twist and turn: *Ted tried to wriggle through the hole in the fence.* **wriggling. wriggled.**

wring (ring) *v.* to twist and squeeze. **wringing. wrung.**

wrinkle (ring′kəl) *n.* a crease in cloth or on the skin. *v.* to become creased or to make creased. **wrinkling. wrinkled.**

wrist (rist) *n.* the joint between your hand and arm.

write (rīt) *n.* to put words or signs on paper or a board so that people can read them. **writing. wrote.** I have **written.**

writer *n.* a person who writes, usually as a job.

writing (rī′ting) *n.* the act of making letters and words with pen, pencil, chalk, etc.

wrong (rong) *adj.* not true or correct; not fair; not good.

X

Xmas *n.* a short way of writing **Christmas.**

X-rays *n. pl.* special rays that are used to take a picture of the inside of your body.

xylophone (zī′lə fōn) *n.* a musical instrument made of wooden or metal bars that are hit with a small hammer.

y

yacht (yot) *n.* a small ship used for pleasure trips.

yak *n.* a long-haired ox that lives in Asia.

yam *n.* a kind of sweet potato.

yard *n.* 1. an area of ground next to or around a building. 2. a unit of length, equal to a little less than one metre.

yarn *n.* 1. thick thread used in sewing, weaving, or knitting. 2. a made-up story: *The old sailor told the children yarns of the sea.*

yawn *v.* to take a deep breath with your mouth wide open, because you are tired or bored. **yawning. yawned.**

year *n.* a measure of time lasting 365 days, 52 weeks, or 12 months.

yearly *adv.* once a year: *The circus comes to town yearly. adj.* coming out or happening every year: *We take our yearly holiday each July.*

yeast *n.* a substance used to make the dough rise when making bread, rolls, etc.

yell *n.* a loud shout. *v.* to shout very loudly. **yelling. yelled.**

yellow *n.* the colour of a lemon, grapefruit, or dandelion. *adj.* having such a colour.

yes *adv.* the opposite of no.

yesterday *n.* the day just past, the day before today: *Yesterday was my birthday. adv.* on the day before today: *We went to the movies yesterday.*

yet *adv.* 1. up to now: *I have not read the book yet.* 2. at some time that is coming: *He may arrive yet. conj.* but: *Helen ran hard, yet she missed the train.*

yield (yēld) *v.* 1. to give way to someone or something: *The enemy yielded to the soldiers.* 2. to produce: *The orchard yields much fruit.* **yielding. yielded.**

yogurt *n.* a thick, creamy food made from milk.

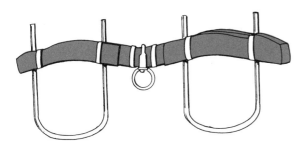

yoke *n.* a wooden frame used to join together two work animals.

yolk (yōk) *n.* the yellow part of an egg.

Yom Kippur a Jewish fast day, observed in September or October.

you *pron.* the person or people you are speaking to or writing to.

you'd short for **you had** or **you would.**

you'll short for **you will.**

young *n.* the baby or babies of a person or animal: *The bird looked for worms for her young. adj.* in the early part of life, not old.

youngster *n.* a young boy or girl.

your *adj.* belonging to you: *Is this your hat?*

you're short for **you are.**

yours *pron.* the one belonging to you: *Is this hat yours?*

yourself *pron.* you alone: *Can you see yourself? pl.* **yourselves.**

youth (yüth) *n.* 1. the time between being a child and being an adult: *In his youth, Father played football.* 2. a young person.

you've short for **you have.**

yo-yo *n.* a small toy that is spun up and down on a string. *pl.* **yo-yos.**

Yukon *n.* a territory in northwestern Canada; capital is Whitehorse. Short form: **Y.T.**

Yule *n.* the festival of Christmas.

Z

zebra *n.* a wild African horse that has black stripes on a white body.

zero (zē′rō) *n.* the number nothing (0). *pl.* **zeros.**

zigzag *adj.* full of short, sharp turns from one side to the other.

zinc *n.* a greyish-white metal.

zip *v.* to close with a zipper. **zipping. zipped.**

zipper *n.* a fastener with a sliding tab, for joining together two edges of material.

zone *n.* any special area: *The Arctic zone is the area around the North Pole. Drivers should go slowly in a school zone.*

zoo *n.* a place where wild animals are kept for people to look at them. *pl.* **zoos.**

zoom *v.* to move or climb suddenly: *The airplane zoomed into the sky, and was gone.* **zooming. zoomed.**

Appendix

Many books have an Appendix. It is a section at the back that gives you extra help. The Appendix in this book has words and facts that you may want to look up quickly. They will come in handy for some of your school subjects and in your everyday writing.

Provinces and Capitals of Canada

Province (from West to East)	Abbreviation	Capital
British Columbia	B.C.	Victoria
Alberta	Alta.	Edmonton
Saskatchewan	Sask.	Regina
Manitoba	Man.	Winnipeg
Ontario	Ont.	Toronto
Québec	Que. or P.Q.	Québec
New Brunswick	N.B.	Fredericton
Nova Scotia	N.S.	Halifax
Prince Edward Island	P.E.I.	Charlottetown
Newfoundland	Nfld.	St. John's

Canada's Territories are:

Yukon Territory	Y.T.	Whitehorse
Northwest Territories	N.W.T.	Yellowknife

The capital of Canada is Ottawa.

Places and People

Afghanistan	Afghans
Africa	Africans
Albania	Albanians
Algeria	Algerians
Angola	Angolans
Argentina	Argentinians
Asia	Asians
Australia	Australians
Austria	Austrians
Bahamas	Bahamians
Bangladesh	Bangladeshis
Barbados	Barbadians
Belgium	Belgians
Bermuda	Bermudians
Bolivia	Bolivians
Brazil	Brazilians
Bulgaria	Bulgarians
Burma	Burmese
Canada	Canadians
Chile	Chileans
China	Chinese
Colombia	Colombians
Costa Rica	Costa Ricans
Cuba	Cubans
Cyprus	Cypriots
Czechoslovakia	Czechoslovakians
Denmark	Danes
Dominican Republic	Dominicans
Ecuador	Ecuadorians
Egypt	Egyptians
England	English
Ethiopia	Ethiopians
Europe	Europeans
Finland	Finns
France	French

Germany	Germans		Paraguay	Paraguayans
Ghana	Ghanaians		Peru	Peruvians
Great Britain	British		Philippines	Filipinos
Greece	Greeks		Poland	Poles
Guatemala	Guatemalans		Portugal	Portuguese
Guyana	Guyanese			
			Romania	Romanians
Haiti	Haitians			
Hungary	Hungarians		Saudi Arabia	Saudis
			Scotland	Scottish, Scots
Iceland	Icelanders		South Africa	South Africans
India	Indians		South America	South Americans
Indonesia	Indonesians		Spain	Spaniards
Iran	Iranians		Sri Lanka	Sri Lankans
Iraq	Iraqis		Sudan	Sudanese
Ireland	Irish		Sweden	Swedes
Israel	Israelis		Switzerland	Swiss
Italy	Italians		Syria	Syrians
Jamaica	Jamaicans		Taiwan	Taiwanese
Japan	Japanese		Tanzania	Tanzanians
Jordan	Jordanians		Thailand	Thais
			Trinidad and	
Kampuchea	Kampucheans		Tobago	Trinidadians
Kenya	Kenyans		Tunisia	Tunisians
Korea	Koreans		Turkey	Turks
Laos	Laotians		Uganda	Ugandans
Lebanon	Lebanese		Ukraine	Ukrainians
Liberia	Liberians		U.S.S.R. (Soviet	
Libya	Libyans		Union)	Russians
			United States of	
Malawi	Malawians		America	Americans
Malaysia	Malaysians		Uruguay	Uruguayans
Mexico	Mexicans			
Morocco	Moroccans		Venezuela	Venezuelans
Mozambique	Mozambicans		Vietnam	Vietnamese
Netherlands (Holland)	Dutch		Wales	Welsh
New Zealand	New Zealanders		West Indies	West Indians
Nigeria	Nigerians			
North America	North Americans		Yugoslavia	Yugoslavs
Norway	Norwegians			
			Zaire	Zairians
Pakistan	Pakistanis		Zambia	Zambians
Panama	Panamanians		Zimbabwe	Zimbabweans

Numbers

Numbers that are used a lot:

1	one	first
2	two	second
3	three	third
4	four	fourth
5	five	fifth
6	six	sixth
7	seven	seventh
8	eight	eighth
9	nine	ninth
10	ten	tenth
11	eleven	eleventh
12	twelve	twelfth
13	thirteen	thirteenth
14	fourteen	fourteenth
15	fifteen	fifteenth
16	sixteen	sixteenth
17	seventeen	seventeenth
18	eighteen	eighteenth
19	nineteen	nineteenth
20	twenty	twentieth
30	thirty	thirtieth
40	forty	fortieth
50	fifty	fiftieth
60	sixty	sixtieth
70	seventy	seventieth
80	eighty	eightieth
90	ninety	ninetieth
100	one hundred	hundredth
1000	one thousand	thousandth
1 000 000	one million	millionth
1 000 000 000	one billion	billionth

Writing out other numbers:

The number 'twenty-one' comes after 'twenty'. 'Twenty-first' comes after 'twentieth'. When writing out numbers like these, use a hyphen between the first and second part of the number.

Metric Symbols

Symbol	Meaning	Symbol	Meaning
cm	centimetre	s	second
m	metre	min	minute
km	kilometre	h	hour
mg	milligram	d	day
g	gram	a	year
kg	kilogram	cm^2	square centimetre
t	tonne	m^2	square metre
mL	millilitre	km^2	square kilometre
L	litre	ha	hectare
kL	kilolitre	cm^3	cubic centimetre
km/h	kilometres per hour	m^3	cubic metre
		°C	degrees Celsius

Days and Months

Days of the Week

Sunday (Sun.)
Monday (Mon.)
Tuesday (Tues.)
Wednesday (Wed.)
Thursday (Thurs.)
Friday (Fri.)
Saturday (Sat.)

Months

January (Jan.) 31 days
February (Feb.) 28
March (Mar.) 31
April (Apr.) 30
May (May) 31
June (June) 30
July (July) 31
August (Aug.) 31
September (Sept.) 30
October (Oct.) 31
November (Nov.) 30
December (Dec.) 31

There are 52 weeks in a year. Each week has 7 days.

There are 365 days in a year. Every fourth year, called a leap year, has 366 days. The extra day is added to February.

Holidays and Special Days

New Year's Day — January 1
Chinese New Year — During the first moon (Jan. 20-Feb. 19) for one week
Valentine's Day — February 14
St. Patrick's Day — March 17
April Fool's Day — April 1
Good Friday — Friday before Easter Sunday
Easter Sunday — First Sunday after full moon that follows March 21
Passover — Eight-day Jewish celebration in March or April
Mother's Day — Second Sunday in May
Victoria Day — May 24
St-Jean Baptiste — June 24
Father's Day — Third Sunday in June
Dominion Day (Canada Day) — July 1
Labour Day — First Monday in September
Rosh Hashona (Jewish New Year) — First day of the Jewish year (in Sept. or Oct.)
Yom Kippur — Tenth day of the Jewish year
Thanksgiving Day — Second Monday in October
Halloween — October 31
Divale — Hindu festival in October or November
Remembrance Day — November 11
Hanukkah (Chanukah) — Eight-day Jewish festival in or around December
Christmas — December 25 (celebrated on Jan. 6–7 in the Ukrainian and other Eastern churches)
Boxing Day — December 26
Ramadan — Ninth month of the Moslem year (Moslem month of fasting)

Pronunciation

Pronunciation is given (in brackets) for some difficult words in this dictionary. The letters and signs are pronounced as in the examples below. These are not the only letters used, but the others should give you no difficulty.

a   as in **bad**, **sang**

ā   as in **face**, **raid**

e   as in **best**, **head**

ē   as in **meet**, **jeans**

ə   called a 'schwa sound'
     as in **metal**, **broken**,
     pencil, **bacon**, **circus**

i   as in **sit**, **give**

ī   as in **find**, **ice**

o   as in **pot**, **on**

ō   as in **rope**, **soap**

u   as in **but**, **other**

u̇   as in **full**, **cook**

ü   as in **rude**, **cool**

th   as in **thing**, **both**

TH   as in **other**, **than**

zh   as in **measure**, **treasure**

ʹ   as in akʹsent (accent)
     or ad vīsʹ (advice).

This mark is placed after the sound with the heavy, or main, stress.

Abbreviations

The following abbreviations, or short forms, are used in this dictionary.

adj.	adjective	*opp.*	opposite
adv.	adverb	*pl.*	plural
conj.	conjunction	*prep.*	preposition
fem.	feminine	*pron.*	pronoun
masc.	masculine	*sing.*	singular
n.	noun	*v.*	verb